WITHDRAWN

Marjorie Hol
of Health, En
and Staying

Marjorie Holmes' Secrets of Health, Energy, and Staying Young

MARJORIE HOLMES

Originally published as *God and Vitamins*

A DOUBLEDAY-GALILEE BOOK
DOUBLEDAY & COMPANY, INC.
GARDEN CITY, NEW YORK
1987

Galilee Books Edition published July 1987 by special arrangement with Doubleday & Company, Inc.

Library of Congress Cataloging-in-Publication Data

Holmes, Marjorie, 1910–
    Marjorie Holmes' secrets of health, energy, and staying young.

    Originally published as: God and vitamins.
    "A Doubleday-Galilee book."
    Bibliography: p. 337
    Includes index.
    1. Nutrition. 2. Vitamins in human nutrition.
3. Exercise. 4. Health. 5. Christian life—1960–
6. Nutrition—Religious aspects—Christianity. I. Title.
II. Title: Secrets of health, energy, and staying young.
RA784.H59   1987   613   87–8919
ISBN 0-385-24145-3

Grateful acknowledgment is made to the following for use of copyrighted material:

Excerpt condensed from *Striper, A Story of Fish and Man* by John N. Cole. Published 1978 by Atlantic-Little, Brown. Reprinted by permission.
Excerpt from *Vitamin E: Your Key to a Healthy Heart* by Herbert E. Bailey. Copyright © 1964 by Herbert E. Bailey. Reprinted by permission of Chilton Book Company.
Excerpt from *Pure & Simple* by Marian Burros. Reprinted by permission of William Morrow & Company.
Excerpt from "Second Opinion Special Report: Laetrile at Sloan-Kettering" by Ralph W. Moss, *Second Opinion*, November 1977. Reprinted by permission of the author.
Excerpt from "New Hope for the Childless" by Emily and Per Ola D'Aulaire, *Reader's Digest*, January 1977. Reprinted by permission.
Excerpt from *Health Preserver*, © 1977 by Wilfrid E. Shute, M.D. Permission granted by Rodale Press, Inc.
Random excerpts from various issues of *Prevention* magazine. Copyright © 1970, 1972, 1973, 1974, 1975, 1976, 1978, 1979 by *Prevention* magazine. Reprinted by permission of Rodale Press, Inc.
Excerpt from James J. Kilpatrick's article "Laetrile and FDA Tyranny," copyright © 1977 by Universal Press Syndicate. All rights reserved.
Excerpt from an article by Jean Carper, the Washington *Post*, February 4, 1979. Reprinted by permission.

87-654   Ingram 8-11-87   8.95

For Lynn

Acknowledgments

I wish to thank the editors of Rodale Press for allowing me to quote from *Prevention* magazine, and for their help and that of their staff in my research. I also appreciate the generosity of the following people who read portions of this work in progress and gave me invaluable critical guidance:

Dr. Linus Pauling, Dr. Richard Passwater, Shreve Spitler, D.D.S., Arthur Alexander Knapp, M.D., Arlin J. Brown, Dominick Bosco and Vere Shute.

Contents

INTRODUCTION by George P. Schmieler, M.D.   xvii

1 GOD WILL TAKE CARE OF YOU   1

The Body Keeps Trying to Tell Us   4
A Lucky Start   6

2 THE WONDERFUL WHYS OF EXERCISE   10

What We Learned   12
Exercise Tells the Body "I Love You"   14
Walking   18
The Doctor Who Changed My Life   19

3 JOGGING, JUMPING AND OTHER FUN
    THINGS   24

Climbing Stairs   24
Running   26
Square Dancing   27
Skipping Rope   29
Swimming   30

Isometrics, Stretching   31
Dancing   32
Other Glorious Activities   34
Making Work Your "Workout"   34
Worship and Exercise   35

4   WATER   37

The Magic of the Cold Shower   38
Why Water Does So Much for Us   41
The Historical Significance of Water   42
Watering Within   44
The Importance of Hard Water   45
Our Poisoned Lifeline   47
Should Fluoride Be Added to Water?   48
Learning to Love Cold Water   51

5   THE DENTIST WHO CHANGED OUR LIVES   53

Vitamins, Minerals and Prevention   56
If Only We Had Listened   58
The People Stories   59
Doctors   61
The Terrible Resistance to Change   64
Why Doctors Don't Tell You About Vitamins   66
How the Drug Companies Court the Doctors   67
A New Breed of Doctors   69
The Public Rebellion   71
Drugs: Where Have All the Billions Gone?   72
The Swiftly Turning Tide   75

6   WHAT IS A VITAMIN AND HOW DOES IT
       WORK?   78

How Vitamins Were Discovered   79
The Evidence   79
How the Enzymes Help   81
Why We Need More Vitamins   82
Which Vitamins Should You Take?   84
How Many Vitamins Do We Need?   86

Natural Versus Synthetic   89
What Vitamins Do for Me   90

7   THAT DANGEROUS CLICHÉ, THE
    "BALANCED DIET"   92

Today's Poisoned Food   94
The Ruin that Comes with "Civilized" Foods   95
The Family Goes to the Supermarket   97
A Look at the Menu   98
Let Them Eat Sawdust   100
How Many Vitamins in Our Balanced Meal?   102
Our Children Are the Victims   104
Hook the Kiddies Early   106
The Nutritional Disasters at School   107
Get the Kids to Sell It   108
Parents Fight Back   109
The Powers that Push the Dangerous Cliché   111

8   VITAMINS AND THE FDA   115

The Vendetta Against Vitamins   117
*The Hidden Giants: A Food and Chemical Who's
    Who*   119
New Battle Lines Drawn   121
"The Myths of Vitamins"   123

9   VITAMINS A AND D—FOR HEALTHY LUNGS,
    SKIN AND EYES   125

And God Said, "Let There Be Light!"   126
The Sun and Vitamin D   128
Which Vitamin D and How Much?   130
The Nature and Work of Vitamin A   131
Vitamin A and the Epithelial Package   132
Vitamins A and D and the Complexion   133
Vitamins A and D and the Eyes   136
*The Remarkable Results of Calcium and
    Vitamin D*   138
Why Won't They TELL Us These Things?   140

How Vitamin A Protects Us   142
Vitamin A and Stress   144
Vitamin A and Sex   145
Vitamin A, Shield and Sword Against Cancer   146
Other Evidence   147
How Toxic Is Vitamin A?   149
How Much Vitamin A Do We Need?   151

10   B, THE HAPPINESS VITAMIN   153

The Breakdown and Vitamin B   155
Who Needs Vitamin B?   157
What the B Vitamins Do for Us   159
The Closely Knit Family of Vitamin B   160
Vitamin B_{12}   162
Folic Acid   164
Vitamin B_1 (Thiamine)   164
Vitamin B_2 (Riboflavin)   165
*Vitamin B_3 (Niacin, Niacinamide, Nicotinamide,
    Nicotinic Acid)*   166
Vitamin B_5 (Pantothenic Acid)   168
Vitamin B_6 (Pyridoxine)   169
Choline   171
Inositol. Biotin. PABA (Para-aminobenzoic Acid)   172
Body, Mind and Spirit   173

11   THE ANTI-CANCER VITAMINS, B_{15} AND B_{17} 177

The Many Roles of Vitamin B_{15}   177
The Fearless War on "Useless" Vitamins   179
All-Out Attack on Apricot Pits   180
Vitamin B_{17} (Laetrile)   181
The Cover-up in the War on Cancer   183
The Government Wants Your Child   186
The Truth about Chad Green   188
The Joey Hofbauer Story   189
No Happy Ending   192
The Man Who Knows There Is a Cure for Cancer   194
Cancer Is No Stranger   197
First, Do No Harm   199

Contents

The Fate of Laetrile   201
Why All the Opposition?   202
How to Prevent and Overcome Cancer   205

12   C, THE WONDER VITAMIN   207

The Stormy History of Vitamin C   209
Vitamin C and the Common Cold   209
The Vitamin C Pioneers   212
The Swine Flu Scandal   213
Just What IS a Cold?   214
How Vitamin C Fights Colds and Flu   216
Vitamin C and Emergencies   218
Have We Really Licked Scurvy?   220
Collagen, the Cement that Holds Us Together   221
The Case of Norman Cousins   223
Vitamin C and Cancer   225
The Cameron-Pauling Cancer Experiment   227
Vitamin C and Energy   229
The Most Important Supplement   230

13   VITAMIN E, FOR YOUTH, HEART AND
     ENERGY   232

Can We Get Enough Vitamin E in Foods?   233
The Rape of the Virgin Wheat   234
The Enrichment Hoax   236
Natural Sources of Vitamin E   237
The Bonds Between Vitamin C and Vitamin E   238
The History of Vitamin E   239
The Heart   240
The Respiratory System   240
Circulatory Diseases of Feet and Legs   241
Arthritis   243
Burns and Afflictions of the Skin   244
Energy, Speed, Endurance   245
Keeping Young   246
Menstruation and Menopause   248
Fertility   250
The Versatile Vitamin   253

The Shutes: Pioneers of Vitamin E   254
How to Buy and Use Vitamin E   258

14   THE MAGIC MINERALS AND ORGANIC
     FOODS   260

Back to the Farm   261
Where the Farmers Failed   262
Why People Are Going Organic   265
Whole Species Are Dying   267
The Public Attack on Natural or Organic Foods   269
How Truth Is Perverted   271
Natural Foods and the Diabetic   273
Why Natural Foods Are So Important   274

15   NINE SUPPLEMENTS THAT CAN SAVE YOUR
     LIFE   278

Bone Meal   278
Bone Builds Bone   280
Dolomite   281
Desiccated Liver   284
Zinc   286
Lecithin (and the Cholesterol Scare)   287
Lecithin (and What It Can Do for Us)   289
Wheat Germ   291
Brewer's Yeast   293
Selenium   293
Kelp   295

16   FOODS THAT HELP YOU "EAT HEALTHY"   298

Simple Meals, Busy Teeth   299
Raisins   300
Nuts   301
Seeds   302
Popcorn   304
Bran   304
When We Skinned Those Orange Peels   305
Bring On the Eggs   307

Garlic   308
Yogurt   310
Sprouts   311
The Fun of "Cooking Healthy"   313

17   NONE OF US NEEDS TO GET *OLD!*   315

A Practically Painless Way to Keep Your Figure   316
It's Not How Long You Live, But How Well   319
Get Outdoors   321
Get Away from Drugs   323
The Dangers of "A Pill for Every Ill"   324
Wean Yourself from Drugs   326
Go Barefoot   327
You're as Old as Your Sense of Adventure   329
Keep Growing and Giving   331
Keep Doing the Work You Love   332
Choose the Nightmare or the Dream   334

REFERENCES AND SUGGESTED READING   337

INDEX   353

Introduction

GEORGE P. SCHMIELER, M.D.

When I met and fell in love with the recently widowed Marjorie Holmes, I had no idea she was the author of this book (then entitled *God and Vitamins*). I knew only that she had written *I've Got to Talk to Somebody, God,* a lovely book of prayers that had literally saved my life at a time when I was almost suicidal with grief over the death of my wife. To my surprise, Marjorie told me her latest book was one about health and energy. As we parted after our first date for dinner, she signed a copy for me.

The next morning I called her in great excitement to tell her, "I've been up half the night reading your book, and I agree with everything you say! I've been using the same principles in my medical practice for years. In fact, when I was at Pitt I was a student assistant to one of your vitamin pioneers, the famous Dr. King. One of my duties, as I recall, was to squeeze the lemons for some of his experiments to isolate and learn more about vitamin C."

But never in my wildest dreams could I foresee that this vibrant little woman and her book would one day actually save my leg from amputation.

Marjorie and I were married after a whirlwind courtship of four months, and although we are seventy and seventy-one years old, took up a full and joyous life together, swimming, dancing, and doing the work we love: I, as a physician, she as a writer.

Two years later, however, despite the fact I have never smoked and am not a diabetic (two of its primary causes), I began to have serious circulation problems. My feet were ice-cold, the right leg swelled, and for months the pain was excruciating. Ulcers were also forming on my foot. When we noticed that the middle toe was also swollen and ulcerated—gangrenous, in fact, I finally realized it was high time I had an arteriogram.

After it was over, the surgeons entered my hospital room looking grave. "Your arteriogram shows virtually complete blockage of the arteries that go down the entire leg from the knee. The smaller arteries of the feet are also almost completely occluded." They could try a bypass, but they didn't recommend it; they doubted if it would succeed. And even if it did, it would only postpone the inevitable. "In our opinion," they said firmly, "the leg should be amputated."

Amputated. My wife and I stared at them, dismayed.

They could begin by taking off the toe, they told us. But that too would be only a stopgap; before long I would probably lose the foot. In their best judgment the whole leg should come off just above the knee, as soon as reasonably possible. Meanwhile, the toe could be treated with medication, and we might want to get a second opinion. But if we agreed, they would like to schedule the surgery for the following week.

That surgery never took place.

Instead, it was Marjorie's turn to stay up half the night, reading everything she could find about circulation in the mass of books and papers she had used in her research. Winnowing and gleaning every bit of advice about therapy for such problems, she made up a list. By the next morning, when she arrived at the hospital to bring me home, she had prepared a program she was convinced could very well save that leg.

My son George, Jr., who is also a physician, agreed. "Dad, since there's no hurry, why not try it?"

Just to be sure, however, we consulted one of the most prominent vascular surgeons at Pittsburgh University. To our pleasant surprise, he too agreed. "While your situation is serious, it isn't life-threatening right now. No harm can be done by trying what your wife suggests. Who knows? It might work. If it doesn't, they will probably have to amputate."

Marjorie's program was, in brief, as follows: 1. Continue treating the ulcerated toe with Betadine ointment and vitamin E oil. 2. Increase my daily intake of vitamin E to 1,200 International Units. 3. Increase vitamin C to 5 grams (5,000 milligrams). 4. Increase zinc to 150 milligrams. 5. Increase bioflavonoids to 500 milligrams. 6. Increase niacin to 100 milligrams twice a day. 7. Apply vitamin E oil not only to the ulcers but to all toenails. 8. Soak feet three times a day in hot salt (or peroxide) water, alternating with cold footbaths. 9. Gentle massage.

While I can't promise this treatment will work for everybody, I can say it worked for me.

Gradually the toe returned to normal, the swelling of legs and feet subsided, the pains relented, the ulcers healed. None of this happened overnight, and there were setbacks—but with patience, prayers, and determination, we won the battle. I still have poor circulation and always will, but now some six years later *I still have my leg.* With Marjorie I walk the dogs every night, swim every summer, and she says I dance better than ever!

As a physician, I do prescribe the wonderful lifesaving drugs science has given us, but always with great care, after making very sure they're safe. I do applaud and utilize the marvelous advances that have been made in medical technology. But even as a young doctor, I was preaching the very things in this book: Thank God for this precious body—take care of it. Exercise, don't smoke, eat sensibly. I also was providing patients with vitamins and minerals long before they captured the public fancy. (I was never criticized for this by my colleagues—they just thought me a little crazy.) For fifty years all the patients who entered my office got a complete physical, no matter how often they came or how long it took, and they never left without a prayer. And they responded, many overcoming serious diseases with little more than B_{12} shots, carefully selected food supplements, and an ever-listening ear. Most have lived long, active lives, many well into their nineties and several have reached a hundred.

In view of all this I am proud to be married to a woman who has kept herself so young, vital, and full of energy, and who can share her discoveries so charmingly. I'm happy to tell you she is just as delightful in person as she is in print. I should know—I live with her!

1

God Will
Take Care of You

One night, alone in a hotel room far away from home, I woke up
deathly ill. Aware, even as I reached for the lamp beside the
bed, that this was serious. *Food poisoning,* I realized, appalled.
The oysters I'd had for dinner; there had been something about
them that made me uneasy, I remembered, but foolishly I
hadn't said anything. . . . And now this. . . . *Oh, no, please,
God, oh, no.*

For this was my first promotion tour. And only my second
night on the road.

I staggered to the bathroom, refusing to believe how sick I
was. But during the terrible hours that followed there was no
denying it. I vomited, I retched. I fainted. Once I found myself
lying on the cold tiles of the bathroom floor, a lump already
swelling on my head. Again, I woke up on the bedroom carpet-
ing, where I'd fallen trying to get back to bed. "Idiot," common
sense told me, "call Mike!" (the publisher's salesman down the
hall). "Call the hotel doctor." Yet common sense also reminded
me both the doctor and Mike would say, "Sick author," and
send me home.

I had wanted so much to make this trip; to meet the people
who were reading my books and writing to me about them. And

I wanted to prove to my publishers I could do a good job of publicizing them, that I could stand the rigors of the road. It would be too humiliating to go down in defeat before I even got started. I didn't dare call for human help, my only hope was to keep calling on God instead. "Listen, Lord," I prayed whenever I was lucid, "you wanted me to come, I know you did. You brought me on this trip. You were back of the decision to send me, you gave me the courage to say yes. Now help me, heal me, give me the strength to go on!"

And strong and clear came the words I'd been hearing in my mind over and over, steadily, for weeks: *God will take care of you.*

That old song we used to sing back in my childhood church. Heard only in fragments before, while I nervously prepared to come—now the whole stanza began to sing itself to me with its cadences, its special emphasis: *God will take care of you, through all the day, o'er all the way. . . . God will take ca-are of you. GOD WILL TAKE CARE OF YOU.* As if a chorus of angels were reassuring me, or even the quiet voice of God himself.

I knew the worst was over. I crept back to the bathroom and washed my face. Then something told me to take the vitamins I'd brought along, to replenish my strength. I did so and this time made it safely back to bed, and slept. When the wake-up call came before dawn I was weak but steady. I knew I could make it. God *had* pulled me through. . . .

Catherine Marshall writes of a similar experience she had with this same song. And I'm sure its old familiar words have sustained thousands of people in crises large and small for generations. Reminding us, as they do, that if we trust God and let him, he can and will support us far beyond anything we can imagine. This message and others in that frayed green hymnal had been inscribed on my mind, sunk deep in my subconscious; and although I hadn't sung or even said those words in years, they had risen repeatedly to calm me from the moment I had first read that tour schedule: Two weeks away from home, twelve cities. *Raleigh, Birmingham, Atlanta, Tampa, Minneapolis, Denver, Seattle . . .* I gasped as my eyes ran down the list. My heart began to pound.

I was not a seasoned traveler, and I felt the hand of dread. Planes, taxicabs, connections . . . *God will take care of you,* a small voice said.

But all these appointments—interviews, talk shows, speeches. . . . I felt weak, stupid, inadequate, an impostor, unworthy of all this attention and unable to cope with it. . . . Yet it came again: *God will take care of you.*

And I'd have to do something about luggage. And my hair and nails and clothes. What to wear? How would I ever get ready? Especially with the needs of a family still to be met. . . . *God will take care of you.*

It was like a promise. Even as I confided my anxiety to my editor I felt sure of that. "Look, if you don't feel up to it, say so now," she told me. "Not everybody can stand the pace. However, you're as strong as anybody I know. If politicians can do it, and a lot of other writers, so can you."

She was right. I have always been remarkably healthy, and blessed with tremendous stamina and drive. Besides, God would be with me.

Later I was to face schedules far more grueling than that first one. Once I toured six weeks, with only one weekend break at home (I hasten to add this was after our last child was in college). I was to travel coast to coast, miss meals and sometimes sleep, be exposed to every kind of cold, virus and malady, without any visible effects except fatigue when it was over. I learned not to be afraid anymore, primarily because I knew what to expect. And because I knew I would not fail. I could depend on myself —and my own creator.

A promotion tour sounds glamorous; it is actually very hard work, but joyful because it provides so many opportunities to witness, to aid and counsel. I have learned to be equal to its rigors, but I never take this for granted. Always before leaving on such a trip I do two very practical things: I pray for strength and ask everyone I know to pray for this as well. And I fortify myself with extra vitamins and minerals. Nor do I ever pack my bags and leave without them. I am convinced God saved my life that night in the hotel; and that the vitamins replenished what my body had lost in its struggle, and gave me the physical energy I needed to go on. . . .

That next morning Mike said only, "You look a little peaked," as we got into the taxi.

"Well, I had an upset stomach last night," I admitted. "Will we have time for some orange juice and coffee?"

"There'll be coffee at the station. And we'll be able to get a good breakfast before the next show."

We did three TV programs that day, two radio broadcasts, two newspaper interviews and an autographing. I felt great. And at the airport where I was leaving Mike for the next city, he exclaimed, "You look better than when we started! Where do you get your energy?"

It was the first time I articulated what I was to say so often. And I said it fervently: "God and vitamins!"

The Body Keeps Trying to Tell Us

I could also have told him, "Exercise. Plenty of really *enjoyable* exercise. And water, lots of water." And minerals and the right food and a number of other things I'm going to share with you in this book. Physical things, yes, but profoundly related to spiritual things. Inseparable, in fact. For everything *is* spirit before it can manifest in the flesh.

God thought this world into existence and *we* have to think into existence everything that happens to the bodies he gave us. For instance, before I can dive into cold water and swim, the inner voices of self—mind and spirit—must decide to do it. Before I can pick a ripe tomato and eat it, someone must have thought to plant the seed. A seed that then joins forces with the mysterious unseen life-spirit in sun and soil so that it can grow, *become.* The same is true of everything we do for or to our bodies. Even so simple an act as taking a vitamin or mineral. Through mind and body I choose; and within that capsule lies a life-force that someone else has thought to harvest and put there. *Nothing that is physical is not first spiritual,* as Frederick Price says in his fine little book *How Faith Works.* I agree, and so does the Bible.

No wonder then that the state of our mind and spirit has such an effect on our bodies, and vice versa. That when we are in top form physically we have fewer mental and emotional problems.

And that anxiety, worry, guilt, fear, despair, can make us physically ill. Long before doctors and psychologists acknowledged this, Jesus was demonstrating it. When he told the man to take up his bed and walk, he added, "Your sins are forgiven." The certain inference being that the man's sense of guilt and sin was a causative factor. When the woman who had bled for years touched his garment and was made well, there is a strong indication that she had been shamed by this condition, felt guilty about it, "unclean." And that healing could occur only when this man of so much power yet so much understanding made her feel whole and pure once more.

There are even cynics who claim that most of the miracles attributed to Jesus were in cases that were "probably psychosomatic" in origin. Which is ridiculous, since he was also dealing with the scourge of leprosy, with epilepsy and demon possession, with people who had been blind or deaf and dumb from birth. He even raised the clinically dead—and a situation couldn't be *less* psychosomatic than that! No, Jesus didn't believe, nor do I, that sickness is always self-induced, our afflictions all our fault. I know—we all do—good, almost saintly people who are crippled by arthritis, multiple sclerosis or a car; people who cry out with every fiber of their being to be well. Certainly such arguments collapse, at least for me, when a baby is born blind or mongoloid or deformed, or when cancer takes its terrible toll of children.

So I don't *blame* people who are ill or overweight or chronically tired, dispirited and ailing. We human beings differ so vastly from each other in our genes, the physical attributes and susceptibilities which we inherit, as well as develop. Nonetheless, a lot of us—yes, most of us—could be a lot more vigorous, healthy, attractive and happy than we are. And we would be if we only cared enough about ourselves, yes, and others, to take the trouble. Too many of us simply fail to value this remarkable gift, our own body, until it breaks down. "We take better care of our cars!" our old doctor friend A. B. Little would fume. "You can always get a new car, but this is the only body you're ever going to have."

The only body. That marvelous vehicle in which the spirit will make its entire journey through life. . . . Listen to it. What is it trying to tell you about its own state—or about you? About your capacity to handle certain foods or drinks; your ability to work, to cope with stress, to love, to play. We ought to become very aware of our body's signals and directives, because when we ignore them we suffer. "I'm full," says the stomach, yet the appetite can't resist more food and we get uncomfortable or sick. The body tells us when we need sleep; if we're driving and don't stop, we may run off the road and be killed. The body that is being abused by alcohol, drugs, hot blasts of tar and nicotine, begs constantly and desperately for relief. These are obvious examples, but there are more subtle ones just as significant.

The body hates to be thwarted, it wants to do the job for which it was designed. Stop, listen. What is your body saying to you? That you are a lazy, foolish, self-indulgent creature, neglecting and destroying the most important possession you'll ever have? Or that it's grateful to you, glowing, glad to have you aboard? . . . And what are you saying to your body? "Shut up, don't bother me, I'll do as I please." Or "I love you, I'm proud of you. I'll do everything I can to keep you well and slim and strong for as long as the Lord wants us here. Together we can make it a glorious trip."

The body will understand and heed. It will do its best, marshaling its own powers of healing, protection and resistance to disease and even injuries. "The body and the soul do respond to the spirit," says medical doctor William Standish Reed in *Surgery of the Soul,* "and particularly when the human spirit is in harmony with the Spirit of God."

A Lucky Start

I started out lucky, although nobody knew it then. My family were the poor relations of a big rollicking, ebullient, quarrelsome, energetic clan. My dad, Sam Holmes, was one of thirteen children. "And eleven of them grew up," Grandma used to boast in those days when infant mortality was high. And most of them lived to a ripe old age. Like his brothers and sisters, Dad was dynamic, volatile, funny, vigorous, always full of inventions, schemes and dreams. In his youth he was handsome, a gay blade. He became bald and bellied but he never lost his enthusiasm, his dash. He worshiped the ground Mother walked on—so much more slowly, daintily, fearfully almost.

Mother was beautiful and witty, but, like her Quaker parents, less highly charged. She tired easily, she sighed a lot. She put things off, she dreaded things. She was a reader and a thinker and it took her forever to get at the dishes, or finish them. My sister and I often snatched a plate from her hands while, talking, she wiped it over and over—gave it a swipe and stuck it in the cupboard. Dreamily, not noticing, she would reach for another. She was constantly astonished, even dazzled, at the speed with which we got things done.

She adored Dad, never ceased to be entertained by his jokes or his caprice. They were very affectionate; they hugged and kissed a lot, and she sat on his lap long after it was a strain for the old wooden rocker to hold the two of them. (It was years before I realized this was a very uncommon practice among couples married to each other.)

There was far more love than money in the house. And although dear faithful Dr. O'Donohugh called whenever one of us got the grippe or more likely a bellyache from green apples, we were seldom sick. In fact, neither of my parents ever spent a day or night in the hospital in their entire lives. That is, until the prostate operation during which Dad died at seventy-one. Mother lived to be eighty-four, teaching her Sunday-school class on Sunday, laughing merrily at church circle Tuesday and going to join Dad the next day.

They were big eaters—most people were. Church picnics, box socials, enormous family dinners with aunts, uncles and cousins swarming and stuffing themselves. There was lots of kidding and practical jokes, and many violent arguments— sometimes with an uncle getting roaring mad and herding his brood home. The air was heavy with the smoke of big cigars. They ate pork and gravy and hot homemade white bread and devil's food cakes and apple pies. My grandmother made sour-cream cookies so rich they melted on your tongue. They downed vast bowls of homemade ice cream churned lengthily on the back porch. They devoured ham and bacon and sausage and side meat and fried potatoes and so many eggs they almost cackled. They consumed quantities of candy—bulging striped sacks of chocolates from the Greeks' Candy Kitchen, and weekly platters of thick homemade fudge. Nobody worried about cholesterol or counted calories—they'd never heard of them. Vitamins were as yet unknown.

Yet God and vitamins must surely have been at work even then. There is just no other way to explain the enormous vitality and good health of my family, despite what would today be considered its wanton ways. True, it was generally either feast or famine at our particular house, and maybe the lean times made up for the fat ones. But love was there in abundance, and God is love. And even if nobody recognized them, we were getting our vitamins.

We were, in fact, eating organic foods. Pesticides weren't even invented then, nor artificial fertilizers. Good old-fashioned smelly manure was spread on our backyard gardens and on the jet-black fields of the farms that bordered our little town. And the vitamins, all unsuspected, were packed in the raw carrots and tomatoes we munched all summer. In the raspberries and blackberries and grapes that choked the fence. In the apples and cherries and juice-beaded plums that bowed the trees and lay rotting on the ground. In the sweet corn and peas and little red new potatoes. Nature poured upon us a veritable cornucopia of foods uncontaminated by artificial colors and flavors, untainted by chemical preservatives.

We were also breathing clean clear air and drinking clean pure water. Well water, usually, free of chlorine and fluoride, and tasting so sweet and cold after you pumped it that you drank several long drafts of it from the dipper hanging there. Air and noise pollution were other terms nobody had added to our vocabulary to be concerned about. The fragrance of hay fields and clover and cut grass . . . of bread baking . . . of apple butter bubbling on a kitchen range . . . or the spicy tang of a neighbor making catsup . . . the musky whiff of cow barns, or of pigs that squealed in the night as a long train with a plaintive whistle drew them toward their doom. . . . These were the sounds and smells we breathed and heard instead of smog and gas fumes and the deafening assault of rock bands and city traffic.

Sure, Mother cooked with lard and white sugar and cocoa and

other things now considered anathema by people conscious of good nutrition. But they never seemed to hurt us, maybe because we were so tough and resilient from all the exercise we got working, walking, skating and swimming in the lake; maybe because we didn't know they could. We didn't worry about what we ate, we thought we had too much else to worry about, such as getting to go to college, making ends meet. We had no idea how much we were being spared of other worries that would one day plague the world.

Girls didn't smoke, nice people didn't drink. An alcoholic was so conspicuous he was known as the town drunk. Drugs were a horror story not even imagined, much less written. There was no TV to exploit sex, no pornography to debase it. There was very little promiscuity, hence few victims of VD. In fact, sex was something to be reserved for marriage; and although plenty of people didn't wait, to be "caught" by becoming pregnant out of wedlock was considered a disgrace. In these areas, at least, we were raised to respect and cherish our own bodies.

The risk of a ruined reputation may have been a stronger deterrent than morals learned in church or home, yet there *were* deterrents which saved people a lot of grief. Certainly we did not have the staggering suicide rates that are given for our presumably wiser, happier, liberated youth. (If they are so much happier and wiser, why is suicide the third leading cause of death between the ages of fifteen and nineteen? [Up 124 per cent since 1961.] The first is accidents, the second homicide.)

As I described in *You and I and Yesterday:* "It was a time of being safe, being sheltered, being loved. A time when the American dream still beckoned." It was also a time when most of us were bouncing with energy and ambition to achieve that dream, when nothing seemed impossible, if only because we always *felt* so good.

2

The Wonderful Whys of Exercise

Sidewalks were plentiful in our town and people walked on them. We walked to school and, no matter how far we lived, even walked home for lunch. Men walked to work, women walked to call on each other and to Ladies' Aid and clubs. We walked to church and downtown to the movies. We walked to lectures at the college and concerts in the park. Pushing heavy lawn mowers, we walked to cut the grass.

Walking was associated with pleasure as much as with purpose. . . . The Saturday-night promenade up and down Main Street. The couples strolling along the lakeshore, arms entwined. Groups of young people or whole families laughing and talking as they "went for a walk." . . . All kids were eager to drive, of course, and it was legal if you could reach the steering wheel and the pedals at the same time, so I learned. But there simply weren't that many cars to go around. A two-car family was rare indeed; many families didn't have even one. The lone car in most families was fought over so furiously it was sometimes easier to walk, and often just as much fun. Even in his final years Dad would often let the car sit in the driveway and walk downtown to visit with his cronies at the courthouse or the pool hall. And although we hadn't the faintest idea that we were doing anything constructive for our bodies (yes, and souls), I know now how valuable all that walking was. By using "Dr. Right Foot and Dr. Left Foot" as is often said, we had few occasions to need any other.

Despite our vigorous background and upbringing, alas my own generation quickly lapsed into the familiar patterns of adulthood. We considered ourselves too busy with jobs, family, community projects, politics and trying to save the world from its follies, to try to save our bodies from conking out through even a minimal program of exercise.

A lot of people groan when you mention the word. They realize it's something they "need" and "ought" to do something about. They admit feeling "guilty" because they may be over-weight and under-energized, but are too lazy to exercise at home, or can't take the time to attend a class or even to play golf as often as they "should." A huge bag of squirming negatives that lead us right back to those not entirely halcyon days I've described. At least the phys-ed part of our schooling: Being herded into big smelly gyms and coerced into seemingly mean-ingless routines of drills, squatting, jumping and flapping the arms because it was supposed to be "good for you." "We grow up to be muscular misfits," as New York educator Eugene Ezer-sky puts it, "because gym was something to be endured, like algebra."

There was also the crowded, messy misery of the showers. To this day one of my editors will not even *try* a cold shower no matter how enthusiastically I recommend it—"Because we had this horrible teacher who made us stand under that icy water. I swore that if I ever escaped I'd *never* take another cold shower!"

When I was a teen-ager we'd do almost anything to get out of gym, even to faking a menstrual period. Yet as I've said, most of us were healthy, vitally physical young animals who gloried in swimming, skating and playing backyard football and baseball with our brothers. It wasn't the exercise we detested, but the fact that somebody could blow a whistle and make us do things for which we saw no earthly purpose and which, except for basketball, weren't much fun.

What We Learned

In all fairness I did learn and still use several wonderful exercises from gym. Here's one which I've done every day for years (once I woke up again to the marvelous, revitalizing power of exercise). It stretches every muscle and tissue of the body, particularly the abdomen. I consider it the most valuable exercise I've ever encountered:

> Lie on your back on the floor. Put both legs over your head, holding them straight and firm. Stretch your arms as far as you can behind your head. Now slowly . . . slowly, lower the feet and legs, letting gravity pull them down. Resist gravity; hold back as long as you can. . . . As the legs and feet continue to lower, feel the pull in your stomach muscles, your back. It will be intense, it will hurt, but that's good. . . . Continue to descend slowly . . . slowly. At one point, about midway down, you will feel as if you are floating over a cavern, almost into infinity. When you are finally but a few inches from the floor, it is as if you will never touch earth again. . . . It is a strange, almost mystical experience.

Perhaps I treasure and am faithful to this exercise because whenever we tried it in class I was always the champion holder-outer against gravity, which gave me a sweet sense of both show-offmanship and power (the only distinction I ever enjoyed in gym). And a sense of power and control as you test and try your body is one of the subtle but profound rewards of exercise.

There was another exercise which my sister and I and Babe, a friend who practically lived at our house, did every night before piling three deep into bed. We called it the Bridge. This too I was faithful to. It's great for toughening those torso muscles that are so susceptible to sagging. I'm convinced it had a lot to do with the easy delivery of my babies and helped me get my figure back.

> Lying on the bed (or better yet, the floor), arch your back and stomach by placing both hands palms down behind your head, pushing upward while keeping the feet flat.

We also picked up and practiced minor forms of gymnastics—cartwheels, splits, walkovers, back bends. We were in love with our own bodies, anxious to be supple and slim. We did these things because we wanted to. We had motives, and we took pride and delight in them.

So we were actually getting more out of gym than we realized. And I do consider physical education one of the most important things a school can teach. I deplore the fact that, according to C. Carson Conrad, head of the President's Council on Physical Fitness and Sports, "more and more school boards are listening to vocal minorities who don't want physical education to be required." His statement came after a University of Michigan study of 7,800 boys and girls between ten and seventeen years old revealed there has been an alarming decline in physical condition over the past decade. "I think this is the beginning of an erosion which can have disastrous effects on the health of this country's population."

Kathleen Maxa, who did a series, "Sound Body, Sound Mind," for the Washington *Star,* calls this a new kind of energy crisis, and asks, "Is this the legacy we want for our children?"

Glenn Swengros, of the President's Council, told me that since Conrad's statement and that study, things have actually gotten worse. "Many schools are reducing their phys-ed programs due to lack of funds. Also, with colleges hard to get into, many kids are concentrating on academic courses instead. Then there are the organized sports, which leave so many out." He went on to say there are two times when you can really interest people in their bodies: when they are very young and have a lot of physical energy; and when they get around middle age and doctors warn them about getting fat and needing to take better care of themselves. Tragically, there is a major drop-off in between. Television, cars and just "hanging around" are depriving youngsters of critical exercise *during the very years their cardiovascular systems are developing.*

A report from the American Academy of Pediatrics warns us: "By the time they enter college a large percentage of young men and women have been shown to be in alarmingly poor cardiovascular-pulmonary condition." A fact born out by the shockingly high incidence of atherosclerosis discovered in young Americans killed in Vietnam.

Happily, in some places a solution is emerging. A program

known as *New Physical Education* is being taught by Eugene Ezersky, Philadelphia's Earle Matlack, Arnold Dort and others. While not eliminating competitive sports, emphasis is placed on "lifetime sports" (tennis, archery, golf, rowing, etc.). And "movement education" which enables every child to explore the joys of sheer movement—with hula hoops and skipping ropes, with ladders, trapezes, parallel bars, or while playing games and acquiring skills he really wants and enjoys. In "Gym Class Goes Natural," Leonard Lear's fine article in *Prevention,* Arnold Dort says, "When I went to school myself I didn't enjoy it because I always wanted to be outdoors. So I made up my mind that when I became a phys-ed teacher I'd try to give my students an outdoor experience that would last a lifetime. That's why I take them hiking, biking, swimming. You can see for yourself how they love it." Earle Matlack agrees; kids who have happy experiences with exercise, he says, will be a lot more likely to exercise as adults when there's no instructor around to make them do it.

It seems doubly deplorable, then, that *any* schools should be cutting back at the very time such imaginative programs are developing! If such things could have helped my generation, just think how much more important they could be to today's kids, who don't have to walk to school as we did, who are stuffed with junk food, and who crouch motionless so many hours before the TV set.

Exercise Tells the Body "I Love You"

Everyone knows in a general way what exercise can do for us. That it is vitalizing and energizing, that it can ease our tensions and even prevent or help cure many ailments; in short, that it can make us happier, healthier, more beautiful people. But just *why* is exercise able to do so much for us?

The reason is both biological and psychological. God gave us these superlative bodies, cunningly complex, artful and awesome in their power, ability and design. Yet with only four fundamental needs to survive: A body has to be fed, watered, rested and used. Beyond that, anything we do for it, even bathing, however beneficial, is not absolutely essential to its organic survival.

Society and the instinctive desire to be acceptable makes us put forth the effort to keep the body clean. But we are prone to assume that the activity it gets through sheer daily usefulness, working for us, carrying us about, is enough. It isn't. It was true in the beginning and is still true of primitive societies like the Hunzas of the Himalaya Mountains, or the Abkhasian peasants of the Russian Caucasus, all of whom do hard physical labor to advanced years; but it is not true of our sedentary civilization, where "progress" has taken the load from our shoulders—and put it right back on our bellies. Relieved in one direction, we are robbing our bodies in another, cheating them of what they crave and need most to stay slender and vigorous and serve us well: genuine, challenging exercise.

Exercise tells the body it's appreciated, worthy of our attention. Exercise, in effect, tells the body, and its Creator, "Thank you, I love you." And the body responds. Not only physically but spiritually, with a feeling of well-being, of peace and delight and self-respect.

More specifically, there are definite biological functions which exercise accomplishes and/or improves. Quite likely we were taught these in school but we just didn't listen, or forgot. Anyway, once we realize how critically important exercise is to the proper functioning of the body, we begin to realize how critically important it is for us to take the time and effort to provide that exercise.

In summary, exercise affects:

1. *The work of the heart.* The heart is a muscle like any other. It is exercised and strengthened by activities which make it beat faster. The faster breathing delivers a fresh and larger supply of oxygen, which makes its job easier. Exercise also opens up new pathways to supply the heart with blood. Studies have proved that physically active people are far less likely to have heart attacks, and three times as likely to survive if they do.

2. *Circulation.* "You're as old as your arteries," the saying goes. Exercise increases the flow of blood to the arteries. It opens the tiny blood vessels in tissues and flesh, and allows

oxygen and nutrients to be released. The blood supply increases throughout the body, which in itself gives necessary exercise to the arteries and veins as well. Enough body movement will enlarge existing blood paths, and if the demand for blood is greater than can pass through clogged or narrow arteries, even create new ones!

3. *Breathing.* The respiratory system. Exercise, especially in fresh air, forces us to draw deeper drafts of air into our lungs, thus cleansing and flushing out impurities. People who have hay fever, asthma and similar diseases are encouraged by many doctors to jog, cycle or do even brief exercises to get rid of secretions and to open air passages. The *Journal of Allergy* reported that at the University of Iowa Medical College doctors Hal Richerson and Paul Seebohm were able to relieve patients of nasal congestion by having them play a game of handball or even do a simple three-minute step exercise. Evidently the blood vessels in the nose would constrict, increasing the air flow. Another study, conducted on heavy smokers at the Army Medical Research Laboratory at Fort Knox, revealed that only a few minutes of exercise before donating blood reduced the carbon monoxide level in their blood by 10 per cent.

In short, those deep drafts of air which flood our lungs activate and help purify the bloodstream—to the benefit of every system and organ in the body. (And this includes the brain.)

4. *Digestion, elimination.* Exercise sends blood scurrying on its way carrying its precious oxygen and nutrients to our cells. (Minerals, vitamins and foodstuffs, whether from a capsule, a steak or a salad, won't do much good if they sit in the stomach or are sluggish in reaching their destination.) Exercise also facilitates the release of this vital cargo by opening up the capillaries which allow it to flow through. And exercise speeds and helps the elimination of wastes. Anyone who is immobilized usually quickly discovers his marvelous plumbing system coming to a stubborn halt. Especially the bowels. Kidneys, bladder, intestines, all demand stimulation through exercise. When we exercise, even the skin can do a better job of helping throw off wastes through perspiration.

5. *The muscles.* Muscles are made up of fibers which are strengthened through exercise, and become more able to with-

stand fatigue. The amount of blood flowing through our muscles *determines our energy and endurance.* Exercise strongly affects that amount. It's been observed that birds such as chickens, who don't fly much, have white meat on their breasts but dark meat on their constantly exercised legs. Whereas ducks, who both paddle and fly long distances, are entirely dark inside. This is because of the heavy concentration of capillaries in the muscles most used.

6. *Bones.* Bones are not static, but consist of living cells which continue to grow throughout life. Bones constantly renew themselves by absorbing calcium through the blood. Exercise helps the blood deliver that calcium. When we don't exercise, bones weaken. If a bone is kept in a cast, it will thin and decalcify. People who must lie in bed a long time, especially in casts, will excrete large amounts of calcium in the urine. Bones also benefit *directly* by the impact of exercise.

One unexpected problem of the astronauts was the loss of bone calcium due to their inactive, weightless state. NASA's Dr. Victor Schneider says, "The body somehow senses that it doesn't need the bone and muscle and they deteriorate." The space agency is conducting experiments to try to overcome this serious complication.

7. *Keeping young.* No lotion, elixir, spa or transplant can equal exercise when it comes to keeping your looks and forestalling "age." Trim and limber bodies; bones that don't break; heart, lungs and digestion in great shape; alert minds. These are what exercise can let us enjoy, instead of submitting to the miseries so many people consider almost inevitable with age. Joan Griffith, director of the Women's Sports Foundation in San Mateo, California, says she has to run to keep in shape. "When I stop for a while I see the deterioration setting in. *Exercise is a positive form of vanity.*" (Italics mine.) Hooray for that form of vanity! And the earlier you start, the better. But it's never too late. The National Institute on Aging is urging the elderly to get out of the Bingo halls and away from the TV sets, into the pools and gyms and streets for some genuinely enjoyable exercise. There are people in their eighties and nineties winning marathons who didn't even start until their seventies. And they are

enthusiastic, rejuvenated. They will live longer, and when they do die, "die well," as one of them laughingly expressed it to me.

8. *Sleep, relaxation.* Exercise tunes up the whole body, releases tension and encourages restful sleep. In his book *Vigor Regained,* Dr. Herbert de Vries states, "Muscle tightness is intimately linked with anxiety and nervous tension." In a series of experiments with older people he was able to establish that when people are tense, unable to relax, there are actual *raised levels of electrical activity in their muscles,* which can be reduced as much as 23 per cent when they are able to exercise.

Exercise is especially relaxing in fresh air. It shouldn't be strenuous at bedtime, but a walk under the stars or brisk run with the dog is like a soporific, at least for me. I come back yawning, almost limp with sleepiness. In the words of the famous Dr. Paul Dudley White, exercise induces restful sleep "more than any medicine, highball or television show."

Walking

Back to my own case history—as I've said, I learned to drive at an early age. But later, during the gas shortage of World War II, I let my license lapse. Walking became a way of life again, so rewarding and in many ways so much simpler that for the next twenty-five years, while my children were being raised, I did not drive.

Our oldest, mother of two, who spends most of her life on wheels, says, "Mother, that's the smartest thing you ever did." I agree. I got out of all that chauffeuring (not that the children didn't get places—I took them by cab or bus, or we walked), and I got in all that exercise. I walked to the shopping center, the hairdresser, the post office, the bank. I walked the youngsters to the houses of playmates. I know some of the neighbors felt sorry for me, and one particular mother thought me quite mad. An enormously fat woman with varicose veins, who would actually back out and drive her Sally the scant two blocks to our house. She was forever generously imploring me to let her drive me on my errands, flabbergasted that anyone should really prefer using legs.

No use even trying to explain how much I got from walking.

How it perks up the spirits, relaxes taut nerves. How problems that seem insoluble beside a sink or at a desk either vanish or work themselves smoothly out as you swing along—in my case usually pushing a stroller or grocery cart or carrying library books. How the sheer rhythms of walking put you back in tempo with the universe—the birds, the clouds, the rain, the wind, the swaying trees. How you observe bits of interest or loveliness you'd otherwise miss: a clutch of violets beside an unsuspected stream, a unique birdbath in someone's yard, the parallel shadows of a board fence on a sunny lawn.

A couple of times I fell in step with our neighbor Dr. Little, making his house calls hatless and coatless, whatever the weather, and we'd have one of our good health talks. From him I learned that walking utilizes every part of the body. Not just feet and legs and joints, but torso, spine, neck, pelvis, ribs. And as the fresh air dilates the lungs and sends a fresh supply of oxygen throughout your body, the heart receives a lift. "That's why we say your legs are your second heart." He informed me further that the heart is a muscle, involuntary, but profoundly affected by everything we do and even feel, and especially responsive to exercise. That 72,000 quarts of blood are driven through our system every twenty-four hours along some 100,000 miles of veins and arteries. As we walk, the abdominal, feet and leg muscles help push the blood toward the heart and brain, against the pull of gravity. "People who refuse to walk or exercise those muscles are likely to have phlebitis or varicose veins."

Hence Sally's mother!

The Doctor Who Changed My Life

Dr. A. B. Little had come into our life shortly after our move to Washington, D.C. Our ten-year-old woke up one morning with a sore throat and high fever. I phoned our next-door neighbor, a beautiful lady in her eighties, for advice. "Call A.B.," she said at once. "Dr. Little. He lives just a block away, and he'll come."

Thank goodness. It was snowing and the walks were slick. I didn't relish thoughts of transporting a feverish child even a block and then waiting through office hours. Soon the old-fashioned doorbell clanged, and without waiting for an answer, he was bounding upstairs in the huge Victorian house we were remodeling. A lean whip of a man, so rosy and fit I assumed he had just returned from Florida, partly because he was wearing a summer suit almost the same creamy white as his hair. As he sat on the bed ministering to the child, he welcomed us to the community, invited us to a party the next evening, asked if we were interested in square dancing—he was getting up a club— pronounced the room too hot and sprang up to fling open a window.

"Give him plenty of fruit juices and water and keep him in bed." He scribbled on a pad. "Give him this every four hours."

I trotted downstairs ahead of him. "Let me get your coat."

He grinned in a half-sheepish, half-proud way he had. "Don't own a hat or overcoat. And I always walk on my house calls."

I gasped. "On days like this? Don't you catch cold?"

"Nope. I've got a Ph.D." He paused, enjoying my confusion. "Perfectly Hard Dermis."

As he stood there, pulling on gloves and rubbers, his only concession to the storm, he delivered the first of many lectures I was to hear from him. "People don't need to catch cold, not if they learn to condition their skin. Wear as few clothes as you can get by with—I don't even wear an undershirt. Start shedding clothes little by little and you'll be surprised how much your body can stand. Your skin adapts to the weather and gets tougher for it, gives you better resistance all over. And think of the time you save. Think how much time I'd be wasting if I had to stop and take off a hat and coat and scarf and overshoes, and then have to pad my body with all that stuff again. Besides, it's a strain on the heart lifting a heavy overcoat on and off all the time." He gave me a thoughtful look. "How old are you?"

"Thirty-eight."

"Good. That's just the age I was when I first taught myself how to live. See you and your husband tomorrow night?"

"Well, if he doesn't have to work late. And if we can get a baby-sitter."

"Nonsense," he said abruptly. "Life's too short for anybody who's worked all week to still be at it Friday night. And don't worry about the sitter, bring the children along. We're putting on a musical comedy in our rec room. I wrote it myself."

That was my introduction to a man who was to change my life. He was then, I learned later, seventy-six years old.

For the next ten years A.B., as people fondly called him, was to be not only physician but friend, father confessor and one-man entertainment committee. His own family consisted of a grown daughter, several grandchildren and numerous nieces whom he was educating, and frequently married off in beautiful weddings to which friends and patients were invited. He had also delivered half the population of our section, Takoma Park. We were told, that first merry, memorable night, that he'd delivered most of the cast!

He was always browbeating people into performing in these theatricals, whatever your talents or lack of them; it was hard to turn him down. They were staged in a huge game room which he'd transformed into a combination little theater and woodland dell. Laboring lovingly into the night (he claimed most people slept far more than necessary), with his surgical shears he fashioned tin lanterns, stars, moons; made his own papier-mâché for the rocks and bridges; created a lustily blooming garden of crepe-paper flowers. "Poor Ruth," some of their friends said of his wife, "that room's all mahogany-paneled, but it's been years since she's seen the walls." Or "Poor Ruth, she'd love to have a fur coat, but A.B. won't let her, he's afraid she might catch cold!"

Yet everybody adored them both, and nobody ever heard a word of complaint from the loyal, devoted Ruth Little.

A.B.'s own story was a triumph over a sickly childhood and youth. He was seriously ill so often "people told my mother she'd never be able to raise me; I remember hearing her and the doctor discussing where I would be buried." Sent to school at six, he was too weak and frightened to stay; his mother taught him herself until he was eight. "A remarkable woman with great patience and understanding, she literally kept me alive." He was far ahead of his class when he went back, and excelled until he was twelve. Then he saw a classmate shoot himself through the heart. The tragedy cost him a nervous breakdown, and again it was his mother who sustained him.

At fourteen he returned to school, led his class, graduated and even went on to work his way through medical college. All this time, however, he was, he said, "puny." Subject to colds, coughs, pneumonia, and so tired most of the time that studying was misery. Even so, he graduated, interned, married and went into practice. By the time he was thirty-eight "I'd begun to have arthritis in my knees and some cardiac arrhythmias, and suddenly woke up. I realized my life was almost half over and I had spent most of it absolutely wretched physically."

It was then he began the exercises that, he is convinced, made him a new man. Their main objective: to improve the circulation. Because, except for the skin, "circulation is everything." Here are Dr. Little's exercises, just as he wrote them for me. It is their aspect of "limp vigor" which distinguishes them from any I've ever encountered. Exercises One and Two (arms and legs) are actually a relaxed yet energetic kicking and flinging of the extremities.

Exercise Number One: The Legs

Lift one leg up high, and let go, letting it plunge relaxed to the floor. Fifty to 100 times, each leg. Or even more times. Repeat four or five times a day.

Exercise Number Two: The Arms

As with the legs (and you can do them together if you can maintain your balance), fling the arms over your shoulders, trying to release the upper spine. Then fling them downward with a limp jerk. Repeat 50 or more times. Then a horizontal swinging of the arms. And lastly a vertical thrust with limp vigor. Fifty times or more.

Exercise Number Three: The Abdomen

Lie on your back on a rug, place feet under a dresser or anything suitable. Place hands around back of neck, then rise to sitting position. If unable to do this, sit down with feet under dresser and lean back as far as you can, then pull yourself up, going back farther as you develop better muscle capacity. . . . This should not be overdone to begin with, as muscles will get very sore.

Exercise Number Four: Breathing

Lie on back or side on bed or couch. Imagine you are blowing a horn. Blow out every possible bit of air in your lungs. You will feel the lower chest muscles and abdominal muscles contracting. Then take in a big breath of air. In the course of time work up to doing this eight or ten times a day.

Exercise Number Five: The Neck*

Lubricate both hands and neck thoroughly with some good cream or soap, using water to make it more slippery. Place thumbs over palms of hands (flexing is the word), and place on neck muscles. Then rotate the head horizontally and rapidly 50 to 100 times. Then do the same vertically (up and down) about the same number of times. This is valuable for keeping your neck muscles developed and your neck looking younger. Also, in certain cases of cardiac arrhythmias it works like a charm. By this technique I cured myself of auricular fibrillation attacks that occurred over a period of twelve years and did not respond to the skill of a cardiologist. It was worth a million dollars to me.

Exercise Number Six: Feet and Toes

While lying on your back curl toes back and under, as if you were making a fist. Then release and draw up in the opposite direction, with ankles moving forward and back at the same time. This can be done anytime you are lying down.

Curiously, those exercises are either relaxing or invigorating, I found, whichever your need. They can be done almost anywhere, anytime, and they are marvelous for the circulation.

On the same pages of exercise, A.B. wrote the following:

Exercise Number Seven: The Psyche

Exercise of the psyche, or spirit, can go on all day long, all waking hours, consciously at times, subconsciously at all times, and should be considered the "raison d'être" of living. Without that we are just a high-class animal. The psyche flowers by the exercise of love, service, unselfishness, courage, etc., ad infinitum.

Relaxation

Daily periods of relaxation, mental and physical, are important.

Diet

Very important. Never, under any circumstances, eat a big meal. Breakfast should be the biggest meal, supper the smallest. Diet should be balanced, plenty of proteins from lean meat and vegetables, and carbohydrates instead of sugar. Avoid fat meats and be sure you get plenty of vitamins and minerals.

---

* My present husband, a doctor, says this actually consists of a thumb massage to those neck arteries, plus finger pressure against the cranial nerve with the fingers released. We both have been trying this ourselves, and it feels good!

3

Jogging, Jumping and Other Fun Things

Eventually, I did learn to drive again and enjoy it. But I will always be grateful for all those years of walking, which gave me so much inadvertent exercise. And I still walk a lot. As Robert Rodale expressed it: "That rhythmic pacing does something for you that no other exercise can, and certainly that no doctor's drug can do. . . . I can't explain it, but it is a fact that regular walking makes people happier."

Climbing Stairs

Meanwhile, I was getting a lot of other inadvertent exercise traveling miles in that huge Victorian house, especially up and down stairs. One of its chief attractions had been its long winding front staircase. There were also broad marvelous steps to the attic, a steep, spicy-smelling back staircase to the kitchen and another set of steps to the basement. Whenever I wasn't actually at the typewriter in my second-floor study, I seemed to be in transit between the activities of four children, from their clubhouse in the attic to their Cub pack meetings in the basement.

People were always commiserating: "Don't you just wear yourself *out* climbing all those stairs?"

"No," I could honestly reply, "I really love stair steps and think they're good for you." To me stairs are lovely and inviting. I've never cared much for one-story houses or even split-levels with a modicum of steps. They may be models of convenience, but convenience is the enemy of exercise. If you have to climb steps, you *will*. Of course, if you're old or handicapped and can't climb stairs, then a one-story house may be essential; and lots of people build or buy anticipating "the day when we can't climb steps." Well, surely you'll postpone that day for years and maybe for always if you keep in the habit of climbing. After all, the National Geriatric Society says, "the only reason we can't do things as we get older is because we stop doing them."

Keith Monroe reported in *Reader's Digest* that "the peppy Charles F. Kettering of General Motors, who worked at full speed until his death at eighty-two, never took any formal exercise; instead, he just didn't wait for elevators. Whenever he had to visit upper-story offices or laboratories he walked up at least two floors and down three."

The famous heart specialist Dr. Paul Dudley White urged people who think they don't have time for long walks, at least to climb stairs. At the behest of its director, Dr. Joseph Wolffe, there was no elevator for at least a decade for either staff or patients at Valley Forge Medical Center and Heart Hospital. "Stair walking involves all systems of the body," Dr. Wolffe wrote. "The body is carried upward by the skeletal muscles. Groups of muscles contract while their antagonists relax. The work that is required is not limited, however, to the lower extremities. Important chemical changes take place, more blood and oxygen is needed by the active muscles. The heart and vessels are gradually strengthened to meet the demands." These and other authorities have discovered that people forced to climb steps also have stronger bones.

When our family shrank and we moved to a smaller house, it was again on several levels. I intentionally placed my writing workshop on a different floor from that other workshop, the kitchen. All this time I was also running up and down steps at the summer cabin in the country that eventually became our permanent home. Here there are steps down to the lake, steps up the hill, steps from my study to the living room. Like a mountain goat, I climb and scurry and exercise all day without even being aware of it.

Running

Walking is pleasant, but running is fun. Jogging came into its own some years ago when people became aware of the science of aerobics, as taught the United States Air Force by Dr. Kenneth Cooper and presented to the public in his books. (Also those of his wife, Mildred, who collaborated on *Aerobics for Women.)* The thesis of this marvelous system is that "endurance is the best kind of insurance" (against ailments, aging and fatigue). "If you'd like to start back down that road to physical fitness, then get active with the kind of exercises that will demand oxygen and force your body to process and deliver it." These exercises include swimming, cycling, walking, all kinds of ball games and running. There is a point system whereby you give yourself credits for the time and distance you expend in any of them.

Since then running has become almost a national obsession. Congressmen and businessmen jog to their offices. Billy Graham jogs to keep in shape for his grueling crusades. So does Robert Schuller, of the dynamic Hour of Power. My nephew, a Sacramento attorney, jogs at least four miles every morning and another two or three during his lunch break. His wife has graduated from jogging to long-distance running. There are running magazines and clubs; marathon races attract enormous crowds. (There were nearly 8,000 official entrants in the 1979 Boston Marathon.) *Publisher's Weekly,* reporting on the many bestselling books on running, estimates that at least 20 million Americans are running.

Richard O. Keeler, also of the President's Council on Physical Fitness and Sports, calls this part of a general renaissance and gives it (together with a new awareness of the importance of nutrition) a lot of credit for the fact that in 1975 American deaths from heart disease were below a million for the first time in ten years.

In some instances whole families are running together—which is just great. But, ironically, this physical fitness boom engages mostly adults, at a time when programs for children are drastically neglected. And, alas, the enthusiasm is far from universal. While running, tennis and other sports are highly visible, especially among the affluent and better educated, government surveys reveal that 45 per cent of all adult Americans do *not* engage in physical activity for exercise; and among Americans past fifty years of age there is not even general awareness of the need!

Well, Dr. Little *was* aware of the need long before aerobics. You might call him literally a forerunner of jogging. Every morning he'd fling open the windows, strap on a pedometer and run in place before breakfast; then walk on his calls, run again before lunch and run the minute the office cleared out. At the end of a day he liked to brag about how many miles he'd chalked up. He urged me to try it, but somehow stationary running didn't send me; if I ran I wanted to *get* someplace, and if possible yell now and then just to let off steam.

Finding our country cabin was the answer. Here we spent summers and many weekends, and here with or without the children I could run, really run up and down the hills. Run until I'm breathless, panting, and the sweat streams down my face. Skip if I feel like it, or revert completely to childhood and run sidewise, heels clicking, or run in vigorous high-kicking goose steps that look idiotic but feel glorious. Nobody's around to see, and nobody would care anyway. Because this kind of personal running is so much more than exercise, it's release. My chance to be alone and utterly myself with the one who created me. Running, I feel as free as the wind, the water, the trees. Running, I rejoice and thank God for them.

I haven't the faintest idea how many points all this would earn on a chart; I run because I enjoy it. I know, my whole being knows, it does something wonderful for me.

Square Dancing

It was A.B. (Dr. Little) who browbeat us into joining his new square-dancing club. I was already doing some of the exercises he recommended—and would demonstrate either in the office or beside a child's sickbed if you gave him the slightest encouragement. But for me it was more from a sense of duty than enthusiasm. So when he proposed the square dancing, I groaned. Both my husband and I had exhausting professional schedules, and were already up to our ears in Scouts and Campfire and PTA. We just didn't see how we could do it. Also, we dreaded learning all those directions. A.B. said nonsense, it was easy, and we owed it to ourselves.

So, at first mainly to appease him, we trudged down the street toward that game room which was to provide so much sheer glorious fun. The caller was marvelous, the music toe-tickling, the other couples likewise novices. And soon we were all sashaying and promenading like old-timers. Square dancing, we discovered, has got to be the most relaxing, rejuvenating, utterly joyful form of exercise. The companionship, the pounding of feet, the patterns, the rhythms. You spin, you swirl, you sweat, you laugh, and often can't resist a shout of pure delight.

Many an evening we'd be so tired it seemed folly to go anywhere but to bed. Yet a walk down the street, ten minutes of dancing and we'd be revitalized; and two hours later having such a marvelous time we hated to say good night. We came home actually rested, restored in body and spirit.

My husband, at that time a heavy smoker, suffered a serious heart attack, which interrupted our square dancing. Then a cruel accident finished it altogether. One day while building a balcony he stepped off into space and fell two stories, breaking his ribs, puncturing a lung and shattering both heels. We were so thankful he wasn't killed and could even *walk* that the loss of dancing seemed small by comparison. Yet we envied the people who were and still are square dancing all over the country. Ten million of them, old and young, from mere children to great-grandparents. They're involved in an activity that can do more for their minds, bodies and spirits than any doctor, psychiatrist or drug. What's more, they're having fun!

Skipping Rope

I began skipping rope one day after reading an article describing its many benefits. Ten or fifteen minutes of jumping rope was rated just as effective as several miles of jogging. Professional athletes, particularly boxers, value it so highly it's a part of their daily program. So what was I waiting for? I'd adored jumping rope as a child—all kids do. Why do we ever stop?

Jumping rope builds up the muscles of your chest, arms and shoulders, is great for the thighs, legs, feet and ankles, enhances circulation, deep breathing, and keeps you nimble, agile and coordinated. In one way it is even better for the whole body than my beloved swimming, because of its direct effect on the bones. Every time you land, the bones that support the body get a jolt that generates a slight electric current "which seems to draw calcium and other minerals out of the blood and into the bone, which is rebuilt and strengthened," science writer Michael Clark reports in *Prevention.* "When the bone is jarred from the bottom, such as would be the case with walking, hiking or skipping rope, the piezo-electric effect causes the bones to become more dense. And increased density means stronger bones." Perhaps this is one reason children do so much jumping; why even as adults we jump up and down to express emotions of excitement or joy. Nature keeps us jumping to preserve our bones.*

The rope I bought at the dime store was too limp. My husband threw it away and cut me a sturdy length of bright yellow water-ski rope. I keep it handy beside the door; and now three times a day, just before meals, whenever it's too cold to swim I duck outdoors and jump.

All exercise should be done outdoors, if possible. Not only because of the fresh air, but because of the life-giving rays of the sun. Artificial light (unless you use full-spectrum bulbs) lacks

---

* To refer again to the astronauts—scientists are afraid this may prove an obstacle to long flights in space. The loss of calcium and bone density was severe after the three Skylab flights (one of eighty-four days) in 1974. Neither exercising in space nor adding calcium to the diet helped. Evidently the earth demands that our bones vigorously contact *her.*

wavelengths that are necessary for the best functioning of the pituitary and pineal glands. If you wear glasses, take them off if you can; eyes too need those essential rays. If it's snowing or actually pouring rain, I jump inside; but sometimes even the rain can be braved to advantage. Its rhythms join those of your bouncing feet, its cool drops are refreshing on your face. I've found there's something special about swimming or jumping or running in the rain—an extra dimension of awareness and wonder, as if nature herself is bestowing a blessing.

A jumping rope can be tucked into your suitcase when you travel and used on the little courtyards or balconies that motels often provide. Or it can be used in your room. I seldom go anyplace without mine.

Swimming

Swimming lacks only one factor to be the perfect exercise: it has no direct impact on bones. They benefit, however, by the increased blood circulation; and swimming engages every muscle of the body. For me it's on a par with dancing for absolute pleasure through exercise.

It was not ever thus. Alas, the child who'd been the blissful water rat became almost water-shy during long dry years of adulthood. When the only swimming to be had was in a crowded, public, chlorine-choked pool, I got in the habit of staying home. By the time we acquired our lakeside summer place I actually dreaded getting wet, getting cold and getting dressed again. I went in only to please the children and have it over with; and even that took will power. It's an attitude I see all the time in guests; even after they get into their swimsuits they sometimes back out, and there's simply no use trying to persuade them. But like love or conversion, a healthy animal delight in water is something that has to be experienced to be believed.

Mine began to come back about the same time I began to reclaim God. I can't say exactly when, only that I'd been having some heavy burdens, struggling with crosses it didn't seem I could bear. And one morning after a restless night I found myself streaking for the water before the family was awake. In an act almost of defiance or at least abandon, I plunged in and swam hard, hard . . . furiously hard, the way I used to swim as a girl. The birds were singing when I climbed out, the sun just beginning to light the world. And as I looked up at that brightening sky I knew somehow that God's eye *was* on the sparrow—and on me. And, drying my tingling flesh, there came a sudden sense of sheer joy and power. I knew, racing back up to duties and trials, that nothing now would be too much for me.

After that I need only dive into the water to be invigorated and restored. Water was like a tonic, giving me help and hope as well as physical energy. It was worth the slight trouble of getting undressed and dressed several times a day. I swim before breakfast, lunch and dinner, usually. A pattern that gradually became a habit. One so strong that I never again dreaded going in or had to argue with myself about it, even on the coldest days.

Habit is your staunchest ally in whatever you undertake, but especially exercise. Do anything regularly enough, long enough, and you've joined forces with something even stronger than will power: simple behaviorism. Something compels you to do it, however uncomfortable, because you'd be more uncomfortable *not* doing it.

So I swim from early spring until the water is almost icy enough to be locked away—and scarcely even feel its fiery baptism, for your body becomes conditioned as well as your attitude. The flesh reacts to the cold but it doesn't mind. The dermis, as our old friend A. B. Little claimed, finally achieves its "Ph.D."

Isometrics, Stretching

I also do isometrics—pulling in stomach muscles, tightening muscles of arms, legs, hips at odd moments while driving, telephoning, or during those times that otherwise can seem both a bore and a waste. And I love to stretch, especially in bed.

During her later years I corresponded with the once famous model and dancer Marguerite Agniel. As a girl she was a near invalid due to heart problems, borderline tuberculosis and internal complications. One day while lying ill, she noticed the graceful stretchings of her cat; and it dawned on her that a cat is one of the healthiest of animals yet it sleeps a lot, getting its major exercise through stretching and relaxing. Concentrated exercise, the concept came to her. She began to emulate the cat's movements until she not only regained the use of her body, but resolved to make it one of the most beautiful bodies in the world.

The photographs in her book *Body Sculpture* reveal how magnificently she succeeded. She became a dancer and artist's model, posing for some of the most distinguished painters and sculptors of her time, including Daniel Chester French. In her other books *Your Figure* and *Creating Body Beauty* and her letters she shared her convictions and personal routines. She attributed most structural defects of the body primarily to bad posture. (One should *not* throw the shoulders back, but rather tilt the chin slightly and carry the rib cage high.) All her exercises were extremely simple, including my favorite, the Cat Arch:

> Balance on hands and knees in a "table" position, with elbows straight, arms and legs at right angles to the body. Then arch your back in the manner of a cat, meanwhile pulling up abdominal muscles and trying to flatten them against your back. Tense every muscle and hold. Then drop to a sway-back position, exhaling and letting the body go limp.

I sometimes vary this by doing some quick panting "belly breathing" while still holding the arch. That is, expanding and contracting the lower abdominal muscles while keeping the upper ones tense. When you exercise, feel free to be creative. It's more intriguing when you try variations or invent new exercises of your own.

Dancing

Dancing is for me the most effortless and beautiful form of exercise. It is also an ancient and instinctive form of worship. I think God planted this love of motion in all of us, so that even babies begin to bounce and "dance" before they're out of their cribs; and no matter what our age, human toes tap to music.

This instinct was strong in my family. Had there been any

dance studios in our hometown, my sister Gwen and I would have been beating at the doors. Both my daughters inherited this passion, and I spent a lot of years around ballet studios watching the fouettés and tour jetés and admiring all those exquisite bodies striving with such dedication for perfection. Lots of times we worked out at home, the girls bemused but patient with my clumsiness. Daily dance sessions became a way of life, so that it is almost impossible for me to hear good music without physically responding.

Usually the first thing I do each morning (in the winter, when not swimming) is turn on our classical-music station or the record player. Suddenly I am awake and alive, in tune with my own body and the day. Feeling like David who danced before the Lord, I "dance" in the shower, dance as I dress, dance in the kitchen getting breakfast. The counter is just the right height for a ballet barre. Facing and holding on to it, I do some pliés to warm up while the coffee is perking:

> Heels together, toes out, knees out, slowly descend to the floor, then rise to the toes, then back to position.

Then, gripping the counter with one hand, I do a series of bends and stretches right and left, with one leg on the counter (or barre). Some of this picked up in studios, some spontaneous, but all to music . . . all with a sense of joy and wonder and thanksgiving that I am here, now, at this moment, able to feel this wonderful body moving and dancing in this way.

I dance as I continue physical tasks of the day. Anything we do, any form of labor large or small, can be easier and more enjoyable if we think of it as an art form to glorify God. The great sculptor and philosopher Walter Russell said, "A menial task which must be mine, that shall I glorify and make an art of it." Think of this as you bend and lean to make a bed; when you crouch to tuck in the covers, make that crouch a plié. Swinging a hammer, raking a garden, lifting a child or a bag of groceries— whatever it may be, put yourself in harmony with your own inner rhythms. Feel their lovely flow. Whenever possible, do these things to music; it will enhance those beautiful rhythms, and put music into your spirit as well.

Other Glorious Activities

Bicycling, skating, tennis. Canoeing, water skiing. These are discussed together because I love them but don't do any of them with regularity. I used to bike and skate with the children, but there's literally no place to ride a bike where we are now. I have resumed ice skating now that our Virginia lake freezes over a few weeks each winter. I admire the many people who take time for tennis. (Never say "have the time"—we all have the same amount, it's the time we *take* that counts.) For us, badminton has proved a pleasant compromise; it can be set up on the lawn and doesn't take as much skill, but uses the same muscles.

I do canoe, but mainly because I refuse to learn to drive the boat. I don't enter races, shoot rapids. Instead, paddle leisurely along, bird-watching or just drinking in the wild sweet fragrance of woods and sparkling water, and soaking up the sun. Learning to water-ski years ago was mainly to prove to the kids I *could;* but I never learned to slalom or do the tricks they swiftly mastered. Once, skiing double, my son swooped past me shouting, " 'Smatter, Mom, can't you ski fancy?" "No," I yelled back, "I'm lucky to ski plain!"

But all these things are peripheral forms of exercise, appealing in themselves. Sports that call to people who enjoy their own active bodies, and theirs to pursue intensely, or as time and desire dictate. There are dozens of others, of course, far too many to list.

Making Work Your "Workout"

Consider any physical job you must perform as useful exercise. Athletes, dancers, boxers, anyone whose vocation depends on the body must "work out." They skip rope, lift barbells, jog. This is imperative if they expect to stay in top professional shape. The rest of us should have a similar, if less strenuous program. And we get additional benefits if we think of our regular tasks as an extension of that workout. The very word *work* takes on a more attractive connotation. You're not only getting the work

out (the yard mowed, the floor scrubbed, the bricks laid), you're
getting another form of workout.

With this in mind you gain an extra bonus from the use of
your body. Stretch, consciously stretch muscles of stomach and
back as well as arms while raking or making that bed. Reach
farther out, pull farther back. Don't forget to think of yourself as
a dancer as you kneel or crouch to wax a floor, to weed or plant.
Feel the harmony of your own muscles cooperating, gaining in
grace and health as you perform this task. Rise and stretch and
crouch again. Rise and stretch and kneel and bend. . . . Love
these things as you do them, and the objects they involve—the
sheets on the bed, the rake, the trowel, the seeds in your hand.
Thank God for them. Rejoice in the marvelous gift of life and
strength that enables you to be here now, this moment, execut-
ing this humble yet important and beneficial task.

If you spend a lot of time at a desk, as I do, hop up often and
walk around the room. Have an extension cord so you can carry
the telephone with you to a different chair for lengthy conversa-
tions. And as you talk stretch your free arm high, do isometrics
with abdomen and hips, wiggle your ankles, draw circles with
your feet.

When you finish typing a document or letter, get up and file
its carbon or pertinent papers right away. It seems easier at the
moment to let things pile up, but that's the surest route to
aching shoulders, a sluggish mind and sedentary spread. Immediate filing, on the other hand, breaks the monotony, and gives
you the benefit of all those little trips to the files. Eyes, mind and
muscles have a change and are refreshed. (Also, you're spared
the drudgery of all that filing later on.)

Worship and Exercise

If you truly respect and cherish this body God gave you, exercise can be an act of worship. And worship itself can add a
significant dimension to exercise.

How remarkable a human body, how incredibly perfect in its
design! That the brain can signal its movements without our
even thinking, and the muscles quicken to action—running,
jumping, lifting, pulling us vigorously through cold waves, or

simply turning us about when a voice calls our name. I will always be awed by the wonder of this, my own body, and striving to express to its creator how grateful I am for having it, and everything that it experiences.

The instant my eyes open I thank him for the gift of another new day. Thank him for the hot and cold water on my flesh in the shower, and the whole body responding, so eager and ready and *able* to do so many things! It seems to me times of pure physical activity are wonderful times to pray.

I never run across the float and lift my arms to dive that I don't call out to God. First, for protection—because I know it's against safety rules to swim alone (but if I had to wait for lifeguards I might as well stay in bed!). So I call on those angels the Bible and Billy Graham assure us are always hovering by. Then: "Bless this swim to my body and my body to your service." And striking off, I begin to pray for people, blessing people and praying for those who are having problems or need healing, and mentally reciting God's healing promises. And by the time I'm back I've accomplished quite a lot of praying.

Jogging and skipping rope lend themselves well to the psalms, to the *Venite,* the *Jubilate Deo* and other chants and readings from the Book of Common Prayer. The beautiful rhythms of words of worship blend well with the cadences of flying arms and legs. If this sounds ridiculous, so be it—but try it. I feel sure God hears and rejoices. Surely the songs of the nimble jumper are just as welcome as the incense of a kneeling saint (especially one who'd let his precious body go to pot).

4

Water

One of my most important secrets of health and energy is water. Gallons and gallons of beautiful, life-giving water. I think one reason so many people are sluggish, ailing, discouraged and eternally tired is simply that they don't use enough water! Air pollution, faulty diets and the daily assaults and pressures we undergo—all are contributing culprits. But if our bodies were properly watered, inside and out, we would flush away a lot of that pollution; our problems wouldn't seem so monstrous, our days so dreary. We would laugh more, exercise more and sleep better. Water is nature's oldest, most available healer, refresher and invigorator: *aqua vitae*.

The Lord made water before he made people. And we swim in water in our mother's womb. Frederick Leboyer, the French obstetrician who is revolutionizing childbirth, considers this fact so important that he eases the baby's transition from its safe amniotic nest by immersing it gently in warm water before introducing it to the strangeness of a dry world. . . . Most babies squeal and crow with pleasure at being bathed, and beg to get back in the tub. Youngsters are never happier than when wading, romping and splashing in water. This is surely instinctive; nature's way of urging us to stay close to our sources, to rejoice in the wonders of water.

Ben Franklin swam all his long, vigorous, productive life and tells us in his autobiography: "From a child I had been ever delighted with this exercise." Writing only a few years before his death at eighty-five, he says: "I went at noon to bathe, and floating on my back, fell asleep. . . . Water is the easiest bed that can be."

Like him, I discovered early the secret peace and energies that lie in water. A born water rat, I learned to swim almost as soon as I could walk, for the broad bright waters of Storm Lake were the focal point of our little town. Most of the other kids who swarmed its shores swam too (some a lot better than I did), but a lot of them would be content with a quick dip or sunning and skirmishing, and some days they didn't go in at all. For me, to miss a day meant a kind of dull depletion, a curious sense of loss. Even when I was pounding the typewriter in an office on hot summer days while the rest of my friends ran free, I looked forward to six o'clock when I could squirm into a suit and head for the lake even if it meant missing supper. For no matter how tired, sweaty, cross or grubby, I had only to dive in and strike out for the diving board to be revitalized.

But just *why* water is able to do so much for us I had no idea then.

The Magic of the Cold Shower

In college I began to revel in showers. We didn't have one at home, and with six in the family you were lucky to get your turn at the tub. I was working my way through school in a law office, where one of my duties on cold days was to build and tend a coal fire. After work I would head straight for the showers—often to the amazement of my roommate, who'd protest, "But you just *took* a bath last night," or "You just *had* a shower this morning." And she'd give me a long speculative look because we were all studying Freud and there was this theory that lots of washing meant you felt guilty about something, like Pontius Pilate. Well, I didn't feel guilty, just grimy and fatigued. A shower was the next-best thing to plunging into the lake. A kind of self-preservation drew me to water.

College was light-years behind me, however, before I learned the magic and the marvel of cold showers. It was Dr. Little who got me started—dear faithful A.B. bouncing up the steps, so vigorously pink and white from head to toe—as if he'd just stepped out of a shower. Which he usually had—a cold one. I groaned, as most people do, when he first urged me to try it. "Oh, no, not me!"

"But you won't feel a bit of discomfort if you do it right," he insisted. "Don't shock your body with the cold water, first turn on the hot to get your skin warm and comfortable, then gradually turn on the cold. And as it strikes your body, don't stand still —move about, wiggle, dance, and slap yourself. The action gets your blood circulating; you won't mind a bit, in fact you'll enjoy it."

"Yes, but you've got a Ph.D., remember?"

He grinned. "That's right, and you can have one too. All it takes is the right attitude and the right habits. Good habits are just as addictive as bad ones, but they build up the body instead of destroying it. If everybody would get the habit of starting the day with a cold shower we'd all look better and feel better. We'd have happier homes and healthier children." He chuckled, plugging again his Perfectly Hard Dermis: "With more Ph.D.'s we wouldn't need so many M.D.'s."

At that time I was suffering from a number of minor afflictions. Upset stomach, nerves, fatigue and a bad case of middle-age blues. A.B. gave me various pills and potions—probably because I expected them, and probably placebos. But we both knew that his lectures and his example were far more effective than any medication. Here was someone who had almost twice my energy at almost twice my age.

The one shower in this enormous, gingerbready house was up on the third floor, adjacent to the gym-sized attic. Only the boys and their dad were stalwart enough to make the journey. A.B. was so patiently persistent, however, that one day I gave it a try after the thundering herd was off to school. And he was right! If you let the cold water come on gradually, and keep in action while it pounds your flesh, you actually begin to enjoy it. Literally, you feel yourself waking up all over, the entire surface of your body coming alive in a delightful new way.

I came downstairs exhilarated, filled with more energy than I'd had since a long-ago swim; and for days was faithful to this brave new routine. Old habits are hard to break, however; new ones hard to establish—especially when they involve inconvenience. I found myself inventing excuses not to make that three-story climb. I did *not* have a Ph.D. like A.B., and probably never would.

It wasn't until we moved to the suburbs and a new, ultramodern house with a shower bath adjoining the master bedroom that I gave Dr. Little's water prescription another try. By then I was not only tired but run-down, and what can best be described as "achy." Headachy, bone-achy, heart-achy, dissatisfied with my life, myself and the world. A common malaise that doctors don't know what to do about and neither do husbands—whom we are prone to blame. Some women try to get over it by going out and getting jobs. Others, who already have jobs, wonder if they shouldn't quit them. Some just go right on being miserable. I took cold showers. . . . Remembering the bounce, the pep, the sheer vitality I'd enjoyed whenever I had forced myself to those faucets under the rooftop, I knew there was no earthly reason for not walking the few steps necessary now to reclaim that vitality and zest. Nobody who *really* wanted to feel better could be that stupid or lazy. So I got into the habit of leaping out of bed and heading straight for the shower. And nothing—I repeat, nothing—apart from God and vitamins, has made so much difference in my life. Wherever I go I preach the gospel of the cold shower.

I don't take showers at night, they are too stimulating. Bedtime is the time to sink into a warm (not too hot) tub sweetened, if you like, with oil or bubbles or bath salts, and just soak away the day's accumulations, physical, mental, emotional. Let the tiredness go, the conflicts, the worries. Wash them away into the soothing, healing water. Cleanse the mind of them and let pleasant thoughts flow in as you prepare for sleep.

Why Water Does So Much for Us

Plants, they say, are like people. And plants do best when they are properly watered—roots, stems and leaves. See how trees and flowers and plants perk up after a shower, how they sparkle, seem to stretch and dance. And people are like plants. We can survive with the basic, essential root or interior consumption of water. But we are fresher and brighter when our surfaces are stimulated and cleansed. Skin gets thirsty too. The skin gives off wastes. Subject to invisible dusts and microbes and frictions, rubbed by our clothes all day and by bedclothes at night, it thirsts for water. And when we plunge it into water or let water cascade down upon it, all its tiny nerve endings respond, like a lively telegraph network sending messages throughout the body. The blood goes rushing to the organs, feeding all the cells and tissues, giving them energy. And one of its most important messages shoots directly to the brain: I'm alive, I'm awake, I feel good!

The brain believes this, it records it. The brain is like a computer that will spew back, and try to prove, everything it's told. Consciously or unconsciously rejoice in being alive each morning, in being awake to this marvelous if often maddening world and in feeling good, actually feeling *good* if only for a few moments under the shower—and a wonderful thing begins to happen. You *do* feel good for more hours each day; feeling good becomes a habit. The physical act of doing something that makes you feel good is simply the beginning. You've started the engine right, given it the right directions, and it's raring to go.

But there are sound scientific reasons why we do feel good. That fountain spilling its merry music in the park, that waterfall in the moist cool woods, that summer thunderstorm that brings such sweet relief from the depressing hot dry air—all are generating negative ions, which counteract the positive ions in the atmosphere. And scientific research throughout the world has confirmed the fact that this negative charge of particles has a rejuvenating effect on all living things. For with each breath we draw in thousands of electrically charged air molecules. When the air is clean and in proper balance there are an average of

2,500 ions per cubic inch, almost equally divided between positive and negative charges. Air pollution, air conditioning and changes of weather, however, can cause "sick air," where the positive ions dominate. This can cause a literal surge in the body's production and release of a neurohormone called serotonin, which throws our whole nervous system out of balance.

Fred Soyka is an American who became fascinated with the subject when he found he was ill and depressed in certain climates. His excellent book *The Ion Effect* summarizes the vast amount of research that has been done and tells us that "ions are also absorbed into the human body through the skin," where the nerve endings act as receptors. He quotes the Russian scientist A. L. Tchijewsky, who said, "Vitamins and ions have similar effects." Soyka states:

> The energy in moving water generates a lot of neg-ions since, as water breaks up, the positive charge remains with the larger drop and the negative charge flies free with the fine spray, forming neg-ions. By the seashore, where waves bounce on beaches or hiss and sputter against rocks, there are always more neg-ions. . . . Waterfalls, too, are surrounded by a beneficial load of neg-ions created by the same process.

Other researchers, in particular A. C. Whitson and E. T. Pierce of the Stanford Research Institute, have discovered the same results occur indoors, in our bathrooms when we shower. The rushing water creates a field of negative electrification which multiplies the negative ions. As we breathe them in and feel them on our skin, there is an enhanced sense of well-being.

For years this idea was belittled; but it has now become so firmly established by physicists and others that the Federal Aviation Agency and the World Health Organization are interested. Meanwhile, people who build shopping malls and apartment complexes usually incorporate a fountain or waterfall, primarily for that reason.

The Historical Significance of Water

There are almost six hundred references to water in the Bible. Water for bathing and baptism, for washing of hands and feet.

Water to cross, to conquer, water in which to fish, or to walk by and be at peace. ("He leadeth me beside the still waters, he restoreth my soul.") Water to quench both physical and spiritual thirst. Water had tremendous significance for people in that arid region; cisterns and wells were priceless. No doubt its very scarcity enhanced its religious symbolism. Water meant purification, washing away not only of desert sands but of disease and sins.

The Romans were great bath lovers. They were also a strong, powerful people who conquered the world. After the fall of Rome (and maybe *because* of the sensuous, bath-loving ex-conquerors) bathing fell too—into disrepute. Throughout the Middle Ages and early Renaissance bathing was considered sinful and downright unhealthy. Even the nineteenth century wasn't noted for hygiene; only the privileged classes could afford the time or leisure to visit the spas and baths. The White House had no bathtub until Abigail Fillmore insisted, in 1850. And we were well into the twentieth century before bathrooms proliferated, especially in the United States. (My Holmes grandparents are said to have had the first farm bathroom in Buena Vista County, Iowa—around 1900.) Yet now almost every American household has one or more, giving us the reputation of being the cleanest people in the world.

"Today most American bathrooms are potential spas, beauty salons and centers of hydrotherapy," authors Guy Remsen and Lawrence Blochman point out in their lively little book, *Wake Up Your Body!* But we're still not as vigorous as we could be if we took full advantage of them. "If you are using your tub for purposes of cleanliness only, you may be getting close to godliness but you are missing a lot of the extra dividends a bath should yield."

One immediate dividend we can give the skin is to rub it briskly and thoroughly as we dry it. This stimulates those nerve endings and refreshes us body, mind and spirit. Gerald L. Looney, M.D., writing in the *Journal of the American Medical Association*, says it's well known that "the entire nervous system of the adult is derived from the surface layer of the embryo, the ectoderm," and that the central nervous system must be viewed as "a highly integrated and unified system" involving every portion of the body, including the tiniest surface of the skin. (A fact basic to the healing arts of acupressure and acu-puncture.)

Again, as with exercise, we are telling this incredible body God gave us, "I'm aware of you, I really care about you." So marvel as you rub yourself rosy; rejoice in every inch of *you*— from the damp fringe of hair that's escaped your cap on down to the smallest nail on your little toe. Anoint yourself with oil, dust with fragrant powder and get into fresh clothes. The whole process needn't take but a few minutes, yet you're ready to face the coming hours revitalized, rejuvenated.

Watering Within

In *Your Body Is the Best Doctor* the famous Melvin Page, D.D.S., tells us, "The average body contains around fifty quarts of water and expels about four quarts each day. . . . Man drinks only a part of this water because the foods he eats are largely made up of water." Fruits, vegetables, even meat and bread. But like plants, we must be watered.

Every cell in our bodies is so dependent on water that with-out it we would die. We see this happen to plants before our very eyes. We also see people so shrunken and shriveled they look like dried-up plants. Lack of water may be only one cause, but I long to give them a good soaking clear down to the roots. For most people simply don't drink enough water. To change the metaphor, we drink merely the water we have to have to keep our engines going; a glass now and then with a meal or whenever the engine complains. No wonder so many of these engines go creaking along until they often stall and break down altogether.

Not that we aren't constantly pouring other liquids into them: coffee, tea. "Soft" drinks heavy with sugar and hard on the teeth, figure and heart. "Hard" or alcoholic drinks which are hard on the entire system. All these beverages that we guzzle all day are water-based, but the water has been so corrupted by syrups, drugs, caffeine and chemicals they only put an added burden on that still plaintively pleading engine.

No, what the body really wants and needs is a goodly quota of pure, unadulterated water. Eight large glasses a day, at least. More in hot weather, and more if you're sick or injured. Just as the body draws upon its precious store of minerals and vitamins during stress, it uses up more water. This is true even of emotional stress. Sometimes we express this accurately in the vernacular: "That burns me up." "I just boiled." Anger, fear, shock, all take their toll. The engine literally heats up; we perspire; kidneys and bowels react. At such times, instead of turning to the coffee pot or liquor cabinet, try to cool off by going to refrigerator or faucet and calmly and slowly drinking a couple of glasses of cold water. Then enjoy the warm comfort of a cup of tea or coffee if you want it, or a glass of wine if you prefer. (The Lord does not expect us to give up everything that makes life pleasant; St. Paul reminds us we are only to use his gifts in moderation.) But first make sure your body is able to restore its vital fluids.

Water, lots of water, is absolutely essential to blood building and cleansing; to the proper functioning of our kidneys, our sweat glands, and to our whole digestive process. Water helps flush the wastes from our body through the most remarkable plumbing system ever invented. People who drink plenty of water seldom have elimination problems.

The Importance of Hard Water

Not many people realize that in addition to carrying molecules of oxygen and hydrogen for our survival, water is a vital source of nutrients: calcium, magnesium, iron and other minerals essential to the blood, the bones and the heart. And the more of these minerals the water contains—especially calcium and magnesium—the better for us. Particularly for the heart.

This has been proved by many scientific studies both here and abroad. In the 1950s Dr. Henry A. Schroeder, trace-mineral authority at Dartmouth Medical School, conducted a survey of water supplies in 1,315 cities. As reported in the *Journal of the American Medical Association*, he found "a striking relationship between soft water and death rates from heart-artery disease." In fact, of twenty-five generally hard-water states, all had lower death rates, with the exception of Indiana and Illinois.

Another famous study was made by Dr. Margaret D. Crawford and her colleagues of the Medical Research Council of Britain in the 1960s. They chose sixty-one British cities, half with hard water, half with soft, and monitored the disease and death rates of men. After twelve years they found "cardiovascular death rates about 50 per cent higher in towns with very soft water." As Ray Wolf points out in *Prevention,* "The *highest* death rate in the hard water towns was significantly less than even the *lowest* rate in the soft water towns." The *British Medical Journal* has also reported a relationship between soft drinking water and birth defects.

Closer to home, residents in Monroe County, Florida, who'd been drinking rain water had their supply changed to well water which was 400 times harder. In a four-year period their heart and blood vessel death rate plunged from a 500–700 range to a 200–300 level.

Hard water is any water which contains high amounts of calcium and magnesium. The water picks this up as it flows through rocks or deposits containing these minerals, especially limestone dolomite. And the worst thing any of us can do is put a water softener into any water used for drinking. The British have halted water-softening treatments and warned the public about their dangers. Our own Environmental Protection Agency has been challenged to take similar steps. Some experts have declared they pose a potential threat greater than cancer.

Water softeners not only deprive us of absolutely essential minerals, they add a dangerous ingredient, sodium (salt), to our bloodstream. Too much salt is already a menace in the American diet, a known cause of Ménière's disease and hypertension. In fact, it was singled out by the Senate Select Committee on Nutrition and Human Needs as one of the main causes of our killer diseases. So it's folly deliberately to add more salt to our bodies via that precious fluid, our drinking water.

If your clothes would be a tattletale gray without your water softener, change the device so that it affects only the laundry. Or buy bottled drinking water if you can find a source which guarantees its freshness, purity and hardness.

Our Poisoned Lifeline

Furthermore, pollution of our water supplies has reached appalling proportions. Pollution from sewage, lead, arsenic, plastic, rubber, drugs, dyes, factory wastes, dangerous radioactive wastes from nuclear-energy plants. Pesticides, chemical fertilizers. Even in midwestern farming communities where the air is still clean, I have been shocked to read headlines calling "Most Farm Wells 'Unsafe.' " One soil conservation report estimated 75 per cent or more of the private wells in one Iowa county had water unfit for human consumption.

The Safe Drinking Water Act was passed in 1974 when the EPA found sixty-six chemicals in New Orleans' water supply—and eighty or more in every city tested thereafter. A number of them known carcinogens. And while the EPA struggles nobly, it is short of manpower and funds. According to United Press reports, its promise to "clean up America's waters by 1983, and to halt all discharges of pollutants into navigable waters by 1985," is becoming less realistic every day. Meanwhile, tests continue to show that alarming numbers of these pollutants cause not only cancer but brain damage, birth defects and other tragic afflictions. And there are literally thousands more of them that haven't even been tested.

Aqua vitae, our liquid lifeline, has become instead a poisonous hazard to both human beings and wildlife. In a beautiful article, "Twilight of A Species," in *Reader's Digest,* John N. Cole describes the plight of a creature my husbands and sons used to catch—the striped bass:

> This fish, once so abundant it clogged river deltas, this resource of such economic importance that its sale helped fund the first public school in America, this creature whose poetry has nourished the souls of men since the Indians . . . is disappearing.

He attributes this to the toxic chemicals that now permeate every creek and tributary of the Chesapeake Bay area.

> From industrial complexes in the Delaware and Maryland manufacturing heartland, chemical wastes have gushed into the Chesapeake for decades. The Hudson is no better. . . . The most recent study

of chemical pollutants in the Hudson . . . says, "The river is awash with deadly chemicals, and it gets worse every day." For me, it is a miracle that any bass still survive. . . .

Have we indeed reached a point where we will allow the demise of this magnificent species? If we have, we have signed our own death warrants. *There can be no extrication of the fate of fish from the fate of man.* [Italics mine.]

Should Fluoride Be Added to Water?

Henrik Ibsen, the famous Norwegian dramatist, once wrote a play called *An Enemy of the People.* It was the story of a doctor who tried to warn his townspeople their water supply was unsafe—and was only viciously destroyed for his efforts. Today, people who fight to prevent disease and disaster through water are also often mocked and persecuted.

This has been especially true of those who oppose compulsory fluoridation. They have been labeled kooks, cranks and John Birchers, they have been vilified and sometimes fired from their jobs. Yet many eminent scientists have grave doubts about dumping a rank poison, sodium fluoride (actually used as a pesticide and rat poison), into the drinking water of an entire population, presumably to benefit the teeth of children under ten years old. Less than 0.4 per cent of that population!

Financially, the whole thing seems preposterous. First, the stuff used is a waste product from aluminum companies who have to get rid of it. In a scheme that surpasses Tom Sawyer's (who conned his friends into whitewashing his fence, remember?) they persuade towns and cities to buy it, then build expensive fluoridating plants. (All, of course, on the taxpayers.) This "corrosive, toxic, most active non-metallic element," according to my Random House dictionary, enters the entire water supply —including that used for bathing, watering the yard and washing cars; and the excess pours into our already polluted waterways, where it becomes an even more potent carcinogen.

All this in the belief it helps prevent tooth decay in a tiny fraction of the population. Now certainly parents who want fluoridation for their children should by all means *have* it. Be able to buy it, have it administered by dentists or even be given it free. In fact, free fluoride tablets could be dispensed to every child in America at one fifth the cost. Yet those who make millions from pouring it out en masse mount furious attacks on all those who object.

The whole thing seems like a Mad Hatter's tea party. Madder when we realize that despite years of fluoridation tooth decay is still rampant, and rising—especially among children. (Researchers at Ball State University in Indiana report that 50 per cent of American two-year-olds have cavities; and 90 per cent by the age of four; that by the time he's sixteen the average youngster has seven decayed, filled or missing teeth.) Because, as David Reuben, M.D., writes in *National Health Federation Bulletin,* "Tooth decay is *not* produced by a deficiency of fluorides. It is produced by eating refined carbohydrates like white flour, white sugar, refined cereals and all the other refined junk that make up the most profitable food products sold to unsuspecting consumers, many of them little kids."

If parents—and the public—were really concerned about children's teeth, they would not *allow* those teeth to be ruined with this deluge of sugared cereals, Cokes, candy and other dental outrages. If adults refuse to stop the *cause* of tooth decay, why spend fortunes on fluorides?

The whole thing would be ludicrous if it weren't so downright dangerous. But sodium fluoride is *not* "harmless as table salt" (sodium chloride), with which it's often compared. Dr. Reuben says, "Generally speaking, adding fluoride to a formula makes a substance explosively active . . . hydrofluoric acid can't be kept in bottles because it eats through glass! Just a little too much sodium fluoride cause convulsions, coma and death." In November 1978 the fluoridation project for Dublin, California (near San Francisco), was delayed because it was feared that a 3,500-gallon tank of fluoride might be sitting on a fault. When a crack showed up, Public Works Director Miles Ferris explained that fluoride is a "dangerous chemical" capable of eating through solid steel, and that to take chances with the public health would be "insane." According to *Public Scrutiny,* he had the fluoride removed and put in a safer holding tank.

In rejecting a mouth-rinse program for Lynbrook Schools, Nassau County, Long Island, the PTA pointed out that a three-year-old in Brownville, New York, had died after accidentally being given an overdose of fluoride at a dental clinic. That the mouth-rinse package itself contained warnings: *Do not swallow. Caution, dangerous if swallowed, keep away from children.* That no medical, dental or public health group contacted would assure them that no harm would come from accidental ingestion. The PTA statement said:

> Fluoridation is compulsory mass medication for a non-contagious disease. . . . It is put into our water although some people are allergic to it, hyperactive children cannot tolerate it, and even though no testing has been done to see how this drug interacts with other drugs or food additives. . . .
>
> It is an enzyme-inhibitor that interferes with body chemistry, can cause genetic damage, is particularly dangerous to those with kidney or thyroid disorders, diabetes, cardiovascular problems . . . and is not the answer to tooth decay. Efforts and tax dollars would be better spent teaching children sound nutrition, and avoidance of junk foods.

I agree. Particularly since a research study of twenty American cities by Dr. Dean Burk (for thirty years with the National Cancer Institute) and Dr. John Yiamouyiannis produced strong evidence that fluoridation also causes cancer. In any case, to force medication on millions of people who don't need it or want it should be unthinkable in a free society. In this we lag behind most of the countries of Europe, who have banned fluoridation. The U. S. Public Health Service gives the maximum safe dose of fluoride as about one milligram per day. A lot of people get almost that much just from toothpaste! Actually there is no safe amount for any poison; and this one combines with other fluorides from exhaust fumes, spray cans, Teflon and even fruits and vegetables that have been *watered* from fluoridated systems. The total effect can be seriously disturbing to some; to others deadly.

How can you protect yourself and your family if you live in a fluoridated area? Boiling water won't help; the fluorine, being a salt, is only intensified. Distilling the water will purify it, but will also take away its valuable minerals. These can be restored to your body, however, by taking mineral supplements. The best solution seems to be getting a device that will really filter out the fluorine, or buying bottled water. One thing sure—if you *are* exposed to fluorine, take plenty of vitamins. Especially vitamins A, C and E, which detoxify poisons.

In any case, we human beings *are* like plants; we must have our quota of water, eight full glasses a day, if we are to thrive and bloom. In this I'm lucky. We dug our own well here in the country woodland, and the water is not only free of pollutants, it is so hard it practically clanks going down. The taste is too metallic for some people, but other water now tastes flat and dispirited to us.

I drink it joyously, for I know it carries a precious cargo of calcium and magnesium and other trace elements which God implants in the rocks and earth for our strength and protection. And as I drink it, I thank him.

Learning to Love Cold Water

Back to A.B. and my personal saga. His Perfectly Hard Dermis lectures continued: The skin could be conditioned to accept even extremes of heat and cold. A lot was in the gradual buildup of resistance, a lot was in the head. Mind over matter. "Lots of times we hurt because we expect to hurt," he insisted. "Pain serves a purpose, it's a warning to take action. But what many people think is pain is merely a sensation they're not used to, something they associate with dread. Cold water is not painful, it does not hurt, and if you have a normal heart it is very good for you."

He and his wife Ruth traveled almost every weekend to their vacation home in North Carolina, where he swam well into the winter, sometimes breaking the ice to go in. We finally accepted his invitation to witness this performance. And later, when I was having sick headaches, excruciating bouts with bursitis, and the whole family was beset with problems, he suddenly tore up the prescription he was writing and handed me the keys instead. "Here. Just go down and spend the week; you'll come back feeling better."

He was right. To wake up and hear birds singing instead of

the roar of traffic, to breathe the tangy fragrance of pine trees along with that fishy nostalgic hometown smell of lake . . . I knew I would never be well in body or spirit until we too had found water. Thus began our search that led to the lake not far from Washington, which became our retreat. Here I could "walk beside still waters" and be restored. And here I began to swim three times a day well into cold weather, and work toward my own "Ph.D."

I also love the ocean. The sea can work miracles, especially when it's cold. It pommels and scours, strips away non-essentials, gives back a mystical power. You emerge from a good bout with it ablaze. Now you are a whole person, tingling from toe to scalp. You are alive in the way you were meant to be, alive as you were in the moment of your first triumphant landing on earth. As you came yelling and fighting out of the waters of the womb at your birth, so you can come shouting out of the sea, claiming the whole earth for your own.

You are truly a child of the universe, a child of the living God.

5

The Dentist
Who Changed Our Lives

Dr. A. B. Little changed our lives in a significant direction—he taught us so much about how to exercise and play. But it was a dentist who finally made us realize the importance of proper fuels and building blocks for our bodies. Quite literally he opened our mouths—and our minds—to vitamins, minerals and organic foods.

After twelve years we had moved to the suburbs, where my husband, who'd been feeling more and more wretched, sought a good dentist to have some teeth pulled. This remarkable man, Dr. Shreve Spitler, took one look in his mouth and read the signals of a lot of things which, in all fairness, A.B. hadn't had much of a chance to find. Mainly because my husband, like far too many men, had a notion that he was indestructible. (And a secret fear, no doubt, that A.B. would prove him otherwise.)

True, as a boy he'd been badly burned by a doctor. In an attempt to cure him of teen-age acne (fortunately only on his back) the physician tried out his new uncalibrated X-ray equipment. Casually, leisurely, this hapless kid was exposed for *hours* —sometimes while the whole staff went out for lunch. There were actually times when he lay on his stomach doing his homework while being irradiated.

The damage didn't show up until he was in his twenties, when the destroyed skin began to redden, thicken and form huge draining ulcers which refused to heal and could only be cut out. New ones were continually forming, inevitably malignant; this meant lengthy skin grafts, taking skin from legs and thighs. So it's probably no wonder that between bouts with dermatologists and surgeons, he felt he had to work harder and longer than other people, and not let a doctor get near him except at parties.

In that attitude I've found he's not much different even from —*doctors.* One of our lifelong friends, who's had a distinguished career in medicine and is now on the staff at National Institutes of Health, is driving his wife crazy because "I know Jack's been having chest pains and hasn't felt right for a long time, but he will *not* see a doctor. He's worse than any patient he's ever had!" In fact, whatever their calling, I'd venture that most men, unless they're downright hypochondriacs, have a fear and resistance to doctors that is almost paranoiac, and sometimes comical. Another friend told me that after many battles she finally got her husband to agree to see a doctor. "But he says he won't tell him what's *wrong*—that's *his* business to find out."

In our case all this was changed by a dentist. "Tooth decay in adults isn't something that just happens by itself," he said. "There is always a reason, often a degenerative disease in progress. The decayed teeth are just one more warning. You'd better get yourself to a good internist."

Another friend, a neurosurgeon, put us in touch with one of his colleagues, and tests were begun. They revealed a long string of problems, the most urgent right then diabetes. My husband was put on a drastic diet and insulin shots begun. The burden of too many cigarettes, too many highballs, too many surgical shocks from all those ulcers and skin grafts and too many years of overwork—all this plus extensive internal damage from that tragic assault of X rays in his youth had begun to take their cruel toll. It was to be worse; he got to the internist just before the first of three serious heart attacks. That skilled and dedicated man, Dr. Saul Holtzman, saved his life. We will always be grateful to him.

And we will bless the day we first walked through the doors of a genuine preventive dentist. Dr. Spitler was a member of the Capital Academy of Clinical Nutrition and the International Academy of Preventive Medicine. He also trained with the famous Melvin Page, D.D.S., whose book *Degeneration-Regeneration* has become a classic. Dr. Spitler's education and practice were dedicated to the whole person. Not merely to fixing and trying to save the teeth, but seeking out basic causes in order to prevent further damage.

How *logical*. For the mouth is the cavity through which our body fuel and building matter first passes. Here the first step in digestion takes place—the breaking down of starches through the salivary glands. In this chamber our teeth grow—root, crown, pulp and bone, all nourished from within. They are gripped by living gums and bone, surrounded by fleshy walls and roof. *All fed by the same blood that circulates throughout the body.* No wonder the first thing a good old-fashioned family doctor used to say was "Open your mouth, stick out your tongue," to get an idea of your problem. A line that seems to have been lost as more physicians specialize, and even the general practitioner is so busy he often reaches for his prescription pad before you've finished telling him where you hurt.

A dentist, on the other hand, hasn't much choice. He *has* to gaze into that chamber (so often a chamber or horrors). And if his interest goes beyond the sheer mechanics of repairing and pulling teeth, he will be curious about the body chemistry which produces the results he sees. He will be eager to teach his patients how to correct their own body chemistry and nourish their often starving body cells by eating the proper foods.

Dr. Spitler was at that time president of the Capital Academy of Clinical Nutrition. With him we attended their meetings, as well as symposiums and lectures of a dozen kinds pertaining to health. He lent or led us to the books of Adelle Davis, Dr. Richard Passwater, Dr. Roger Williams, Carlton Fredericks, Dr. Weston A. Price and others. One of his idols was his teacher, Dr. Page, who wrote in *Your Body Is Your Best Doctor!*:

> We should not only consider what we eat but also its quality. Does it have the needed nutrients for sustaining optimum nutrition? . . . nutrition is the controlling factor . . . the patient must be treated

not just for the specific part of the body which noticeably ails him, but for his entire body since each minute part is merely an interacting part of the whole. When body chemistry is functioning properly, one has good health—hence resistance to disease is at its maximum . . .

Vitamins, Minerals and Prevention

It was Shreve Spitler who got us started at long last on a program of minerals, vitamins and organic foods. He gave us our first subscription to *Prevention.* It was like stepping into an enthralling new world. And just as I urge would-be writers to subscribe to their trade journals, *The Writer* and *Writer's Digest,* if they hope to learn their craft, I urge everyone interested in health and well-being to subscribe to this magazine or others in the field. There are a number of excellent ones, including *Let's Live, Nature's Way, Health Quarterly, Better Nutrition* and others.

Prevention was the pioneer, though, its founder, J. I. Rodale, the granddaddy of all the "health nuts." Through his own experiments Rodale proved the superiority of foods grown in soil which is rich in humus (organic matter). For "in that moist woodsy part of the soil exist the uncountable millions of bacteria, fungi and other minute organisms which give soil remarkable powers to feed tremendous amounts of minerals and vitamins and other nutrients to plant roots," writes his son Robert Rodale:

> He had read the work of the English agronomist Sir Albert Howard, who had perfected the basic and useful theory that organic material was the most vital ingredient in the fertility of soil and that destruction of soil organic matter by modern farming practices was the cause of both production and health problems. Sir Albert also spoke out bluntly against the use of chemical fertilizers and poisonous insecticides. . . . He was an advocate of whole foods, not adulterated by additives or unnecessary processing.

This was in 1942, long before the public had been aroused to the growing dangers of polluted air and water, and how ruthlessly food supplies were being stripped of their nutrients. Rodale, a successful businessman and publisher rather than farmer, bought a run-down farm, began to build up the soil by composting and mulching, and to eat only its natural products. He also decided to publish a magazine on the subject, *Organic Gardening and Farming,* with Sir Albert his across-the-seas collaborator. In 1950 *Prevention* followed, its aim to extend the concept into organic living. "All our articles will be based on facts," he said. "And heaven knows there are tons of facts important to health which are buried in the medical literature, not even being used by doctors, let alone by the public."

Not just theories, but facts, backed up by sound research, lab reports, news of any and every finding in the field of human health. They would be very careful also about ads, spurning anything doubtful, kooky or far-out. At first they accepted *no* advertising, until it became evident that the natural food supplements they recommended just weren't available to many people. (This was long before the proliferation of so-called natural or health food stores.) In fact, at that time, except for vitamin and mineral concentrates used to improve animal feed, only a few were being manufactured, and most of those were synthetic. Thus it was that Rodale began to concoct his own: Bone meal tablets, for instance, made from ground calf bones—a rich source of both calcium and phosphorus in the right proportion. Vitamin C using rose hips instead of citrus, which he considered too acid. And for magnesium—dolomite, a mineral which farmers long had mixed in feeds or used as fertilizer.

Today the magazine is sometimes criticized because it's so full of ads for all these products, the reader can be confused. "And Rodale *owns* most of those companies," I heard a woman scold. This is not true; but even if it were, the articles are so valuable I wouldn't care. (I have learned that the Rodale firm owns a company which sells vitamins in England, but does *not* sell vitamins in the United States.) After you have established your own most effective intake of supplements, just patronize the firm that gives you the best value for the money. Usually it's cheaper to order by mail, but if your supplies run out or you don't want to take the trouble, pick them up at a health food store, or a pharmacy that guarantees them to be natural. Some people don't think this is important, but I do; I'll explain why later.

Reading this magazine every month was like a revelation. (Rest assured I have no personal or commercial connection with the publishers, or any product or publisher mentioned in this book.) We became converts, ready at last to receive the good news that had been preached to us for so long. For alas, there has to be a certain readiness in people before they are willing to accept anything, whether it's Weight Watchers, AA, vitamins or God.

If Only We Had Listened

Years before, my husband's sister Margaret had sent us a bottle of multiple vitamins, which we dutifully swallowed, to please her. But we noticed no special difference, and they seemed too expensive for us to replenish. . . . Years before—long before *Silent Spring*—some Iowa friends, Ken and Pearl Hinde, warned us of the dangers to food, water and wildlife from chemical pollutants. Even then they were resisting the blandishments of fertilizer salesmen, and being criticized and ridiculed by neighbors and farm agents for stubbornly refusing to add anything to their already rich farmlands but old-fashioned manure. "Well, good for you!" we cheered their story. But when they began to extol the virtues of vitamins, minerals and natural foods, we smiled. . . .

Years before, my New York agent Ruth Aley did her utmost to interest me in the writings of Adelle Davis and Carlton Fredericks and other nutritionists ahead of their time. She cooked superb gourmet meals using things like soybeans and wheat germ and tofu. I ate them with delight and went back to French fries and chocolate-chip cookies. She was then perhaps fifty, with the figure of a teen-ager, the face of a young mother and the pep and zip of a colt. Well into her eighties she retained her size 6 figure, looked better than most people in their sixties and was still zapping all over New York accomplishing more than others a third her age. Most important, in over thirty-five years *I never knew her to be sick a single day.*

If only we'd listened to them—Margaret and Ken and Pearl and Ruth Aley. But no, we only smiled and nodded and privately murmured the usual fond if condescending clichés:

"Food freaks." "Health nuts." "Faddists." Those labels so easy to pin on things we don't understand and won't try to learn because they seem a threat to our lazy and comfortable habits. Now I can only regret the precious time lost, especially when the children were growing up. I am absolutely convinced that all of us would have been spared incalculable pain, misery and even emotional problems, not to mention a mountain of medical and dental bills. But far more important, our sons and daughters would have faced life with stronger, healthier, more disease-resistant physical equipment.

Fortunately, as adults they are all on the Mother Earth bandwagon. Like a great many of their generation, they recognize the profound and delicate balance that relates every living thing on this planet, and their personal responsibility to honor and help maintain this vital chain of life. This includes a responsibility to their own bodies. Furthermore, they are keeping a vigilant watch on *their* children, protecting them as much as possible from the empty, damaging junk foods that glut the market (and are so seductively advertised), and making every effort to see that they are properly nourished. In short, our progeny realize, as we their parents failed to, that prevention *is* possible, and infinitely superior to cure.

Gradually we began to reform our eating habits. And gradually we added vitamins to our daily program. Then minerals and other supplements. At first just the much touted vitamin C. Then vitamin E. Then vitamins A and D. Then the B vitamins in various combinations. Then bone meal and dolomite, and lecithin and zinc. Then garlic perles and alfalfa tablets and kelp. Until one day my husband's internist laughed, "Lynn, you've become just a walking drugstore."

"But these aren't drugs," my husband told him. "These are foods, and they're making me feel a whole lot better."

"Well, *something* is."

The People Stories

Among the rewards of reading magazines like *Prevention* are the letters to the editor describing readers' own experiences and discoveries: The parents of a child so hyperactive the schools were drugging him into a zombie—"Seven years old and on seven different drugs!" Now on a strict additive-free diet —"He's a totally different little boy. At last he's able to learn, to play peacefully with other children." . . . A teen-age daughter deemed seriously schizophrenic; hospitalized, drugged, shocked. "Then we found this doctor who discovered she was allergic to chocolate, milk and wheat. By eliminating them and using megavitamin therapy he's restored her to glowing health. In fact, she's just won a scholarship to college." . . .

Letters from people in their seventies and eighties who are still working, dancing, jogging—sometimes falling off a roof or ladder without even *breaking* anything, thanks to calcium. . . . Stories of acne cured, ulcers healed, depression overcome, vitality regained—simply by restructuring the diet to exclude that which is injurious, and adding the natural substances which that particular body was literally starving for. . . . Tales of people who turned to vitamins in sheer desperation after doctors had given up. "My husband had open heart surgery," one woman wrote. "The doctor said it was the heart muscle, he couldn't possibly get well. I took him home and started him on vitamin E. . . . He now drives, goes fishing, works in the yard. People stare at this miracle in disbelief. He's literally been snatched from the grave."

Sometimes the letters are tragic, describing years of agonizing search before help was found. Sometimes they are funny. But always they are helpful as people share folk remedies that work for them, or their own discoveries in the cure of warts, ingrown toenails or the maladies of pets. I've clipped and filed this information for years, used it myself and often passed it on. "Anecdotal medicine," the AMA would call it. But the dictionary defines it in more accurate and dignified terms: *"Empirical evidence. Anything provable or verifiable by experience or experiment."*

I wish we could have written a similar testimonial about my husband's health. But destruction that deep, that lasting, seldom yields totally to human solutions. I *can* say it's remarkable he lived such a long full life (outlasting many friends who dropped off in their fifties and sixties), thanks to good doctors, good nutrition and an awful lot of prayer and supplements. In short, God and vitamins.

Certainly I can speak for myself. In the fifteen years since beginning this program:

• I have had only one case of flu. (During the first year, before I'd had a chance to build up resistance.)

• I have had only one cold. (After ten years of vitamins. I had gone on a trip without my vitamin C, got chilled, stayed up late and ate a lot of meat and sweets. Even so, it lasted only four days.)

• I have been freed of all my ailments, including the miseries of Menier's disease and the agonies of bursitis.

• My energy, productivity, stamina and endurance have been immeasurably increased.

Doctors

This book does not encourage anyone to "play doctor" either for himself or for others. We all need the wisdom and support of trained physicians. As I hope is evident, my husband and I love and admire our doctors. Ever since college, doctors have been among our closest personal friends; while professionally they have cared for our wounds and afflictions with skill and dedication. The medical profession as a whole, however, is geared almost entirely toward trying to help people *after* the harm has been done.

We come dragging our sorry wrecks of bodies to them, begging or demanding to be fixed. And they do exactly as they've been trained—and as most of us expect: Give us shots and/or prescriptions. If we still hurt, or the offending part doesn't improve, cut it out. X rays and a battery of ever more dazzling and expensive devices and therapies are also turned on us. But generally only the most cursory consideration is given to what kind of fuel the patient is putting—or not putting—into the tank to cause the engine to break down; or how the proper fuels and building materials could repair and regenerate the whole machine.

True, thousands of doctors do advise people to "eat a bal-

anced diet," to exercise, lose weight and cut down on foods high
in cholesterol. Also, to give up such obviously bad habits as
smoking and drinking. But doctors work at a double disadvan-
tage. Too often they are confronted with patients who won't
cooperate. And very few doctors have been trained in nutrition!
"Clinical nutrition is not even taught in most medical schools,"
says N. S. Scrimshaw, M.D., of Massachusetts Institute of Technology, "and not really adequately done in any of them." The
AMA itself was aware of this fact as long ago as 1963 when its
Council on Food and Nutrition acknowledged that "medical
education and medical practice have not kept abreast of the
tremendous advance in nutritional knowledge"; that medical
schools give "inadequate recognition, support and attention" to
this subject which should be "integral to the practice of medicine."

Yet a survey of 60 medical schools taken in 1976 showed little,
if any, improvement. Dr. Esther S. Nelson reports in the *Journal of the American Medical Association* that questionnaires
were sent, asking for information on what nutrition courses
were offered. Sixteen failed to reply; 7 admitted they had none.
One hour was offered by 2 schools; in 11 schools 2 to 10 hours
were offered; in 9 schools 11 to 19 hours; 3 schools offered 20 to 40
hours. Only one could claim a complete department of nutrition. The rest responded that the subject was "touched upon" in
various ways.

Ironically, when a similar survey was taken of the animal
husbandry departments in 30 agricultural colleges, all 30 responded, all assuring that the teaching of animal nutrition was
very much a part of their curriculum. The proper feeding of
animals is of more concern to our medical institutions than the
proper feeding of people!

In his famous book *Nutrition Against Disease*, biologist Roger
J. Williams, who discovered pantothenic acid, writes:

> The most basic weapons are those most ignored by modern medi-
> cine: *the numerous nutrients that the cells of our bodies need.* If the
> cells are ailing, as they must be in disease—the chances are excel-
> lent that it is because they are being inadequately provisioned. The
> list of things that these cells may need includes not only all the
> amino acids and all the minerals . . . but about 15 vitamins. . . .

Physicians, with their background of knowledge as to how our bodies are built and how they function, are precisely the ones who should qualify to develop expertness in this area. Yet because medical education has developed a strong orthodoxy that excludes cellular nutrition, the research necessary for this expertness has never been undertaken.

In fact, a large segment of the medical establishment is actually hostile to any suggestion that cellular malnutrition may very well be the cause of many of our afflictions. It's easier to blame germs or stress or environment or almost anything else that can be attacked by drugs.

Dr. Michael Lesser, an orthomolecular psychiatrist testifying before the Senate Select Committee on Nutrition and Human Needs, stated:

Clinical nutrition should be a mandatory course in every medical school. . . . I'm afraid it's only being taught in two or three, if that many. When I went to medical school, which wasn't that long ago, we spent one day discussing vitamins, and I can recall my professor finishing his lecture with the statement, "But since we live in the richest country in the world and we eat a well-balanced diet, all Americans receive all the vitamins and minerals they need from their diet, so it isn't necessary to take any supplements."

At this writing the Senate Nutrition Subcommittee has been hearing testimony on this very subject. In his opening statement Senator Robert Dole said, "The antidote to rising health care costs is plain and simple. More nutrition education for medical students, more applied nutrition by practicing physicians, and more positive attitudes toward nutrition by all medical personnel." Most impressive was the testimony of Jack Rutledge, on behalf of the Medical Student Association, saying the medical students themselves are very much interested in seeing more and better nutrition courses included in the curriculum.

Mandatory nutrition courses will *not* be a panacea, however, if we allow them to be endowed and influenced by the food industry, which is true of the nutrition departments of so many universities.

The Terrible Resistance to Change

Dr. Dwight Kalita, of the Huxley Institute for Biochemical Research, says, "It is important to realize that the greatest enemy of any science is a closed mind." Yet from its very beginning the science of medicine has been notorious for its fiercely locked minds. Had they succeeded, we would have no microscopes, no X rays, no antibiotics, no inoculations. Almost every technique and treatment today considered essential to the practice of modern medicine was dogmatically resisted, its discoverer persecuted:

• Paracelsus, now recognized as the greatest physician of the sixteenth century, was abused as a heretic whose writings could not even be published. Because he dared to suggest that his colleagues should continue to study and observe; that they did *not* have all the answers to disease.

• When Anton van Leeuwenhoek (1632–1723) invented the microscope and described what he saw, doctors refused to look. Because his findings conflicted with their common belief in the spontaneous-generation of life cycles.

• In 1854 the English physician John Snow was bitterly denounced even after he'd proved—against fierce opposition—that the epidemic of cholera ravaging London was being spread by the filthy drinking water from the Thames. He had to fight orthodox medicine in order to finally stop a plague that had devastated cities for centuries.

• Dr. William Harvey was still being attacked by his peers forty-three years after he first published his accurate descriptions of the circulatory system. He was hated for showing them something they hadn't been taught.

• Edward Jenner, the Scottish physician whose vaccination for smallpox wiped out the disease, was read out of his medical society and forced to flee.

• Dr. Emil Grubbe, co-founder of X-ray therapy, was bitterly attacked by orthodox surgeons who "controlled medicine," as he put it, and "considered X ray a threat to surgery."

• When Dr. Frederic Gibbs introduced the EEG (encephalograph) to an AMA meeting in 1934, he was declared a fake, his instrument laughingly called a "quacker box."

• There was a long and bloody struggle *even to get doctors to wash their instruments or their hands*. Both the British surgeon Joseph Lister (considered the father of modern antiseptic surgery) and the Austrian Ignaz Semmelweis tried in vain to persuade their colleagues that this could reduce the terrible toll of infections. They were jeered. Semmelweis, horrified by the fact that women were dying like flies after childbirth in hospitals, discovered the doctors were going directly from autopsies and shoving their contaminated hands into still bleeding wombs. In *The Body Is the Hero,* Ronald Glasser, M.D., relates that Semmelweis was so maliciously attacked for his plea to stop this practice, his desperate protests were so futile, he went mad. . . . A young Harvard medic, William Stewart Halsted, returned from Europe in 1886 with this same plea. Dr. Glasser describes what happened when Halsted challenged Jackson, his professor, to wash in a bowl of dilute carbolic acid before beginning surgery in an open amphitheater before other surgeons— all dressed in street clothes:

> They agreed with Jackson, who angrily poured the carbolic acid out of the basin . . . ordered the "impudent" young surgeon out of "his" operating suite and began the operation, cutting into the breast of his young patient with his filthy hands and filthier instruments.

• Louis Pasteur was resented as an interloper by the medical profession because he had no medical degree. Despite his other achievements, his proof that microbes could cause illness infuriated the hierarchy; it was mocked and opposed for a generation. Once accepted, however, the doctors fastened so firmly on the conviction that germs were the *only* cause, they would listen to no other.

It was this dogmatism that caused delays and blunders in the treatment of beriberi, rickets, scurvy and pellagra—all vitamin-deficiency diseases.

Here's what happened:

In 1553 both the explorer Cartier and Admiral Richard Hawkins found that scurvy yielded to something in citrus fruits. Their reports were ignored. . . . Two hundred years later a British naval surgeon, James Lind, published his own findings that scurvy could be prevented merely by giving sailors lime or lemon juice. He was ridiculed. . . . Captain Cook finally took his advice, and received recognition in 1776 for saving his seamen from this horrible disease by simply adding fruit to their diet. But it took the British navy, under royal physicians, another twenty-five years to follow his example. And even then the French Academy of Medicine was scornful.

Finally, *fully three hundred years after this simple fact was made known, it was generally accepted by medical science.* Another ninety years were to pass, however, before the "something" in citrus fruits was identified as ascorbic acid or vitamin C.

The same years of tragic blundering, disavowal and mistaken treatment were to delay the conquering of other devastating diseases: Beriberi—caused by lack of vitamin B. Pellagra, a disease much like it—caused by lack of the B vitamin niacin. And rickets—caused by lack of vitamin D. Primarily because the belief that *all* diseases were bacterial in origin had become so much in vogue.

Why Doctors Don't Tell You About Vitamins

Having learned that vitamins not only exist but are so vital that lack of any one of them can cause serious illness, it would seem that the medical establishment would have pounced upon this fact and looked to it for further answers. Or at least considered the possibility that other diseases might be due to the body's need for specific nutrients.

No such thing happened. The microbe theory could be embraced because it involves *medication.* And physicians are, by their very title, definition and training, *medical* doctors. It would be going against centuries of orientation to turn their attention to nutrients instead of drugs. The very possibility that a number of other diseases, including some forms of mental illness, might be prevented or cured merely by supplying the missing nutrient or nutrients, has been almost too direct and uncomplicated for them to accept. They have gotten far away from the admonition of Hippocrates: "Let thy food be thy medicine and thy medicine be thy food."

Furthermore, doctors deal primarily with disease instead of health. Their training is not in how to prevent the affliction, but in how to relieve or cure it. For this they rely on a vast arsenal of drugs. As expressed by Dr. Roger Williams in *A Physician's Handbook on Orthomolecular Medicine:*

> The basic fault of these weapons is that they have no known connection with the disease process itself. . . . These drugs are wholly unlike nature's weapons. They tend to mask the difficulty, not eliminate it. They contaminate the environment, create dependence on the part of the patient, and often complicate the physician's job by erasing valuable clues as to the real source of the trouble.

In the Senate hearings referred to earlier, Dr. Michael Lesser went on to say, "The physicians in medical school are taught to use drugs, not vitamins." If you don't hear about them there, and almost nothing about nutrition, then are visited by drug salesmen who suggest that if you use nutrients you'll be considered a charlatan, you are wary. "I think many of the doctors are afraid to try nutrients for fear they will be looked on as charlatans or witch doctors."

It is the multibillion-dollar drug industry which poses the greatest obstacle, compounding the problem for both doctors and the public.

How the Drug Companies Court the Doctors

Doctors are under enormous pressure from the drug companies, who court them all through college. Such gifts as bags, stethoscopes, drug samples, theater tickets and even free luxury trips are not uncommon. "The gifts are part of the estimated minimum one billion dollars a year the drug industry spends for advertising and promotion of prescription drugs," writes Morton Mintz in a series which appeared in the Washington *Post.* Promotion to which he (the doctor) will be subjected for the rest of his professional career; for the courtship continues: Free subscriptions to medical magazines (funded entirely by pharmaceutical advertising). Free video tapes and closed-circuit television, touting drugs. According to Dr. J. Richard Crout, director of the FDA's Bureau of Drugs, testifying before a Senate committee, the industry pays for 80 per cent of the scientific exhibits at AMA meetings, and "otherwise provides physicians with the bulk of their post-graduate medical education."

Dr. Gaylord Nelson, the committee chairman, found "irreconcilable conflict between good medical practice and the industry's commercial interests." And Dr. Quentin K. Young, of Cook County Hospital in Chicago, said, "It is just such practices that have resulted in unnecessary cost to the entire public, as well as inappropriate and excessive use of drugs in our health care system."

The sums of money involved in this drug-doctor marriage are mind-boggling . . . and going up! In his 1979 State of the Union address, President Carter said: "We must act now to protect all Americans from health care costs that are rising *$1 million an hour, 24 hours a day*—doubling every five years." Such figures are almost impossible for the human brain to comprehend; but here are some more:

• Our annual medical bill will soon be $200 billion.

• We are spending $35 billion dollars a year for doctor bills. (Compared to $2.7 billion in 1950.)

• Use of medical drugs has increased 400 per cent since 1950. We are spending $7 billion a year on these drugs.

• Hospital costs have gone up 1,000 per cent during that period.

• "Health care" (more accurately *disease* care) is now costing the nation more than we are spending on defense. This comes to $740 for each man, woman and child, or $2,500 for a family of four. If we were getting value received, the money would be well spent. Yet more people are dying from preventable diseases than have died in our wars.

Health is not big business. *Disease* is big business. It would be unrealistic if not naïve to expect those in the business of disease to support, let alone applaud, efforts to stop or curtail such a highly lucrative monopoly. Not that there is a conscious conspiracy. *I believe most doctors are sincerely dedicated to the relief of suffering.* Rather, that they have been taught there *is* no other

way. And while admittedly there is very little money in prevention, they have also been taught to doubt and distrust the very
methods of prevention. *Of course* they will belittle the role of
nutrition and attack nutritional supplements.

In this they have government backing. Despite all the hearings and hand-wringing speeches about "proper health care for
the people," and more recently "prevention," our government
is actually penalizing people who are trying to stay well. One of
its own agencies, the FDA, is allowed to slander the organic
movement, to harass and raid health food stores. Medicare and
Medicaid (and most health insurance companies) will reimburse
you for drug, doctor and hospital bills; but not a cent of your
money will you get back for the vitamins and minerals which
are keeping you healthy; or for *any* form of natural therapy.

How ironic. These agencies will spend your money *only* for
the very brand of "health care" that has allowed us to become
an arthritic, diabetic, hypertensive, schizophrenic, cancer-rid-
den nation. And which is responsible for those very "million
dollars an hour" cost rises the President deplored.

A New Breed of Doctors

I want to be fair. We can thank orthodox medicine for some very
important things. Primarily, through drugs (and improved sanitation) our most serious infections and communicable diseases
have been largely overcome. Tuberculosis and polio are under
control; we no longer have epidemics of cholera, smallpox,
diphtheria, typhoid fever. Diseases caused by germs. *And drugs
kill germs.* But today you have only to read the obituary page of
any newspaper to realize that heart attacks and cancer *are* an
epidemic in this country. Degenerative diseases account for
more than 70 per cent of all deaths. These are not diseases that
can be conquered by drugs. They are diseases which can be
prevented and even corrected by a change of lifestyle.

And if the entire AMA were suddenly to do an about-face—to
throw out 90 per cent of its medications, encourage people to
come to doctors only for instruction and help with that lifestyle
(exercise, nutrition, mental attitude), or for emergencies—I believe the entire profession would be happier. Not quite as rich,

maybe, but happier. Doctors are already overworked; they would have fewer hypochondriacs on their hands, and they would have more time to heal people. As for the money—well, there will always be those who abuse their bodies, who manage to maim and cripple themselves; there will *always* be enough business for doctors.

Granted, getting away from the excessive use of drugs would cut down on the exorbitant profits of the drug companies. (The annual list of industry profitability rates issued by the Federal Trade Commission has ranked drugs at the top or next to the top ever since 1961.) But they certainly won't go bankrupt. We will always need antibiotics, antiseptics, anesthetics and vaccines; need drugs to control certain diseases. And there will always be people who *won't* take care of themselves.

Fortunately, there have also always been a few brave individualistic doctors. Men like our beloved A.B. Like the pioneers Albert Szent-Györgyi and Evan and Wilfrid Shute; like Fred R. Klenner, who for years has accomplished such impressive results with vitamin C. Men and women who dared to march to a different drum, and survived. And gradually, but more and more visibly, a new breed of doctors has evolved, until now we have a veritable explosion of professionals practicing "wellness," "wholeness," natural, orthomolecular, metabolic healing, instead of the traditional drug-or-operate. Many of them are young new doctors who feel cheated that they have not been taught these things in medical college. They have banded together to teach themselves and others. They are publishing books and magazines. In England there is the McCarrison Society—named for Sir Robert McCarrison, who discovered the remarkable health and longevity secrets of the Hunzas. In Philadelphia there is the Health Alliance for Progress. There is the Southern Academy of Clinical Nutrition, whose founding statement said:

> Many of us have concluded that we know more and more about sickness and disease, and less and less about health, and that our failure in prevention ensues from this general lack of knowledge concerning optimum health.

There is the International Academy of Preventive Medicine and many more. And a public fed up with the ever mounting expense and misery of illness is beginning to beat a path to their doors.

Many doctors now seriously concerned about nutrition had practiced conventional medicine, sometimes for years, until they too rebelled at the futility of their own efforts. Dr. Alan H. Nittler, author of *A New Breed of Doctors,* came to believe drugs only mask symptoms. He began instead to test patients exhaustively to see what nutrients they lacked. "The building blocks of repair must be supplied by the diet or supplements if the body is expected to do the healing." Dr. Nittler says it was his own patients who introduced him to vitamins and got him started on metabolic nutrition. That even the few courses offered during a medical education are woefully out of date. "And what's more, the public knows it! . . . They are watching others, laymen and a few doctors, who are reversing illness. They are beginning to do the same things themselves through the newer concepts of nutrition which teach that the body is only as strong as what's put into it."

The Public Rebellion

It's true that thousands of laymen have been taking their health into their own hands—often with the active encouragement of progressive doctors, but over the indignant protests of others who denounce the movement as faddism. Yet even the most orthodox cannot ignore the failings and often flagrant abuses that have helped stimulate this revolt. Let's go back to the cost of modern medicine and what we're getting for our money:

Hospitals, for instance:

• Sick or injured people are the *most* in need of healing, body-building food. Yet one of the things most hospitals will do (not all) is take away your vitamins and minerals. If you have surgery, you are put on intravenous feeding, generally a glucose-salt solution, which may be necessary, but so lacking in nutrients it can be dangerous if prolonged. Then follows all too often a diet that would be poor fare for a *well* body: dry, overcooked meats and canned vegetables; instant potatoes, instant gravies, instant puddings; Jell-O, canned fruit, pastries and white bread. Meanwhile, Coke and candy machines are available in every hall, even in the children's hospitals associated with famous universities of medicine.

In a report published by the *Journal of the American Medical Association* itself, Bruce R. Bistrian, M.D., and three Boston colleagues found that *half* the surgical patients in one Boston hospital were undernourished, and a third of them seriously deficient in both proteins and calories. Another physician, Dr. George Blackburn, testified before the Senate Agriculture Subcommittee on Nutrition that a shocking number of patients who die in hospitals are victims not of their injuries or illnesses, but have literally starved to death.

• Extravagant waste and duplication as hospitals compete for business, and spend fortunes on machines such as $600,000 scanners. One hospital in our area has built a new million-dollar wing *just to house its equipment.* As I write, two more are hurling charges at each other as they battle for a lucrative dialysis center, where patients have to be hooked up three times a week. "Doctor's Hospital could charge $176 for each treatment, while Mid-Atlantic offers the service for $150," writes the Washington *Star.* "A difference that could cost each patient up to $8,000 a year." Just the *difference,* mind you. Each kidney patient represents an annual income to the hospital of $23,000 or more.

• Exorbitant costs that seem unjustified. My sister's husband was rushed to the hospital with a fatal heart attack. He was kept in the hospital exactly three hours—my sister billed for $1,500. *Five hundred dollars an hour.* Weeks later, to add insult to anguish, she received another bill. This time for lab tests that hadn't even been performed until after her husband's funeral.

Drugs: Where Have All the Billions Gone?

• Thalidomide babies. . . . Blood clots and strokes from the Pill. . . . Cervical tumors in the daughters of women who were given DES* during pregnancy; and possible abnormalities in their sons.

* A hormone given to some 4 to 6 million women to prevent miscarriage. Now banned for that use, at this writing *it is still being prescribed for other problems.* A number of the women whose daughters developed tumors have

• The disaster of MER/29, which was to help prevent heart disease. Prescribed for some 400,000 persons; at least 5,000 suffered cataracts, loss of hair and skin disease—the same afflictions that had showed up in test animals but had never been reported.

• Addiction and a grim harvest of death from tranquilizers, sedatives, mood changers, barbiturates and sleeping pills. . . . The pain killer Darvon, third most widely prescribed drug in the country, now linked to thousands of deaths—more than all deaths from morphine, heroin and methadone combined.

• Four antidiabetes drugs (Diabinese, Orinase, Dymelor, and Tolinase) for which doctors have written millions of prescriptions over the past five years, now revealed to be "dangerous and essentially ineffective," according to Dr. Sidney M. Wolfe, director of Ralph Nader's Health Research Group. Two others, Meltrol and DBI, were finally banned after HEW findings that the death rate among users was "far higher than has been regarded acceptable for any other drug approved for use in the United States for a broad patient population."

OTA Priorities 1979 (Office of Technology Assessment, U. S. Congress) states that although use of prescription drugs has increased 400 per cent since 1950, as much as 25 per cent of them "may be ineffective, unnecessary, or even harmful. Adverse drug reactions . . . may kill as 'few' as 24,000 or as many as 130,000 people annually."

Surgery? Here are some things that are shaking public faith:

• Unnecessary surgery. An estimated 2 million cases in 1977, says Representative John Moss, chairman of the subcommittee that investigated. With a resulting loss of 10,000 lives. During the Los Angeles doctors' strike in 1976, there was actually a significant drop in the death rate—due, it is believed, to unnecessary surgery that wasn't performed.

• Ghost surgery. Where the physician engaged to operate only supervises, or allows someone else to do it in his absence. One woman, terrified before the prospect of a colostomy, shopped for the most skilled specialist—only to learn that while

---

sued the manufacturers. Former HEW Secretary Joseph Califano warned that sons too should be carefully checked.

he was supposed to be wielding the scalpel he was appearing live on a local TV show; her husband saw the program. . . . My husband once had a similar experience. Even in his groggy state he recognized that a total stranger was preparing to operate. "Oh, Dr. S. has a lecture this morning," he was cheerily assured. "He says you won't mind. I'm his assistant."

The most shocking evidence of ghost surgery made headlines —and an astounding book, *Salesman Surgeon: The Incredible Story of an Amateur in the Operating Room.* William McKay, a high school dropout, became not only a top salesman for ortho-pedic devices, he regularly scrubbed in with the surgeons to implant them. When the doctor botched the job, got the artifi-cial hip, knee or other device in wrong (it was frequently the first time he'd even attempted the procedure), McKay took over. At times he performed the entire operation. He also sold instruments and describes assisting in a brain operation where the drill kept breaking in the man's skull.

> What really astounded me was the lack of preparation for surgery. Here they were opening up a man's head and exposing the most vital and irreplaceable part of his body—the brain. And the sur-geons, for starters, did not know how to operate the major piece of equipment used in this procedure . . .

In the course of an investigation after McKay's exposure, it was brought out that it was very common practice for drug or equipment salesmen to be in operating rooms.

There are other assaults on both our public pocketbook and our trust:
• The $135 million swine flu fiasco in 1976. What we got from that was 300 people paralyzed by the inoculations (the Guillain-Barre syndrome); an unknown number died.
• The mammography fiasco. A national program to have women under fifty X-rayed for breast cancer; only to discover more cancers are *caused* by such X rays than are revealed.

It's almost impossible to pick up a paper without reading of startling wrongs. People are becoming alarmed. Aroused not only to the dangers in our environment but to the dangers inherent in our own medical system. The very system supposed to protect and help us! In sheer desperation we are insisting there has to be a better way.

Not that we've turned our back on hospitals and doctors. *And nothing I say in this book is to be construed as an indictment of either.* The hospitals where I had my four babies treated me so grandly I didn't want to come home. Whenever we needed them, doctors, hospitals and nurses have been angels of mercy to my family; especially during the countless operations and crises that often meant life or death to my husband. I have known doctors and nurses I'd nominate for sainthood. But if the medical profession as a whole is too bound by its own traditions and organizations even to investigate methods of healing most people can afford, or to provide services guaranteed to "first, do no harm," then laypeople must take more responsibility for our own health. We must learn more about the needs of our own bodies, turn more and more to nature to heal us and help us stay well.

The Swiftly Turning Tide

There have, of course, been mistakes in the nutrition industry, as in anything else. Outlets known variously as "health food," "organic food," "natural food" stores and restaurants have proliferated. Their aisles swarm, cash registers ring. No doubt there has been opportunism and some misrepresentation. But certainly far less than the gross and flagrant misrepresentation that has gone on for years in the advertising of soft drinks, processed foods and drugs. (For example, in a classic test by Dr. Roger Williams, an "enriched bread" widely proclaimed as providing all nutrients necessary for life was fed to 64 baby rats for 90 days; 40 of them died, the rest were severely stunted.)

"The natural health movement has to be the success story of the century!" writes Betty Franklin in *Let's Live.* And, ironically, the very industry that drove consumers to create it is now clamoring to get on the bandwagon. Breads, drinks, cereals and other foods capitalizing on the words "natural" or "organic" have been rushed into the supermarkets, are touted on TV.

Even "vitamin" is no longer a dirty word but an asset; some products courageously claim, "No artificial preservatives."

The validity of these claims and the true definition of "organic" and "natural" must be firmly and legally established. The Federal Trade Commission has recommended that the terms apply only to products grown without artificial fertilizers or poisonous sprays, preserved without chemicals, and with a minimum of processing. Several states have passed Organic Foods Acts which spell these out, also prohibiting dyes, artificial flavors and such additives as hormones and antibiotics in meat or poultry. Since 1970 there has been a growing movement of organic farmers; they have organized throughout the country, with strict standards for certification to protect both themselves and the people seeking honest, natural, uncontaminated food. The kind God meant for these marvelous bodies.

Finding and preparing it takes a little time and effort, but it does *not* cost more, as some people think. Not in comparison with the high-priced steaks and cold cuts, the pizzas, pastries, package mixes, TV dinners, fake cream whips and other concoctions that fill so many grocery carts. Certainly it's far less expensive in the long run than the time and money spent on sickness that might have been prevented.

Happily, the tide which came in so slowly, under so much attack, is gaining both converts and momentum. More people are reading labels, showing concern. More people are trying to protect themselves by taking vitamins and minerals. And fewer doctors scoff. More and more physicians—certainly those with open minds and a willingness to learn, a genuine desire for the total well-being of their patients—are using nutritional tools. Even those once skeptical.

One day I was amused but delighted when my husband's internist questioned him carefully about his diet. Then, after making some suggestions, urged: "Now, Lynn, are you sure you're getting enough vitamins and minerals? How about zinc? That's very important to healing. And are you taking plenty of vitamins C and E?"

I could have hugged him; in fact, I think I did. This same wonderful doctor who'd once kidded my husband about being a walking drugstore was now earnestly recommending supplements!

6

What Is a Vitamin and How Does It Work?

Vitamin. I love the very sound of that word because it comes from the Latin word *vita*, meaning *life*. And from it stem other lovely words—vital, vitality, signifying that we are truly vigorous, vibrant, vivacious, alive. This is truly one of the most intriguing marvels of the universe. That God would secrete this mysterious life-force in all edible plants and animals and leave it to us to discover how essential it is for us to survive.

But just what is a vitamin?

In *The Chemicals of Life,* Isaac Asimov explains: "The body cannot manufacture all the compounds it needs out of the simple substances it gets by digesting fats, carbohydrates and proteins. The additional compounds it needs must be gotten ready-made from the diet, and they are known as vitamins." In short —a vitamin is not the food itself but an organic substance found in food which enables the body to *utilize* its food for energy, resistance to disease and the building and repair of body tissues.

Vitamins are absolutely essential for health and growth. Without enough of them to do an effective job our bodies get run-down; our cells cease to replenish themselves; our blood can't deliver its proper load of nutrients. Then our entire system becomes vulnerable to disease; and *lack of certain vitamins can be the direct cause of certain diseases.*

How Vitamins Were Discovered

It was this, in fact, which led to the discovery and naming of vitamins. In 1886 a Dutch physician, Christiaan Eijkman, was sent to Java to find the germ thought to cause beriberi—an agonizing disease common to rice-eating people. Instead, he observed that the disease struck only those rich enough to eat the white polished rice, bypassing those who were forced to eat the husks. *Something* in the brown rice gave protection. The "something" was later isolated by a Polish biochemist, Casimir Funk, and labeled a vitamin *(vita* for life, *amine* for the chemical believed to be a part of it). Funk even propounded his vitamin hypothesis: that pellagra, scurvy, rickets and other diseases could be caused, not by microbes, but by lack of some vital element in the diet. A theory that was bitterly rejected for years; although Eijkman did finally receive the Nobel Prize for first unearthing vitamin B.

It will soon be a hundred years since vitamins were originally recognized and at least tentatively labeled. Since then at least fifteen have been cited, and knowledgeable people believe there are more. "Vitamin Q, which aids in blood clotting, was discovered as recently as 1972," says Dr. Richard Passwater in *Supernutrition—Megavitamin Revolution,* "and who knows what will be discovered this year or next?" A number of vitamins which are benefiting other countries around the world are still not recognized or accepted in the United States by the FDA. For instance, vitamin U, which the Russians use to prevent and cure gastric ulcers, and the controversial B_{17}, or Laetrile.

The Evidence

In any case, nearly a century has passed during which there have been thousands of experiments and studies firmly establishing the fact that vitamins not only exist and are useful, but are absolutely essential to the survival of man, woman or ani-

mal. To this end countless millions of test rats, mice and monkeys have been subjected to every conceivable disease and
deprival in order that we might know how a vitamin works and
what its presence or absence in the system means. In addition,
thousands of human subjects have participated in similar studies.

In every test where careful controls were used *and sufficient
vitamins given*, results established beyond the slightest doubt
that vitamins were effective in preventing and controlling disease. Furthermore, that a good supply of vitamins and minerals
maintained in our bodies contributes immensely to a vibrant
state of health.

These findings are facts. They are well documented. Enough
books have been written about them to fill a vast library. For at
least fifty years they have been presented in papers read before
the most learned professional societies; they have been reported in the most reputable medical and scientific journals.
What's more, new and equally important discoveries and verifi-
cations are being made and currently reported, some hundred a
month, in such publications as: *Journal of American Medicine,
Canadian Medical Association Journal, Journal of Immunol-
ogy, Journal of Pediatrics, Journal of Nutrition, Medical Press,
Nutrition Reviews, Annals of Allergy, American Journal of Digestive Diseases, Journal of Dental Medicine,* the British medical publication *Lancet* and others of equal stature. Hundreds of
distinguished sources which one would assume the "authorities" would at least be slightly familiar with.

It seems incredible, therefore, that any spokesman for the
community of nutrition or medicine would continue to deny or
ignore what the scientific community has long established. Declare on television or in a magazine piece, "There is no evidence." In the *Medical Tribune* for February 1979, Arthur M.
Sackler, M.D., discusses this strange phenomenon. Some years
ago Dr. Sackler and his aides were developing a new therapy
for schizophrenia:

> After publishing about 10 reports we heard our friends say, "You
> have no proof." After 10 more papers we still heard, "You haven't
> got proof." Still more work and more published papers, and we

continued to hear, "You haven't got proof." This, of course, raised the question, "What is scientific proof?"

Being the editor of a psychiatric journal, I decided to have a symposium on "What Is Scientific Proof?" I wrote several leading scientists for their participation. The first reply came from a man who sent a very humble note. The question, he said, was much too difficult. He doubted he could make a significant contribution to so complex an issue. . . . The letter was signed—*Albert Einstein.*

To state arbitrarily there is "no evidence" that vitamins have therapeutic value is, in effect, to pretend that all this expensive and exhaustive research has never taken place. Surely this is as absurd and irresponsible as it would be to still ignore or deny that penicillin can combat infection or that vaccination can prevent smallpox. (Both rejected for years by the medical profession.)

Again, the only conceivable reason must be that whenever there are finally accepted breakthroughs in *medicine,* the doctor is given tools he can use on behalf of the patient. But he is understandably skeptical of breakthroughs which give patients tools they can use for themselves.

How the Enzymes Help

Vitamins and minerals don't perform their miracles alone, however.

This marvelous body of mine must have energy—and so must yours. Otherwise, we'd be helpless; our hearts couldn't even beat. And energy is provided solely by the food we eat; food which provides not only fuel but building matter. God, who created the earth, took care of all that by richly covering it with plant life on which both people and animals must feed, then allowing us his children to eat an abundance of the animals. He also designed a cunningly complex and awesome set of machinery by which we are able to convert that food into energy-giving fuel, and into the stuff that constantly repairs and rebuilds this precious and amazing structure in which the spirit journeys through life.

The whole system is called our metabolism. Yet, like a fine car that sits at the curb filled with gas and oil—it couldn't even *start* without the spark plugs, let alone keep going. For us, these are three critical elements—vitamins, minerals and enzymes. We'll be talking a lot about minerals and vitamins, but it's important to understand the enzymes too. Because they all work together.

Enzymes are tiny elements found in all living cells—plant, animal and *us*. In other words, we eat them in food; but unlike vitamins, our bodies also manufacture them. And while there are a limited number of known vitamins, there are literally billions of enzymes. Every cell has at least 1,000 enzymes causing about two million biochemical reactions to take place every minute. For enzymes act as catalysts which ignite and speed up everything that happens in us. Another difference is that the vitamins, though few by comparison, do many different jobs in the body. Yet every single tiny enzyme is a specialist, specifically created to perform a single task. (To me, this is thrilling.) There is one important similarity between vitamins and enzymes, however. The enzymes in food are also destroyed by air, processing and cooking. Temperatures of 120 degrees or over will kill them. Another reason we should strive to eat our fruits and vegetables as fresh and raw as possible.

Remember, we simply can't function without these vital sparks, the enzymes—which are produced in the body by the pancreas. If your pancreas isn't producing enough of the right kind, or you are not getting enough living enzymes in your food, then your body can't utilize the vitamins and minerals. The three are interdependent, they can't work without each other.

Right now, let's look more closely at vitamins.

Why We Need More Vitamins

There are two kinds of vitamins: Those which dissolve in fat (for instance, the vitamins in liver and eggs); and those which dissolve in water (most of the vitamins in fruits and vegetables). The fat-soluble vitamins are A, D, E and K. The water-soluble are vitamin C, the various vitamins in the B complex, vitamin P and no doubt others yet to be identified. Vitamins A and D are the two primary vitamins which are stored in the liver for future use, much as our livers store other nutrients. For this reason vitamins A and D are the only two that could cause trouble if taken in supplements in excessive amounts. (Excessive, however, means well beyond the 50,000 international units of vitamin A and 4,000 units of vitamin D which are considered safe by most doctors.)

Our supply of vitamins is constantly being diminished by their own activity in the body. And they are very rapidly used up by all the following:

> tobacco, alcohol
> salt, sugar, rancid fats
> estrogen, antibiotics
> sleeping pills, tranquilizers
> mineral oil
> surgery, sickness, accidents
> emotional strain
> fluorides
> polluted air or water
> pesticides
> food additives
> extremes of heat or cold
> pregnancy, nursing

Every one of these puts extra demands on our vitamins. They must work extra hard to keep the machinery of metabolism functioning correctly; to help throw off the poisonous invaders; to build up our resistance to others such as germs; and to restore our assaulted flesh and nerves. If we are to maintain even reasonably good health, these vitamins *must* be replaced. And if we want to enjoy a state of really glowing health, we will not only avoid as many of the poisons and stresses as possible, we will be *sure* that our bodies are amply supplied with vitamins and minerals. (Pregnancy and nursing are, of course, "happy stress" situations as the body strives to provide for both the mother and the little new life.)

Ideally, all the vitamins we need should be available in their original source, food. They once were. Our ancestors got along without supplements. But take a look at that list. Only three or four of those hazards would apply to our predecessors. Yes, they had babies and broke bones and maimed each other in battle;

they were also sometimes felled by plagues from polluted water or other illnesses caused by germs—usually due to lack of sanitation (one reason their infant mortality was high). But they were not captive to chemicals in the air and practically everything they consumed; nor subject to the intense social stresses we endure. Their food, furthermore, was unrefined, retaining all the life-giving elements the creator put there. And when they needed remedies they had the native wisdom to find those too in growing things.

Today, unless you and I live in a monastery on a mountain and raise our own food, we are simply not going to get the vitamins and minerals we need. If I want to stay well, vigorous, energetic, productive, truly able to enjoy this enthralling world and contribute something to it, I must make up the difference. I must fortify my body with extra vitamins and minerals.

Which Vitamins Should You Take?

The first question people ask is: "Which vitamins do you take?" My answer is: "All of them"—meaning all that are available in over-the-counter supplements. This excludes the blood-clotting agent vitamin K; and vitamin P, commonly known as the bioflavonoids. These occur abundantly in fruits and vegetables, and are less subject to processing; it isn't considered necessary to isolate them for private use. Otherwise, I take the entire complement, because vitamins work in teams. They support and enforce each other.

Up to the time we met Shreve Spitler, I had been rather hostile toward swallowing anything besides food, which no doctor said I had to. Such supplements might be okay for sick people, but if you are blessed with a healthy constitution, who needed them? I was reflecting the common either/or attitude: either you're sick or you're well. Failing to consider the countless maladies which don't put us to bed or yield laboratory evidence, yet keep us from feeling and doing our best. The vague aches and pains, depression, nervousness, fatigue—symptoms which are often dismissed as hypochondria. In his introduction to Richard Passwater's book *Supernutrition,* Raymond F. Chen, M.D., says:

> This "two state theory" runs counter to common sense. Health has many gradations, not just two. . . . There are great variations in the way we feel on different days, and there are great differences in the amount of energy people possess . . . vitamins and other dietary nutrients may be critical in accounting for these differences.

I was beginning to find this out for myself. But the thing that really convinced me was what supplements did for my husband's arthritis. It had begun with some of those vague aches and pains, and gradually gotten worse. Finally his neck was so stiff he had to turn his whole body to see to back down our steep driveway. And the joints in his hands and knees hurt so much it was hard to bend over to shine his shoes. One day only *two weeks* after he had begun his new regimen, he suddenly realized that for the first time in years he was vigorously shining his shoes without pain. He was so surprised he called my attention to it. And when he left for the office he honked and waved and demonstrated how freely he could move his head as well.

Since so many people ask, here is what worked for *him*. (Remember, there are many different kinds of arthritis. Also, no two people are identical in their needs.) The following, taken three times a day:

500 mg. of vitamin C
500 IU vitamin E
One tablespoon wheat-germ oil
500 mg. vitamin B complex
50 mg. pantothenic acid
A vitamin-mineral capsule

The wheat-germ oil provides additional vitamin E as well as minerals and other valuable nutrients; it also seems to lubricate. The pantothentic acid is an important member of the vitamin B complex; he took extra because it directly affects inflamed nerve endings.

In any case, we were both so elated I decided to try the formula for my bursitis. *And I never had it again.* After a few years, however, when I got cocky and careless, I began to have twinges in my shoulders and elbows. In fact, one elbow would sometimes ache severely in the night. "Well, I guess we can expect a little arthritis as we get older," sighed a friend—a remark that made me so mad I marched right back to the vitamin cupboard, declaring, "I will *not* have arthritis!" And here is a curious thing: For the next couple of weeks, whenever an arm or elbow would begin to ache, all I had to do to stop it was to get up and take a capsule of wheat-germ oil.

I haven't been bothered since, not so long as I am faithful to my full program of vitamins.

How Many Vitamins Do We Need?

I also began reading the books Dr. Spitler recommended. And one of the major things I learned was that to get full benefit out of vitamins you have to take *enough.* Taking too few is like throwing a few teaspoons of water on a blazing fire. (That's what was wrong when we were dutifully swallowing one capsule a day for a few weeks to please my husband's sister. Nothing happened.) Among the books were those of the famous biochemist Richard Passwater. Later I was lucky enough to meet Dr. Passwater personally and attend his lectures—one on this very subject. Here are some highlights:

> What do we mean by *need?* To be able to breathe, be average—or superior in health? Some people think it's all right to be sick several times a year. The FDA thinks a normal healthy person misses several days work every year, and has a serious illness every couple of years. That's actually the attitude they have in determining the recommended daily allowances for the "average" person. But health should be freedom from disease, and a lifestyle free of doctors, medicines or things that keep me from doing what I want to do when I'm well.

He says there *is* no average person.

> They give us several categories and try to fit everybody into them. Yet there are eighty different body types—not three or four; at least twelve different "average" stomachs. Surgeons have found greater differences *inside the heart* than they do with people's exteriors. Even our enzymes are different. . . . The only way to make RDA's helpful is to make them higher, so that people *will* get more than

they need, but everybody will get *what* they need. There is essentially no harm in too many.

The effects of vitamins are long-term. If I make an error, to be safe it should be on the high side; if I err on the low side, I may get cancer. The National Cancer Institute has many experiments showing that vitamin A protects against cancer, but people don't get enough. By the time they discover the shortage it may be too late. Of course, vitamins A and D can be moderately toxic, but only in excessive amounts and not if you use common sense.

Dr. Passwater described how the RDA's are set:

The Food and Nutrition Board looks at the number of people in the country, decides how much food they consume, then divides, saying that's how many vitamins we need. They divide the food supply by the population, and say what we have is what we need. No allowances for loss of vitamins in cooking and storage, no allowances for sick people who may need more. And these RDA's repeatedly change; amounts have appeared, disappeared, reappeared—there have been up to seventy changes since 1968. Yet the needs of people haven't changed.

And here's an irony—the RDA's for animals are ten times higher than for human beings. And remember that the animals, especially test animals, are fed good balanced diets of chow, not the junk the rest of us eat. Why do they want to ensure that animals get ten times more nutrients than we do?

We're all responsible for our own health. To discover how many vitamins we need, we have to observe, experiment. Give yourself a mini-physical, Dr. Passwater says. Check when you're tired, depressed, or when you're feeling great. Ask, "Body, how am I? Listen to your own body wisdom." It will soon tell you whether you're getting too little or too much.

Luckily, when we were beginning this program we had our enthusiastic dentist friend to guide us. And our regular doctors could not have been more cooperative and encouraging. Several times when my husband's condition was desperate, we proposed and tried some very unorthodox treatments. In each instance his internist and other specialists were open-minded, wanting to learn all they could and to see the experiments succeed. I don't think it can be repeated too often—most doctors want, above all, to have their patients get well.

If you are just starting out, the best way is to find a good nutrition-oriented M.D. Such doctors are known variously as holistic, (also spelled "wholistic"), metabolic or orthomolecular physicians. *(Holistic* is from the Greek philosophy that people are more than the mere sum of their parts. *Orthomolecular,* the prevention and treatment of disease using the natural chemical substances of our bodies.) Such doctors emphasize nutrition and other natural means; but they recognize there are situations when drugs, surgery and radiation may be necessary. He or she will run a survey on your diet, and give you the hair and blood tests which will reveal any vitamin or mineral deficiencies. With this information the doctor can make accurate and specific recommendations as to what supplements you may need.

Generally health food stores can put you in touch with such doctors in your area. Most have a list of them in a booklet titled *Nutrition-Minded Doctors in the United States and Canada,* published by Alacer Publications. Or you can learn about those in your area by attending meetings of the various nutritional societies. Information is also available by writing:

International Academy of Preventive Medicine
10409 Town & Country Way
Houston, Texas 77024

International College of Applied Nutrition
Box 386
La Habra, California 90631

International Academy of Metabology
1000 East Walnut Street #247
Pasadena, California 91106

Society of Orthomolecular Medicine-East
1125 State Road
Princeton, New Jersey 08540

Huxley Institute for Biosocial Research
1114 First Avenue
New York, New York 10021

Natural Versus Synthetic

In Rodale's *The Complete Book of Vitamins* the story is told of some sea-water fish that were brought to an aquarium in London. There wasn't enough sea water available for them, but one of the curators said "no problem"—he knew the chemical formula for sea water and would whip up a batch. When it was completed, however, the fish put into it promptly died. Other batches were prepared, each more carefully, yet the fish would not survive. Then someone suggested adding a small amount of real sea water to the product. "This they did, and the fish could live in it! Evidently in real sea water there is a gleam of some substance which is too tiny to measure, and which is not in the published formula for sea water, but which is needed by fish in order to live."

Even scientists disagree, but I go along with those who believe that natural vitamins likewise contain something which no synthetic can duplicate. The very word holds the secret in its root—*vita*, of life. It is this potent quality that is missing in chemical combinations put together in test tubes. No matter how identical the basic compounds, no man-made substance can completely duplicate the God-created essence that exists in a living source. For instance, an apple seed might be chemically copied, but it would never produce an apple; if planted it could not grow.

We are often told, "A vitamin is a vitamin, the body doesn't know the difference." But any living body, human or animal, *does* know the difference between a dead inorganic substance and one in which the life-force stirs. Hundreds of experiments with animals have proved this—with chicks, guinea pigs, mice. Weight gains, vigor, survival rates were markedly different. Synthetic vitamins were better than none, but the natural were more effective and less toxic. This is mainly because nature always gives us her vitamins in groups. If one is extracted it is bound to incorporate fragments of others, which both enhance it yet dilute it and give it balance.

Britain's Dr. Isobel Jennings, researcher at Cambridge University, points this out in her book *Vitamins in Endocrine Me-*

tabolism. Her major objection to synthetics, however, is that "they have only a fraction, whether large or small, of the biological activity of the natural plant."

Some people are also allergic to the chemicals used as a base for many synthetic vitamins. Some of them toxic, including nicotine, coal tars and alloxan. If the product is properly made they will be refined out. Nonetheless, no poisonous substance is used in preparing natural vitamins.

True, today so many people are taking vitamin C there simply are not enough natural sources to meet the demand. Therefore, even the so-called natural form of ascorbic acid is manufactured from glucose with rose hips or citrus added to bring it as close to the original as possible. But even the glucose used as the common base for vitamin C is itself a natural compound, the sugar found in corn or potato starch.

The very best source of any vitamin is, of course, the foods in which the Creator first put them. Milk and eggs and butter and meats of every kind, but especially the organ meats such as liver. Fresh fruits and vegetables. Nuts and seeds and unprocessed grains. The health-dedicated person will seek these first and use them, whether he takes supplements or not. But since so few of us can get our foods genuinely fresh and unadulterated, practically all of us need the boost of supplements. And if we're going to buy them it doesn't make sense to settle for an impoverished substitute.

What Vitamins Do for Me

I take vitamins for energy. With them I can work harder.

I take vitamins for vitality. They make me feel better; life has more zest.

I take vitamins for resistance to disease. They protect me from the poisons in our air, water and food. (Since beginning some fifteen years ago, my sick days could be counted on one hand.)

I take vitamins for self-control. They calm my nerves.

I take vitamins for rest. With them I can sleep better.

I take vitamins out of sheer healthy vanity. I *look* better (skin, hair and nails); and I know from observation and experience that people who take vitamins simply don't age as fast as the calendar claims.

In addition to all these physical benefits there is a psychological lift in simply doing something regularly that is like a little gift to your own body. Not a candy bar, which can make you feel guilty. Not a medication because you're ailing and this is what the doctor ordered. But something you're doing from choice; another way of telling your body "I love you." All this leads to a new awareness of your own health and the things you can do to maintain it.

The end product is bound to be a more vigorous, happy human being!

7

That Dangerous Cliché, the "Balanced Diet"

Why do I take vitamins and minerals? I am a healthy person. What's more, I can hop into my car and drive to any supermarket, where almost every foodstuff ever grown or concocted is available from which to choose. Into my big wheeled cart I can pile everything necessary for a so-called balanced diet. This is the incessant theme song of the "experts" who cheerily assure us we're the best-fed nation on earth. "Just eat a variety of foods and you'll get all the vitamins and minerals you need with a knife and fork."

The ludicrous lengths to which this is carried was dramatized by four nutritionists from a big nutrition convention in Washington, D.C. During an interview on the evening news, all were spouting the cliché of the balanced diet. "But what about the people who have to eat out and patronize fast-food places?" they were asked. One smiled straight into the camera and proposed this little gem: "Well, you could vary the *places*. One day eat at a hamburger shop, the next day fish 'n' chips, the next fried chicken, the next day a pizza parlor—then start over."

Never mind the high salt, sugar and fat in fast foods, the white flour, the lack of fiber—just *vary* them and you'll get a balanced diet!

Oh, goody. If they're right I can drive home and put my groceries away knowing my family will be properly nourished. For I have gone the fast-food lady one better and stuck to the groups known as the Basic Four: Milk, meat, fruit-vegetable and grain. For some twenty-five years these have been the approved USDA standard, the "magic yellow brick road" to eating correctly; and since we *are* what we eat, we'll be healthy.

But wait, something's wrong. Is it a safe road, after all, this one marked BALANCED DIET? If so, why do we meet so many sick people dragging themselves along it? Why so many ambulances screaming toward hospitals? Why do we have:

- 1,200 people a *day* dying of cancer? (More cancer than any other country in the world.)
- Nearly a million people a year dying of heart disease?
- 50 million people suffering from arthritis—with a quarter million new cases every year?

Why so much diabetes, mental illness, kidney and liver disease? Why are so many sterile? Why so many birth defects? So many hyperactive children? Why are so many people miserable with colds, ulcers, viruses? Why are we chronically fatigued?

If simply eating a variety of foods is the answer—*why are we spending almost as much on sickness as we are on the foods that keep us alive?* For our medical bills have reached a point where they are threatening to equal or surpass our $200 billion grocery bills!

The U. S. Department of Agriculture's own Carol Foreman (Assistant Secretary for Food and Consumer Services) says, "It is no longer enough merely to recommend a regular diet from the four basic groups. People today are getting a lot of questionable information about foods through advertising, and this has produced a nation malnourished in a new way, by being overweight." In a speech to the American Association for the Advancement of Science, Joan Dye Gussow, president of the Society for Nutrition Education as well as chairman of nutrition education at Columbia, pointed out:

> One reason we and the food industry have lived so long and happily together with the four food groups is that it is a vague enough

classification to be able to tolerate all kinds of food horrors. Purple breakfast confections with magenta marshmallows are taken in as part of the grain-cereal group, for example, and Hi-C Dairy Fresh Red Punch—containing little or no fruit—can masquerade as part of the fruit and vegetable group. The Basic Four, in short, turns out to be totally undiscriminating in a world of fantasy foods—hence, no one's ox gets gored.

Good health does indeed depend on a varied diet. And the variety in our supermarkets makes us the envy of the world. But the simple truth is—the diet is bad, no matter how varied, if the food itself is bad. And the food is bad if it lacks the essential nutrients and if it contains chemical poisons.

Four other California nutritionists studied twenty menus made up of the Basic Four; all failed to provide even the RDA's for half the nutrients analyzed. Writing in the *Journal of Nutrition Education*, they reported that the foods contained 60 per cent or less of the recommended daily allowances (which themselves are woefully low) for vitamin E, vitamin B_6, magnesium, iron and zinc, and gave little energy.

Today's Poisoned Food

Worse, today's processed foods are loaded with sugar and drenched with chemical poisons. I was privileged to know Rachel Carson briefly, at the time she published *Silent Spring*. (Her adopted son and our daughter attended the same small school.) At that time she said that if any of us made a list of the additives on the labels of the food we buy, and took it to the neighborhood druggist, he would demand a doctor's prescription or make us sign a poison register before allowing us to have them.

That was a long time ago, at a time when our individual consumption of these additives was estimated at a "mere" two or three pounds a year. Since then these chemicals have gradually increased. According to Dr. Passwater, by 1974 we were each ingesting an annual five pounds of them; by 1977 nine pounds; now it is ten poisonous pounds and rising. To get another perspective—he says the food industry spent some $853 million on them in 1974; and has budget estimates of $1.3 billion for chemical food additives by 1984.

These are the people who put the food on our table. Their power is enormous. They own us, body and belly. But they also want to own our minds. To that end they also spend billions selling us on the marvels of the food they sell us to eat. They have billions to spend on advertising; on lobbying and political contributions; on endowing the nutrition departments of universities; on scholarships and favors; on a vast army of media spokespeople all eager to spout their self-righteous and scathing clichés: "There's no nutritional superiority in natural foods." "All foods are health foods." "Vitamins and minerals are a waste of money; you'll get all you need if you just eat a balanced diet."

No wonder Americans are confused. Because other voices are gravely warning that that selfsame diet is killing us. In his opening statement before the now famous hearings of the Select Committee on Nutrition and Human Needs, Senator McGovern stated: "The simple fact is that our diets have changed radically within the last 50 years, with great and often harmful effects on our health. . . . In all, six of the ten leading causes of death in the United States have been linked to our diet."

We'll take another trip back to that supermarket; but first let's look at what that highly touted American diet has already done to other people.

The Ruin that Comes with "Civilized" Foods

Many studies have now been made of primitive people like the Hunzas, citing their remarkable longevity and health *so long as they remain "nutritionally uncivilized."* Many books have been written about them. One of the first, however, remains the classic: *Nutrition and Physical Degeneration* by Dr. Weston A. Price. Dr. Price was a dentist who set out in the thirties and forties to find people who were then still isolated and forced to live on native foods. He and his wife traveled the globe, studying at least thirty-five different groups, ranging from the Eskimos of Alaska to the Australian islanders of the Torres Strait. Their original purpose was "to find out why savages have good teeth." They found out even more—*in every instance* such people had perfect bodies as *well* as perfect teeth. They were almost entirely free of disease.

The Prices made careful control studies, comparing these people with those in the nearest communities who had access to sugar, white flour and other processed foods. The contrast was screamingly evident. Although of the same racial stock, and sometimes living as near as across a river or beyond a mountain range, those who had lost their isolation and adopted the foods of modern civilization not only lost their teeth but their immunity to disease!

Dr. Price chemically analyzed the vitamin-mineral content of all the various foods consumed, no matter how diverse. He found it didn't matter what the source of the minerals and vitamins might be, *so long as the supply was adequate.* Whether the food came from mountain pastures, the jungles or the sea, whether it was goat's milk, nuts, berries, octopus or caribou, *all* the foods which came straight from nature were rich in body-building elements.

There were other common denominators among the people themselves, whether they lived near the North Pole or the wilds of Africa: They did hard physical work. They were healthy, happy, peace-loving. All believed in a divine creator. All were highly intelligent. All demonstrated an intuitive sense of their own physical needs and had the will power to fill these needs, at whatever cost in time and energy. Dr. Price states: "One of our greatest difficulties in undertaking to apply the wisdom of the primitives to our modern problems involves a character factor. The Indians of the high Andes were willing to go hundreds of miles to the sea to get kelp and fish eggs for the use of their people. Yet many of our modern people are unwilling to take sufficient trouble to obtain foods competent to accomplish the desired results."

We are not only too lazy, we also hate to be called "faddists" for trying to eat foods the way God created them, and practically crazy for taking supplements. Put-downs found so freely for so many years in so many government publications, insisting that all anybody needs is to choose from among the marvels of the supermarket. (This dictum, however, was so severely challenged by the Surgeon General's Report on Disease Prevention,

Healthy People, published in July 1979, that the Department of Agriculture has since released a booklet, *Food.* The first of its kind to tell the blunt truth about diet and disease.)

Writing in *Prevention,* Dominick Bosco cites the research done by a California team among the Hopi and Papago Indians, testing commercial foods against traditional Indian foods. "The mineral content of food grown and prepared by the Indians in Arizona was compared with that of supermarket variety food *supplied by the government under the supervision of a Nutrition and Dietetics Branch established to upgrade Indian health."* All the Indian breads and dishes were enormously higher in calcium, magnesium, zinc and other nutrients. "What the Hopi *were* getting from the government experts responsible for their nutritional welfare were barrels of white flour, white rice, degerminated cornmeal, hydrogenated fat . . . barrels of *junk!* . . . This has been going on wherever Indians procure their food from white men. And it hasn't been without recurrent degeneration of health." Obesity, tooth decay and diseases like diabetes, once rare, have become rampant among them.

The Family Goes to the Supermarket

Let's say I'm a young mother who, like most mothers, must take my children along while I shop for that "balanced diet." First I must drag them past the booby traps cleverly planted just as advised in *Supermarket News:*

> Snack foods are a high profit item and we are hopeful that after placing the merchandise in a better location (the front of the store) volume will jump from 33 to 50%.

Having denied frantic pleas for potato chips, pretzels, filled crackers, twisties and crunchies, I pick up rolls, a cherry pie and three loaves of bread. We make it to the fruits and vegetables, only to be confronted by a huge revolving rack of candy bars. *Progressive Grocer* has urged:

> Focus on the demand—kids. Try massive floor displays in high traffic aisles or large related product ends; candy in the toy departments; candy in produce; candy at the checkout counter.

And right on cue, the kids demand!

From then on, the journey to get to meats, dairy products and other essentials is an obstacle course of fizz drinks, artificial fruit drinks, cookies, sugar-coated cereals, chewies, loopies and other food frivolities advertised on TV. "But they're *good* for you!" their fan club desperately pleads. Valiantly, I resist; my big brown bags are finally loaded with bread and cereal; milk and meat; butter and eggs; and plenty of fruits and vegetables—fresh, frozen or canned. All four food groups.

By now, though, the kids are sulking or weeping. I buy them off with doughnuts, and console myself by munching one too as I cross the parking lot. There to discover somebody has crushed a fender. I'm so upset I nearly hit another car backing out. "Turn that radio down!" I order a son whose horrendous music further assaults my nerves—and an argument follows. Meanwhile, we get stuck in traffic behind a bus whose nauseous leaden fumes must be inhaled all the way home. By the time we get there I have a tension headache, and reach blindly for the aspirin, Excedrin or one of the other remedies whose incessant ads are at that very moment screaming, "Strong, STRONG, STRONGER!" If I'm Mrs. Average American, I may also try to relax with a cocktail.

I then start dinner by peeling, boiling and frying things, adding plenty of salt and throwing any extra liquid down the sink. I will make coffee for the adults, let the children lace their milk with chocolate syrup and yield to the teen-ager's insistence on a Coke. Unless we're lucky, somebody will spill the milk, the meal will be interrupted by phone calls, its peace further assailed by more arguments and sometimes tears. During all this the food actually consumed, however, should qualify as a balanced meal:

Meat and potatoes. Cooked carrots. A tossed salad. Bread and butter. And for dessert a cherry pie served a la mode. Can I then cheerfully assume my family is getting all the vitamins and minerals it needs?

A Look at the Menu

First, consider the meat. Whether steak, pork or chicken, it's probably from poor creatures who've never been allowed to set foot on the ground. They've been raised as prisoners in cruelly crowded cages where they're pushed to their limits. Dr. Michael Fox, director of the Institute for the Study of Animal Problems, says in *The Humane Society News,* "Broilers may put on so much weight they collapse because their bones are too weak to support them." The stress of confinement often makes animals so restless they attack each other and must be debeaked, their tails docked. They've been pumped full of hormones for growth, their feeds laced with arsenic for appetite and antibiotics against disease. Dr. Fox says that in 1976 one out of every ten hogs tested for antibiotics had illegally high residues. Nitrate fertilizers, herbicides and pesticides also infect both the animals' feed and their flesh. "These substances may be stored in the animals' fat, muscle and internal organs or be concentrated and excreted in milk, and then be ingested by humans." Although most of them are known to be cancer-causing, they're allowed because they reduce production costs! (A cost saving I've never seen passed on at the meat counters, have you?)

If, instead of meat, I've served fish, there's a very real possibility it contains mercury, PCB's, Mirex or other pollutants from contaminated water. (Fish condemned as unfit for human consumption in Canada is actually sold in the United States.)

The potatoes were raised on chemically fertilized soil. This *does* reduce their supply of selenium, zinc and other vital minerals, because chemicals destroy the earthworms and other life forms which make minerals available to the roots. If the soil was generally poor, the protein was also diminished. Agricultural experiments have proved this, despite violent claims to the contrary. The potatoes have lost some of their nutrients in storing, more in the peeling, cooking and salting. The same goes for the carrots. The tomatoes in the salad were picked green, which didn't allow nature to finish her job of filling them with vitamins. They were literally bred for the gas chamber in which they were artificially reddened or "ripened." Then waxed. No wonder they taste like golf balls.

Worse, all these vegetables have been subjected to pesticides so poisonous the EPA warns they should be carefully washed and peeled—but even so, the poisons may have penetrated.

They have also been subjected to a lethal fungicide, ETU (ethylene thiourea). A Washington-based news release states:

> ETU gets on vegetables and fruits because it is a residue of what government officials say are the most widely used fungicides in the United States. . . . They degrade in the environment to the pure cancer-causing residue ETU, which is left on foods. These cancer-causing residues cannot be completely washed off food, according to EPA scientists. And unlike bacteria, EBDC residues only break down quicker into pure ETU when vegetables are cooked.

Let Them Eat Sawdust

Well, how about the bread? I'll try to play safe and serve my family three different kinds: White. Wheat. And that low-calorie, high-fiber kind so widely advertised.

The white bread or rolls? Their flour has been stripped of 75 per cent of its minerals, 90 per cent of its vitamins; then "enriched" with only three (of the more than twelve) B vitamins, plus inorganic iron. (A nutritional contradiction since, unlike meat, bread is one of the few foods reluctant to release its iron.) No vitamin E, sorry.

The wheat bread? It may be only 25 per cent wheat, the rest dyed white flour. My good friend Marian Burros, food editor of the Washington *Post*, writes in her additive-free cookbook, *Pure & Simple:*

> Usually it's impossible to tell by looking if the product is 100% whole grain or just colored with caramel to make you think so. . . . That phrase "wheat flour" has been turning up more and more on bread products and it's easy to believe the term is meant to confuse you. . . . For 100% whole-wheat bread, look for *"whole-wheat flour."*

Well then, we'll eat that high-fiber bread. We need to take off a few pounds, and everybody knows fiber is good for you. . . . Or *is* it if the fiber comes from wood pulp? Or, as Senator McGovern called it at a hearing, "sawdust." For the fibrous ingredient, powdered cellulose, is actually a cheap by-product of the pulp industry, which can absorb a lot of water. Beatrice Trum Hunter cites the possible dangers of excessive artificial fiber, which, unlike that found in fruits and vegetables, has no food value whatever. And which the human body was never designed to digest.

Writing in *Consumers' Research*, she says that FDA approval of this filler was given after only brief three-month tests, none involving children. "Such studies are inadequate to demonstrate possible long-term effects. . . . The studies, limited to adults, fail to give any indication of possible effects on growing children." We are also told:

> The consuming public now stands on the threshold of having powdered cellulose incorporated into a wide variety of processed foods and beverages as a substitute for more costly ingredients with nutritive value. Powdered cellulose is being sold to food processors by paper mills as a unique "bulking agent" for flour-based products such as cookies, cakes, breakfast cereals, and pastas, as well as bread.

This at the time when the HANES Report (an extended government health and nutrition survey) is concluding with the information that at least half our population is getting less than even the low recommended daily allowances of the nutrients tested for. (Vitamins A and C and the minerals calcium and iron.)

As for dessert: The pie crust is made of white flour, salt, sugar, hydrogenated fats and chemical preservatives. Inside, there are barely two dozen cherries; they have been stretched with fake fruit made of a seaweed derivative artificially colored and flavored, the whole thing swimming in a glutinous dyed red mass concocted from petroleum synthetics and sugar. The ice cream, which one child doesn't finish, won't even melt like genuine old-fashioned ice cream, but only becomes a gluey mess, because it's primarily stabilizers, emulsifiers, buffers, artificial coloring, flavoring, sugar and air. (In 1977 the producers tried to take out even the little bit of real milk they were using, and substitute cheaper caseinates or whey—ingredients commonly used in non-dairy creamers, imitation milks and cheeses. The FDA actually backed the proposal until both the national dairy associations and consumers had a fit.)

Let's say I've tried to avoid all the chemicals in non-dairy cream, however, and bought real cream for my coffee. It says so right on the package: Grade A Homogenized, Ultra-Pasteurized TABLE CREAM. From one of our leading dairies. But wait, why then the list of ingredients?

> Guar gum, mono- and di-glycerides, edible salts, microcrystalline cellulose, cane sugar, carrageenin, cellulose gum.

They don't even mention cream!

(In real life, I wrote a protest to the dairy. Who assured me it was indeed cream because an 18 per cent minimum butterfat was required by law. And those other ingredients were merely stabilizers "to give the product a little more body." Gee, the cream from my uncles' cows had so much rich body it thickened; and the cows would have been embarrassed to think anybody had to add *sugar* to their sweet cream. Could it be to disguise the taste of the gums and glycerides? And what about *my* body?)

How Many Vitamins in Our Balanced Meal?

There's no earthly way of knowing how many vitamins and minerals such a family was actually getting even if we had a nutritional chart beside the table. Such a chart tells me there are 12,500 international units of vitamin A in a three-ounce serving of cooked carrots. Which carrots? I wonder. Pulled fresh from my garden, or awaiting my purchase in the market? And how cooked? With or without salt, and for how long? These charts are inaccurate. We are told nutritionists reduce the value of raw foods only 25 per cent. This does not truly account for the loss of nutrients.

There are simply too many variables. The soil and conditions under which the food was raised; time spent in storage. Heat, light and air take their toll. Dr. R. E. Hein, Manager of Food Research for the H. J. Heinz Co., says in both the Chicago *Tribune* and the *Congressional Record* that vitamins disintegrate in those conditions. And when vegetables are cooked, "the losses range up to 40% for vitamin A, 100% for vitamin C, 75% for niacin, 80% for thiamine, 55% for vitamin E." As for the FDA's preposterous claim that modern processing technology does no harm—any scientist from the Agriculture Department will tell you that's bunk. Nutritionally it's disastrous. By the time our balanced meal reaches the table it's been freezed, dried, radiated; leached and bleached; salted and sugared; embalmed, adulterated, dyed, waxed and polished. And the assault on its nutritional integrity is even more complete if I depend on "instant" or convenience foods.

What remains may be protein, fat or carbohydrates, but without the vitamins and minerals which are absolutely critical if our bodies are to build and draw energy from these materials.

So actually our "balanced meal" is woefully *out* of balance because it is woefully deficient in the very substances our hypothetical housewife needs most, particularly the vitamins her body has been desperately burning up as she strives to cope with stress:

Emotional: Behavior of the children. Shock and indignation at her damaged car. Worry—will the insurance cover it? What will her husband say?

Noise: From car radio, traffic and kids.

Pollution: Some twenty minutes of breathing lead, cadmium and carbon monoxide fumes from other cars, especially the bus. . . . Chemicals in the food.

Drugs: The headache remedy. The cocktail, if she had one. Sugar and salt—both vitamin-destroying drugs. Caffeine.

This is just a typical end-of-day situation which in real life probably would have been preceded by other stress or crisis situations, some of them more serious. Every member of the family would have had his or her own problems, been exposed to the same environmental hazards, and likewise failed to receive from that good "balanced meal" enough vitamins and minerals to replace those which had been destroyed. And unless those elements are replaced through reasonably fresh, untreated foods, or supplements, their bodies will suffer. Their resistance will be low. They will be susceptible to colds, fatigue, depression, infection, and they will be laying the groundwork for serious degenerative diseases.

John M. Ellis, M.D. (who wrote *Vitamin B₆: The Doctor's Report*), says in *Natural Food and Farming*:

"Mr. Balanced Diet" is correct to a degree—if he is advocating use of pure food, grown on fertile soil, that provides all the nutritive substances, in sufficient quantity, not overcooked, and fed to a perfectly normal human who has never in his life been denied proper nutrition, and who has never breathed or swallowed toxic nutritive antagonists.

He is talking about a diet for a person who is not pregnant, does not smoke, drink alcohol to excess, take birth control pills, or take any number of drugs that deplete the body of vitamins and minerals. . . . Very frankly I am sick and tired of the term "balanced diet" as it is used in the United States today.

Our Children Are the Victims

Tragically, the degenerative diseases once associated with age are devastating the ranks of the young.

Before the turn of this century most people died of accidents or infectious diseases. Tuberculosis, smallpox, typhoid fever, pneumonia, measles—such caused the church bells to toll. An 1876 issue of *Scientific American,* reporting the causes of death in New York City, doesn't list a single case of cancer. From 1890 on, when coronary thrombosis began to surface here and there in America, the symptoms were so unusual nobody knew what it was. Doctors came from England to study this strange new disease. At about this same time the aching agonies of arthritis began to attack people.

All this within a ten- to twenty-year period after millers began stripping flour of its wheat germ. All after white sugar, once expensive, became available to the masses.

The era of degenerative diseases had begun.

• Today, one person in four is suffering from cancer; and two thirds of these will die. Despite the billions of dollars spent on research and treatment, *there has been no improvement in the overall rate of cure for cancer for the past thirty years.*

• Today, although the number of deaths from heart disease is declining (dropping below one million for the first time since 1967), our cardiovascular death rate remains among the highest in the world, claiming most victims before the age of sixty-five. It is felling men and women at the beginning or height of their careers. One year my husband and I attended both the wedding and the funeral of a brilliant and promising naval officer, twenty-seven years old. Another friend, a beautiful young mother of four, had a stroke at thirty and is still paralyzed.

• Cancer is the chief killer of children. In the poignant opening sentence of his book *The Greatest Battle,* Ronald J. Glasser, M.D., says, "During the Christmas holidays last year, of the twenty-three children admitted to the largest pediatric ward of the University of Minnesota Hospitals in a single day, eighteen had cancer."

• At least 200,000 American children are afflicted with juvenile rheumatoid arthritis. "More than were struck down by paralytic polio in any 10 years of annual epidemics," writes Lawrence Galton in *Parade*—"more than those with leukemia."

Such things were unheard of when I was growing up. Paralysis. Arthritis. Cancer. Heart failure? These dread afflictions were visited only on the old!

Something is appallingly wrong; clearly we're failing our children. Despite our affluence as a nation, and a scientific technology that has put men on the moon, we have reverted; we are "in the dark ages of human nutrition," as Deputy Agriculture Secretary John C. White expressed it. Addressing a Community Nutrition Institute Conference on "Nutrition and the American Food System," he said:

> It is a fact that within the U.S. Department of Agriculture we have more knowledge about the dietary needs of a cow or a pig than we have about the kinds of foods a pregnant woman should eat to assure the health of her unborn child or herself. It is true today that we know more about the nutrition requirements of our pets—the poodle I have at home—than my own children.

Government ignorance, however, is no worse than that of parents, who'll feed the pets carefully, while letting the kids eat junk. I saw this demonstrated to ludicrous perfection recently at a dog show. A little girl stood eating a candy bar with one hand, holding the leash of a prize Afghan with the other. When the dog whimpered, the child reached down to share the candy— only to have it slapped out of her hand.

"Don't feed him that!" the mother scolded. "You know we don't allow our dogs to eat stuff like that."

Hook the Kiddies Early

The annual American appetite has a $200 billion price tag. And the battle to profit by it is waged in advertising. The food industry spends some $6 billion a year to pitch its products; another $26 billion for colorful packaging. Naturally, they don't take full-page ads for milk and eggs, or sponsor TV shows for fruits and vegetables. Such aren't high-profit items. No, the big money goes into things like Tang, Twinkies, Kool-Aid, Cokes, Pepsis, Pop Rocks, Fruit Loops and Sugar Smacks. And the largest, most vulnerable audience is children.

Hook the kiddies early—as soon as they're able to sit up before the television set. Bombard them with cartoons and commercials for sugary, chocolaty concoctions they'll nag parents to buy. They'll be sugar junkies by the time they get to school.

Challenges to this crass exploitation of children have made headlines for years. No less than forty-six different groups have protested—dentists, pediatricians, parents; most vigorously a coalition, Action for Children's Television. The chairman of the Federal Trade Commission, Michael Pertschuck, has himself said he's convinced something should be done. But so powerful is the food lobby and its lawyers, nothing but hand wringing and rhetoric follows.

Joan Gussow summarized the futility during a seminar on children and advertising held at Georgetown University in Washington, D.C. She said she spoke with a sense of *déjà vu*. That she'd addressed them on the same subject five years before—and nothing had changed. The same "nutritionally disastrous array" of sugary products was being advertised; and companies demanding that we prove the "harm" to children:

> These people are using *our* airwaves to exploit *our* children for profit. Why should they not be required to prove the harmlessness of their activities? . . . What we do know is that Americans as adults are not healthy, that they are dying in frightful numbers from a variety of degenerative diseases linked to a diet high in calories, high in sugar and fat, and low in fiber, fresh fruits, vegetables and

whole grains. . . . The products advertised to kids on television are, overwhelmingly, precisely the kinds of products any responsible nutritionist would warn adults away from eating.

The Nutritional Disasters at School

Nor is there any escape when the kids get to school. Our educational system has become, in fact, a vast showroom, mecca and marketplace for the food industry. For here the kids can actually buy the TV-huckstered junk from vending machines, or from school stores where the kids themselves may work. They can even eat it as part of the school food program. Except for a number of cities now rebelling, gone are the days when motherly women prepared hot food in the cafeteria; today it's spouted out of dispensers onto foil trays, then frozen. Food so bland and formula-ized many kids dump it and head for the nearest candy machine. "The frozen food may not be reheated and served to the hungry youngsters for as long as six months," writes columnist Jack Anderson. "Officials concede that some vitamins are lost in the freezing-reheating process."

Anderson had sent his aide Jim Mintz to the Morton Food factory, an International Telephone and Telegraph subsidiary which prepares foods for thousands of schools, including the one attended by Amy Carter. Mintz sampled the lunches. The first was an aluminum bag containing a sandwich which showered so much grease on him the embarrassed officials had to mop it up. He says the rest of the lunches were bland but good. However:

> Mintz also sampled Morton's new super-nutritious donut, which is supposed to supply school children with many of the vitamins of a home-cooked breakfast. But to hold the vitamins, Morton had to load the donut with extra fat. And to keep the fat from going rancid, a preservative had to be caked on. . . . Another thing. The nutritious donut is expected to bolster the sales of Morton's run-of-the-mill donuts, which are heavy on sugar and light on vitamins.

Such pastries, manufactured by seven different firms, and bearing names like Astro Food, Super Donut, etc., have been the subject of controversy ever since their introduction. Their manufacturers claim that with a glass of milk they meet the government requirements for a good breakfast. Responsible nutritionists are appalled. Dr. Ross Hume Hall, Canadian biochemistry professor and author of *Food for Nought: The Decline in Nutrition,* pointed out that they don't have all the vitamins and are totally lacking in both fiber and minerals. Mary Goodwin, of the Montgomery County, Maryland, Health Department, is quoted in *National Enquirer:* "They are certainly not equivalent to a proper breakfast. We are promoting tooth decay and poor lifelong eating habits."

There have been petitions, speeches, hearings. There have also been threats of lawsuits, demands for more studies, delays. Thus far, those who make fortunes on the appetites of children have been able to block every proposed regulation or deadline for change.

Get the Kids to Sell It

To add insult to injury, the food barons also use schoolchildren to pitch their products: General Foods encourages pupils to collect Post cereal and Kool-Aid tops, to be redeemed by their schools for cash or sports equipment. . . . Hershey sponsors an athletic program, with emphasis on candy bars for energy. . . . Pepsi-Cola has a "Learn and Earn Project." Students learn about business by selling Pepsi at games and other school functions, then write their success stories for a national competition. The prizes are shares of Pepsi stock! And since many schools are usually strapped for funds, many are glad to go along.

Nor is the classroom itself off limits. It is in fact inundated with "educational" materials designed solely to solicit. *Sugar Through the Ages,* a book for students published by the Savannah Sugar Refining Corporation, is sprinkled with such statements as "Scientists have found that generous amounts of sugar are a valuable part of well-balanced diets for growing children." Not a word, of course, about sugar's making you fat or causing tooth decay. Kellogg, Campbell Soup, Safeway Foods, Betty Crocker, Dr. Pepper, Coca-Cola, Kraft, the National Dairy Council—all these and many more produce similar nutritional booklets, workbooks, lesson plans, film strips and audio-visual aids; each touting its own product in every chart, illustration or recipe.

Often the material boldly and righteously "corrects" any foolish criticism about empty calories, the dangers of sugar or chemical additives, calling such objections misleading, wrong. "Let's set the record straight—" they say.

Never mind that all this is sheer propaganda to brainwash young minds; it is slick, professional, colorful, pictorial, enticing —and free. And most teachers are delighted to have it, says Sheila Harty, who has made a study of this form of advertising for Ralph Nader's Center for the Study of Responsive Law.

Even math classes are no longer sacrosanct. In an article titled appropriately "Whatever Happened to Apples and Oranges?" (in *Nutrition Action,* published by the Center for Science in the Public Interest, Washington, D.C.), Susan Parry calls attention to a textbook called *Mathematics Around Us,* published by Scott, Foresman, which names fifty-eight different brands and businesses.

> On one page, 15 Coca-Cola bottlecaps are used to illustrate the division of five into 15. On another, under a box of Jujyfruits that costs 12 cents in the illustration (but 20 cents in most stores) is the mathematical problem: "How many boxes of Jujyfruits for 75¢? How much money is left?"
>
> So while parents are battling to ban junk food vending machines and non-nutritious lunches from school hallways and cafeterias, in the classrooms their children are confronted daily with advertisements for ice cream, soft drinks, candybars, and a host of other products.

Parents Fight Back

Parents, however, are becoming concerned. Our kids, we've noticed, have been getting fat but weak. And why are so many hyperactive, delinquent, disturbed? Why the shockingly low Scholastic Aptitude scores? Why the scandalous numbers of high school graduates who can't get jobs because they can't even *read?* These children God gave us—are they really that *dumb?* Or physically and mentally half sick? *Can it be poor schools or poor food?*

Allan Cott, M.D., author of *The Orthomolecular Approach to Learning Disabilities,* says that research has proved that many learning problems have organic causes, most often traced to an improper diet lacking in enough vitamins and minerals. He warns that the number of children with learning problems is very large, that few childhood disorders are so painful or long-lasting. That if not corrected early they can cause suffering for a lifetime.

Over and over the Select Committee on Nutrition and Human Needs heard testimony from teachers, psychologists, officers of juvenile courts—that not only learning disabilities but criminal actions are profoundly affected by what the child consumes.* Yet, tragically, as pointed out by Dr. Carolyn Brown, executive director of The Growing Mind (a behavior and learning center in Berkeley, California), almost no testing is done in schools or juvenile institutions to discover the child's nutritional needs.

Dr. Brown cited the terrible decline in both the physical and mental health of children born during the past twenty-five years, and challenged the senators to help reverse the disaster course on which we have been headed in feeding our offspring.

Throughout the country, parents are fighting back. In some areas they've petitioned to have commercially slanted texts and teaching materials barred. Many are getting rid of the junk-food machines. "We were getting a percentage, which we spent for uniforms and athletic equipment," one junior high principal told me. "But it doesn't make sense to have a phys-ed program and try to teach health if we're also profiting on stuff that ruins their bodies." In places like the Gilroy, California, school district, the candy, Cokes and cookies were phased out, nutritious snacks like nuts, raisins, apples, fruit juices, phased in. And to everybody's surprise most kids love it.

The National Parent Teacher Association has passed a strong resolution calling for more nutritious school meals. Individuals

---

* Dr. K. E. Moyer, professor at Carnegie-Mellon Institute, is convinced that food allergies affect the nervous system and cause a brain swelling which can trigger aggression. . . . Studies by the Canadian psychiatrist Dr. Abram Hoffer indicate that 70 per cent of the inmates imprisoned in Saskatchewan for serious crimes have vitamin deficiencies.

have been rolling up their sleeves, converting the cafeterias to natural, fresh, truly nourishing food. Wherever this has been tried the rewards more than justify the effort. For there is always obvious improvement, not only in grades but in how the kids behave. A program in San Pablo Elementary School, Jacksonville Beach, Florida, is typical.

When a diet of natural foods minus sugar and additives was introduced for forty hyperactive children, their attention span was increased; poor readers were soon outstripping those in regular classes. Results were so spectacular, in fact, that now about 350 other students are on it; the rest bring their natural foods from home. Dr. Wright Worden, the county school psychologist, conducted evaluations of all the children. "The academics went up," he said. "The other thing that showed improvement was the kids' behavior."

Wherever improving the food at school has been tried—in cities like Bloomington, Indiana, Dallas, Atlanta, New York—in suburbs or small towns, everything else improved. Educators report less truancy, less hostility and rambunctiousness, better obedience, better grades.

The Powers that Push the Dangerous Cliché

But the fight is a tough one because of the gargantuan commercial interests. Every effort of parents has been fiercely opposed by the makers of soft drinks, candy and other confections. By the vendors. By the sugar and cereal companies. By the TV networks and their advertising agencies. Bailey Morris, writing in the Washington *Star,* describes how a group of industry lobbyists met in a Washington restaurant to plot strategy to keep the Federal Trade Commission from ruling against their $600 million worth of TV commercials known as "Kidvid." "Seated around the table were representatives of the sugar, broadcasting, advertising and cereal industries"—a small command team back of a larger coalition which includes major law firms, toy manufacturers, the Grocery Manufacturers of America and more.

A "war chest" of some $30 million was raised with which to defeat the FTC in its power to restrict advertising aimed at children. They succeeded. In November 1979 the Senate Commerce Committee bowed to the power of the industry lobbyists. "A tragic defeat for consumers but above all for children," said Peggy Charron, director of Action for Children's Television.

These are the people who buy and shape public opinion. And one of the easiest, simplest, yet broadest and most damaging ideas they've been able to spread is that Americans are well fed. "All you've got to do is eat a balanced diet." Experts will tell you so.

How often we hear that naïve cliché from doctors, who admittedly had no training in nutrition in medical school. How often from nutritionists on the staffs of distinguished universities. A fact prominent on their credentials, while failing to mention that the very chair they occupy was funded by Kellogg or General Foods. How often we read and hear it from syndicated health columnists, who may also hold stock in Monsanto, or are paid advisers to Nabisco, Nestlé or other food giants. Certainly it's the theme song of countless "nonprofit" groups with scientific- or educational-sounding names. Presumably unbiased, they publish journals, sponsor information programs, court food editors from leading newspapers and offer scholarships to budding nutritionists or other professionals. Quietly hidden is the fact that most of their funding comes from the large food and chemical companies. Writing in *Nutrition Action*, Greta Bunin says:

> In fact, dues from Dow Chemical, Monsanto, Hoffman-LaRoche, and 94 other companies make up half of CAST's (Council for Agricultural Science and Technology) income. Adding the dues of sustaining members (National Corn Growers Association, Florida Fruit and Vegetable Association, and 106 other similar associations) and grants from Dow Chemical, Ralston-Purina, General Mills, and others, we now have accounted for over 60 per cent of CAST's income. Nowhere in CAST's published reports or news releases is this connection to industry noted, though all the member scientific societies are prominently listed.

The selfsame industries sponsor the radio and TV programs and sustain the newspapers and magazines with their advertising. No wonder we continually hear how well fed we are. And despite grave pronouncements about the state of American health, despite committees, investigations and highly publicized congressional hearings, our government is often putty in the hands of lobbyists (witness the Kidvid decision) and scared to death to do anything that might jeopardize economic interests.

For instance, when the Senate's Select Committee on Nutrition and Human Needs finally issued its report, *Eating in America: Dietary Goals for the United States,* in 1977, it boldly announced that what we're eating is killing us. And the things directly related to our most widespread and fatal diseases are: fat, salt, cholesterol and sugar. Yet the Department of Agriculture continues to award fat-marbleized beef its highest "prime" rating, and the sugar growers actually got their multimillion-dollar subsidies increased. Furthermore, those dietary goals came under so much attack from both the food monoliths and the AMA the committee knuckled under. The goals were watered down to try to please everybody, and a revised, weaker version published a year later.

Senator McGovern, chairman, had told his committee that at the beginning of this century almost 40 per cent of the nation's calories came from whole grains, fruits and vegetables, while today that figure is less than 20 per cent. It was pointed out that now every man, woman and child in America consumes 125 pounds of fat and over 100 pounds of sugar per year; downs nearly 300 cans or bottles of sugared, caffeine-laced soft drinks; and far more salt than the body requires, mostly from salted snacks and processed foods. A diet squarely responsible for most of our health problems. (Since then the Surgeon General's report on Health in the United States reiterates this fact in a chapter on diet and disease prevention.)

I don't know whether it's sad, funny or simply ironic—because that is exactly what the National Nutritional Foods Association, the health magazines and people mocked as "health nuts" have been saying for years. Charlotte Gerson Straus is the daughter of the late Max Gerson, M.D., who was so successful curing cancer by natural methods ("restoring the body's ability to cure itself") that he was cruelly persecuted. Mrs. Straus says the Dietary Goals sound familiar; they are precisely what her father told a similar Senate committee thirty years ago. And the American Medical Association reacted then with almost the very same words that they are using now: "These goals should not be adopted because there is no proof that they are related to disease."

To that I must again quote Dr. Roger Williams, one of the most distinguished scientists of our century. Writing in *A Physician's Handbook on Orthomolecular Medicine*, he says:

> It seems unthinkable that medical science will be inclined to reject, without trial, the hypothesis that promoting the health of all body cells and tissues will result in general health. . . . It is my considered belief that medical science has taken an extremely important and unfortunate wrong turn in its neglect of nutrition and that this wrong turn is evident in connection with the thinking about all diseases, including cancer.

8

Vitamins and the FDA

Another agency that preaches the cliché of the balanced diet is the FDA. While one branch of government warns that our foods are killing us, this other branch assures us the food is great. "Foods can and do supply most Americans with adequate nutrients," claims the slick, scoffing FDA publication *Myths of Vitamins,* "and consumers should not expect any major physical benefits from multivitamin pills, contrary to the myth." The first edition also contained a statement later revealed to be an outright falsehood: "that 4,000 cases of vitamin poisonings are reported each year, with some 3,200 involving children."

There was such a demand for explanation the statement was retracted; yet the publication still warns that taking vitamins is not only foolish but dangerous. And, tragically, many people believe this propaganda.

The history of the FDA goes back to 1906, when the first "Pure Food Law" was enacted. Its purpose, to prevent the sale of adulterated or misbranded foods. *Adulterated* meaning that no valuable element had been removed and nothing harmful added. Shortly afterward the word *pure* was deleted, and the door blew open for a storm of chemical adulterants. Until today the Food Law is a joke. For we are captive consumers of a food supply deliberately stripped of critical elements. The vitamins and minerals from flour and cereals, for instance; or the vitamin E which is destroyed in processing vegetable oils. (Ironically, there are reports that vitamin E is sometimes salvaged and sold back to vitamin companies.)

We also swallow literally thousands of alien chemicals in both food and drugs. "To illustrate how far out of hand things are," write Dr. Jacqueline Verrett and Jean Carper in *Eating May Be Hazardous to Your Health,* "the government does not even know how many additives are being used or by whom, or for what; official estimates range from three thousand to ten thousand."

Yet the agency paid to protect us has chosen to protect the adulterators instead. And guess who they've decided is really Public Enemy Number One? The natural food and vitamin industry! Not those responsible for nitrates and cyclamates—or pesticides in milk or poisonous dyes in cake and candy; not the makers of drugs that cripple and kill. What this country really needs protection from is quackery and food faddists. Those idiots who try to avoid this chemical feast and think vitamins and minerals are necessary.

Why? I'm often asked. Why in the world would any bureau attack anything so harmless? And if they're so good for you, why isn't the government backing them instead?

Well, it's common knowledge in Washington that government agencies provide revolving doors to and from jobs with industry. The FDA is no exception. Michael Jacobson, crusading director of the Center for Science in the Public Interest, found that, in 1976, 30 per cent of its top executives left for jobs with food or pharmaceutical firms. That, in 1978, of the last fifteen lawyers to leave, thirteen had gone either directly with those industries or with firms that represented them. Often they simply change hats.

Sometimes they almost bump into each other going in and out the doors. In a flagrant example, a lawyer who'd represented the FDA for thirty years left to become a top executive of the Institute of Shortening and Edible Oils. His place was taken by an attorney who had been counsel for a huge cosmetics conglomerate, chewing gum manufacturers, Continental

Baking and—the Institute of Shortening and Edible Oils. . . . Then, after eight years with the agency, *this* counsel departed for the sweeter fields of Hershey Corporation, where he promptly led its fight against parents trying to get junk food out of schools.

At the time of the earlier oil switch, Ruth G. Desmond, president of the Federation of Homemakers, wrote Elliot Richardson, then Secretary of HEW: "Significantly, at this very time FDA is considering the labeling of processed foods . . . particularly fatty acids. What is taking place? An Alphonse and Gaston Mutual Benefit Act performed by protégé and benefactor? But what of the captive audience (consumers) in this game of musical chairs?"

Congressional investigators have also found that many FDA officials enjoy research grants from these companies. According to Jack Anderson's column in the Washington *Post*, in 1978 there were 104 consultants collecting research money from the same companies whose products they were regulating. Earlier, twelve scientists rebelled at the coziness that went on, they claimed, with the drug industry. If they approved a drug they were praised, they charged; if they disapproved they were punished. The agency investigated, and whitewashed, itself. But in 1977 a special government panel finally upheld their complaints of pro-industry bias. Dr. Donald Kennedy, the then new FDA director, even took the unusual step of issuing the scientists a public apology.

Less publicized were the new rules laid down. As reported in *Chemical Engineering News,* one was to stop FDA officials from lying.

The Vendetta Against Vitamins

This is important to remember. Because for years the FDA has conducted a program of harassment and false propaganda against vitamins. For years their avowed purpose was to put the whole health food and supplement industry out of business.

Repeatedly, they have issued autocratic rules and regulations intended solely to make these products difficult if not illegal to obtain. In 1965 an all-out attack was mounted on "vicious food faddists and nutritional quacks." Here were the "final" dictates:

Supplements could not be sold whose potency exceeded the official RDA's.

• Only certain combinations and vitamins and minerals would be allowed.

• Labels would not be allowed to say whether the product was natural or synthetic.

• It was forbidden to state that the supplement could prevent or help any condition.

• It was forbidden to state or imply that any Americans were suffering in any way from vitamin or mineral deficiencies.

• It was forbidden to state that foods are affected in any way by storage, processing or the soil on which they were raised.

• Every container must bear what was known as the "crepe label," stating that nobody needed to take vitamins and minerals since they were already abundantly available in foods. (In short, this product is worthless, don't waste your money.)

Ironically, that very year national government surveys had revealed that most American families had diets that didn't meet even the low recommended daily allowances; that the quality of diets had been declining seriously. Another survey, in New York City alone, showed that 73 per cent of the children tested had low blood levels of vitamins C and B, were generally poorly nourished, and *it was affecting their reading scores.*

There was a storm of protest. It's said over 55,000 letters poured in within a few weeks (one of them mine). The pressure was so intense that finally, in 1968, the FDA conducted a hearing—to show once and for all that an ignorant and gullible public was being defrauded by taking "useless" vitamins. To their dismay, the majority of witnesses, which included outstanding pediatricians and nutritionists, declared that the danger of vitamin deficiencies was actually far greater than any danger from overdoses. That, in fact, there were no cases on record of deaths from vitamins, but plenty of people died because of lack of them. And why pick on vitamins, when drugs were advertised so freely?

In the words of California congressman Craig Hosmer (who later introduced a bipartisan bill to prevent the regulations from going into effect): "I have been told there has never been an accidental death due to vitamin overdosage, but it's said one person dies every three days from taking lethal doses of aspirin, which the FDA permits to go unlabeled."

The Hidden Giants: A Food and Chemical Who's Who

For years the battle raged, while the government tried to clap its handcuffs on any dissenters. For instance, in February 1974 Clifford Wasem, proprietor of a pharmacy in Clarkston, Washington, was ordered to face TV cameras and make the statement: "There is no need for most people to supplement their diet with vitamins and minerals," or pay a fine of $10,000. His crime? He had advertised some vitamin B saying it could make you feel better, with a money-back guarantee.

Vitamin B is, of course, important in preventing and treating iron deficiency; and that very week newspapers were announcing, "A preliminary Public Health Service report shows about 95% of all preschool children and young women don't have enough iron." Never mind that—retract, say what we dictate or be fined $10,000!

"I had to read their prepared statement at my own cost in prime time each evening for a week," Mr. Wasem told me. "The actual result was a great deal of sympathy for my problem in the community. While the sales of that product fell off because I couldn't advertise it anymore, the publicity really brought more business into my drugstore."

Meanwhile, millions of letters about vitamins were pouring into Congress. Repeatedly, the Hosmer bill was introduced; each time it failed. Things looked bleak when Hosmer was about to retire. Then Senator Proxmire took up the cause, co-sponsoring a bill with Senator Richard Schweiker. It was a critical last stand, for had it lost, most vitamins would be classified as drugs, available only on a doctor's prescription.

Proxmire warned the Senate on May 8, 1975, "What the FDA did was to come down squarely on the side of one group. If you disagreed with the FDA you could go to jail." In December he presented some impressive evidence: That the Recommended Daily Allowances as prepared by the Food and Nutrition Board were capricious, unscientific and invalid, even fluctuating from year to year. That "It is in the interest of the food industry to have low RDA's so they can print on the side of their breakfast food packages that the breakfast food—which may in fact be almost totally lacking in vitamins and minerals in quantities to provide for optimum health—contains 100% of the so-called RDA's."

He then introduced for the *Congressional Record* (over vigorous objections) a list of the industry liaison panels which had advised the Food and Nutrition Board. And it reads like a Food and Chemical Who's Who. I won't name all the giants who are influencing the FDA, but you'll recognize a few:

Abbott Laboratories	Heinz
Allied Chemical	Hormel
American Can	International Flavor &
Amstar	Fragrances
Armour	Kellogg
Borden	Oscar Mayer
Campbell Soup	Mead Johnson
Carnation	Merck
Coca-Cola	Miles Laboratories
Continental Baking	Nabisco
Continental Can	National Starch & Chemical
Del Monte	Nestlé
Dow Chemical	Pepsi-Cola
E. I. Du Pont	Pillsbury
General Foods	Proctor & Gamble
General Mills	Quaker Oats
Gerber	Ralston Purina
Green Giant	

Thanks to the heroic efforts of Senators Proxmire and Schweiker, backed by the largest avalanche of mail ever received in the halls of Congress, the bill passed by an overwhelming majority.

New Battle Lines Drawn

Other restrictions are still in effect, however. Although vitamins and minerals are now being advertised more freely, it is still illegal to advertise them as *good* for anything. Illegal even to state on the label what the substance is *for*. Meanwhile, we're treated to an incessant bombardment of TV ads claiming the wonders of drugs for headaches, colds, indigestion, arthritis, hemorrhoids, constipation, insomnia—thousands of them drugs dubbed useless by the World Health Organization, many of them actually dangerous. Even as I write, the Associated Press reports warnings from doctors that many of the widely advertised sleep aids contain potent cancer-causing substances. I seem to recall these same drugs were "investigated" a few years ago, but they are still being freely advertised and sold.

Why the discrimination?

And the FDA is persistent—at least in its fierce determination to stamp out natural, non-toxic substances. Since the Proxmire decision, it has tried unsuccessfully to control the amounts of vitamins A and D which can be sold over the counter; and even come up with a devious ploy which would circumvent the entire Proxmire decision: to get control over vitamins, plus a number of other nutrients (selenium, tryptophan, ginseng), by having them declared "food additives."

In a long stern letter Proxmire challenged this obvious device, concluding, "I thought this battle was over. . . . The FDA tried for years to treat vitamins and minerals as drugs. The FDA was beaten decisively in both Congress and the courts. Having failed, they are now trying to treat vitamins and minerals as food additives. Isn't it time to put a stop to this?"

Evidently not, because an even more recent strategy is an attempt to regulate vitamins and minerals as over-the-counter drugs—"if intended for therapeutic use" in the prevention or treatment of a deficiency. "This definition creates a serious problem," says Milton A. Bass, counsel for the National Nutritional Foods Association, "in that vitamins and minerals are most certainly sold to prevent a vitamin and mineral deficiency."

Furthermore, the new regulations would prohibit the sale of vitamin E by itself. Prohibit the sale of pantothenic acid by itself. Prohibit ingredients like biotin and choline. And impose limits on combinations and potencies. "The potency limitations raise very substantial questions," says Bass. For example, vitamin C for deficiency could only be within the range of 50–100 milligrams.

The proposed rules also strike out at freedom of speech. Such words as *stress, superpotency* and even *geriatric* and *natural* would be banned. And the label must state the product should be used only "when the need for such therapy has been determined by a physician."

"We have gone through a long period of court actions and congressional enactments directed to this very problem," Bass points out, "and apparently we are now faced with another struggle on this very same question."

It would seem that the FDA has better things to do: About saccharine and nitrates. About Red Dye Number 40 and BHT and BHA. About cancer-causing hormones, and antibiotics in meat. About the staggering list of chemicals we are ingesting. About labeling alcoholic beverages. About radioactive materials in our food and drink. About dangerous drugs like Darvon.

About making sure baby formulas are safe.

In the summer of 1979, when a lot of babies began getting mysteriously and seriously ill (some died), the cause was traced to an infant formula that had been prepared without chloride— a salt compound essential to life. The FDA was notified, the manufacturer ordered to remove the formula from the stores. Yet months later Lea Thompson, of WRC-TV in Washington, went shopping—and found the dangerous product still being sold. Not only in the Washington area but nationwide.

Her exposé gave the scandal national publicity. Congress investigated, FDA spokesmen were interviewed on the air. They admitted the crisis hadn't been given top priority; nobody had bothered to follow up the recall orders. More shockingly, it was revealed that *there was no mandated pretesting of baby formulas in this country.* *

"But this isn't just *any* food," Lea Thompson protested. "This is the *only* food. Has the Food and Drug Administration ever asked for pretesting authority on baby foods?"

"No, not specifically." As for the situation of dangerous products that should be recalled, the spokesman acknowledged, "I can't guarantee this is not going to happen again. The FDA has limited resources."

I submit, this agency should call off its expensive, time-wasting war on vitamins. It has more important things to do.

"The Myths of Vitamins"

Part of that war on vitamins has been a scare campaign, paid for with our tax money. Including the mocking, cartoon-illustrated publication I referred to earlier: *Myths of Vitamins.* It was launched in January 1978 with a story which went out over all the news services headlined "Vitamins Can Be Dangerous." In it the statement was made: "The FDA's National Clearinghouse for Poison Control Centers reveal that 4,000 cases of vitamin poisonings are reported each year."

I wrote the FDA asking for permission to study the case histories of these "poisonings." And received a prompt, if almost ludicrous reply:

> As you will note in the attached erratum slip, the statement about which you requested further information was in error.

The erratum slip reads:

> This is a clarification of a statement made in Paragraph 3 of the attached publication, "Myths of Vitamins," which reads: "His experience was added to the statistics compiled by FDA's National Clearinghouse for Poison Control Centers which reveal that 4,000 cases of vitamin poisonings are reported each year." Although there were over 4,000 cases of vitamin ingestion overdoses by children reported to FDA's National Clearinghouse in one year, *the vast majority of these children had no symptoms.*

* Since the exposure, this appalling negligence is finally being corrected.

Italics mine! Because, I ask you—if these children "had no symptoms," how, in heaven's name, could they be considered *poisoned?* This question I carried direct to the Poison Control Center, asking at the same time if the false information would be corrected in future editions of the booklet and in the media where I first read it. Their response was to send me data which confirmed that there had been no fatalities, few hospitalizations, and that in almost every case there were indeed "no symptoms." Yet here is the accompanying letter from John J. Crotty, M.D., Director:

> Dear Ms. Holmes: The original publication substituted the word "poisoning" for "ingestion." Obviously there is no way of correcting the information that has been previously distributed.

Think about *that* for a minute.

Hopefully, with new leadership, all this will change. The agency paid to protect us will focus its "limited resources" on the many real and severe threats to our health, rather than attacking the very substances on which our health depends.

Meanwhile, I feel it's important that people should know the truth. Otherwise, they will continue to be intimidated, to believe the scare stories and other false propaganda, and possibly miss something that could very well change or save their lives.

9

Vitamins A and D—
for Healthy Lungs,
Skin and Eyes

One reason we were so healthy as kids, I'm convinced, is that
we devoured so many carrots and downed so many eggs. Like
rabbits, we raided the gardens, wrenched the orange stalks
from the rich black earth and crunched, sometimes not even
bothering to rinse them under the pump. Although we didn't
know it, we were warding off colds, putting roses in our cheeks
and enhancing the brightness of our eyes.

Okay, so everybody knows carrots contain a lot of vitamin A
for eyes; but *eggs?* Yes, eggs. We had at least one or two for
breakfast, often a hard-boiled egg for lunch. Even supper might
be an omelet, and if we were hungry at bedtime it wasn't
unusual to scramble a couple of eggs. As for that supposed
baddie, cholesterol—which I'll deal with later—nonsense. An
egg contains enough lecithin to keep its cholesterol fluid, which
is all that counts. And if you eat an onion with your eggs, it will
cancel the cholesterol even more. (Our favorite sandwich, the
Denver or western, *was* mostly onions and scrambled eggs.)

But the main thing about eggs is that they're the best food
source of both vitamins A and D. Eggs also contain iron and
trace minerals, and vitamins B and E. Better yet, an egg provides all 32 amino acids, including some 12 grams of albumin,

the protein absolutely necessary for *transporting* vitamin A from the liver into the blood, where it can be used. Eggs have been called the perfect food.

Furthermore, the soil which nourished the carrots—as well as the grains which fed the chickens which produced the eggs—was not at that time poisoned with nitrate fertilizers. And nitrates combine with other elements to form the deadly nitrosamines—which do double damage: Nitrosamines are not only potent carcinogens, they destroy our major protector, vitamin A.

We were also sun nuts long before it was fashionable to be. But I don't remember ever *seeing* a pair of sunglasses until a glamorous lady got on the bus taking me to college. (I was sure she must be a movie star; only celebrities who "didn't want to be recognized" wore them.) We'd never heard of a vitamin, let alone a hormone; we had no idea the sun was bestowing a marvelous gift of vitamin D by way of our skin; and controlling our hormones by way of our eyes. We just knew we were healthy, even sexy little savages. What's more, our teeth were in great shape, and only one member of our family ever broke a bone. (Dad when a motorcycle fell on him.) Nor did any of us ever have arthritis. A blessing I now relate to the fact that none of us wore glasses. Not even our parents and grandparents.

Not many people did. Look at any group photograph taken during the first third of this century, or before. The noses sprouting spectacles are so rare they're conspicuous. Contrast with such pictures today. Today it's the faces *un*disguised by glasses that stand out.

It would be years before I began to learn the reasons back of all this.

And God Said, "Let There Be Light!"

I'll get back to vitamins in a minute, but let's pause to marvel at the role of God's very first creation—light. God said, "Let there be light!" because there cannot be life without it. Every one of his creatures, from fish that swim deep in the sea to birds that fly high in the sky, depends upon it. Light controls life. Either directly or indirectly light enters the organism and enables it to live. For most of us this life-giving miracle enters through the eyes.

Actually, our eyes are gateways to three important glands. When sunlight strikes the retina and the optic nerve, messages are shot to the brain. Thence to the hypothalamus and the pituitary—that tiny master gland which controls the thyroid, our adrenals and our sex glands. All of them critically important to vigor, growth, resistance and sexual health. Scientists say it's for this reason children born blind develop more slowly; that youngsters in torrid climates mature early; that during long months of darkness in the Arctic, explorers often have physical and emotional problems, and Eskimo women don't menstruate or conceive.

It's light that causes birds to migrate and even bestirs them to mate, ornithologists say. Their studies are responsible for the poultry industry's trick of "lengthening" days with full-spectrum bulbs so hens will lay more of those wonderful eggs. In his fascinating book *Health and Light*, John Ott writes, "The response of the hens is due to the light energy entering the eyes and stimulating the pituitary gland."

Ott, who pioneered in time-lapse photography, was one of the first to discover the relationship of light and body chemistry. It was also Ott who made the connection between sunlight and arthritis. After breaking his glasses on a Florida vacation, he decided to do without them—even dark glasses for a while. To his amazement, his arthritis improved. "Something was stimulating the glands that lubricated my joints without artificially injecting any of the prepared glandular extracts. The effect was as beneficial as the injection of one of the extracts right into the hip joint."

Now a word of caution about the sun. We lived in the Midwest, far from the intense sunlight of desert or ocean beaches, where it would be folly not to protect both skin and eyes. Too much sun can cause wrinkles and cancer; sunburned eyes can lead to blindness. All our farmers wore big straw hats in the fields, and many times we wore them too.

The Sun and Vitamin D

"The sun," wrote Galileo, "is 92 million miles from the Earth; it is the center of the solar system and by the power of gravity holds every planet in its orbit. Yet that very same sun can ripen a bunch of grapes as though that were all it had to do."

Miraculously, this distant sun "ripens" us as well. For its ultraviolet rays shining on our skin create from the fats there (primarily the cholesterol) the vital substance known as vitamin D. The process is precarious, however. Water, even cold water, will wash it away. (So always take your sunbath *after* your swim.) And once the skin is deeply tanned the sun can't form any more. Also, the winter sun gradually loses its power, so that even a hot sun on a December ski slope is creating about a tenth as much vitamin D as the suns of July.

Curiously, this vitamin has only three food sources: An egg yolk (sun-round and sun-yellow); the seeds of sunflowers, which, mysteriously, always keep their faces lifted to the sun. And, even more mysteriously, saltwater fish like cod and halibut, which swim deep and far from the sun, yet have rich stores of it in their liver, along with vitamin A. Fish like sardines also contain some vitamin D; but it is cod-liver or halibut-liver oil—oils we associate with babies—that are the major sources we have for vitamin D.

Some scientists say vitamin D has been mislabeled since, unlike other vitamins, it isn't found altogether in foods; that it functions more like a hormone. But whatever we call it, we *must* have it; it is absolutely critical to the health of our skin, our eyes and the building of strong teeth and bones.

This was starkly demonstrated during the Industrial Revolution when rickets began seriously to deform the bodies of children working in factories. At first this bone-crippler was blamed on lack of calcium. Then recognized as lack of sunshine—for even when these youngsters went outdoors the air was thick with coal smoke. (Rickets and its adult counterpart, osteomalacia, are not uncommon even today in backward countries where babies are still swaddled and women kept robed, veiled and mostly confined to their homes.) By 1919 it was discovered the disease could be prevented and cured by cod-liver oil. But it was many years before vitamin D was identified as the healing substance in the oil.

Without this vitamin the body can't utilize calcium. Calcium can't be absorbed into the bloodstream or deposited in the bones. Nor can it be withdrawn from the bones as needed. And although we think of calcium primarily as important to teeth and bones, *calcium is in constant demand for every activity of the body.* Vitamin D sees that calcium gets where it's needed, even if that calcium has to be stolen from the very structure of the bones. When this happens bones begin to weaken, teeth deteriorate—afflictions which do beset the aged, but which are not solely the result of aging. Rather, simply a lack of vitamin D.

Tragically, the two extremes who most need vitamin D are those who are most often deficient in it—the aged and growing children.

Thousands of elderly people are shut up in houses or nursing homes where they get very little sunshine. And unless they are drinking quantities of D-enriched milk or taking fish-liver oils, they are prime candidates for broken hips and other casualties. A great many need more calcium as well; but it's not just calcium they may lack, but the vitamin D which makes the calcium available to the bones.

Mothers, however conscientious about giving babies their drops, usually stop when children get older. Which would be okay if the kids consumed plenty of eggs and milk, and could play outdoors as much as we did, in unpolluted sunshine. But an awful lot can't, or don't. Physicians have been astonished to find rickets among hospitalized children today, often from affluent homes. And even when there is not actual deformity, the deficiency shows up in other ways—bad skin, bad eyes, bad teeth and weak bones.

The rest of us don't come off so well either. Look at how many people work and play and go to school in windowless, air-conditioned buildings, locked away from natural light. How we huddle in sealed-up houses, often in the dark before TV. And when we do get outdoors the sun is often blocked from us by buildings, or the air so choked with smog its rays can't penetrate. To compound the problem, at least half the population wears glasses, and practically everybody slaps on a pair of dark ones the minute the sun is spied. Some people even wear them indoors.

No wonder dentists and eye doctors drive Cadillacs. No wonder millions of dollars are spent just on the *ads* for the pastes that hold false teeth in place. No wonder some 17 to 20 million Americans are tortured by arthritis, and uncounted millions more break hips and other bones every year. We are a nation woefully crippled by too little vitamin D.

Which Vitamin D and How Much?

Adding vitamin D to whole milk is one commendable case of fortifying food. However, the form is the synthetic or vitamin D_2, which is less potent, yet at the same time more toxic, than the natural form found in fish-liver oil—vitamin D_3. Even the vitamin D_2 in whole milk is easily destroyed by light; and there is no vitamin D at all in skimmed milk, used by so many people who are worried about both weight and cholesterol. The vitamin D in fish-liver oils is preferable to any other, because it is the very same vitamin D_3 substance manufactured by the sun. As such, it is far less toxic.

Vitamin D, like vitamin A, is a fat soluble, which the liver stores. But reports of the dangers of toxicity from taking too much have been vastly exaggerated. *The Merck Manual,* that classic guide for physicians and pharmacists, says it would take 40,000 IU a day to produce ill effects in babies. (An amount no mother in her right mind would give.) And 100,000 IU a day, taken for months, to cause any trouble for adults. "Treatment consists of discontinuing the vitamin, placing the patient on a low calcium diet, and keeping the urine acid."

A far cry from the warning screams from the FDA about the awful possibilities of too much vitamin D. Furthermore, if the body is also well supplied with vitamins C and A, any toxicity will be negated.

Now let's look at vitamin D's major partner, vitamin A.

The Nature and Work of Vitamin A

Vitamin A too is a fat-soluble vitamin which the liver stores for future use; and it depends on at least small amounts of fat to be absorbed. It must also have plenty of protein to function. Yet the more proteins we eat (and most Americans eat a lot), the more vitamin A we need. *The body can't use one without the other.*

Vitamin A is actually a pair of twins. *Pre*formed A is present in butter, meat fats and fish oils; and once digested it's ready to go into action. . . . *Per*formed, the "A" we speak of in leafy green vegetables, or those with bright colors like carrots, isn't really vitamin A until it's been changed from its original form—appropriately named carotene.* A process that takes six or seven hours.

To accomplish this conversion you have to have a healthy bile flow and plenty of fat-splitting enzymes in the intestines. You also have to have the proteins necessary for vitamin A to be merged into the bloodstream, then transported to its target. If your body lacks any of these things you will still be deficient in vitamin A no matter how much you consume. You could be like my friend who owns a gift shop and knows I'm writing this book: "Marj, something terrible seems to be happening to my eyes. You know how I love carrots, I eat them every *day;* yet when I step outside the store anymore I can hardly *see!*"

I urged her to consult her doctor. Yet whatever else he finds, it seems highly probable her body may not be using its vitamin A.

Many conditions interfere with both the conversion and the assimilation: Diabetes or other serious diseases, for instance. Cortisone, too much iron, even physical exertion after eating. And vitamin A is quickly depleted by the same things which use up other vitamins: alcohol, smoking, drugs, air pollution, surgery, any emotional or physical stress. One particularly dangerous enemy of vitamin A is mineral oil. Never use the stuff; it can

* Vegetables with yellow or orange colors like sweet potatoes contain the largest amounts of vitamin A. Those with paler colors such as turnips contain almost none.

damage your intestinal tract, and it will dissolve and waste your fat-soluble vitamins.

Vitamin A is absolutely essential. Its presence in our bodies means the difference between sickness and health. For this vitamin stands guard against infections; it is vital to the entire immunity system which rejects and fights off disease.

Vitamin A is also responsible for: Healthy eyes. Healthy teeth and bones. Every aspect of our sexual health. And for the complete epithelial system, which means every tissue in our bodies, especially the skin.

Vitamin A and the Epithelial Package

How the Lord must love us, he wrapped us in such a lovely package! Pause a moment, look at your skin—on the palms of your hands, for instance, or the soles of your feet, or the smooth soft skin of your tummy. Turn and rub an appreciative chin across the warm flesh of your own shoulder. Never mind the wrinkles elsewhere; never mind the blemishes you may see in the mirror. From head to toe you have been covered with a fine and sensitive sheath, both to protect you and to give you pleasure. For it is through the skin you experience the sense of touch, of comfort and caressing. Oh, the skin is such a marvel I'd like to write a whole chapter about it.

But wait, there's more. Our creator has taken just as much care inside, where we don't even see it. For every entrance, every orifice is likewise wrapped in materials just as precious. They cover the eyes, line the mouth and throat and nose and passages to the lungs, the rectum, the vagina. More deeply, every body cavity is likewise guarded. No inch of you has been left exposed to attack from germs or poisons; for those tissues have been impregnated with something to keep the flesh always moist, pliant and resistant—mucus. It is called the mucous membranes.

The entire package inside and out is called the epithelial system. And the one substance absolutely essential to its health and proper functioning is vitamin A. Without sufficient vitamin A those membranes will dry out and degenerate. Instead of producing mucus they begin to manufacture keratin, a hard scaly protein that can't protect us and can actually do damage. The body is then left vulnerable before invading bacteria, especially via the mouth and nose and the vagina.† The tissues of the eyes will begin to dry out, leading possibly to cataracts, even blindness. The nasal passages, lined normally with mucus and tiny hairlike fibers to catch and repel dust, germs, chemicals and other invaders—these too will become hard, dry, useless, leaving you susceptible to colds and infections. Thus, to change figures, the enemy will have stormed the gates and be free to advance even deeper, where it is even more critical that we be well fortified with vitamin A.

Before going into that, though, let's examine the outside of the package.

Vitamins A and D and the Complexion

Those two partners vitamins A and D are a complexion's best friends.

Vitamin A helps keep the skin moist; it prevents flaking, scaling and premature aging. Without enough vitamin A there is a pile-up of keratin and wastes which plug the pores and oil sacs to form blackheads and pimples. This affliction, acne, strikes, if at all, during adolescence when glands and hormones are struggling to bring the body into balance. And what a cross it is.

I know, because I carried it from about twelve into my twenties. "Poor kid," Mother would try to comfort as I desperately tried every salve, soap and mudpack on the market, "you get it from me. But, honey, mine was *much* worse as a girl."

"Our other kids don't have it!"

"They take after Dad." She was right. Good or bad complexions are inherited; my father and all his clan had skin like newborn babies. But even bad complexions can be helped. (If only we'd known then about vitamins and minerals.)

The only relief came with summer. Mysteriously, when the

---

† It is a mistake to wash out the vagina with douches or to use deodorant sprays. Nature has its own methods of cleansing and getting rid of excess mucus, *if* supplied with sufficient vitamin A. It's also unwise to use nasal sprays, except on rare occasions. Their drying effect irritates the passages and interferes with the normal production of mucus.

orchards and gardens bestowed their abundance, and the sun its vitamin D, my skin would clear. With winter, however, the agony returned, fluctuating with stress and menstrual cycles. Bitterly I had to face the fact—I was different from my brothers and sister. And there was nothing, absolutely nothing to do but try to cover the curse with cosmetics, and pray.

My husband had the same problem as a boy, except that his was confined to his back. (Thank God no doctor ever got to his face—or mine—with the X rays that nearly destroyed him.) So it was probably inevitable that our children inherited the same affliction, in varying degrees. Naïvely believing that if we just spent enough *money* science would provide the answers, we had each one under the care of a dermatologist by twelve or thirteen. By then there were lots of new drugs, new gadgets, but, alas, no answers. As one doctor cheerfully admitted after he'd been seeing our teen-ager for years, "One nice thing about this work, you get to be such good friends with your patients; they never get cured, so they always come back." I must have winced, for he added, "Well, at least we're preventing scars." He was wrong even about that.

By the time of our last, belated chick, they were using tetracycline and birth control pills. These helped briefly, until she began to have such blinding headaches and erratic menstrual cycles we got scared; especially after a girl her age had an allergic reaction to the same treatment and became schizophrenic. Enough's enough, we agreed. "You'll just have to live with it awhile, but at least you won't be in a mental hospital!"

Looking back, I am appalled that we had to go through all this because of sheer ignorance. These people were *skin specialists.* It seems shocking that in all those years not *one* even mentioned vitamin A. They did issue the usual dictum about diet: cut out chocolate, sweets and greasy fried foods. And they recommended sunbaths—so they had heard about vitamin D. But vitamin A, whose *primary job* is to keep all tissues of the body healthy? Not one word. Pills and potions, salves and lotions, peeling, lancing, diathermy (we balked at X rays)—all these—but not a single word about simple old-fashioned cod-liver oil, so rich in the two elements vital to a clear glowing skin—vitamins A and D.

I had to find out about them from reading, and that blessing, "anecdotal medicine." A young neighbor told me she'd had terrible acne until her pregnancy, when her doctor put her on A and D capsules. "My skin cleared up, but I thought it was just my condition, especially when it got bad again after the baby came." Then one day while giving her baby his cod-liver oil, she decided to take some herself because she was so tired. To her surprise, she not only felt better, her skin improved. "Look at me, I don't have a single blemish anymore. I know it's the A and D in the cod-liver oil. If I feel a pimple coming on I just take an extra capsule. Believe me, my children aren't going through what I did."

Using vitamin A for acne isn't new. As far back as 1943, Dr. John J. Straumfjord of Astoria, Oregon, wrote in *Northwest Medicine* that he had used it successfully. Of 100 patients, 36 became entirely free of acne and 43 free "except for an occasional pustule." Doses were from halibut-liver oil, 100,000 IU taken at bedtime. (Far larger doses, of course, than ever should be given except by a physician.) He said the skin may get worse at first, and a cure takes time—as much as a year—although improvement was generally noticed within three months. There have been other studies since then, and the ultimate result became a vitamin A acid solution applied directly to the skin. A process only a dermatologist should undertake, however.

I know now that the best thing to do for acne is to stay away from things that will destroy the vitamin A in your body: sweets, Cokes, cigarettes and drugs, even prescription drugs. To eat plenty of the fresh fruits and vegetables, eggs and lean meats (especially liver) which contain not only vitamin A but vitamins B, C and E. Brewer's yeast is also a good source of the vitamin B your body needs to regulate its hormones, and to help blot up the extra oils your body is generating. Take vitamins A and D either in capsules or liquid form from fish-liver oils. And zinc and calcium are a *must* if the vitamin A is to work. It's also very important to get plenty of sun on your skin.

I'm going into all this in detail because today acne is actually more common than ever before. Thanks to early smoking, drug taking, junk foods and sunshine starvation, acne afflicts over 86 per cent of our youngsters between the ages of twelve and seventeen. According to the National Center for Health Statistics, that leaves only 27.7 per cent who *don't* have bad skin, "without significant lesions or scars." What a tragedy for these poor kids. For this is the age when the desire to be attractive is most intense, and the scars of adolescent acne can scar the personality as well for years.

Vitamins A and D and the Eyes

Nothing God has given us could possibly be more precious than sight. Eyes are our windows to the world. Yet millions of people grope through life in darkness. Tragic, yes, but not surprising when we think of the hordes in backward countries where both starvation and infectious diseases ravage the eyes. But what about the United States, where we've overcome such diseases and are supposed to be well fed? Why are more than half a million of our own citizens blind? And the numbers are not declining, but growing by nearly 50,000 new cases every year! Why does at least 10 per cent of our population begin to find the lights going out from glaucoma, cataracts and general retinal degeneration after the age of sixty-five? *Is* this simply "old age" as we're so often told, even by the medical profession—or actually malnutrition?

The good Lord also gave us two nutrients designed to prevent all this from happening; two eye-building, eye-protecting substances, vitamins A and D.

One of the first signs of a vitamin A deficiency *is in* the eyes. Redness, itching, burning, dimming vision. Especially the inability to adjust to changes of light. We call this night blindness, and I used to think it was something inconvenient but not serious, like color blindness. I now realize it's a symptom of grave deterioration which can lead to total loss of sight.

Actually, night blindness is one of man's oldest afflictions. Ancient Egyptian records refer to it and prescribe the eating of raw liver for it. So they knew the right treatment even then. It wasn't until World War II, however, that the modern world realized its dangers. Pilots on night missions were having so many crashes, there were so many night accidents among the drivers of trucks and tanks, that the Armed Forces Vision Committee conducted investigations. It was found that most of the trouble came from men who'd been to bright beaches while on leave or exposed to brilliant snow light. Others who had had excellent vision before submarine duty failed eye tests when they came to shore. Their eyes were not getting enough vitamin A to compensate for the contrasts of light.

Night blindness continues to have dire consequences today. Although at night there is far less traffic, the National Safety Council tells us there are far more deaths from accidents, mainly because people just can't *see*.

Vitamin A has been used to prevent night blindness, and to restore vision if such blindness is not too far advanced. Experiments with rats showed they could see fine so long as their livers were well supplied with vitamin A; but as the supply dwindled, so did their vision. Sight could be regained by giving them large doses of vitamin A within the first eight weeks; after that, however, it was too late to keep them from blindness or death. The rats in these experiments were also rendered sterile by their vitamin A deficiency.

Similar results were obtained with people, although individuals vary. Some people develop night blindness very quickly when deprived of this vitamin; others take longer. Some recover faster than others when A is restored to their diet. It all depends on the amount of the vitamin in the liver, and the person's ability to use it. (Naturally no human subjects were allowed to go blind or to die.) Some cases of night blindness are genetic, but scientists believe such cases involve an inherited inability to convert and metabolize vitamin A.

The reason for all this lies in our retina, the "film" that takes the picture in those two marvelous cameras, our eyes. This retina is composed of cones and rods; the cones sensitive to colors and bright light; the rods sensitive to dim light and to black and white. The rods depend on a protein made of opsin, and retinene—a form of vitamin A. Together they form rhodopsin (also called visual purple), which splits in the presence of light. This destroys some of the vitamin A, which must immediately be replaced. When we suddenly find ourselves in the dark, the process is reversed; the opsin and retinene join each other, so that gradually we can see. In both these cunning processes the visual purple must be replenished, and this depends on a constant supply of vitamin A.

Vitamin A serves and protects our eyes in other ways. This vitamin, remember, is responsible for the health of the tissues which keep out irritants and germs; and for the fluids which bathe those tissues. A severe lack of vitamin A in the diet leads to the disease so prevalent in Middle Eastern countries—xerophthalmia, a dryness and inflammation of the membrane which covers the eyeball.‡

The Remarkable Results of Calcium and Vitamin D

Despite the studies I've cited, a very famous New York ophthalmologist, Dr. Arthur Alexander Knapp, insists vitamin D should get top billing for the eyes, instead of vitamin A. Vitamin A has been overrated, he told me. "Its only importance to the eyes stems from its secondary effect from a vitamin-deficient body treated with vitamin A. If the body lacks vitamin A, so do the eyes. In that instance, vitamin A may be beneficial clinically.

"Before vitamin D was isolated," he continued, "it was combined with vitamin A, both oil-soluble. When presumably A was given for the eyes, actually D was also administered. And it was the D and not the A that primarily helped the eyes. So came the belief that vitamin A is the eye vitamin."

It is vitamin D and calcium that are the true heroes, in his own experience. Dr. Knapp has been using them to correct eye disorders and prevent blindness for more than forty years.

Dr. Knapp began his own original research with animals in the 1930s at the College of Physicians and Surgeons, Columbia University, followed by human research at other New York hospitals, in Sing Sing Prison and in private practice. As described in his many published papers and lectures, dogs and rats were placed on low-calorie and vitamin-deficient diets. All developed retinal vascular disease—in contrast to a well-fed control group, which didn't. But it was *only those deficient in cal-*

‡ The United Nations World Health Organization estimates that 25 per cent of the victims of this disease go totally blind, the rest partially blind.

cium and vitamin D which consistently developed eye diseases similar to those of humans: myopia, keratoconus, cataract, optic nerve atrophy and retinitis pigmentosa. "Naturally, then, humans suffering from these diseases as well as allergic conjunctivitis, a frequent complication, were treated with vitamin D and calcium." In literally thousands of cases this therapy corrected the conditions, many times when blindness seemed almost inevitable.

Keratoconus, for instance, where the cornea protrudes like an ice-cream cone and reduces vision. Dr. Knapp says this deformation of the eyeball simply reflects a deficiency in the body, creating a weakness of the cornea "which then yields to the normal eye intra-ocular pressure." He found that "given sufficient D and calcium, the cornea loses fluid and actually shrinks." In his first use of them with human beings he observed a definite change within six weeks. "Every patient had improved eyesight, accompanied by a flattening of the cone."

Myopia likewise yielded, whether mild nearsightedness or the progressive myopia that can lead to total blindness. To establish what was happening Dr. Knapp took before-and-after pictures of the eye interiors, and made plaster casts to demonstrate the shrinking back toward normal size. Afflictions such as allergic conjunctivitis also were greatly improved, sometimes within twenty-four hours. He has even been able to reverse advanced cases of retinitis pigmentosa, the classic example of night blindness which often leads to complete loss of sight. "Without exception, every patient improved."

Dr. Knapp emphasizes that his therapies are not a cure-all. "In many cases advanced clinically irreversible pathological changes have taken place which presumably preclude return to normal eyes." (Yet even these may show improvement.) He will use traditional methods—lenses, medication and surgery—when necessary. "But isn't it wiser to try to solve a problem by first attacking the cause?" More often than not it is the body's lack of these two substances critical to sight.

He prescribes 50,000 IU of vitamin D taken orally, along with a gram of calcium a day. Amounts considered staggering—yet Dr. Knapp states, "For the past twenty years and more I have seen no toxicity." The FDA once sent him a long bibliography "on the supposed toxicity of vitamin D. I chose about twenty references at random—and the only toxicity they could come up with occurred in infants under a year old! This may be true of babies, but I know from my own experience it's not true of children or adults."

Dr. Knapp began publishing his findings in 1934. Since then some twenty of his papers have appeared in such publications as the *Journal of the American Medical Association, American Journal of Ophthalmology, Journal of the International College of Surgeons* and many more. He has lectured before the most distinguished medical and scientific groups around the world. The day I was fortunate enough to interview him in New York, he had just returned from addressing the International Congress of Ophthalmologists in Kyoto, Japan. He has, in fact, spent a lifetime sharing what has been done and can be done to restore sight to those who might otherwise be blind.

Tragically, ophthalmologists are not being taught nutrition. And despite large, learned audiences, the techniques Dr. Knapp has found to be so effective are not even being tried.

Why Won't They TELL Us These Things?

Obviously, all this information has been available for a long, long time. Years ago the London surgeon James Doggart stressed the importance of vitamins and calcium to the eyes. Writing in *Medical Press* in 1958, he pointed out that the body can't fully utilize calcium without vitamins A and D; that vitamin D regulates the amount deposited in the bones—and *any bone disorder in the skull area can affect the eyes.* Not just the protective sockets, but the bones of nose or jaws, even misaligned or decaying teeth.

In short, *for years* scientific journals both here and abroad have reported the evidence of what the proper nutrients can do for the eyes. Journals you and I don't normally read. But doctors do—or should. Yet I had never *heard* of such evidence until I began research for this book. Not once had an ophthalmologist, optometrist or anybody else who specializes in the science of vision ever mentioned their usefulness to me—until recently, at my own request. I was having my eyes examined and reading glasses checked by a young woman ophthalmologist. When I asked her what she thought about vitamins and eye health, she hesitated. "Well, I just never bring it up unless the patient does." Then, discovering I was an enthusiast, she nearly fell into my arms. She is an enthusiast herself.

Hopefully, these young new doctors will have the courage to take a stand. To speak out. To share what they know to be true. That so many eye problems could be prevented; and that many could be corrected without surgery or drugs.

Even the Prevention of Blindness Society, with its disease-detection programs, its warnings about having regular eye examinations and avoiding accidents, has nothing whatever to say about nutrition. When I asked the Washington, D.C., director about this, he replied, "Well, we take the traditional approach, urge people to do the more common things. Vitamins are controversial. We have to go along with the doctors who say vitamins may be all right, but they don't have anything to do with glaucoma or other diseases of the eye."

The National Eye Institute (a division of the National Institutes of Health) takes the same position. A spokeswoman for them told me, "We have never advocated vitamins. Most of the information we have, and the authorities we agree with, state that there is not enough lack of any vitamin to cause visual problems in the United States. True, a lack of vitamin A will cause visual problems, but these occur mostly elsewhere in underprivileged countries where people don't get enough vitamin A in their diets. Here there is almost no lack of vitamin A, so it isn't much of a problem. As for vitamin D, there's no lack of that either; but then vitamin D isn't generally considered important to the eyes."

Studies and actual human experience, however, have proved that vitamins A and D *are* important to the eyes. And if they are so generously supplied by the great American diet, why is there so much myopia, and why do we have so much blindness? Why does more than half the American population wear glasses? A percentage that goes up to 88 per cent for people over forty-five! Educators will tell you that at least half our school-age children have less than 20-20 vision. Eye patients make up more than 10 per cent of all hospitalized patients; there are 750,000 major eye operations each year. More than 2 million Americans over sixty-five have problems due to cataracts.

According to government surveys, however, the great American diet is not providing sufficient amounts of these nutrients, particularly vitamin A. The well-known HANES report (First Health and Nutrition Examination Survey) found that the range of "below-standard intakes" of vitamin A were as follows:

For children age 1 to 5	37 to 52%
For males age 18 to 44	46 to 65%
For women age 18 to 44	50 to 79%
For adults 60 or older	52 to 62%

In other words, at least half the people tested were not getting enough of this vitamin so critical to our immunity system, our body tissues, and many believe to our eyes. As for vitamin D —sun starvation (due to indoor living and air pollution), and the fact there are so few food sources, make a deficiency of vitamin D equally serious.

How Vitamin A Protects Us

Vitamin A is known as the resistance vitamin. No other substance except vitamin C does so many things to defend us against disease. Working with vitamins C and E, it detoxifies poisons, particularly in the polluted air so many of us must breathe. It also lubricates, moistens and strengthens the respiratory tract; and this alone can give us relief from many lung, throat and nasal problems.

My neighbor used to set off for what she called her "hell trip" —to have long sharp needles probed way up into her blocked sinuses. The pain was so excruciating she would come home in tears. I would comfort her with coffee; and share the box of tissues I myself couldn't be without because of a lesser ailment —postnasal drip. Not in the same class with her misery, but inconvenient—and embarrassing. Especially later when I had to make more frequent public appearances. I would start to make a speech, or face an interviewer on TV, and suddenly be choked with phlegm. (Like most things, it was worse in times of stress.) Nasal sprays only created mouth dryness (besides, they can become addictive). Nothing helped.

Then, only a few months after starting to take vitamin A for general health, I realized I was no longer bothered with postnasal drip. Not even at night, when it wasn't unusual to go through a whole box of tissues. *Something* had finally gotten my mucous secretions in balance. As for my friend: when we met after several years' separation, she had the same good news about her sinuses. "You'll never guess what fixed me up!" But I could, and did. She was now going to a nutrition-minded doctor, who was giving her vitamin A.

Vitamin A provides our best defense against bacteria, and an even more tricky invader, viruses. Repeated experiments, at the National Institutes of Health and elsewhere, have proved that vitamin A can rout the most stubborn and dangerous organisms. The *Journal of Infectious Diseases* for May, 1974, reports that at NIH Drs. Ronald J. Elin and Benjamin E. Cohen protected some groups of mice with vitamin A before injecting them with deadly bacteria. In every instance, most of the group given vitamin A survived, while the control group perished. At Einstein Medical College in New York City the same protective powers of vitamin A were demonstrated even against viruses.

Viruses are parasites so tiny they can't be seen even under a microscope. They attach themselves to a cell, "hatch" and send out hordes of offspring. Our most potent antibiotics have been helpless before viruses, which cause so many illnesses. Yet in similar experiments with vitamin A and several strains of virus, the mice given the vitamin had fewer symptoms and recovered faster. Dr. Eli Seifter, who reported the results before the American Chemical Society in Chicago, stated, "A general picture emerges that vitamin A is very protective. We don't know exactly how vitamin A works but we find it enhances the immunological response of the body . . . and this has broad implications."

The scientists who performed these experiments on animals were surprised, however, that they couldn't duplicate the results in test tubes; vitamin A had *no direct effect* on either bacteria or viruses. Their conclusion is, therefore, that vitamin

A works by stimulating the body's own immunity system. In short, this vitamin protects and defends us in several ways: First, by fortifying our epithelial armor to keep enemies *out*. But once they get *in*, by providing the ammunition and strategy to fight for us.

Vitamin A and Stress

Vitamin A stimulates the production of our own germ-destroying antibodies. And it has a powerful effect on two important glands: the thymus (located just under the chest), and the adrenals (located one over each kidney). The thymus, for many years considered useless after we reach maturity, is at long last recognized as playing a very important role in our immunity machinery. In fairly recent years it has been discovered that these two glands react curiously in unison, yet in contrasting ways, to stress:

The thymus actually shrinks, while the adrenals swell. Both actions cripple their ability to cope with whatever assault we may be suffering. The thymus can't send out its special messengers to trigger the right response to infections. The adrenals, which can actually enlarge to a point of bleeding if the stress is prolonged, can't produce the proper hormones. Again it was Dr. Seifter's work at Einstein Medical College that established that simply having enough vitamin A in the system will keep these two sets of glands in balance, reducing the swelling of the adrenals, while at the same time enlarging the thymus.

All this makes it easier to understand how some diseases, such as gastrointestinal ulcers, are believed to be caused or aggravated by stress. And how and why vitamin A can help. Why this vitamin is so important to the healing of wounds, burns and breaks. In fact, any accident, surgical operation or sickness puts great stress on the body; and so do fears and emotional conflicts. All these situations demand tremendous amounts of vitamin A if we are to resist and to recover as we should.

Vitamin A can even help with the stress of menstruation.

Vitamin A and Sex

A few years before I discovered vitamins I was having some typical "female problems." Nothing serious, but enough to inspire my doctor to urge, "Come on, Marj, why not just get rid of the whole business? You've had your family, you don't need that baby carriage anymore."

"You mean have a hysterectomy?" I gasped. "Look, that baby carriage is a part of *me!* I'm not getting rid of it unless I have to."

Not all women feel this way; and it's that doctor's kind of reasoning which propels so many into surgery—some 700,000 hysterectomies a year at last count. Only 10 to 20 per cent because of a threat of cancer (the only sane reason, surely), but most because of problems with menstruation, especially after stopping the Pill. Certainly excessive bleeding can cause anemia, and cramps can be debilitating. But there is almost no problem associated with a woman's cycles that can't be corrected by simply getting enough vitamins A and E. Hospital studies have shown that women with menorrhagia (excessive bleeding) were invariably woefully deficient in vitamin A. By giving such women 60,000 IU of vitamin A a day for a month, doctors were able to cure 90 per cent of them, and the rest were helped. Pain, spotting and irregularity also were corrected.

Vitamin A is actually responsible for our sexuality. Without it the gonads can't manufacture our sex hormones, then release them into the bloodstream to targets that announce whether we are male or female and what we are going to do about it. For on these hormones depend our sexual desires and abilities. (*Hormone* comes from the Greek word *hormán*, meaning "to excite.") For males—plenty of healthy sperm and virility. For females—responsiveness, and the ability to conceive, then to carry the fetus to full term in the womb. In her classic *Vitamins in Endocrine Metabolism*, Isobel W. Jennings tells us that for some reason women are able to store vitamin A longer than men, and so are less vulnerable; that for men, however, an advanced vitamin A deficiency is equivalent to "virtual chemical castration."

In the whole marvelous mystery of our reproductive system,

everything *depends* on vitamin A. Without it there would be no sperm, no seminal fluid, no lubricating solutions in the cervical passages and uterus. For this vitamin, remember, is responsible for the health of the mucous membranes. Responsible, in fact, for the entire epithelial package inside and out. And that includes that precious and sensitive covering filled with tiny nerve endings which respond to the touch—our skin. And without touching and caressing—well, there would be no babies! And a whole lot less pleasure in the world.

Vitamin A, Shield and Sword Against Cancer

In view of its tremendous powers of resistance and defense, it should be no surprise to learn that vitamin A is one of our most potent weapons against cancer.

Yet this crucial weapon has received little attention in the so-called War on Cancer. A crusade which has already cost $3 billion (not counting the untallied billions spent by the victims themselves), but has accomplished so little it has been called "A Medical Vietnam." Because (with the exception of a slight decrease in leukemia) the death rate is *not* going down. Lung cancer alone has increased more than 25 times in the last forty years.

In April 1978, the National Center for Health Statistics released figures which, in the words of Robert Hadsell, an official of the National Cancer Institute, "end the suggestion last year that the overall cancer rate might be dropping." He attributed the overall increase in mortality rates to "the large increase of deaths from respiratory cancers (mainly lung cancer) among women." Dr. Warner Winkelstein, dean of the School of Public Health, University of California at Berkeley, also says this biggest cancer killer of men "will shortly become the biggest killer of women."

Now our government's same National Cancer Institute has proof from experiments around the world, *and its own scientists,* that vitamin A protects against this very form of cancer.

Here's just one, as reported in the *International Journal of Cancer,* 1975: In 1969 the National Cancer Institute and the Norwegian Cancer Society undertook a five-year study. In it

8,278 Norwegian men were carefully observed to see if there was any relationship between their intake of vitamin A and lung cancer. (Smoking habits and other factors were considered.) Two thirds of the group consumed relatively large amounts of vitamin A; the rest didn't. At the end of five years, results showed that this latter group, the men lacking in vitamin A, had developed far more cancers. The report states:

> A lower lung-cancer rate in those with the high values of vitamin A index is seen in all age groups, and in both urban and rural residents.

It concludes:

> Thus, the present findings do suggest that vitamin A active compounds or some closely associated dietary factors may modify the expression of pulmonary carcinogens . . . in man. In view of the difficulties of influencing smoking behavior, the suggestion that ingested agents may be potent prophylactics against the effects of smoking should be of more than theoretical interest.

Other Evidence

At least sixty other studies with vitamin A have proved its efficacy in fighting cancer. Some of the earlier and most impressive were performed by Dr. Umberto Saffiotti at the National Cancer Institute.

In one, smoke containing carcinogens was actually blown into the throats of test animals. Those whose diets were rich in vitamin A did *not* develop cancer even then. It was also demonstrated that lung cancer could be reduced if the vitamin A was swallowed. Applied locally, vitamin A was able to stop vaginal tumors.

In these and other studies it was discovered that *if vitamin A was first mixed with the cancer-causing agent,* these carcinogens could be applied directly to the neck of the cervix, the prostate glands and other areas without causing cancer. In an address before a symposium on vitamin A at the Massachusetts Institute of Technology some years ago, Dr. Saffiotti made a significant statement:

These observations can be interpreted as indicating that vitamin A can exert a control over the ability of certain cells to undergo neo-plastic transformation [cancerous changes]. . . . The interesting implication here is that there may be a common mechanism affected both by the carcinogens and by vitamin A acting in opposite directions.

"Isn't this exactly what the world has been waiting for?" asks *Prevention* magazine, which has faithfully reported such findings for more than twenty years. "If carcinogens and vitamin A act in opposite directions, then certainly vitamin A must be an important prophylactic to prevent the formation of malignancies."

Yet have you ever seen a newspaper headline to that effect? Heard it announced on radio, television, or in a general-circulation magazine? I've been clipping health articles for years; yet not until this past week did I ever encounter a single piece informing people that vitamin A was known to be a powerful deterrent to cancer. Finally, a long article by Jean Carper in the Washington *Post* for February 4, 1979, devoted two columns to it. Particularly to the work of Dr. Michael B. Sporn, also of the National Cancer Institute, using retinoids, a synthetic form of vitamin A.*

Scientists tried natural vitamin A and found it did have some protective effect and that people with vitamin A deficiencies were higher cancer risks. . . . According to Dr. Sporn, numerous animal studies show the retinoids can dramatically halt the progress of cancer in animals exposed to carcinogens. "In some cases," he says, "the risk was cut in half, three-quarters or by 90 per cent." The retinoids worked against cancer of the lung, breast, skin, bladder—almost all common cancers.

Moreover, Dr. Sporn remarks that the vitamin-A-like derivatives not only can arrest the cancer process but can actually repair cells damaged by carcinogens, thus reversing what was thought to be a relentless march toward cancer. The animal studies were so successful that an experiment is now under way in five cities (Boston,

* Dr. Saffiotti also used retinoids in many of his experiments; he found them safer and more effective. This is one exception to the general rule that natural vitamins are better. It does prove, however, that *there is a difference* between natural and synthetic.

Chicago, Iowa City, Richmond and Seattle) with 100 persons who have had bladder cancer surgery. . . . The purpose is to determine if retinoids will prevent the recurrence of cancerous lesions.

Now hear this. The article continues:

Despite persistent campaigns by the federal government, notably the FDA, to denigrate the role of massive doses of vitamins to combat any disease, vitamin C also has potential for preventing cancer.

In short, while one branch of government is producing mountains of evidence which prove the importance of vitamins in fighting disease, even a killer like cancer—another branch persists in campaigns against them. And one of the chief weapons to denigrate vitamins is the claim they are dangerous—particularly vitamins A and D.

How Toxic Is Vitamin A?

Let's slay the straw dragon of all those dire dangers right now. Too much vitamin A *can* be toxic, but only in absurdly high amounts. In all medical literature there aren't two dozen proven cases of serious vitamin A reactions; and practically all on record are children.

Turning to our trusty *Merck Manual:* "Acute toxicity in children has resulted from taking large doses (300,000 IU). *Recovery is spontaneous with no residual damage; no fatalities have been reported.*" (Italics mine.) The FDA itself is hard put to provide reasonable examples. Typical are two- or three-year-olds who'd been given 250,000 to 500,000 IU a day from birth. (More than 100 times the recommended daily allowance). As Carlton Fredericks dryly remarked in his column: "Those cases do not prove vitamin A to be toxic; they demonstrate that astronomical doses of the vitamin are toxic to small children; they also reveal that some mothers are ignorant."

Dr. Thomas Moore, the British scientist who wrote the chapter on vitamin A for another highly respected reference, *The Vitamins,* says the adult human liver can safely store at least 500,000 IU of this vitamin. Not that vitamin A or *any* vitamin should be taken in excessive amounts; but that overdoses among adults are extremely rare. So rare, in fact, as to make the whole issue almost ludicrous.

For instance, when the FDA announced its program to control the labeling and sale of vitamins as non-prescription drugs, it published the recommendations of an "expert advisory panel." The panel not only recommended that "vitamin E should not be sold by itself because it has no proven therapeutic value and vitamin E deficiency is virtually unknown"; it also stated:

> Some vitamins and minerals, though required by the body, can be dangerous at high levels. For example, large amounts of vitamin A taken over a long period can cause irreversible liver and bone damage.

I wrote to the panel chairman, Dr. Irwin H. Rosenberg, of the University of Chicago Medical School, asking: How many cases are on record of irreversible bone and liver damage? How much vitamin A was taken, for how long? And where can I obtain copies of the case histories for study?

A prompt and cheery reply was forthcoming, together with citations from the *Journal of the American Medical Association* and *New England Journal of Medicine.* The opening sentence of the first source reads:

> Hypercalcemia caused by excessive ingestion of vitamin A has been reported only three times. We report a fourth case . . .

It was that of an eighteen-year-old girl who'd taken 152,500 units a day for three years for acne. Two of the other three cases were: a sixty-three-year-old man who'd taken 400,000 units a day for eight years; and a woman who admitted working up to doses of 1,250,000 units of vitamin A a day for five years! (I could find no information about the other case.)

Now I ask you—*only four cases?* (None of them fatal.) And in amounts that any normal person would consider preposterous. To paraphrase Carlton Fredericks—these examples don't prove vitamin A to be toxic, they show that astronomical amounts are toxic to people who lack common sense.

How Much Vitamin A Do We Need?

The recommended daily allowances of vitamin A are absurdly small: 1,500 IU for babies, 3,000 for children and 5,000 for adults. Bear in mind these RDA's are estimated for "average" daily needs. They don't take individual differences into account; nor special circumstances like accidents, illness or other forms of stress which *immediately* use up enormous amounts, leaving the liver's supply depleted. Doctors who realize how critical this vitamin is to our defense system will give massive doses at once in cases of such emergencies. Doses as high as 400,000 IU a day have been given for brief periods, with no ill effects, and excellent results. (Of course, doctors and *only* doctors should administer such amounts.)

All of us are so different. In our habits, our lifestyles, in our reactions to stress. Different even in our bodies' ability to convert and utilize vitamin A. Taking such things into consideration, the best-qualified medical sources agree that most adults should be getting from 20,000 to 30,000 IU of vitamin A a day, with safe limits up to 50,000 or even 60,000. And instead of screaming about the dangers of getting too much, our government should be far more concerned about the dangers of our getting too little. As rampant disease figures indicate, and its own statistics show, a great many Americans are seriously deficient in vitamin A.

This critically important substance is destroyed by the nitrate fertilizers which now pervade every phase of the food chain. Food processing robs us of more. Smoking and air pollution take a heavy toll—the body uses up huge amounts of vitamin A just trying to combat their poisons. Then there is the cholesterol scare; many people have cut down drastically on their consumption of butter and eggs, so rich in vitamin A. Meanwhile, the propaganda spewing from the FDA has succeeded in frightening these same people away from the very supplements they need to compensate for the loss.

If our government were truly determined to stop cancer, it would stop subsidizing the growth of tobacco. Since that's not likely to happen, it should take another look at Dr. Saffiotti's cancer-smoked hamsters. It should reexamine the study of over 8,000 Norwegian men which was performed by the National Cancer Institute together with the Norwegian Cancer Society. Particularly its conclusion which recommends: that since it's difficult to influence smokers, at least *tell* people there *is* a "potent prophylactic agent" to protect them against the effects of smoking.

It's not enough just to put warnings on cigarette packages; people should also be advised: IF YOU MUST SMOKE, BE SURE TO CONSUME PLENTY OF VITAMIN A. . . . Certainly our government should do everything possible to stop the pollution of our air and water and soil. But it should also inform its citizens that there are natural substances which can detoxify these poisons and fortify the body against them. And chief among them are vitamins C and A.

Either there is a conspiracy of silence against vitamins, or there is appalling ignorance in positions of authority. One of the greatest things that could happen would be for every agency concerned with health to become informed. And then to unite in a vigorous crusade to release the truth. To get the thousands of scientific studies out of the libraries and professional journals, and let people *know* what they *say*. To translate the results of research projects into *action,* so that real live human beings can be spared needless suffering.

Let's face it, we're starting late. Irreparable damage has already been done to our beautiful planet. So many toxins and pollutants have been released we will probably never be rid of their terrible carcinogens; they permeate our earth and air, our very food and water. But God has given us a marvelous immunity system. It can and will fight off these perils if we keep it strong. But for this it must have ammunition—the proper nutrients.

Vitamins are nutrients. And one of the most powerful protective nutrients we have, especially against cancer, is vitamin A.

10

B, the Happiness Vitamin

One night I'd just gotten to sleep when the phone rang. It was a long-distance call from a man asking me to pray for his wife. She was only thirty-seven but either on the verge of a nervous breakdown or becoming an alcoholic, he wasn't sure which. "Yes, of course I'll pray," I told him, "but what does her doctor say?"

"He thinks she may be having an early menopause and wants to perform a hysterectomy." She cried a lot, he told me, which wasn't like her; had become irritable, moody, depressed. "And the more pills the doctors give her—tranquilizers, anti-depressants—the worse she gets; I finally threw them away. Now she's drinking, hardly able to get dinner on the table anymore, so I open a can of something for the kids or we all go out for a hamburger."

"And this is hard on the children, and you too."

"It's terrible!" He went into their problems. Like most people, he needed somebody to talk to; and a writer, particularly anyone in the inspirational field, is presumed to have all the answers—which we don't. "What do you think? Maybe it's all my fault, I admit I haven't been as patient or attentive as I should be. Or maybe she needs to go out and get a job. Say, do you think it could have anything to do with Women's Lib?"

No, I wanted to tell him, I think it could be simply lack of vitamin B. But I can't and don't diagnose or prescribe for anybody.

I did ask, "Does she take vitamins?"

"Whenever she remembers." He named a popular brand which is supposed to take care of all vitamin and mineral needs for the day. I looked it up later. While it contains six components of the B complex (there are eleven), the amounts are so small it's hard to see how they could be much help to anyone who wasn't getting a proper diet. Especially to anyone who had turned to alcohol—so often a warning signal of vitamin B deficiency.

I urged him to get some books on nutrition and study them, particularly the role vitamin B plays in the nervous system. I told him what this vitamin had done for me at a time when I could hardly drag myself out of bed in the morning and felt I might explode if I had to cope with another day. I told him wheat germ, liver and brewer's yeast had become staples in our kitchen, simply because they are the richest natural source of the B vitamins, which are so essential to nervous health and energy.

After he hung up, I kept my promise to pray. And part of the prayer was that this whole family be led to good nourishing foods—and vitamin B.

A year later a letter proved the prayer was answered. "No hysterectomy! In fact, we're awaiting our third child. (You didn't warn me about *that.)*" He had looked up some of the books I'd recommended, and had found another doctor, who said his wife was indeed undernourished. "He began giving her B_{12} shots, which helped so fast we could hardly believe it. Also put her on B_6 and niacin and some others. He also told us to eat more eggs and liver. Since we don't like liver we all take desiccated liver tablets. We've given up Cokes (which I'm ashamed to say I used to buy by the gallon) and cut down a lot on sweets. No more white flour and sugar. Jane's taken a new interest in baking—using honey and whole-grain flours. Well, the results are like a miracle, for all of us. Even the kids are doing better in school."

The Breakdown and Vitamin B

This story is only too typical. All over America families are in trouble. Nervous breakdowns, alcoholism, drug addiction, hyperactive children, runaways, delinquency. Mental illness (schizophrenia attacks more people than heart disease, cancer and arthritis combined). Infidelity, divorce, the epidemic of teen-age pregnancies, VD. . . . Obviously we've been assaulted by the demonic influences in society—sex and violence in books, in movies and on TV, the drug culture, the general breakdown of moral fiber. As a nation we are physically and spiritually ill—and God knows we need his help. But isn't a sick society merely a lot of *sick individuals?* And if we are to survive these influences and live as stable people, we've got to keep our *physical* fiber healthy. The literal tissues of our brains and nerves, and the chemistry that enables them to perform properly.

I am passionately convinced that three fourths of our mental-emotional problems are the direct result of cellular starvation of the brain and nervous system. One of the most important sessions of the Senate's Select Committee on Nutrition and Human Needs was that devoted to Nutrition and Mental Health. Dr. Michael Lesser, a psychiatrist from Berkeley, California, told the committee, "Schizophrenia means some kind of chemical disease of the brain," and that frequently schizophrenics are living on junk food. By giving hospitalized schizophrenics large doses of vitamins—especially vitamin C and the B vitamin niacin—and putting them on a high-protein, low-carbohydrate diet, Canadian psychiatrists Humphrey Osmond and Abram Hoffer were able to help 82 per cent of their patients. Their work went largely unnoticed, Dr. Lesser said, because of the popularity of tranquilizers. Which are lucrative for the drug companies but only put people in straitjackets. "I now treat all my patients by first examining their biochemical nutritional status." He has found that 67 per cent of his patients suffer from hypoglycemia (low blood sugar), "a very common and generally undiagnosed condition which is impairing significantly the health of a large percentage of the population."

Blood sugar problems have been positively correlated with violent behavior. This was vividly confirmed by Mrs. Barbara Reed, a probation officer from Cayahoga Falls, Ohio, who also testified. Some years ago, using a test devised by an orthomolecular psychiatrist, Dr. John Baron, of Cleveland, Ohio, she began to keep records of the physical symptoms and eating habits of prisoners sent to her. Old or young, drug addicts, people arrested for violently antisocial behavior—she found that *most* of them were seriously ill with low blood sugar. "We had fantastically dramatic results just by changing their diets and adding vitamin supplements," she told the committee. So that now even the judges warn them either to stay on Mrs. Reed's diet or go back to jail. *"We have not had one single person back in court for trouble who has maintained and stayed on the nutritional diet."* Perhaps most rewarding of all, she receives letters and visits from former criminals who tell her, "I was dead, but now I'm alive!" That for the first time in their lives they feel like happy, decent, worthwhile, *well* human beings.

Now what are the dietary villains in this vast tragedy of mental-moral breakdown? Undeniably, the refined carbohydrates—white flour and sugar. The sugar and other food industries *will* deny this, of course; in fact, they'll scream bloody murder. And so will their well-paid "experts." But the evidence is glaring. These are the two items that are *always* removed from any genuinely corrective diets.

Sugar as it occurs naturally in fruits and vegetables is absolutely essential to our body's energy and survival. That's why nature has given us such an intense desire for it. And if we could eat sugar in its raw natural form—even sugarcane—it probably wouldn't do us any harm. But when sugar and flour are refined they are stripped of their bulk or fiber. Then they are stripped of their minerals and vitamins.* Yet, *sugar must have vitamin B for its own metabolism.* Refined sugar, robbed of its original

---

* There is so much fiber in sugarcane that in some mills it's the only source of fuel used in boiling down syrup. Dr. G. D. Campbell, a South African physician, says another factor lost in refining is the active, highly protective chromium.

vitamin B, commandeers it from the rest of the body. At the particular expense of the nervous system.

This is a serious loss when we realize that vitamin B is the one vitamin *most* critical to the health of the nerves and brain.

Who Needs Vitamin B?

The vitamin B complex has been called "the middle-age vitamin" because it can do so much to relieve both men and women of middle-age miseries. It could just as aptly be called "the teen-age vitamin." Because adolescents, poor kids, go through even more radical physical changes than we do, even more shattering emotional and nervous upheavals, which vitamin B can help. But actually everyone needs vitamin B:

Children need vitamin B for growth. . . . All women need large amounts of vitamin B, especially when they're menstruating, pregnant, nursing babies or on the Pill.

Anyone over fifty needs plenty of vitamin B to help prevent loss of memory and the senility which so often accompanies aging. If you're taking cortisone or other steroids for arthritis, you need extra vitamin B because these drugs play havoc with the body's supply.

And nobody in the world needs vitamin B more desperately than the alcoholic. Alcoholism has been called our number one addiction. In America alone there are an estimated twelve million victims of this disease which devastates the liver and central nervous system, and which causes so much heartbreak. After generations of misunderstanding, authorities now recognize that alcoholism *is* a physical sickness caused in part and definitely made worse by a deficiency of the B vitamin thiamine. And the more liquor consumed, the greater the need; for alcohol literally wipes out the body's supply. This is because "the grain from which the alcohol was made lost all its vitamin B complex factors during the distilling process," explains Lelord Kordel in *Health Through Nutrition*, "and it soaks up thiamine like a prune does water."

There are enormous amounts of chromium in the dark molasses which cane workers devour with no ill effects whatever.

Alcoholics Anonymous recognizes the value of the B complex vitamins in treating this serious illness. Bill Wilson, co-founder of AA, distributed a paper to physicians about it. He had been impressed by the successes of Russell Smith, M.D., in treating over 500 chronic alcoholics who had failed to respond to everything else, including AA. Over 85 per cent of Dr. Smith's patients recovered and remained abstinent after being treated with large doses of the B vitamins, vitamin C and other nutrients. . . . Incidentally, I consider AA one of the most inspired and effective organizations in existence. If you are concerned about your own drinking or that of anyone dear to you, I urge you to call them. They offer fellowship, support and help from "the God of your understanding." I have heard ministers say their own churches could benefit by following such an example.

In addition to all these special needs, remember that most people exist on a diet of white flour; and that Americans are now devouring an average of 128 pounds of sugar per person per year. Not just people who eat a lot of sweets, mind you, but all of us. Due to the fact that sugar has become a major ingredient of practically everything in the supermarket. According to *Consumer Reports,* Heinz Tomato Catsup is 29 per cent sugar; the non-dairy creamer Coffee-Mate, 65 per cent; Shake 'n Bake Barbecue Style, 51 per cent; even a Ritz cracker, 12 per cent. Sugar in one or more forms is added to hot dogs and cold cuts; to canned and frozen vegetables. Until recently an average infant could get eight pounds of it a year in baby foods. The hidden sugar in some items is even more than in ice cream or candy bars.

Consumer Reports states:

> We now have far less control over the amount of sugar we eat than did previous generations. In 1930, 64% of the sucrose used in this country was purchased directly by consumers for home use, while only 30% went to industry. By 1970 those percentages were more than reversed, with just 24% being bought by consumers directly and 65% going to industry. This means that most of the sucrose we eat has already been added before the food is brought home. Sugar is the leading food additive in the United States today.

The irony of all this is compounded when we realize that one major reason for using the sugar is to disguise the flavor of all the *other* additives.

In short, we've become captive consumers of the very enemy that can throw our entire nervous system out of balance, because it knocks out vitamin B. We are also downing literally tons of drugs, legal or illegal, which likewise destroy this vitamin so essential to our health, our happiness and even our sanity.

Add up all those categories and it's easy to see why so many people are so wretched. Their misery could be caused or aggravated by sheer lack of something their bodies may be screaming for.

What the B Vitamins Do for Us

Primarily, the B vitamins light the fuse that enables the body to convert nutrients into energy. In his marvelous book *Food Facts and Fallacies,* Carlton Fredericks writes: "If the food you eat has been deprived of the B vitamins you are asking your body to burn sugar, flour and similar foods without wicks. The result is that you fill the furnace (your body) with fuel (carbohydrates) which will not burn fully. The furnace will then be filled with the smoke of partial burning. . . . This 'smokiness' translates into nervousness, indigestion, constipation, or any of a thousand common disorders."

The B vitamins also enable the body to use its fats and proteins for energy and body building; to create red blood cells; and to synthesize nucleic acid, an element closely related to how soon we age.

The B vitamins have another unique and critical function, which illuminates the connection between mental and moral breakdown and lack of vitamin B. Some of them produce *a definite chemical reaction on the nerve endings.* Thus affecting the "neurotransmitters," those chemicals which activate networks of nerve cells and *allow messages to reach the brain.*

Vitamin B has such a profound effect on mental and emotional stability it could also stand for Brain.

The Closely Knit Family of Vitamin B

I've been speaking of the B vitamins because, unlike other vitamins, vitamin B is not a single substance. When Christiaan Eijkman and Casimir Funk first discovered that lack of it in the diet could cause beriberi (and, as they later learned, pellagra and other diseases), they thought it was. Actually what they first isolated was vitamin B_1, the first of a whole family of substances which scientists kept subdividing. Although individually identified by name and number, they are grouped under the term *B complex*.

The B vitamins are a closely knit family; they can't and won't work without each other. Their duties often overlap, but they perform in different ways. Deficiency symptoms are much the same. All but one (B_{12}) are water-soluble, excreted in the urine, and *must be replaced every day*. All are easily destroyed by overcooking, especially in water, and the addition of baking soda, which some people mistakenly add to vegetables. As I've said, alcohol, drugs and sugar are their archenemies.

All are richly contained in a few basic foods: wheat germ, brewer's yeast, eggs, whole untreated grains, liver, brown rice and milk whey. If you ate such foods every day it is unlikely you would ever have a vitamin B deficiency. Most people don't however; and the only way most of us can get enough vitamin B for the kind of energy, vitality and joy in life we all want is by taking a B complex supplement. (Just to be doubly sure I do both.) It isn't wise, however, to take the individual B vitamins without a doctor's direction. They can't hurt you, but he's the only one who can tell which ones you may lack, and prescribe accordingly.

Fortunately, the medical profession has not resisted the B vitamins as long and vigorously as the others. There was no denying their usefulness in treating beriberi and pellagra. Then in 1934 two physicians, George Richards and William Parry, won a Nobel Prize for demonstrating that eating enough liver could save people otherwise doomed by pernicious anemia. (A fact that saved at least 10,000 lives a year in America alone.) Scientists at the Merck laboratories and elsewhere finally iso-

B, the Happiness Vitamin 161

lated the "something" in liver in 1948, and proclaimed it another B vitamin, B_{12}. Since then many medical doctors have been in the vanguard of vitamin B therapy.

Many now routinely give B_{12} shots for anemia and nervous disorders and prescribe choline and niacin for the heart. Geriatric specialists have discovered what pantothenic acid, niacin and others can do for the aged. And vitamin B has become one of the foremost weapons in a whole new field known as orthomolecular psychiatry—treating mental patients with megadoses of vitamins. An approach that is still a long way from acceptance among the ranks of the conventional old guard, but one that is gaining new converts every day.

In his opening statement before the Senate Hearing on Nutrition and Mental Health I referred to, Chairman George McGovern said: "Achieving recognition of the relationship between nutrition and mental health is still very much a struggle. Established scientific thinking remains weighted against those few scientists and practitioners who are striving to understand the complex links between the food we consume and how we think and behave as individuals. For example, the newly appointed Mental Health Commission has no member with experience in this vital area. I find this oversight both surprising and distressing."

Even so, the orthomolecular movement is growing.

Many doctors, revolted by the painful, often futile cut-burn-poison treatment which is all they can offer cancer victims, and appalled that despite thirty years of research and billions of dollars spent, there has been almost no improvement in the survival rate of cancer—that, instead, the terrible scourge is growing—such doctors are rebelling. . . . Many psychiatrists, frustrated at the wretched cure rate for schizophrenics, discouraged by their own inability to do more for the mentally ill than keep them drugged and/or locked up, have begun to realize that the brain *is* a physical organ that must be properly nourished or it can't function.

Jonathan Winer, writing in the Boston *Globe*, reports: "Ostracized from the medical community as heretics, the orthomolecularists have fought back, by founding their own medical societies publishing their own medical journals. . . .

Whether or not megavitamin treatments and orthomolecular therapy work, they are here to stay, at least for a while."

Now let's get acquainted with the members of this remarkable family, the B vitamins, starting with the so important B_{12}.

Vitamin B_{12}

This vitamin first gained attention as a cure for pernicious anemia; then as a pick-me-up for tired or neurotic women. Now it is recognized as critical to the functioning of the entire nervous system. For it maintains the strength of the myelin sheath—a delicate protective substance *covering all our vital nerve centers, including spinal cord and brain.* Just how is not yet known, only that without B_{12} serious and sometimes irreversible damage is done.

Heavy smokers need extra B_{12} because the same myelin sheath protects the optic nerves. Unless there is enough B_{12} to maintain it, the cyanide in tobacco can destroy the eyes. A condition known as "smoker's blindness." . . . Pregnant women need plenty of vitamin B_{12} to guard against postnatal depression, and to build up immunity in their babies. . . . Children have special needs, not only for growing strong vigorous bodies, but for mental and emotional stability. . . . People who have had abdominal surgery have extra needs, because it is the gastric juices which produce a substance known as the "intrinsic factor," which allows B_{12} to be absorbed. (Some people don't have this intrinsic factor anyway and must have B_{12} shots to compensate; it also declines in all of us as we get older.)

Unlike the other B vitamins, which are found primarily in fruits, vegetables and whole grains, vitamin B_{12} is found only in animal products: meat, eggs, milk, butter and cheese; and in soy milk. An awful lot of people eat an awful lot of meat and dairy products, so deficiencies of this vitamin are assumed to be less common than some others. But the same people also often eat an awful lot of B-destructive sugar. Furthermore, the test of any nutrient is not how much we consume, but how much we are able to assimilate. Often people who are always tired, irritable, nervous, "blue," don't know they simply lack vitamin B_{12}.

Many times their complaints are considered psychosomatic

and treated with placebos or tranquilizers and anti-depressants. If the symptoms become severe, the victims are sent to a psychiatrist, who may probe the background and subconscious for years without discovering the "switch," as Freud called it, that has caused the neurosis. A switch that more and more people are discovering may actually be biochemical: low blood sugar, allergy to certain foods or chemicals, or lack of certain vitamins, particularly B_{12}. Tragically, cases of outright insanity may go on for years without their true cause being detected.

Hundreds of such cases have been documented (and successfully treated) by Dr. Hoffer and others; but here is one I'm familiar with personally. My friend Beth knew, when she married Bob, that his older sister had had a mental breakdown at twenty-two and been psychotic for twenty years. After periods of hospitalization and shock treatments, which hadn't helped, the parents were determined to keep her at home and cope as best they could. "A tough job," Beth told me, "as she was maniacal at times, and self-destructive. Between the psychiatrists and tranquilizers they managed. But I begged them to let Bob and me take her awhile and see what could be done here in D.C."

Reluctantly, the parents agreed. "Bob and I spent another two years in the same futile battle, until we discovered the Washington Schizophrenia Foundation, who put us in touch with an orthomolecular psychiatrist in Annapolis. The first thing he did was give her hair and blood tests. He said they showed the lowest vitamin B_{12} of anybody he'd ever seen! He began giving her B_{12} shots and also folic acid. Within *two months* there was marked improvement. Her own parents could hardly believe it.

"Dr. Dozinang was then called away and we went to a wonderful neurologist, Dr. Dora Nicholson, who kept up the B_{12} and other vitamins. For more than three years now, Jean has been as normal as you or I." (She certainly is. I've met her. A gracious and attractive woman, albeit a bit insecure about getting a job and taking her place in life. But who wouldn't be, after being kept out of circulation for over twenty years?) "The best years of her life!" Beth protests. "And the really sad part is that it *all* could have been avoided."

Folic Acid

Folic acid (or folate) is essential to the multiplication of cells, especially red blood cells; and it enhances the assimilation of B_{12} —the reason they are so often used together. In the body its highest concentration is in the fluid of the spinal column, where messages are relayed to the nerves and brain. It's easy to see why any lack in this central switchboard could cause a short-circuiting, with resulting emotional and mental problems.

Because folate is so good at producing hemoglobin, the FDA reasons it might hide symptoms of pernicious anemia, and forbids tablets of more than 1 milligram to be sold, even on prescription. In Canada, however, you can buy 25 milligram tablets even without a prescription; and some doctors have their patients get it there. The American limits seem senseless, in view of the fact that a deficiency of folate is far more common than even a deficiency of vitamin B_{12}.

A survey by the World Health Organization revealed this deficiency in up to a third of all pregnant women. This is doubly tragic because when mothers lack this vitamin their babies are threatened by mental retardation. . . . Another study of teenagers found 90 per cent of the girls and 85 per cent of the boys in low-income families consumed less than half the RDA of 0.4 milligrams. While in girls of upper-income groups, the lack was 100 per cent! Old people also were found to be getting woefully little in their diets.

The major food sources of folate are fruits and leafy vegetables. (The very name comes from *folium,* meaning leaf.) People who can't or won't eat plenty of fruits and vegetables, and aren't even *allowed* to get enough folate in vitamin preparations, should return to the other basic sources: Wheat germ (powdered, capsule or liquid). Liver (fresh or desiccated). And brewer's yeast in any form.

Vitamin B_1 (Thiamine)

Thiamine or B_1 was the first vitamin to be discovered and named. It is sometimes called the morale vitamin, it has so much to do with intelligence and a good disposition. It's important to hormone balance, health of the digestive tract and the nourishment and repair of nervous tissues.

A deficiency of thiamine can cause a wide range of symptoms and afflictions: Acne. Numbness and tingling in hands and feet. Indigestion, nausea, constipation. Insomnia, depression, fatigue. Forgetfulness, inability to learn. Neuritis. Infant convulsions. Edema. Nervous breakdown, mental illness. Alcoholism. Beriberi.

Studies have revealed that a great many people are deficient in this vitamin so critical to emotional and nervous health. Especially to the health of girls, pregnant women and women over fifty. One released in the *Journal of the American Dietetic Association* found deficiency in 40 per cent of the college girls tested.

Again we must look to the diet. The best food sources of thiamine (in addition to whole grains and liver) are oatmeal, potatoes, pork, beef heart, peas and beans. Today people are eating far more steaks than pork. And while I don't recommend pork, it *does* contain ten times more thiamine than beef. (Except for beef heart—but where can you even *buy* a beef heart anymore?) Beans and potatoes are no longer popular (too fattening); and oatmeal has given way to dry "enriched" cereals which still contain less than half as much thiamine as their old-fashioned country cousin.

In view of all this, it seems not only ludicrous but appalling that the current RDA for thiamine is a mere 1.5 milligrams for the "average" person, and only 1.7 milligrams for pregnant women. Authorities who understand its importance consider 10 milligrams necessary to maintain health; and to correct thiamine deficiencies doctors use from 50 to 2,000 milligrams.

Vitamin B₂ (Riboflavin)

Riboflavin, like the other B vitamins, is necessary for energy and growth. It's also essential for absorption of iron. And it sees that the soft tissues of the body properly exchange their oxygen. (In short, "breathe.") This makes it especially important to the health of the eyes and brain.

Early symptoms of a deficiency of riboflavin are often cracks at corners of the mouth, burning eyes sensitive to light and a scaly skin. A severe lack may lead to trembling, dizziness, mental problems, poor vision and cataracts. Some scientists believe a lack of this vitamin may be a contributing cause of cancer. Injections of riboflavin have reduced tumerous growths in laboratory animals.

The RDA for riboflavin is 1 to 2 milligrams. Actually, we need at least 5 milligrams a day, much more than most people get in foods.

Vitamin B₃ (Niacin, Niacinamide, Nicotinamide, Nicotinic Acid)

This is the famous vitamin that conquered pellagra, a disease that killed thousands of people all over the world for centuries. In America it was found mainly in the Deep South, where people lived mainly on corn and starches, which lack vitamin B. Its symptoms long identified it with the four D's—dermatitis, diarrhea, delirium—and if unchecked, insanity and death.

The major role of niacin is to stimulate blood circulation. It has been compared to an electric charge which propels the oxygen-carrying blood cells toward their targets—the ear, heart, muscles and joints and brain. It is especially important to the brain, which *has* to have enough oxygen or it can't think straight or run the body properly.

In his classic *Nutrition Against Disease*, Dr. Roger Williams relates a case which clearly demonstrates "that insanity may accompany pellagra and may be cured by supplying the missing nutrient (niacinamide)." The patient, in addition to other symptoms, saw and heard vile things. When admitted to the hospital she was having maniacal outbursts. "About twenty-four to thirty-six hours after receiving niacinamide, her mind began to clear and she knew that the 'craziness and foolishness in her head' was unreal." He continues: "This vitamin is absolutely essential for the metabolism of brain cells and unless the nervous mechanisms have been damaged beyond repair, their function returns promptly once the malnutrition is corrected."

Doctors now prescribe niacin for a number of things—arthritis, hearing loss, cardiovascular disease. Orthomolecular psychiatrists have found it invaluable in treating senility, schizophrenics and autistic children. In fact, it is in the field of mental illness that the most dramatic results have been achieved.

Nearly thirty years ago, Abram Hoffer and Humphrey Osmond began to notice the similarities between many symptoms of pellagra and schizophrenia. Hallucinations, depression, often manic or erratic behavior. Although at that time schizophrenia was still considered solely a psychological illness—might not such patients respond to the same treatment? "We turned our attention to the biochemistry of schizophrenia," Dr. Hoffer writes in his book *Orthomolecular Nutrition*. "Osmond and I undertook pilot studies of vitamin B$_3$ in the form of nicotinic acid to determine a dose range that would not be toxic and would have an effect. The first 8 acute or subacute patients treated showed a prompt and sustained response to 3 grams of nicotinic acid per day given over a one month period."

These eight cases are described. All had failed to respond to electro-convulsive therapy or insulin coma. Some had been placed in restraint, doomed to spend the rest of their lives in mental institutions. *All got well. Some within four days, some within four weeks.* One woman recovered, but on three occasions during the next five years she discontinued the vitamins, and each time relapsed within three weeks. When she again took her vitamins she was restored to sanity.

A number of double-blind studies with large numbers of other patients, who were then evaluated by their own psychiatrists, left no doubt. This therapy, combined with proper nutrition and other forms of psychiatry, doubled the recovery rate for schizophrenics.

The National Institute of Mental Health says that schizophrenia is attacking more and more young people. That it's the most common form of mental illness to hospitalize adolescents and young people today.

Mental illness, whether it stems from the pellagra we associate with poverty (and there's still plenty of it!) or the breakdowns of the privileged, *cannot be divorced from the lack of proper nutrients.*

Additional food sources of niacin are poultry—especially the white meat of turkey; peanuts, mushrooms, tuna fish and mackerel. Very little is contained in cow's milk or dairy products. (Mother's milk is the only good source for babies.) Niacin is restored to flour, but in insignificant amounts. And the more sugar and white flour we consume, the more niacin we need.

Vitamin B₅ (Pantothenic Acid)

Pantothenic acid occurs in all living cells, plant or animal, even bacteria. Its name derives from the Greek *panthos* meaning universal. It is one of the two vitamins manufactured by your own body as well as found in food. (The other is vitamin D, manufactured by sunlight using the cholesterol in the skin.) Pantothenic acid is vital to the adrenal glands, whose hormones help fortify us against the stress and shocks of life. For this reason it's sometimes called the anti-stress vitamin.

Without enough pantothenic acid you could very well suffer from: Low blood pressure. Stomach and intestinal distress. Respiratory infection, allergies. Fatigue, fainting, breathlessness. Insomnia. Arthritis. Nervous anxiety, depression. Premature aging. (Test animals deprived of pantothenic acid turned gray, hair fell out, many became bald, wrinkled, bent. I know a man whose hair returned to its natural color after he took pantothenic acid. Mine didn't; but there are numerous cases where hair does.)

Pantothenic acid has been found to be as good for arthritis as the drugs cortisone and ACTH, without their dangerous side effects. It is a powerful antihistamine, again without side effects. . . . The body *must* have it to produce acetylcholine, a vital chemical transmitter at the nerve endings. When you sometimes feel as if you're going to pieces, your nerves exploding, they could be—due to lack of this critical stuff. I used to take hormones for nerves; now I know better. Pantothenic acid is good for any condition where hormones help, and is a whole lot safer.

All foods contain this vitamin, but the amounts are small and easily lost in processing. The pasteurization of milk destroys it; none is replaced in baby foods or formulas. (This may be one reason so many children are allergic.) It is *not* restored to flour.

Antibiotics, injuries, surgery and X rays all take a tremendous toll. And any emotional crisis, from a fight to a scare to a loss, or even the joys of a wedding, can drain our defenses.

Scientists who have investigated pantothenic acid declare we need at least 50 milligrams a day just to resist stress and disease; and from 500 to 1,500 milligrams to fight them when they strike us.

Vitamin B₆ (Pyridoxine)

Vitamin B_6 is critical to energy and to mental and emotional health. Without it we can't use our protein properly, especially tryptophan. This can lead to serious problems.

Vitamin B_6 is so important, especially to women, I wish I could write a whole book about it. Since I can't, I urge you to read John M. Ellis' *Vitamin B₆: The Doctor's Report.* In it Dr. Ellis traces its history, and his own experiences in using this "priceless jewel" among all the vitamins.

Dr. Paul György "discovered it, independently isolated it, and finally named it pyridoxine, thus closing out what he was later to classify as 'one of the most intriguing chapters in the rapid development of vitamin research.'" Only a few months later in 1939 three Alabama doctors reported astounding results in using it to treat pellagra and Parkinson's disease. Patients responded within a few minutes of injections. Then, in the words of György, "with all the rich history of vitamin B_6, approximately twenty years passed before its requirement by the human organism had been definitely established and recognized."

One reason was World War II, keeping doctors and scientists busy in other fields; by the time the war was over attention was focused on the more glamorous technology and wonder drugs. An episode in 1952, however, shocked people into an awareness of the importance of B_6. "That year an excessively heated commercial milk formula caused convulsions in infants. It was subsequently proved that naturally occurring vitamin B_6 in the formula was destroyed by heat to the point where a resulting deficiency caused serious impairment of brain function. When their formulas were changed, the convulsions disappeared."

Doctors in Lancaster, Pennsylvania, then discovered that injections of B₆ actually stopped convulsions, and prevented further ones. Other hospitals and clinics were learning that vitamin B₆ would relieve neuritis, especially in tuberculosis patients being treated with certain drugs. That there was a relationship between the need for B₆ and mental retardation. Radiologists found this vitamin relieved nausea in patients being treated for cancer; obstetricians, that it helped the nausea of pregnancy.

Dr. Ellis became interested in 1961, when there was (and still is) "a prevalent concept that B₆ deficiency did not exist in the United States." Worried about the great American junk-food diet, he began putting his patients on low-fat diets, substituting lean meats and lots of fruits and vegetables, as well as peanuts and pecans. All improved so fast he realized there was something *in* the diet itself—the B vitamins. He decided to work with the B complex vitamins themselves; then by a process of elimination to discover the most effective for certain ailments. It proved to be vitamin B₆.

Here are some of the symptoms and afflictions which Dr. Ellis and others trace to a lack of this vitamin, and which respond to its use: Numbness and tingling in hands and feet. (I had this myself before trying vitamins.) "Carpal tunnel syndrome," a disabling condition of the wrist (carpus) involving the small bony compartment where nerves and ligaments control the fingers.

Neuritis. Arthritis. Trembling in the hands of the old.

Acne, especially at menstruation. Edema and swelling in pregnant women. Tension, nervousness and depression of menstruation, pregnancy or menopause.

Infant convulsions. Mental retardation.

Nausea, motion sickness.

Anemia. Epilepsy. Kidney stones.

Excessive fatigue. Nervous breakdown. Mental illness.

Drugs, particularly hormones, are very destructive of vitamin B₆. Millions of women are still taking the Pill, one of whose side effects is depression. London physician P. W. Adams, addressing an International Congress on Hormonal Steriods, spoke of how widespread and serious is this upsetting of the brain's chemistry. He reported clinical studies which showed that depression is relieved, balance restored by administering 20 milligrams of vitamin B_6 twice a day.

Vast numbers of people are also taking steroids such as cortisone for arthritis. According to the Arthritis Foundation, more than 17 million Americans are being medicated for this disease. There are many kinds of people, many kinds of arthritis; estrogens are often necessary. But Dr. Ellis believes they should always be accompanied by B_6.

Despite all the foregoing, the recommended daily allowance for pyridoxine or B_6 is a mere 2 milligrams for the average person and only 2.5 milligrams even for pregnant women. Dr. György deplores such amounts, which he considers hopelessly outdated, and says they should be increased at least tenfold. Another physician, Dr. Robert Atkins, author of *Super Energy Diet*, says, "I consider B_6 to be one of the most essential vitamins for energy. When I evaluate a B complex formula or a multivitamin pill, the first thing I look for is the B_6 content. I find little use for those that contain less than 25 milligrams."

Choline

Choline, like vitamin B_{12}, is found primarily in meat and eggs; another good source is fish. Choline is important to the liver, kidneys, gall bladder, glands and brain. It is one of the few nutrients which are taken by the blood directly to the brain. So those old quips about certain foods being "brain foods" were right. Choline helps the brain manufacture an important nerve signal transmitter, acetylcholine. It is now known that the person who consumes a goodly amount of eggs, fish or lecithin, will soon have an extra supply of this lively transmitter in his brain.

Quite literally—and to me amazingly—in order for a message to leap from one nerve to the next, this chemical must be released from the nerve endings and into the synapse (gap) so the nerve impulse can cross. Here again may be an explanation of why we sometimes feel as if we're "flying to pieces"; we may simply not have enough.

Doctors use choline in treating diabetes, heart trouble, gallstones, muscular dystrophy, and a wide range of nervous disorders, including uncontrollable tics and twitching. Most recently choline has shown promise as a learning and memory aid. Tests at the National Institute of Mental Health revealed that subjects given added amounts of choline improved "significantly."

A vitamin B complex preparation should include 50–100 milligrams.

Inositol. Biotin. PABA (Para-aminobenzoic Acid)

These three members of the vitamin B complex are less well known and are not yet fully acknowledged to be "essential." But common sense tells us if they weren't the good Lord wouldn't have put them in foods or set them to work in our bodies.

The sources of inositol are fruits, vegetables and organ meats —especially liver, beef heart and brain. In our bodies inositol shows up, logically, in the tissues of the heart, brain, liver, kidneys and spleen. (Primitive peoples in their wisdom always eat these organs when they kill game.) Inositol has a tranquilizing effect; like vitamin B_{12}, it fortifies the myelin sheath which protects the nerves and brain. It also helps to reduce cholesterol.

A good formula should contain from 50 to 500 milligrams.

Biotin helps metabolize fats and is associated with a healthy skin. Skin problems are usually the first sign of a lack. It may show up as dermatitis in bottle-fed babies or those whose mothers don't have enough biotin in their milk. Fortunately, deficiency of biotin isn't common. From 10 to 50 milligrams is plenty for any vitamin combination.

PABA isn't even contained in most B complex capsules; to get it we need to eat plenty of liver, yeast and eggs, as well as vegetables. PABA stimulates the intestinal bacteria and helps break down and utilize proteins. It too is associated with healthy hair and skin. PABA ointment is believed to be the best protection you can use against sunburn, wrinkles from sunning and even sun-caused skin cancer.

Body, Mind and Spirit

There are two more B vitamins to be discussed, but they are controversial, and I want to end this chapter by emphasizing the importance of the vitamin B complex to human happiness.

This is not to discount the importance of our thoughts and attitudes. Jesus said, "As a man thinketh so is he." Adelle Davis said, "We are what we eat." Both are right, because the two are inseparable. *We are what we eat. And we are what we think.*

When we harbor destructive thoughts—anger, resentment, remorse, jealousy—any of the long black gamut of self-concerned emotions—our sympathetic nerves react. (How appropriately those nerves are named!) Chemicals are poured into the system (those flight or fight juices) which affect every organ —stomach, heart, nerves and brain. And these chemicals can make us literally sick. So it *is* very important to control our emotions and our thoughts.

Here is where good counseling can help. Here is where the books and courses on self-improvement apply. Here above all is where we need the Bible, prayer and God. Even so, we still need enough vitamins in our body to resist those self-engendered poisons; and we need vitamins to replace those we have burned up in our battle with our own emotions. Otherwise it's almost impossible to break the old self-destructive habits of thinking. Because when we are *physically* ailing the whole nervous system is affected, and this includes the brain with which we think.

For the same reason, our mental and emotional miseries can begin just as often in the breakdown of the physical tissues of the brain itself. "The brain," writes Linus Pauling, "provides the molecular environment of the mind." The mind, being an abstract, can't get sick. It is the *brain* that gets sick. (And of course the conflicts none of us escape can make it sicker.) If the brain isn't getting enough oxygen or nourishment, it can't think right. If it isn't receiving the right messages via those neurotransmitters and the central switchboard in the spinal column, it can't operate in a healthy manner. The results can range from the normal self-pity, "blues" and moods to depression, confusion, senility and all the other torments, even madness, that we call mental illness.

The old school of psychiatry still violently resists all this. Ignoring Freud's own warning that one must never forget the chemistry of the brain, they insist patients belong only on the couch and/or drugs. They are particularly hostile to megavitamin therapy. "Today, after more than twenty years' success with more than thirty thousand schizophrenics, alcoholics, addicts, and autistics, there are still those who denounce the concept," Richard Passwater says in *Supernutrition —Megavitamin Revolution.* "Megavitamin therapy is so opposed to what they have been taught that they refuse to consider seriously the possibility that it could work. This is mega-ignorance!"

Curiously, they find no inconsistency in condemning nutrition and vitamins as "dangerous experimentation" at the same time they are turning people into zombies with psychotropic drugs which sometimes do irreparable damage. "What is worse, these mind-bending drugs are symptomatic treatment, the practice of medicine at its worst, creating a drug-dependent population which, under its artificially induced calm, is as sick as it ever was." This quote is from Carlton Fredericks' book *Psycho-Nutrition.* Dr. Fredericks, like Dr. Passwater, is an outstanding authority on nutrition. Dr. Fredericks has researched, taught, written and lectured on the subject for more than forty years—long before many in the medical profession had even heard of a vitamin. His books are filled with fascinating case histories of people whose lives were dramatically changed or saved by them.

If you have problems in any of these areas, help is available. If you have a wife or husband who is alcoholic, or whose moods and behavior are causing serious concern . . . if you have a disturbed child, a problem child, or one with learning difficulties . . . or if you yourself are exhausted, confused, nervous, depressed without strong cause (in short, manifesting symptoms associated with the body's need for vitamins, especially vitamin B), don't delay. Write or call one of the following agencies; they can put you in touch with a doctor who practices orthomolecular (megavitamin) therapy:

The Academy of Orthomolecular Psychiatry, 1961 Northern Boulevard, Manhasset, New York 11030. Telephone 516-627-7260. (This Academy is a meeting ground for professionals and physicians seeking training, but it provides an active referral list for others.)

The Canadian Schizophrenia Association, 2135 Albert Street, Regina, Saskatchewan, Canada S4P 2VI.

The American Schizophrenia Association, 1114 First Avenue, New York, New York 10021. Telephone 212-759-9554.

The Huxley Institute for Biosocial Research, also at 1114 First Avenue, New York, New York 10021. (The Institute publishes and distributes all pertinent information in this area. It has launched a campaign to stimulate biochemical research "and to educate the afflicted regarding the nature of their illness and the availability of treatment.")

National Health Federation, Box 688, 212 West Foothill Boulevard, Monrovia, California 91016. Telephone 213-357-2181. (Every American family should belong to this Federation, whose purposes are to support freedom of choice in health matters, reduce the cost of health care, oppose food additives unless proved safe—among others. They publish a bulletin concerning issues of nutrition legislation and holistic health care.)

The phone books of most large cities list the addresses of the local Schizophrenia Associations. They also contain the addresses of the central offices of Alcoholics Anonymous.

There are also medical societies whose members include physicians and dentists practicing orthomolecular therapy:

The International Academy of Metabology, 2236 Suree Ellen Lane, Altadena, California 91001.

The International College of Applied Nutrition, Box 368, La Habra, California 90631.

The International Academy of Preventive Medicine, 871 Frostwood Drive, Houston, Texas 77024.

Institute of Preventive Medicine, Suite 400, 2139 Wisconsin Avenue, Washington, D.C. 20007.

The doctors associated with these groups can give you the hair, urine and blood tests which are remarkably accurate in determining whether you have any deficiencies of these vitamins and minerals so critical to the health of our minds and bodies; and, if necessary, put you on a program to restore them.

11

The Anti-Cancer Vitamins, B_{15} and B_{17}

There are two more B vitamins which have proved invaluable in fighting disease around the world but which our government doesn't want us to have.

Vitamin B_{15}, also known as pangamate or pangamic acid.

And vitamin B_{17}, known as amygdalin or Laetrile (also spelled laetril).

In America these two vitamins were first researched, and B_{17} isolated, by a California physician, Ernest T. Krebs, Sr., and his son, Ernest, Jr. Yet their discoveries brought them only twenty-five years of harassment and persecution. Why? Because the FDA says amygdalin is toxic. *Even though amygdalin is not listed in any government registry of toxic substances.*

As for B_{15}. They don't even claim it's toxic, merely "useless." (Just as for more than twenty years they claimed vitamin E was useless in human nutrition.)

Let's look first at this "useless" vitamin.

The Many Roles of Vitamin B_{15}

Dr. Richard Passwater devotes an entire chapter to B_{15} in *Supernutrition for Healthy Hearts.* He states:

Pangamate improves the available oxygen content of the blood, enhances the circulatory blood volume, lowers arterial pressure, normalizes the heart's balances of potassium and sodium, suppresses heart pains in coronary disease, and accelerates heart and vascular system repair.

Studies were establishing these facts as far back as 1964. At an international symposium in Moscow that year, thirty-four scientific papers on pangamate or vitamin B_{15} were presented. Russia and its satellites give it generously to their athletes. They have found it relieves muscle pains, helps heal torn ligaments and gives stamina and energy.

The Russians—who have an even greater drinking problem than we do—also believe it has great promise in treating alcoholism. In her book *B-15: The "Miracle Vitamin,"* Brenda Forman describes the work of a Moscow psychiatrist, Dr. I. V. Strelchuck, who gave 80 to 100 milligrams of B_{15} to fifty men who had a pathological craving for drink. After twenty to thirty days they actually became indifferent to alcohol! "He concluded that pangamate interrupted the chemical process in alcoholics that leads to their addiction, and thus eliminates their craving." He also discovered that among these men such diseases as hepatitis, cirrhosis of the liver and heart problems went into remission.

Pangamate also lowers cholesterol, and plays a role in cancer prevention by detoxifying cancer-causing chemicals. It has even helped autistic children.

Dr. Allan Cott, a New York psychiatrist, described just a few of many cases to the International Academy of Preventive Medicine. Two concerned seven-year-olds. The first had never spoken and was withdrawn. After daily doses of pangamate (200 milligrams) the little boy began to speak—at first a word or two, then sentences. Soon he was dressing himself, playing with other children. The second youngster not only wouldn't speak but was hyperactive. After being given vitamin B_{15} he was eager to try words, and his disposition changed. Withdrawal of the vitamin made him revert to his frenzied, helpless behavior. He improved immediately once it was restored.

Vitamin B_{15} is thought to be involved, as well, in slowing the process of aging. The famous Russian researcher Dr. Y. Yu. Shpirt has said, "I believe the time will come when there will be calcium pangamate on the table of every family with people past fifty."

I take it every day.

The Fearless War on "Useless" Vitamins

The vitamin which helped those alcoholics, helped those children, *can* be purchased legally in the United States. It is not a toxic substance, not against the law. Such facts have not deterred the FDA, however, from trying to stop its sale. Pangamic acid was specified in the search warrant which allowed nine government agents to ravish the premises of S&S's Health Hut in West Covina, California, in their search for Laetrile. (While they were at it, they seized supplies of zinc, enzymes and other nutrients; all books having to do with cancer; and private records.)

Horrifying as this was, the co-owner, Carroll Leslie, considers the attack less terrifying than an earlier raid when two San Diego policemen broke down the door of her home one night and dragged her to jail without even allowing her to dress. "For ten years I'd been active in freedom causes," she told me. "I really thought I could empathize with people who were the victims of tyranny. But I really didn't realize how it felt—the sheer horror, until it happened to me. Nothing prepares the decent, law-abiding citizen for such abuse!"

She went on to say that it is the *policy* to arrest "health criminals" on Friday nights, after midnight, when banks are closed, lawyers aren't available, and you can't appear before a judge to post bond. "It cost me $25,000 in bail, and the most appalling experience of my life, to be exposed to all the brutal inhumanities of jail."

Such incidents are not uncommon. In Orlando, Florida, over $4,000 worth of vitamin B_{15} was confiscated. In Cincinnati, drugstores were forced to recall more than 15,000 bottles of this perfectly legal substance. "The problem is power," says Mrs. Leslie. "Man cannot handle unrestrained power, and those men who arrested me, and their bureaucratic bosses, have too much power."

This is the agency, remember, that permits the sale of 161,000 drugs, only 200 considered essential by the World Health Organization. (Americans spend an estimated $700 million a year on cold remedies alone, most of them totally ineffective in treating the common cold.) The agency that allows millions of prescriptions to be written for drugs whose side effects—their own manufacturers warn—can sicken, cripple, blind and even kill you. The Congressional Office of Technology Assessment states in *OTA Priorities, 1979:*

> Unfortunately, as much as 25 per cent of prescription drug use may be ineffective, unnecessary, or even harmful. Adverse drug reactions, many of which are predictable, may kill as "few" as 24,000 or as many as 130,000 people annually.

For instance, Darvon, the third most widely prescribed drug in the country, has been linked to more deaths than all deaths from heroin, morphine and methadone combined.

Why, then, the savage attack on vitamins?

With all that power at its disposal, I again submit—surely this public protector has better things to do.

All-Out Attack on Apricot Pits

Vitamin B_{15} is found in the same foods which contain the other B vitamins: wheat germ, liver, brewer's yeast, whole brown rice and nuts. I wonder how long it will be before war is declared on them? That remark is not as absurd as it sounds, because the FDA *has* said it would even seize shipments of lettuce, lima beans, cherries, apples, pears and fruit seeds (all produce containing vitamin B_{17}) should there be any likelihood they would be used to manufacture Laetrile.

And a few years ago it actually began seizing apricot pits.

These seeds became a part of our family diet when a neighbor, Lenore Winfield, brought me a little bag, saying, "Scott and I eat a few every day. They're a known cancer preventive, and we think they're delicious." We thought so too. Apricot kernels have a bitter almond flavor which bakers have used for years.

(They are on the FDA's own Generally Regarded as Safe list.)
We especially like them in cookies or sprinkled on desserts. It
was good to know that among the Asian Hunzas, a people who
have eaten these kernels daily for generations, *there has never
been a single case of cancer.*

Imagine my consternation, then, to pick up newspapers and
read of the daring raids the FDA was making on the purveyors
of apricot pits. In Manitowoc, Wisconsin; in stores throughout
New York State; in Knoxville, Tennessee. In the Knoxville case,
however, the judge ordered 6,700 cases returned to the owner,
saying he himself had eaten apricot kernels since he was a child.
"They are not poisonous, not misbranded, not deleterious to
your health, but a food fit in every way for human consumption.
Mr. Heinsohn is no criminal." The owner, however, had to
borrow $10,000 to retrieve his own seized property.

(A word of caution, even so. Apricot pits are not to be eaten in
quantities, like peanuts. Their flavor is so strong it's unlikely
anybody would want to. But if you didn't use common sense and
ate a lot at once, you could indeed get sick. We enjoy and feel
protected by half a dozen or so a day.)

The company from which we had been ordering our own
supply was not so lucky. After years of harassment, they were
put out of business. Meanwhile, my family and other presumably free Americans were deprived of a perfectly legal food we
wanted. Finally, after a lot of effort, we found another source.

Vitamin B_{17} (Laetrile)

Now, why all the furor about apricot pits? Because they are the
primary source of vitamin B_{17}, scientifically known as nitrilosides, amygdalin, more popularly as Laetrile. And amygdalin
contains minute amounts of cyanide. That's the excuse back of
all those LAETRILE WARNING posters you may have seen in
post offices and doctors' waiting rooms. "Indicating that Laetrile is a poison because it contains cyanide," says Dr. Harold
Manner, former head of the biology department at Loyola University. "If the FDA were truthful they would also tell you that
lima beans contain cyanide, buckwheat flour contains cyanide;
in fact, vitamin B_{12}, which is used so widely, is one of the richest

sources of cyanide! Because, you see, cyanide is not a poison, not when it's part of a complete molecule."

Laetrile is itself a component of at least 1,400 foods. The pharmacopeias have considered it non-toxic for nearly 150 years. It does not appear on the registry of toxic compounds published by the Department of Health, Education, and Welfare. Arlin J. Brown, a physicist who has led a long fight for freedom of choice in natural, non-toxic cancer therapies (Laetrile is only one of many), says, "Laetrile is not new, it is not a drug, it's not toxic, and it's not illegal." Yet mention Laetrile to almost any orthodox doctor or scientist and he runs screaming for cover.

When Dr. Manner first began his work with Laetrile at Loyola, he realized he was entering forbidden territory when he called friends in the medical or science field. "All went beautifully until I mentioned the word Laetrile. Then it was as if I'd used the most unmentionable word in the world. Dead silence—followed usually by an invitation to meet them somewhere. During the first few years I met in so many parked cars or so many basements I began to feel like the star in some undercover spy movie."

As for supplies to conduct his studies, Dr. Manner says, "I wouldn't have believed what I had to go through to get started with this work. I hold both federal and state Hard Drug and Controlled Substances licenses. There is no drug or pharmaceutical I can't purchase." Yet through a program of harassment and delays the FDA did everything possible to keep him from getting the substance he wanted to test. "I have never, during thirty years of researching, had any trouble buying anything in the world until I tried to buy the extract of an apricot pit!"

The lengths to which its opponents will go to deny either use or research of Laetrile have been paranoiac. During the Johnson administration a high school boy whose experiments with Laetrile on mice were winning first place at science fairs, was warned to desist or he'd be kept out of medical school. When he continued his project (a demonstration that ultraviolet light enhances its effectiveness) and was competing at the national fair in Texas, the warnings were sternly repeated. Shortly afterward he was shocked to be notified that he was being rejected by the same medical school that had already accepted him. And no other school would take him. It took the intervention of Senator Robert Kennedy and the President to get him into medical college.

In other cases, science teachers have been so brainwashed and bullied they have refused to allow their students even to perform any experiments with Laetrile. In short, twentieth-century public schools are saying to young inquiring minds, "Lay off, kids! We don't want any Galileos showing us things we'd rather not know."

The Cover-up in the War on Cancer

In 1971, "with a fanfare comparable to that accorded the moon shots," in the words of *U.S. News & World Report*, the War on Cancer was launched. Now, literally billions of dollars later, cancer victims are still dying like flies. "Hoped-for break-throughs failed to materialize. . . . Even the highly touted million-dollar mass screening program for breast cancer is now largely discredited after scientists pointed out that X-ray mammography may have caused as many cancers as it was detecting."

At that time all females were urged to have radiation, regardless of age. In some cities there were even portable units set up in vans, where teenagers could walk in and have themselves tested, for kicks. Poor records were kept . . . Let me emphasize that mammography is a safe and very important tool for detection of breast cancer, especially in older women. On the advice of my present husband, an internist, I have a mammograph once a year. But during the government program it was grossly misused.

Dr. James A. Watson, a Nobel Prize-winning biologist, has called the war on cancer "a total sham." The former commissioner of the FDA itself, Dr. Donald Kennedy, pronounced it: "A medical Vietnam. People are disgusted. Having been told that the investment of funds produces a technical fix for a problem, they're now being told there is no fix, and instead their environment is not completely safe and they shouldn't drink or smoke."

What they are *not* being told is that *there have been break-throughs*. Because there has also been a massive cover-up. And the greatest cover-up of all has been the suppression of the evidence concerning Laetrile.

"In cancer we have a thousand Watergates all rolled up into one," says Arlin J. Brown in his *Cancer Victory Bulletin,* where all forms of cancer therapy are examined. "If just one major newspaper, magazine or TV network would do a total investigation of Laetrile and metabolic therapy, and keep telling the truth about it, we would be winning the war on cancer and saving lives."

But like the three monkeys who simply refuse to see, hear or speak of evil, the cries of "No evidence!" go up from those who refuse to look or listen. Even though at least twenty independent institutions around the world have produced mountains of evidence that amygdalin or Laetrile *can* prolong the life of test animals and gain remission of tumors.

Here are just a few:

> Pasteur Institute in Paris
> Scind Laboratories, University of San Francisco
> Southern Research Institute in Birmingham, Alabama
> Institute von Ardenne in Dresden, Germany
> Department of Biology, Loyola University, Chicago
> Sloan-Kettering Cancer Center in New York

Sloan-Kettering? Yes, the same prestigious institute which on June 15, 1977, announced it had "found no evidence that Laetrile cures or prevents cancer or is beneficial in treating malignant tumors." Yet here is the text of a handwritten letter sent to the Arlin J. Brown Information Center by the eminent researcher Dr. Kanematsu Sugiura, *who conducted virtually all of the Laetrile experiments there:*

> I have tested the effects of Laetrile isolated from apricot pits on the growth of spontaneous mammary cancers in mice many times and on the development of lung metastases. I found that prolonged intraperitoneal injections of 2,000 mg/kg/day of Laetrile inhibited the growth of small tumors (less than 1.5 cm in diameter), in many cases temporary.
>
> Laetrile had a strong inhibitory action on the development of

lung metastases—approximately 80% against approximately 20% in control mice. The general health and appearance of Laetrile-treated animals were better than those of the control animals with large tumors.

The Arlin J. Brown Information Center was understandably shocked, therefore, at the highly publicized "no evidence" release. (So was I, because I happened to hear Dr. Sugiura make quite the opposite announcement a day or two before on a network TV show.) Mr. Brown, who had invited Dr. Sugiura to address a cancer convention in Washington, D.C., in September, called him to repeat the invitation, only to be told, "I'm very sorry, I can't come." When pressed for a reason: "At the moment everything is all upside down. I don't want to get into any more trouble."

Dr. Sugiura had done cancer research at Sloan-Kettering for more than fifty years. During that period he had had some 250 papers published; never before had officials refused to release results of his studies. Yet it became evident that this great scientist had received his orders. During the course of the conversation he was guarded in his replies and obviously apprehensive.

The whole story of the successful Sugiura experiments and the suppression of their results is described in fascinating detail by Ralph Moss, both in his lectures and his book *The Cancer Syndrome*. Moss was fired from his job as assistant director of public affairs because he tried to get the truth before the public. He refused to tell reporters the tests had failed; in fact, joined the scientists and other employees who were publishing an underground newsletter *Second Opinion*. In *Second Opinion* Special Report: Laetrile at Sloan-Kettering, the scientists made some serious charges:

> The 1974 Sloan-Kettering Institute Annual Report, belatedly published in December 1976, . . . omits the main Laetrile experiments which took place during that year and which indicated a positive role for the substance. . . .
>
> Dr. Sugiura carried out some of his most important work on the effects of Laetrile in mice with spontaneous mammary tumors. In general, he found that Laetrile inhibits the spread of cancer, stops the growth of small tumors, and leads to a general increase in health and well-being. Yet all of his work, still unpublished, is mysteriously

missing from the 1974 SKI report, which supposedly is a complete
record of the hundreds of projects performed that year. This raises
some serious questions about the honesty and intentions of the SKI
administration. . . .

We believe there is a coverup of Laetrile experiments at SKI. The
reason for this coverup is the long-standing hostility of the drug
companies toward this and other substances which are cheap and
plentiful, nontoxic, easy to manufacture and nonpatentable. The
SKI administration, intertwined with the corporations for whom
cancer is big business, has been hamstrung by Sugiura's surprisingly
good results in Laetrile tests.

In other issues of *Second Opinion* these scientists state they
don't believe anyone is maliciously sitting on a cancer cure;
rather that "with the passage of the National Cancer Act and
the disbursement of billions of dollars in research funds, an
extensive cancer bureaucracy has grown up to administer those
funds." The bureaucrats jealously guard their own territory,
while the medical profession resists anything that poses a threat
to their prestige, and in many cases their livelihood.

The Government Wants Your Child

Even more appalling—our government is using Hitler-Stalin
tactics to tear children away from their parents. Good, loving
mothers and fathers are being charged with neglect, even child
abuse. They are being forced to kidnap their own children and
flee to avoid prosecution. Their crime—refusing to submit their
cancer-stricken youngsters to treatments dictated by the medical establishment and the FDA.

In Florida four-year-old Nikki Finn was only getting worse
under radiation and chemotherapy. Bloated, nauseated, losing
her hair, beginning to hate her father because he could only
stand helplessly by while strangers held her down for the painful spinal taps. Desperate before her agony, the parents found a
physician willing to administer Laetrile, along with vitamins,
enzymes and a fruit and vegetable diet—*the only way it will
work for human beings.* The child was immediately relieved,
the disease in remission. Yet the state charged these parents
with criminal negligence, demanding they turn their little girl

over to them for more of the same torture under which she'd been disintegrating. Only after long, expensive court battles were they allowed to keep their own child and continue the treatments that had saved her.

Mrs. Betty Kehrer of Dallas hid out for a month with her sixteen-year-old son Dwight, moving from state to state to keep authorities from forcing him to have more radiation for a brain tumor. "His very first session almost turned him into a vegetable," she is quoted in news stories. "His head and eyes turned to the right, he couldn't walk and couldn't even feed himself." As treatments continued he became paralyzed. Horrified, the parents took him to another doctor, who gave him Laetrile; after one treatment "he was able to walk for the first time since he'd had the radiation." Instead of rejoicing at the boy's improvement, however, the Dallas County courts demanded custody. Only after weeks of living as fugitives could mother and child return—when the case was dropped.

One of the most publicized cases is that of two-year-old Chad Green of Scituate, Massachusetts, whose leukemia was responding well to natural therapy when the state discovered the heresy and demanded "medical custody," or the right to force chemotherapy on him. He was given spinal injections of a drug so toxic "it turned him into a wild animal," as his mother expressed it. "You'd be holding him in your arms and he'd suddenly bite and scream." He became hoarse, his motor abilities were affected, he dragged one foot, began bumping into things.

After a number of court battles a compromise was reached: the state would continue the drugs, while the parents were allowed to keep the boy at home and use nutritional therapy in an attempt to counteract their terrible side effects. In January 1979, however, when Chad was three, a Massachusetts Superior Court judge ruled their child to be the property of the state, and forbade the parents from using Laetrile and its accompanying program of enzymes and vitamins. A few days later Gerald and Diana Green escaped with their son to Mexico. They left a poignant message for Chad's grandparents:

> When you find this note we will be safely gone. We all know that we cannot endanger Chad's life and comply with a court order that

would not allow us to give him nutritional support. It is clear that the politics involved would take our son's life . . . and that we are to be public examples.

Our country was founded in freedom by free thinkers. We are no less free thinkers than our forefathers, but the country has changed and wants total control even over the food we eat. This ruling should be a warning to all our friends across the nation and angry voices must be heard if anything is to change . . .

The Truth about Chad Green

The Greens put Chad under the care of the holistic oncologist Ernesto Contreras, M.D., whose Tijuana clinic administers physically and spiritually to thousands of cancer refugees. (Many of whom have tried everything else and are in the last stages before they arrive.) Dr. Contreras is a devout Christian; he has built a church, where he personally conducts services all day Sunday and several times a week. He and his staff consider spiritual counseling as important as physical treatment for his patients. Also, contrary to general belief, Dr. Contreras uses conventional therapy when necessary.

In Chad's case, small amounts of chemotherapy were contin- ued, in addition to enzymes, diet and Laetrile. The child imme- diately improved, his health seemed "excellent," according to those who saw him, "no different than any active healthy child his age." But as the months passed the little boy began to grieve; he missed his puppy and his grandparents, began pleading to "go home." He refused to eat, his grandmother says, refused to take his pills. And suddenly, in October (only a few days after a bad fall from a tree), the littlest refugee died.

The loss of this "public example" seemed to fulfill the predic- tions of the courts. Chad Green did not, however, die from lack of chemotherapy; nor did he die from cyanide poisoning. The autopsy showed no cyanide whatever in his system; and actually very little leukemia. In fact, the pathologists could determine no obvious physical cause for his death. But it has been well established that the emotions of a cancer patient play a critical role in recovery. And children are especially prone to stress. Little Chad Green was under tremendous stress. He had been traumatized by the battles over him; he was afraid of the police, who had once taken him physically from his parents, and knew it was dangerous for the family to return to the United States. Yet he longed to "go home." The psychologist who questioned the little boy shortly before his death told the parents of this conflict. "In my opinion the child is destroying himself."

I think it important to note some statistics from the National Cancer Institute: Only one child in five (under fifteen years) with acute leukemia will survive three years—*regardless of what therapy is used.* Two out of three die within three years.

I don't think it unreasonable to conjecture: that had the Greens not been molested—first in their home state of Nebraska, then in Massachusetts, where they had moved in the mistaken belief of more liberal laws there—had they and their doctors been allowed to continue the program under which their son was improving, he could have lived longer. Possibly even been healed. Certainly the whole family would have been spared the agony they so futilely endured.

The Joey Hofbauer Story

"The government wants your child." Another victim, John Hofbauer, spoke those words in opening his address before the Third Annual Cancer Victory Conference in Washington, D.C.

"What is happening to me concerns every parent, because the grounds on which my child was taken from me is Orwellian in concept. It was said during the hearings that all children under the age of eighteen are wards of the state. That all children belong to the state, and when the state wishes to exercise its power it has only to make a phone call or sign a court order. That's exactly what happened to me."

In October 1977, John and Mary Hofbauer of New York State received heartbreaking news. The node on the neck of their seven-year-old was malignant. Joey had a cancer of the lymph glands known as Hodgkins disease. Years before, cancer had struck another of their five children, baby John. The Hofbauers, however, have a strong faith both in God and in the powers of the body to heal itself. With lots of prayer and good nutrition the cancer vanished—to the amazement of the doctors.

Now the doctors were describing what they planned to do to Joey. "The diagnosis alone," says the father, "would have included removal of his spleen, removal of a piece of his liver, the injection of radioactive dye between his toes—which would surround the liver and stay in his system two years—and bone marrow extracts, which are very painful. Five to ten per cent of those who go through the staging procedure, as they call it, die just from the procedure. When children have their spleens removed their chances of dying from infection are enormously increased. Then they would have embarked on a program using nitrogen mustard gas, which was internationally outlawed in World War I as too toxic and inhumane even for the soldiers.

"I was told Joey would be dead within two weeks if I didn't do immediately what they said." When the father hesitated the doctors warned he'd be in serious trouble with the law if he took any other action.

John Hofbauer isn't easily intimidated. He rushed home and began making phone calls, investigating every form of treatment, orthodox and otherwise, both here and abroad. He had been reading about the medical kidnappings; it was partly for Joey's safety that he decided to fly Joey to the Fairfax Medical Center in Montego Bay, Jamaica. The hospital is staffed by West German physicians, biochemists and nutritionists trained by the famous oncologist Dr. Joseph Brown. Laetrile is only a part of the treatment, which includes vitamins, enzymes and diet. Joey responded, and after two weeks he and his father returned, to continue the therapy under the direction of Michael Schachter, M.D., who specializes in holistic medicine. (Later Dr. Schachter was himself the target of health officials, who attempted to seize the records of all his patients and destroy him professionally.)

They found Mary Hofbauer almost on the verge of nervous breakdown. She and her husband were being charged with child abuse! A few evenings later the sheriff and two social workers were at the door. "With a court order to take Joey from us, put him in a foster home that night, and start their barbaric treatments the next day. Resistance meant arrest." After a long confrontation an agreement was reached. The parents would bring their child into the hospital, but no bodily invasion would be made on him until the issue was settled in the courts.

The Hofbauers had little choice. They have other children; they knew if they fled the state all their children might be taken from them. But John Hofbauer called a press conference on the hospital steps. "My son is being imprisoned," he said. "His rights and my rights not to have him poisoned are being violated."

Joey was kept prisoner for ten days. The term is no exaggeration when we realize the hospital threatened to put an armed guard at the door to keep his parents from smuggling in the Laetrile and enzymes Joey needed; and the father himself stationed a twenty-four-hour guard on his son to be sure the doctors did not break their promise not to begin their dread assault. After an unprecedented hearing, Joey was released. The judge ruled his parents could have their son treated metabolically for six months, submitting monthly reports to be checked by an independent oncologist. If during that time Joey seemed to be regressing, the judge could order chemotherapy begun.

The state and the FDA were furious. A battery of thirty lawyers was put to work to have the decision overturned. By February 1978 they had instituted hearings, which dragged on until June, when full hearings were begun. By that time John Hofbauer, "child abuser," had lost his job with the insurance company where he'd formerly been a top man, and was deeply in debt in his fight to save his son. Desperate, he called the National Health Federation, who not only guaranteed legal expenses but provided the expert counsel of Kirkpatrick W. Dilling to back up the family counsel, Leslie Couch. They also brought in some very impressive witnesses who'd had long experience with both Laetrile and nutritional therapy. Among them: Dr. Dean Burk, for thirty years chief cytologist with the National Cancer Institute. Former army surgeon Dr. Thomas J. Roberts, who'd found Laetrile effective in hundreds of cases. And Dr. Harold Manner, who had achieved such impressive results at Loyola.

As phrased by the National Health Federation, "It was the first time orthodox medicine had to defend its course of action." It too was ready, with some of its biggest guns. Seven specialists appeared, to jeer at nutritional therapy as quackery, and pronounce Laetrile "as efficient in curing cancer as Roquefort cheese." Ironically:

One of them was the same doctor who'd first said that without chemotherapy Joey would be dead within two weeks.

Another, that if the first court order were sustained he'd be dead within six months.

A third had actually signed an affidavit that the boy could not survive nine months.

Meanwhile, a robust and lively Joey had to be summoned from school and the baseball field to be examined for traces of the disease.

On cross-examination these doctors were forced to admit: That chemotherapy is toxic enough to kill, can cause sterility and dwarfism, destroy the body's immunity system, and increase up to 29 times the chances for another cancer to develop. That they could give the Hofbauers no assurance that such things wouldn't happen to Joey; in fact, the parents would have to sign a waiver relieving the doctors of responsibility. That they didn't know how much radiation would be required; were woefully ignorant about the proper diet for cancer patients; and knew almost nothing about vitamins A and C, not even the government RDA's. Finally, although claiming cures ranging from 85 to 90 per cent, actually *they don't even have such statistics on little children.*

Judge Loren H. Brown ruled in favor of the parents. In his ten-page decision he made a landmark statement: "Metabolic therapy has a place in our society, and hopefully its proponents are on the first rung of the ladder that will rid us of all forms of cancer."

Important as that is, another part of his decision is vitally important to the Hofbauers. Joey Hofbauer, he ruled, *is not a neglected child.* (The charge on which the state had based its claim.) Rather, the Hofbauers "are loving parents who have devoted more time and energy and have given more thought and concern to the care of their child than would be expected of the ordinary parent."

No Happy Ending

But this victory was short-lived. The New York State Health Department, backed by the FDA, refused to accept defeat.

Instead, they announced they were carrying the case to higher courts—not because they had a better treatment to offer, but because they wanted to confirm their "right" to do what they pleased with this man's child. Their fifteen-page brief argued that the decision set a dangerous precedent in depriving the government of this "right" to overrule parents and attending physicians.

Again they failed. Judge Brown's decision was unanimously upheld. First by the Appellate Division of New York State's Supreme Court; then by its highest court, the Court of Appeals. In all, thirteen New York judges voted to uphold the rights of parents.

It would be nice if this story had a happy ending. But meanwhile terrible harm had been done. John Hofbauer lost his job. The long legal battles cost the family their home; they had to sell and move several times, to meet expenses and avoid harassment. Finally, fearing the decision might go against them, the family was divided, the mother taking Joey to the Bahamas to be sure his treatments could continue. And although Joey had been improving, he developed shingles from the strain, was sometimes afraid to come downstairs for fear "somebody will come to take me away!"

John Hofbauer is outraged by something else that has frightening implications for all parents. "Despite my vindication in court, the state refuses to take my name off the register. . . . Because I chose not to have my son cut up, burned with radiation or poisoned, I'm still accused of child abuse."

He concluded his very moving lecture: "When Joey was first admitted to the hospital for his biopsy, there was a four-year-old girl named Michelle who was diagnosed as having lymphoma, almost the same disease. When we brought Joey back a month later he still looked like a normal, healthy little boy. That little girl who had embarked on the chemotherapy was no longer walking up and down the halls with her grandmother, she was now lying in bed. She'd lost most of her hair, and she was vomiting. And part of what she was vomiting were pieces of her intestines!

"Child abuse? I charge the state of New York with child abuse!"

The Man Who Knows There Is a Cure for Cancer

Dr. Harold Manner, for years chairman of the biology department at Loyola University and still on its staff, was once "about as orthodox as they come." As he tells in interviews, lectures and his book *The Death of Cancer,* he was working on a study of the pollution in Lake Michigan, when he discovered that *all* the pollutants were carcinogenic. This led him into reading in the field of cancer—and a little book that was to change his life. *World Without Cancer,* by Ed Griffin, presented the Laetrile theory:

> That the extract of an apricot kernel—Laetrile or vitamin B_{17}—when taken into the body, circulated around in the blood stream until it met a cancer cell. At the site of the cancer cell, an enzyme, produced by the cancer cell, triggered the release of a deadly compound, called hydrocyanic acid (HCN). This cyanide compound killed the cancer cells. Any cyanide not so used was converted by another enzyme, found primarily in normal cells, to an innocuous compound, sodium thiocyanate, which was promptly excreted in the urine.

Dr. Manner said he laughed—"that anything so simple could even be suggested for anything as complex as cancer." The idea haunted him, however, and he decided to abandon other projects to test it.

His first experiments revealed that Laetrile is *not* toxic, as the FDA claimed. Laboratory mice, injected with ten times the amount of Laetrile ever given human beings anywhere, thrived. None got sick, none died. In fact, after twenty days they were healthier than the control group that hadn't got it! Dr. Manner's report, *The Nontoxicity of Amygdalin,* was published, and copies sent to the National Cancer Institute and the FDA. As I've said, the FDA had done everything possible to balk these tests. Dr. Manner had been involved in legal and scientific confrontations; and on each occasion a certain spokesman made this point firmly: "Gentlemen, the FDA cannot approve this because it is very poisonous." After the publication of Dr. Manner's findings, however, the statement was subtly changed.

"Gentlemen, the FDA cannot approve this because it is an unsafe material."

He was challenged by Dr. Manner. "Dr. Young, you read my report, you know Laetrile isn't toxic." "I didn't say it was *toxic*," the man replied. "I said it was *unsafe*. By unsafe we mean that anybody that uses Laetrile might not use conventional therapy. For this reason we consider it an unsafe compound!" (Exclamation point mine!)

Dr. Manner was now determined to try Laetrile on cancer. It should work. It didn't. To his dismay, he got the same negative results as a number of his colleagues in other institutions. Yet he knew that elsewhere Laetrile was proving successful. Accordingly, he visited Laetrile physicians and clinics around the world. He discovered two things: First, to be effective, *Laetrile was never used by itself,* always with a complete nutritional program. Second, most experiments that failed were using "an improper tumor system." The usual method was to grind up the tumors from cancerous mice, inject those cells into healthy mice, then treat the new tumors. "But that's not the way people get cancer. It usually takes years."

Dr. Manner began ordering thousands of mice from a strain genetically predisposed to breast cancer. A group of graduate students were assigned to do nothing all day but feel the mammary glands of the mice. When a tumor appeared, and only then, the animal was moved to the laboratory. "We never induced cancer." Dr. Manner had also taken a common denominator from all the successful clinics. The Laetrile must be accompanied by vitamin A in emulsified form and a series of enzymes.* When this treatment was followed with his mice a strange thing happened. After four days a white pimple appeared on the tumorous mass; two days later it broke. The pus was analyzed by the pathology department; it proved to be dead cancer cells. As the pus continued to ooze, the tumors shrank. At the end of five weeks 90 per cent of the mice were totally free of cancer, autopsies proved. The other 10 per cent had their cancers in regression.

_____

* Emulsified vitamin A can be safely given in very large doses, since it bypasses the liver. Vitamin A stimulates the body's own immunity system. The enzymes attack the protein shield protecting the tumor.

"I was thrilled," says Dr. Manner. "And you can imagine how my graduate students felt."

These remarkable results were presented in September 1977 before 2,000 people at the annual meeting of the National Health Federation in Chicago. The story made headlines around the world. One, however, was a joint release from the AMA and the FDA: *A blistering attack.* Not on his methods, not even on results, but on the heresy of announcing his findings at a public forum. "These agencies, you see, wanted me to go through the normal scientific channels which I had always used. But I had a specific reason, and I'd do the same thing again. I wasn't about to play games with cancer. It would have taken approximately two years to clear the various medical journals, another two or three for a laboratory to approve and repeat my studies. That's four, maybe five years—and I submit to you that cancer patients don't *have* five years!"

Almost immediately physicians began calling from all over the country. Patients, particularly women with breast cancer, were begging them to try this treatment. Dr. Manner agreed to act as consultant, with one stipulation—that he receive complete reports, which he is filing in a bank vault for evidence. He is now working with many doctors, and thus far most of the patients with breast cancer have recovered as completely as the mice. Two major clinics in Chicago have also been established. One, the American International Hospital, in Zion, Illinois; the other, an outpatient clinic, the Bridgeview Anti-Cancer Center; both using Laetrile therapy with excellent results. The staffs of other hospitals have "come over" to Laetrile-nutrition therapy, Dr. Manner says—for instance, Whitestone General in New York City. Dr. Manner is now president of the Metabolic Research Foundation composed of forty-five physicians who are using this therapy for the patients in their clinics. He also keeps a list of sympathetic physicians, which is growing all the time.

These doctors and these clinics have offered all their data to the FDA. "We can give them every case that comes in, give them the information they need. The interesting thing is—*they know it, and they don't want it.* They're even making every attempt to keep us from continuing. Right now, knowing the enzymes have to be used together with Laetrile and vitamin A, they have banned the enzymes! The intra-tumoral enzyme is no longer available in this country. And I wonder how the FDA can go to sleep at night with the thought of festering women's breasts, women whose tumors were going down, suddenly deprived of the help they need."

Dr. Manner has invited the American Cancer Society to come to the Chicago hospitals and see for themselves. He has challenged the FDA to send their own people, set up their own protocol so there can be no doubt. "All I ask from them is to let the material come into these clinics unimpeded while the tests are going on. And at the end of that time we'll know how effective Laetrile therapy is. If they don't accept that challenge then it's a clear-cut mandate to the people of the United States that *the FDA does not want to know* anything about the efficacy of Laetrile therapy in the treatment of cancer. The most effective anti-cancer treatment I believe that has come along in this entire decade."

Cancer Is No Stranger

Cancer is no stranger to this family. Cancer, caused by radiation, riddled my husband's body, first showing up the year we were married. Young, naïve, taught to blindly "trust your doctor," we went back to Texas, to the physician who'd burned him. Surveying the terrible damage, the doctor advised *even more*. This time ultraviolet lamp treatments and long sunbaths at noon. And blindly we obeyed. Shortly thereafter, this doctor died, leaving us to our lifelong battle. We simply lost count of the many operations to gouge out the huge draining ulcers, then to graft skin from my husband's thighs to his back. Then, when the cancer spread, began to attack deeper areas—more surgery—and more X rays.

It was a vicious circle we should have recognized long before we did. Because what causes cancer, spreads cancer. Except for God and vitamins and an organic diet (as well as the support of dedicated doctors, whatever their methods or convictions), he would not have survived the last twenty years of his life. A time when we saw so many of our friends—many of them younger—

die of heart attacks, strokes or cancer. Often after unspeakable suffering during cancer therapy.

During all this we read almost everything published about malignancy, and attended many cancer conventions, lectures and symposiums. There we were astonished and thrilled to hear the personal stories of people alive and well, who were supposed to be dead! People who'd had "inoperable" cancers. People who'd run the gamut of surgery, radiation, chemotherapy, and—since their own doctors said their cases were hopeless, they had only a short time left—decided, in sheer desperation, to try something else. Or people who, despite dire warnings, simply refused to submit to what seemed to them even more dire treatments.

One was a lovely Australian girl, Louise. After four years of the great American diet she began to feel tired; a malignant breast was discovered and removed. Then a scan revealed bone cancer. She had a year to live; chemotherapy must begin at once. Three different drugs would be used, and there would be side effects. "I'd lose my hair, but they had a drug for that. There would be nausea, but I'd be given an anti-nausea drug. I'd be depressed, but they had a drug for depression." She decided to return home for one last visit, "while I still had my hair, wasn't nauseous and wasn't depressed." The delay, she was warned, could be fatal. And when she returned, the cancer indeed had doubled; it was now in the spine, cervix, lymph glands, whole bone cage. She was about to begin the chemotherapy, even knowing it to be futile, when a friend put her in touch with Dr. Howard Lutz, who had just opened his Institute of Preventive Medicine in Washington, D.C.

He put her on a strictly vegetarian diet, and began giving her massive doses of enzymes and vitamins, "which I believe can control cancer," she said. "This was nearly four years ago. Since then I have never taken a drug of any kind, never had radiation, never been sick a day, never spent a day in bed." (She also had all her hair, which hung in long shining braids.)

Another was Jim, who'd had a malignant tumor removed from his groin. A few months later it came back, even bigger. This time the surgeons removed chunks of muscle and bone, and ordered months of daily X rays, "which made me feel so weak and sick I could hardly stand. Then they discovered the cancer was spreading, they'd better amputate the leg, including the hip, and might have to go after a kidney and the bladder. After that they'd put me on chemotherapy, which would make me very sick, but just might save me. I started to pray—I still had a family to support, it was a very tough time."

Reservations were made at the hospital. But before he could keep them a friend called to tell him about her uncle, a college professor, who'd once had a brain tumor that was supposed to kill him. When all else failed he'd flown to Dr. Krebs in California for Laetrile treatments. "He recovered and went back to teaching—in fact, had just retired after a long career."

Jim didn't have the money to go very far, so he began frantically trying to find a doctor nearby who could obtain the Laetrile and was willing to try it. "When I canceled that reservation at the hospital my original doctor said I was crazy. He got my wife on the phone and told her she'd be co-signing my death warrant if she didn't stop me. . . . My new doctor completely changed my diet—no more fats whatever, and mostly raw vegetables, gave me vitamins and enzymes and some chelation." (An IV procedure that cleanses the blood.) "That was over two years ago. I've been back at work for a year, in a job that requires climbing in and out of trucks. I've still got two legs to do it with, thank God. In fact, my wife and I have started disco dancing.

"I don't say I'm cured—not yet. But I can say I'm alive and feeling great—something nobody would have believed a few years ago."

First, Do No Harm

Inspiring, yet sobering, is the testimony of doctors who spent years in the practice of orthodox medicine before realizing there *are* effective alternatives. Dr. Ahmad Shamin, himself a surgeon, is one. He says surgery is sometimes necessary, but in most cases it just removes the symptoms, it doesn't eliminate the disease. "If you survive the surgery it's not because of surgery, but because of your own immunity system. You survive *in spite of* the surgery." He told the story of a boy whose cancer had spread from his arm to his shoulder. The doctors decided he was too far gone to operate. "He was fortunate. He's alive and well today—ironically because he was beyond the reach of the surgeon's knife!"

Even a simple biopsy can spread the cancer. There are equally reliable blood and urine tests for malignancy.

Dr. Shamin has led in the fight to legalize Laetrile and to recognize the value of nutritional therapy. (Shockingly, the National Cancer Institute did almost no nutritional research for thirty-five years, until Congress ordered them to in 1974. Only to discover that at least half of all cancers are caused by a bad diet.) Dr. Shamin says nutrition, the oldest form of medicine, will be the medicine of the future.

Even more sobering are the experiences of medical doctors of the highest caliber who have been persecuted, raided, their supplies confiscated, their hospital privileges denied, their licenses revoked, their clinics closed. Physicians who have even been jailed for the crime of offering their patients hope and relief by any method not officially approved. In some cases for simply providing the Laetrile which gave them relief from pain, and which might and often did prolong lives.

I want to be fair. I know there are a lot of women (some of them my friends) who have had mastectomies, some of them years ago. No doubt the procedure saved them. I also know there are countless other people whose cancers may be under control after going the traditional route, with no discernible damage from the methods used. *Methods that any good, scrupulous metabolic doctor will also use when absolutely necessary.* Always fortified, however, by the proper vitamins, minerals and nutrition.

Such people are the fortunate third. Remember that the majority—two out of three—who submit to orthodox methods do *not* survive. I have also been very close to cancer victims who were mutilated, burned, violently poisoned, starved, given no supportive nutritional help and suffered the torments of the damned before they died.

The stern admonition of Hippocrates was: "First, do no harm." Laetrile, even if it never saved a human life, does not inflict such harm.

The Fate of Laetrile

Laetrile has been legal in at least twenty-seven medically advanced countries for years. Nineteen of our own states have approved its use; and in 1978 a landmark decision by Judge Bohanan in western Oklahoma ruled that it was *not* a new drug, as claimed; that the FDA's banning of its interstate sale and shipment was "arbitrary, capricious, an abuse of discretion . . . and not in accordance with the law."

The case had been brought on behalf of Glen Rutherford and other terminally ill cancer patients, to establish their right to have this medication. The FDA carried the case to the Supreme Court. On June 18, 1979, the court announced a decision widely interpreted as a victory for anti-Laetrile forces; certainly as a victory for all those who want to deny patients that right. The court ruled that federal drug laws make no exception from their safety and effectiveness requirements just because somebody is believed to be dying.

This in a nation that has always been the whole world's model of personal liberty.

Even before this decision, syndicated columnist James J. Kilpatrick expressed it well:

> Our government's position is unbelievably pompous, dictatorial and hoity-toity. Imagine, if you will, a patient who falls victim to cancer. The patient goes through every treatment recommended by the medical establishment. . . . Nothing works. The patient is dying. . . . In desperation, he says, "I have heard of other cancer victims who seem to get relief from pain, and sometimes remission, from laetrile. Please, may I try that now?" Our government's response, to put it plain, is precisely: Go to hell. Die! We say laetrile is worthless, therefore you can't have it, and we will prosecute any doctor or supplier who tries to make it available to you.
>
> The gut issue here is freedom. By every rational indication, amygdalin is harmless. . . . In the name of a free society, why can't a free people have it if they want it?

What was not brought out by the news media, however, is the fact the court did *not* reverse the Bohanan decision. Rather, dealt only with the issue of making exceptions for the gravely ill.

The case was sent back to lower courts for consideration of the "grandfather" clause (concerning the right of a government agency to judge a substance used before the FDA came into existence; whether or not amygdalin is really a new drug, as claimed).† It may not be settled for years.

Why All the Opposition?

There will be other lawsuits, other court decisions. Meanwhile, people will suffer. Because, as pointed out by Congressman Ross MacDonald (a medical doctor himself, who was viciously attacked and almost lost his license for prescribing Laetrile)— "When a medical mistake is made by an individual only the patient and his family are affected. But when a mistake is made on a national scale thousands of people are hurt and time is wasted. It takes millions of dollars and sometimes years of court battles before that mistake is corrected."

Eventually, however, truth prevails. I predict that someday the cut-burn-poison methods of treating cancer will be considered as barbaric as bloodletting or throwing the mentally ill into pits of snakes. That the vendetta conducted against nutritional therapy and Laetrile will seem as preposterous as the persecution of Pasteur and Semmelweis and Harvey, the horsewhipping of Edward Jenner, or the jeering at a "moldy bread" called penicillin and a "quack gadget" now known as the indispensable EEG. That someday use of simple but successful vitamin B_{17} will be as common as allergy shots or inoculations. Moreover, that other non-damaging methods of treating cancer (Laetrile is just one of many) will be in common use.

To name only a few:

Vitamins A and C, discussed in other chapters. . . . Mercenene, an extract from clams discovered by a Dominican nun, Sister Arlene Schmeer. . . . Benzaldehyde (one component of amygdalin), giving promising results in Japan. . . . Blood serum injections, developed by Dr. Lawrence Burton, which help the body's own defense system destroy the cancer

† Maureen Salaman, president of the Coalition for Alternative Therapy, cites drug industry records dating back to 1907 which refer to amygdalin (Laetrile), and even antique apothecary jars stamped *Amygdalin.*

cells. . . . The trace mineral selenium, found to be effective by a number of scientists and physicians, especially Dr. Emanuel Revici at New York's Institute of Biological Research.

But why did the War on Cancer turn out to be a "war on cancer cures"? as expressed by Gary Null in a very important series in *Penthouse* in the fall of 1979 (a magazine I don't normally read). And why did it turn its biggest guns on Laetrile, instead of the enemy it was declared to conquer? The reasons are complex, but not really very hard to understand.

For one, sheer face. The FDA, the AMA, the National Cancer Institute and the American Cancer Society all came out strongly against Laetrile twenty-five years ago. (In fact, despite billions spent on "research" these agencies resist *any* therapy that does not include expensive drugs and technology. A stated purpose of the American Cancer Society is to strengthen laws against "worthless cancer remedies *and tests.*" Italics mine.)* To produce a simple solution to so monstrous a killer after all the denunciations—and all that money—would be a devastating blow. Public confidence in their authority would be shattered.

Enormous bureaucracies, fund-raising groups and research institutions devote their entire time to cancer. A cure, especially a simple one, would be worse than an embarrassment— they would have no further excuse for being.

For another, cancer is big business. Our number two killer. Our most expensive disease. And according to official statistics, *over 1,200 Americans are dying from it every day.* In fact, even that appalling number may be conservative. A spokesman for the National Cancer Institute acknowledged it is probably much higher, could very well be as high as 475,000 a year.

Yet more people make their living from cancer than die from cancer. The American Cancer Society alone takes in mind-boggling sums from donations. Its 1978–79 budget was

---

* The American Cancer Society's book *Unproved Methods of Cancer Management* appears to be a euphemism for "quackery." Gary Null writes, "This unproven-methods list is in effect a blacklist of remedies that include some of the most promising methods for control of cancer in the world today . . . Once a treatment gets on this list, it becomes virtually impossible for any of its proponents to continue their research." This despite the fact that 90 per cent of those proponents hold bona fide medical or scientific degrees.

$149,171,000. (Try for a minute to visualize nearly *a hundred and fifty* million dollars!) It maintains a huge staff with generous expense accounts and handsome salaries; spends millions on administration, public relations, parties, publications, fund raising and advertising. While the actual victims of cancer are multimillion-dollar consumers of enormously expensive services, technology, hospitalization, medical fees and drugs.

As far as Laetrile is concerned, I am neither a scientist nor a doctor. I can only report what I have experienced, or learned from my research. But it seems to me flagrantly unfair that these agencies and the FDA should practice a double standard. Laetrile should not be used, they claim, because it is toxic. Yet Laetrile is "remarkably non-toxic, compared with virtually all cancer chemotherapeutic agents," says Dr. Dean Burk, whose long experience at the National Cancer Institute should make him an authority. The government's own brief before the court could come up with only three instances of presumed "toxicity." One the death of an eleven-month-old girl, whose hospital records don't show she ever swallowed Laetrile at all. A toxicologist from the Division of Poison Control wrote me, "I have reviewed the details of this case and am not convinced they showed what they were purported to."

Actually, *every other substance commonly used in treating cancer* is violently poisonous. If in doubt, read *Physicians' Desk Reference,* where the horrible dangers of these lethal drugs are graphically spelled out for pages; together with the admission they may actually *cause* cancer, and even kill patients.

It seems to me preposterous that the FDA should license such drugs as "safe and effective" at the same time it denounces Laetrile and tries to deny people their right to get it. Certainly there should be no persecution of doctors who try to provide it. In fact, when any qualified physician wants to try *any* thoroughly tested therapy he has investigated and believes to be effective, there is no moral justification for the government to interfere.

Laetrile is not a patented drug. Such doctors are not getting rich on it. (Or on selenium or diet or any of the other non-drug therapies.) Indeed, they could make far more money and spare themselves endless time, expense and grief by simply following the party line. It is not these courageous men and women who are profiting from cancer. But a lot of people are.

The Washington *Post* reports a symposium for stock market analysts in Philadelphia. A featured speaker was Dr. Stanley Crooke, whose company, Bristol Myers, manufactures cancer drugs. He reminded the investment-minded that cancer "is the second most common cause of death in developed nations," and as its incidence increases so do the number of doctors and others specializing in its treatment. "The number of patients receiving appropriate chemotherapy will increase, and is increasing exponentially," he promised. "The impact of these changes [sales] is obvious." The title of his talk: *Cancer Chemotherapy: Market and Product Opportunities.*

How to Prevent and Overcome Cancer

Don't become an "opportunity." Hundreds of cancer cells swarm our bodies constantly; yet God has given us a marvelous defense system against all disease. He also expects us to defend *ourselves*. As Dr. Ronald Raven, chairman of the Royal College of Surgeons in London, has stated, "75% of all cancer can be prevented if we utilize the facts we now possess." Here are the major ones:

• Exercise. Exercise delivers oxygen to the cells. Cancerous tumors, like fungus, grow best where there is little oxygen.

• Don't smoke. Or breathe the smoke of those who do.

• Don't take any drug, even aspirin, unless absolutely necessary.

• Avoid radiation. It accumulates. Submit to X rays only when absolutely necessary.

• Avoid alien chemicals in your body. Insofar as possible eat foods organically raised, foods free of cancer-causing substances.

• Cut down on meats. This not only cuts down on chemicals, it cuts down on proteins. Cancerous tumors are protein. Less meat frees your pancreatic enzymes to "digest" them so they can be expelled.

• Eat plenty of fruits and vegetables, especially raw. Cooking destroys their precious enzymes, so important to preventing and overpowering cancer. Eat some raw fruits or vegetables with every meal.

• Build up your body's immunity system with vitamins and minerals. Cancer victims are generally found to be very low in both. The minerals selenium and zinc are especially important; so are the detoxifying and oxygenizing vitamins A, C, E and B_{15}.

• Eat whole grains and seeds. Especially the seeds of fruit—apricot pits, if you can get them. Grains and seeds (with the exception of seeds of citrus fruits) contain the vital nitrilosides or vitamin B_{17} that will destroy cancer cells.

• Think positively, hope, plan. Believe God wants you to be well. Visualize the remarkable defenses of your own body. Thank him for them—and for your smallest blessings. Refuse to harbor destructive thoughts. Rejoice, forgive, love. When we walk in harmony with the creator and giver of life, we exist in a state of healing.

All these are things any good metabolic doctor will tell you to do to protect yourself from cancer—and to overcome it, should it strike.

12

C, the Wonder Vitamin

Let's suppose somebody announced the discovery of a new wonder drug. One that would make most of the other drugs on the market obsolete. A product for which the following claims could be made. That it:

Boosted energy
Built strong bones
Healed wounds and burns
Cleared the blood of poisons
Lowered cholesterol
Aided diabetics
Relieved and cured allergies
Prevented blood clots, strokes, heart attacks and cataracts
Prevented and cured cancer
Prevented and cured the common cold
Relieved arthritis
Overcame infections
Helped epileptics and schizophrenics
Relieved backache, muscle spasms and disc lesions
Repaired the damage done by smoking, alcohol and drugs
Prolonged life

The FDA wouldn't allow it. The drug manufacturers would be furious. Cries of "snake oil!" would go up; nobody would believe it. The inventor would have to break the stuff down and aim for single ailments; and *it would have to be expensive.* That is one of the major drawbacks to establishment acceptance of vitamin C, which can and does accomplish all the above. (In *addition* to its job of aiding every process in the body.) Good heavens, a substance that can be extracted from common foods! The hierarchy in any field have always felt threatened when someone dares to reveal that what they have made complicated rare and costly can be replaced and even improved on by something simple, available and cheap. If vitamin C could be manufactured from expensive chemicals and sold for the prices we pay for drugs, it would be the most widely advertised remedy on the market.

Yet name any human affliction, including cancer, and you will find a cluster of scientists who have shown that one of its major causes was lack of sufficient vitamin C. And that, by restoring enough of that vitamin, the condition can be cured or tremendously relieved. Their papers multiply like the guinea pigs on which they experiment so often.* Hundreds of articles and whole books are written about their findings. Yet the more the evidence accumulates, the louder the denials from those who do no research themselves and refuse to acknowledge the research of others: "There is no evidence!" An attitude that brings to mind the rhyme written about the famous Dr. Jowett, erstwhile master of Balliol College, Oxford:

> My name is Jowett,
> I am the master of this college.
> There's no knowledge but I know it.
> If I don't know it, it isn't knowledge!

* Guinea pigs are ideal for such experiments, since, like man, they are one of the few animals which can't manufacture their own vitamin C. Ironically, to keep these guinea pigs in good health, they are given 50 times more vitamin C than the official recommended daily allowance for man.

The Stormy History of Vitamin C

Poor vitamin C. This first child of the vitamin family came to light more than four hundred years ago, yet was among the last to be named. In 1536 Jacques Cartier, who discovered the St. Lawrence River, found his men dying of scurvy, just as thousands of sailors before had perished after spending many months at sea without fresh food. His men recovered only when friendly Indians fed them a tea brewed from the arborvitae tree —a plant now recognized to be rich in vitamin C. It was not until our own century, however, in the 1920s that the acidic substance which prevents scurvy was finally isolated by Dr. Albert Szent-Györgyi and christened ascorbic acid—or vitamin C. (His achievement won him the Nobel Prize in 1937.)

During that four-hundred-year interval countless wars had to be waged before medical authorities finally acknowledged there *was* something alive and well in fruits and vegetables which was absolutely essential to overcoming that fatal disease. Nor have the battles let up much in the half century since the poor kid was finally *named.*

That vitamin C can also do a lot of other things for us has been the subject of fervent claims and scornful denials. This faithful servant has been praised and damned, declared worthless and a cure-all; been debated, discussed, written about and fought over perhaps more than any other single issue in the field of health. Maybe because it's the most commonly found vitamin in food; maybe because, in addition to its basic task of triggering the mechanism that makes that food usable, so many people are convinced of its versatile therapeutic powers. But the thing that gets most people worked up is whether or not it really helps knock out mankind's oldest enemy, the common cold.

Vitamin C and the Common Cold

In 1970 Dr. Linus Pauling's book by the above title made headlines and added fuel to the fires of debate. In his book he presented a staggering amount of data to prove that vitamin C *can and does.* Now this man was no quack. The American College of

Physicians had given him a gold medal for his contributions to internal medicine; the French Medical Academy another for his work in anesthesiology—to name but a few of his worldwide honors. Furthermore, he had twice won the Nobel Prize, the only person to be so distinguished. It seems amazing, therefore, that so many of his colleagues denounced his work as worthless, and continue to do so to this day.

Pauling was a controversial figure; his book commanded attention in much the same way as Rachel Carson's *Silent Spring.* In both cases these highly qualified researchers were simply making the public aware of things which others had been trying to tell us for years: Chemicals are poisoning our planet. And vitamin C (ascorbic acid) *is* an answer to our most chronic tormentor, the cold.

They succeeded in arousing people. The Carson book added so much vigor to the ecology movement that many thought she'd started it. Pauling's sent so many converts rushing to the store for ascorbic acid the supplies ran out. A lot of those who hadn't read his book but heard about it actually had the impression he had discovered this "marvelous new cure."

The fact is, as Pauling relates in that book and its successor, *Vitamin C, the Common Cold, and the Flu,* he didn't become interested in vitamin C until 1966, when he and his wife began taking it, on the recommendation of the biochemist Irwin Stone. "We noticed an increased feeling of well-being, and especially a striking decrease in the number of colds that we caught, and in their severity." Intrigued, he began an intensive investigation of all the experiments that had been made with this vitamin, dating back to the forties.

> I found that a number of excellent studies had been carried out, and that most of them showed that vitamin C does have value in controlling the common cold. My concern about the failure of the medical authorities to pay the deserved attention to the existing evidence caused me to write my book.

Those studies are detailed in his later volume, which may be even more valuable, for in it he shows how effective vitamin C can be against the flu as well. Pauling also reports on an article which appeared in *Fact* magazine for July–August 1967. The author, Dr. Douglas Gildersleeve, reported that he personally had been able to suppress colds with his own patients using 20 or 25 times as much vitamin C as had been used in previous studies, stating: "It is my contention that an effective treatment for the common cold, a cure, is available, that is being ignored because of the monetary losses that would be inflicted on pharmaceutical manufacturers, professional journals, and doctors themselves."

Dr. Gildersleeve backed up his contention by pointing out that a previous paper on the subject had been rejected by eleven professional journals, one of whose editors frankly told him it would be unwise for them to print it, since a large part of their advertising came from the makers of cold remedies. (Americans spend $700 million a year on non-prescription cold remedies, not counting aspirin; and even more on prescription drugs to fight the common cold.)

After Pauling first published his findings, a number of scientists rushed back to their laboratories; some, as they later acknowledged, in an attempt to prove him wrong. One, conducted by Canadian doctors Anderson, Reid and Barton, was of particular interest since Dr. Barton had attacked Dr. Pauling's book in a review. The doctors had tested the vitamin using doses of only 200 milligrams—amounts Pauling told them were too small. The three decided to meet Dr. Pauling's challenge to use more. As reported in the British medical journal *The Lancet,* and the *Canadian Medical Association Journal,* the results were "entirely unexpected," confirming the fact that large doses of vitamin C "were indeed effective in preventing and curing colds."

Another test, conducted in Glasgow, caused *The Lancet* again to report: "The results obtained are clear-cut in favor of vitamin C as a positive agent in reducing the incidence and duration of the common cold." In *every* experiment where *enough* vitamin C was given, the results were exactly as Pauling predicted. Yet even today detractors still talk about the tests that "failed." A particular favorite is an experiment at the University of Minnesota, where 400 students were given 200 milligrams a day for six months; "and most of them still got colds." In a popular version the figures are grossly distorted; and the fact is always ignored that even on so small an amount, 15 per cent were helped.

Dr. Pauling has pointed out that doctors are programmed to think of ascorbic acid in the tiny amounts that prevent scurvy— 5 to 15 milligrams. To them 200 milligrams seems a lot. Yet in combating colds the tissues must be saturated; it takes at least a gram a day (1,000 milligrams) and in some cases three or four.

The Vitamin C Pioneers

Every vitamin C advocate is, of course, extremely grateful that a Nobel Prize winner was finally able to wake people up to its wonders. But Dr. Pauling himself is the first to admit that the real credit should go to those who were busy in their laboratories and reporting their findings long ago. For one, his own friend Dr. Irwin Stone, who spent ten years on his book *The Healing Factor: Vitamin C Against Disease.* Another, J. W. McCormick, M.D., who was publishing his discoveries about what vitamin C was able to do for disc lesions in 1954. Certainly the North Carolina physician Fred R. Klenner, who began using massive doses of vitamin C to fight infections and detoxify poisons (including snakebites) in 1950. Dr. Klenner has given his cold patients 10 grams or more of vitamin C for years, without side effects and with 90 per cent cures.

All these men, and others, have lectured widely about their findings, and presented their evidence in leading scientific journals repeatedly. It seems incredible, therefore, that both the medical establishment and the FDA have remained completely impervious to this knowledge that could help so many, and even continue to denounce and scorn the use of vitamin C.

One of the earliest people to point out that this vitamin was an antihistamine that could be of great benefit in treating colds and allergies was not an M.D., however, but a nutritionist and Ph.D. Carlton Fredericks was declaring this in his columns and his broadcasts way back in 1941. And leafing through my accumulated issues of *Prevention,* I find articles dating back to the fifties reporting on scientific studies which proved beyond any reasonable doubt that ascorbic acid was not only the best possi-

ble treatment for colds, but successful in treating every affliction listed at the head of this chapter—and more.

The Swine Flu Scandal

If more people had listened to Linus Pauling and others who
warned against mass vaccination, we might have been spared
the 1976 swine flu scandal. A fiasco which cost taxpayers $135
million for a worthless vaccine which was administered to 40
million people, sickened and paralyzed thousands and claimed
some 120 lives.

Only a few people in command of the health and welfare of
the nation took into consideration a fact that almost any school-
child should know: That colds and flu—any kind of flu—are
caused by viruses; and the first stage of flu is always a cold.
Hence, whatever protects the body against the cold in the first
place, is more likely than not to protect the body against the flu.

One exception was Dr. Theodore Cooper, then Assistant Secretary for Health. He publicly stated that, although backing the
immunizations, he and his family took vitamin C. As reported in
Medical Tribune, they took it

> as a most valuable adjunct to enhancing human resistance to influ-
> enza and other viral infections. . . . I believe Pauling's thesis. . . .
> I believe that C adequacy may be helpful in reducing or preventing
> infections. . . . I think you will find many people in practice em-
> ploy vitamin supplementation. In the absence of specific data to the
> contrary, they do not wait for the full evidence required for official
> actions by government agencies.

He felt it was his duty to support President Ford's program, but
he felt another duty to inform the public that he was hedging
his own bets with vitamin C. Taken "in fairly large doses" too.

He was, of course, contradicting the AMA, which had issued
this statement only the previous year: "Vitamin C will not prevent or cure the common cold." Of more immediate conse-
quence, he was bucking the FDA, who immediately retorted,
"There is no scientific evidence and never have been any mean-
ingful studies indicating that vitamin C is capable of preventing
or curing colds (much less flu)."

There were other voices which opposed or seriously questioned the inoculation program. Dr. Sidney M. Wolfe, director of the Public Citizens Health Research Group, exposed a widely publicized story of an "outbreak" of the disease at Fort Dix as untrue; and cautioned, "The vaccine against swine flu has not yet been tested for safety and effectiveness in human beings." He was ignored. According to *The Swine Flu Affair* (an investigative report by HEW in 1978),† government epidemiologists who were skeptical or unenthusiastic were "lambasted for disloyalty." While Anthony Morris, an FDA virologist whose job was to evaluate the effectiveness of vaccines, was fired. (He'd said he had never seen a vaccine that worked against any kind of flu.)

The government went bulling on with its program even after the vaccinations began felling victims; and didn't call it off until the toll was high enough to arouse public outrage.

From the beginning, Dr. Pauling had advised: "It now seems quite unlikely that there will be a swine flu epidemic." There wasn't. "And there is now little justification for recommending mass vaccination." Nobody listened.

As a result some 500 people were stricken with Guillain-Barre syndrome (a form of paralysis), more than 100 died, and the government is facing several thousand lawsuits by the victims, which will cost at least an estimated $2 billion.

Just What IS a Cold?

Let's look for a moment at the malady which makes so many people so miserable on an average of three times a year. This curse, which may be "just a cold" lasting a few wretched days—or may be the first symptom of more serious troubles: bronchitis, pneumonia, strep throat or several varieties of the flu, some of them killers. As Pauling says, nobody ever died of a cold; "influenza (the flu) on the other hand is a very serious and dangerous disease."

† By Richard Neustadt and Harvey Fineberg, two Harvard professors commissioned by HEW Secretary Joseph Califano. They sharply criticize the haste with which the program was put together and the high-pressure tactics used on President Ford by doctors at the Center for Disease Control.

The common cold itself is caused by a virus known medically as *rhinovirus. (Rhino* is from the Greek word for nose.) Medical textbooks tell us there are at least 100 strains of this virus, plus a number of other things non-viral in origin, which can invade the respiratory tract. There the virus tries to take over the cells, and if it is successful, produces more viruses. The body fights back in the very ways that make us most miserable—raising the temperature and washing out the invaders by means of mucus (in which are also embedded our own white blood cells slain in the efforts to defend us). We ache, sweat, shiver, cough, sneeze, blow our noses until the battle is finally over. And unless we are well fortified by strong tissue cells in the beginning, plus plenty of white blood cells, the battle may be long and fierce.

The exact number and variety of cold viruses isn't known, which is why no single cold vaccine helps much—it can attack only one virus, which may not be the one you have. Vitamin C is effective against *most* of them—at least 90 per cent, it is believed—but that still leaves 10 per cent that may not yield. There is, therefore, no guarantee that ascorbic acid will prevent every cold for everybody at all times. It is also true that a few lucky people seldom if ever get colds, simply because they are immune to most of these viruses.

The vast majority of us *are* susceptible, however. Personally, from childhood, I could count on at least two major colds a year, one of which was almost certain to put me in bed for a week or more with the flu. Not to mention the in-between miseries of minor colds. No more. For years now I've been able to stop every cold in its tracks by immediately taking plenty of vitamin C. Often just before some important occasion when the stress involved seems to aggravate the symptoms.

Once a TV station called saying they'd had a cancellation; could I possibly do their early show the next morning? I accepted when they said they'd provide a limousine for the two-hour pre-dawn ride. By dinnertime I realized, to my horror, I was coming down with a cold. Chills, stuffy nose, even a sore throat. Resolving, "I can't, I won't!" and rebuking the invader with prayers—which are just as important—I began the attack: Gargling with vinegar and salt, and taking a gram of vitamin C, followed by 500 milligrams every half hour until bedtime; then a gram every time I awoke. By morning every symptom was gone, and never returned.

I have had similar experiences before a major speech or just before starting a tour. *In every instance* God and vitamins, but particularly vitamin C, have made it possible to go on. It's also important to remember that my whole immunity system has improved. Thanks to exercise, a better diet and all the vitamins and minerals, I have built up my own resistance until now I very seldom have even the first symptoms of a cold.

How Vitamin C Fights Colds and Flu

Just *how* vitamin C fights colds for us is intriguing. Let us count the ways:

• First, through *interferon*. That incredible stuff which the cell manufactures literally to keep hostile bacteria from penetrating and multiplying. (Or "interfering.") For this the cell must have copious amounts of vitamin C. Dr. Benjamin Siegel, a research scientist at the University of Oregon Health Sciences Center, calls interferon the body's first line of defense. He told Dominick Bosco, writing in *Prevention,* "Before the body is even producing any antibodies, interferon can just wipe out the disease. But the body has to be producing *enough* interferon."

A husband-wife biochemical team at Stanford University demonstrated how vitamin C affects this process. Dr. and Mrs. Carlton Schwerdt treated human cell cultures with vitamin C for several days, then infected the cells with rhinovirus. They discovered that the viruses went through one growth cycle, then were inhibited in their ability to reproduce. The cells without vitamin C, however, merrily multiplied 40 times over.

Ironically, the drug companies have awakened to the wonderful possibilities of interferon. They are calling it a "medical breakthrough," and a "wonder drug in the class with penicillin," as they busily try to duplicate it in their laboratories. They are backed by statements such as that of Dr. Thomas Merigan, chief of the Division of Infectious Diseases at Stanford University—"This is the first agent known to protect against common cold infections in man"—and of Dr. Eliot Larson, of the Clinical Research Center in London, who called it "the first really useful anti-viral agent." Yes—the industrialists acknowledge—the body itself manufactures interferon, but not enough for practical purposes, they claim.

There's money in them there pills. Nobody bothers to mention that your body *will* manufacture enough of this "miracle drug" if you give it plenty of ordinary vitamin C.

• Our *white blood cells* compose the second line of defense to which vitamin C is vital. It's well known that these cells which fight infection accumulate ascorbic acid. But only recently have scientists found that additional vitamin C stimulates the lymphocytes and leukocytes to greater activity. And that it can prevent actual further damage from the phagocytes—those white cells which engorge and destroy enemy bacteria, but sometimes merely deposit the infection somewhere else. Researchers at the Bowman-Gray School of Medicine in Winston-Salem, North Carolina, discovered that when such cells were isolated and treated with ascorbic acid, their disease-fighting capacities were intensified. And the greater the infection, the greater the need for vitamin C.

• A third way in which vitamin C fights colds is in its capacity as an *antihistamine.* This has been graphically demonstrated. When vitamin C and the histamine are put together in a test tube they will destroy each other. Some people even dissolve a vitamin C tablet and squirt the liquid up the nose to relieve congestion.

• A fourth way, closely related, is in the effect of vitamin C on our *adrenal gland.* This gland contains and uses more vitamin C than any other part of the body. It also produces the hormones we need in times of stress. The stress of a cold, an allergy or any viral infection makes the adrenal work so hard it quickly runs out of vitamin C. Carlton Fredericks writes: "It is possible that the high dosage of vitamin C is not only destroying histamine, but helping to support the one gland that secretes the most powerful antiallergy hormone known, the cortisone group."

To me, all this is fascinating; and in view of it I marvel that anyone with any pretension to authority could still declare vitamin C to be useless in fighting colds. The proof, however, rests in the results. Dr. Robert Cathcart III, a Nevada orthopedic surgeon, told the California Orthomolecular Medical Society that he doesn't know exactly why vitamin C succeeds so well when other remedies don't, but that he does know that if *enough* vitamin C is given it will detoxify the virus and leave the patient well without any side effects.

He also threw light on the possible reason so many elderly patients died from the swine flu vaccine. First testing himself and his daughter to make sure there was plenty of vitamin C in their bodies, he then administered the vaccine. Testing again the following day, he discovered the vaccine had practically wiped out their supply of this vitamin! Elderly people are often very deficient in vitamin C. It is his hypothesis that there may not have been enough ascorbic acid in their systems to protect them against the stress of inoculation; for immunizations, no matter how necessary, do present the body with severe stress.

Not a one of Dr. Cathcart's 5,000 patients ever had to be hospitalized because of a viral disease. And although he has administered massive doses, he has never seen a case of vitamin C-caused kidney stones, gallstones, anemia or any of the other complications critics claim. Patients sometimes do develop diarrhea—a harmless signal they're getting more than they need.

Vitamin C and Emergencies

I wish I had time and space to deal with each of the items listed at the head of this chapter. There is recorded proof of what vitamin C can do for every one of them, and even more. Right now let me share a personal experience of what God and vitamin C can do for burns.

One night when my husband was out of town the oil furnace stopped. By morning the house was cold, and puddles of black oil were seeping out under the furnace-room door. My husband drove up right after I'd phoned the fuel company, but unfortunately he tried to fix it before they arrived. Suddenly the whole thing blew up in his face with a window-rattling *boom!* Then black smoke, then flames. He grabbed a throw rug and tried to beat out the fire while I ran for the salt (somehow remembering that sodium chloride is a good extinguisher). In a few minutes we had the blaze stopped, but his hair was singed off, his face and arms were as black as the oily pall settling through the house. He was, we saw, badly burned.

It was Saturday, and as usual he refused to let me call a doctor. I did call Shreve, however, who told me to give him plenty of vitamin C. "At least 500 milligrams every half hour, he's got to replace that cortisone. And use vitamin E ointment if you have it; if not, break the capsules open and rub them on."

We cleaned my husband up and did just that. He also drank lots of liquids and rested that afternoon—*so we could go to a party that night.* It was madness, I protested, he should be in a hospital; but as I've said before, he was a brave and stubborn man. We went—and his scorched cheeks and singed hair were the conversation piece of the party. Sunday he continued to rest, meanwhile consuming large quantities of liquids and all his vitamins, particularly C. Through all this he had almost no pain. He didn't even blister. Monday he was back at work. I had, of course, been praying. It was an almost incredible combination of God and vitamins.

I realize this can be scoffed at as "anecdotal medicine." Yet the healing power of vitamin C for burns and other emergencies is being demonstrated in medical circles every day. Dr. David H. Klasson, surgeon of Greenpoint Hospital in Brooklyn, reported in the *New York State Journal of Medicine* that by applying vitamin C solutions to the skin, or giving it by mouth or injection, he had found this vitamin superior to the most powerful drugs. Even better than sulfa for healing, or morphine for pain.

Any emergency requires copious amounts of vitamin C. Cuts, surgery, broken bones, shocks or overdoses, even snakebites or stings—all draw instantly and heavily upon the body's supply. Every inch of us is held together by a cement known as collagen, which can't be manufactured or maintained without vitamin C. When a bone or muscle is injured this collagen must be promptly repaired and replaced; flesh can't grow back around the wounds otherwise. This alone requires vast amounts of ascorbic acid. Vitamin C is also needed to detoxify poisons, whether swallowed by mouth or received from a venomous bite or sting.

No matter what the emergency, vitamin C sends out its rescue squads to prevent infection, to reject the foreign substance, to heal, rebuild. It is able to do so much partly by triggering the vitamin C-rich adrenal gland into producing more of the hormones we need to combat the stress. Because any kind of accident or shock creates tremendous physical and emotional stress. Scientists like Irwin Stone tell us that animals which produce their own vitamin C actually triple it in times of stress.

Our whole endocrine system begins to burn up vitamins. And this is true not only of the victim, but of other people who are emotionally involved. In our fear and concern, we too use up lots of vitamin C, which has to be replaced.

Have We Really Licked Scurvy?

It is commonly assumed that scurvy is a disease of the history books, like the black plague. True, sailors no longer die of this dread affliction which claimed more lives than all the sailors lost in battle in all the wars.‡ Yet doctors are finding symptoms of scurvy in patients today, even among the well-to-do.

Typical is the case of a retired army officer, as reported in *Annals of Thoracic Surgery.* He was suffering with a hiatal hernia, stomach problems and depression. The physician also found lesions on his legs; his gums bled and his wounds healed slowly. He admitted living mostly on mashed potatoes, peanut butter and baby foods. No fruits and vegetables, no supplements. He was developing scurvy just as surely as those ancient sailors—due to lack of vitamin C. His doctor, Clement A. Herbert, said, "The study of human scurvy (vitamin C deficiency) can be frustratingly slow in an affluent society"—where it's assumed everybody gets enough vitamin C.

Prevention magazine sent Joan Jennings to England to interview the distinguished researcher-physician Dr. Geoffrey Taylor. "Chronic intermittent scurvy," he told her, far from being obsolete, is becoming a commonplace disease. During his years with the Indian Medical Service he had observed famines throughout the world and become familiar with the *look* of

‡ People on land also suffered from scurvy. It was their scurvy-weakened condition which made millions so susceptible to the Black Death during the Middle Ages. Scurvy also took a cruel toll of the Crusaders.

starvation. He was dismayed to find this same look on faces when he returned to his own country, where physicians and government officials assumed people were well fed. "Among other things they ignore the heavy consumption of sugar and refined flour in industrial countries at the expense of vitamin-providing fruits and vegetables and whole grains."

He cites research studies other than his own—in the Scottish medical journals, for instance—to confirm the fact that insufficient vitamin C in the system is dangerous. It can lead to serious problems, with signs any good physician can detect: varicose veins, blood that won't clot, poor teeth, weak bones, high cholesterol and sometimes senility. He calls this intermittent scurvy because it comes and goes, higher in winter, when fresh produce is scarce and expensive. "Or a person will have marginally adequate vitamin C intake for normal circumstances, but his body stores will dip to scurvy levels if he becomes ill or injured. Over the years the damage builds up. I have seen the evidence." To forestall this, he strongly advises taking ascorbic acid supplements.

The "look of starvation" Dr. Taylor mentions is evident to anyone who begins to observe. I've seen it on the streets both here and abroad. It's evident in the faces of many of the young people who smoke, drink, use drugs and live mostly on junk foods. It is mute and tragic testimony in the faces of old people, whose teeth don't allow them to eat as many fresh fruits and vegetables as they should. Many times they live in institutions which serve little fresh produce, or cook most of the vitamin C out of the vegetables they do serve.

Vitamin C is critically important to the strength of the blood vessels and capillaries which deliver food and oxygen to the brain. It's easy to see why those who study geriatrics are becoming convinced that lack of vitamin C can be a major cause of senility.

Collagen, the Cement that Holds Us Together

There is, as I have said, a kind of mucilage which keeps us from falling apart. This stuff, a glycoprotein known as collagen, cements the cells into their orderly arrangement, strengthens all the connective tissues, including those in the ligaments, joints and muscles, and gives the blood vessels the tough casing they need to carry their precious cargo. In fact, no part of our body could cling to any other part without it; and it is so totally dependent upon vitamin C that it has been said, "We *are* vitamin C."

The importance of vitamin C in this respect is demonstrated by looking again at scurvy. In advanced cases the tissues break down altogether, teeth get loose, joints give way, people can't stand. James Lind, writing in 1753, described the muscles that fell apart during autopsies, ribs separating from lack of cohesion, and "instead of finding in the cavities of the joints the usual sweet oily mucilage, there was only a greenish liquor." Even in subclinical cases blood vessels weaken and break, cartilage gives way, there is a general disintegration. All this because the body lacks *a single essential element—vitamin C.* Without it collagen cannot be manufactured or synthesized. And if the supply of vitamin C runs low this collagen liquefies, becomes soft and mushy, so that tissues, cartilage and bone can no longer support the body.

The effects of this become evident in many ways. Dr. W. J. McCormick, internationally recognized expert on vitamin C, and one of its pioneers, showed that a deficiency of this vitamin was a strong contributing factor in rheumatism, arthritis, hernia, hemorrhaging, hardening of the arteries and back problems. He published a number of papers on these subjects (primarily in the *Archives of Pediatrics* between 1954 and 1959), blaming disc lesions on a breakdown of this intercellular cement, due to lack of vitamin C. He stated that diseases of the heart and blood vessels were less likely to be caused by cholesterol than by a weakness in the walls of the blood vessels themselves. He even theorized that vitamin C could have something to do with cancer, because of the cellular breakdown that occurs without it. A theory that seemed to be dramatically demonstrated years later by the Cameron-Pauling tests on cancer victims in Scotland.

Most of McCormick's contemporaries scorned his arguments and evidence; but not all. And today a great many doctors corroborate their validity. Shortly after Dr. McCormick's findings, Dr. James Greenwood, chief of neurosurgery at Houston, Texas, Methodist Hospital, published his own research on vitamin C and back problems. He had been suffering from hip and back pains himself. After reading that people who died of scurvy always showed a dissolution of the back tissues and vertebrae, he decided to try vitamin C. His own relief was so swift and lasting he began prescribing the vitamin for muscle soreness or any back trouble, including ruptured discs. Not all cases, but many, were able to avoid surgery.

Medical texts tells us that providing collagen is one of vitamin C's most important jobs. At least a third of our body is composed of this critical protein which keeps us neatly meshed together. Without enough ascorbic acid the supply of collagen runs down. Then quite literally we begin to go to pieces. With sufficient vitamin C to supply the collagen, however, we remain upright, resilient and strong.

The Case of Norman Cousins

The distinguished author and editor Norman Cousins learned all this very painfully for himself. The story is told in his book *Anatomy of an Illness As Perceived by the Patient.*

In August 1964 he returned from a month's assignment in Moscow suffering from a disease diagnosed as "a serious collagen illness, a weakening of the connective tissue." He had trouble moving his limbs, there were nodules on his body and gravel-like substances under his skin. At times his jaws locked. The doctors leveled with him—he had one chance in 500 to get well.

Seeking causes, he attributed some of this to stress—*a factor which always affects the adrenal gland.* Knowing that negative emotions can cause negative body reactions, his first step was a resolve to be as affirmative and happy as possible. His second was to question his medication. The hospital had been giving him 26 aspirin tablets and 12 phenylbutazone tablets per day. Tests proved that he was actually hypersensitive to these anti-inflammatory drugs; while his own study warned him that "aspirin warrants considerable care in its use . . . that the chemical composition of aspirin impairs platelet function. Did the relation between platelets and collagen mean that aspirin, so universally accepted for so many years, was actually harmful in the treatment of collagen disease?"

His decision was to stop these medications. "I could stand pain so long as progress was being made in restoring my body's capacity to halt the continuing breakdown of connective tissue."

He persuaded his doctor to move him to a hotel and start administering ascorbic acid through slow intravenous drip, increasing the doses by several grams each day. Although worried about possible complications from such large amounts, his physician agreed. "To know whether we were on the right track, we took a sedimentation test before the first intravenous administration of ten G of ascorbic acid. Four hours later we took another test. There was a full drop of nine points. Seldom had I known such elation. The ascorbic acid was working."

The dosage was gradually increased until it reached 25 grams. Meanwhile, he began to sleep pain-free, without pills, and by the eighth day discernible progress had begun. He could move more freely, the nodules were shrinking. Within two weeks he was enjoying the surf at Puerto Rico and gingerly jogging. "The connective tissue in my spine and joints was regenerating. I could function, and the feeling was indescribably beautiful." All his infirmities didn't disappear overnight, he makes plain. But gradually he improved until he was working full-time and even riding horseback.

He attributes his recovery to two things: A sense of positive joyous affirmation, including laughter. And vitamin C. (God and vitamins!)

Before his book appeared, Cousins had written an article about his experience which was published in several magazines —*New England Journal of Medicine* and *Reader's Digest*, as well as his own *Saturday Review*. As a result of that article, some 3,000 letters poured in, from doctors around the world. And he says that without exception they applauded what he had done, agreeing that modern medicine had become too dependent on dangerous drugs. Many sent him medical tracts "supporting the use of ascorbic acid for a wide range of disorders beyond the reach of antibiotics or other medication." He also received such material from several prominent research laboratories.

Norman Cousins says that in going through the mail he was encouraged to see "the growing evidence of a balanced attitude about nutrition in general and ascorbic acid in particular. The negative views that many doctors held only a few years ago are now being replaced by a willingness to examine new findings and apply them."

They were also emphatic in their agreement that sheer faith, hope and happiness play a significant part in getting well.

Vitamin C and Cancer

In current medical practice there are only three accepted methods of treating cancer: surgery, radiation, chemotherapy. All subject the body to severe and terrible stress. All are very destructive. As in warfare, although you may hit the target you generally destroy the countryside. In each of these treatments there is also a risk the cancer cells will reappear somewhere else. It's like burning down a barn to get rid of the rats; they only scatter. For this reason even a biopsy can be dangerous.

Yet there are natural, non-toxic ways to protect the body from cancer in the first place, and to keep the cancer from recurring. They are the nutrients that fortify our entire immunity system, and that *build* the tissues instead. And one of the most important is vitamin C.

Tests show that cancer victims are always significantly deficient in vitamin C. This is particularly true of bladder cancers. With very few exceptions, the people are heavy smokers. And smoking simply wipes out vitamin C.

Studies relating smoking to bladder cancer go back many years. In 1955 the publication *Cancer* reported that when tobacco tars were applied to the mouths of mice, instead of the expected cancer in cheeks or lungs, they developed bladder cancer. . . . In 1956 the *British Medical Journal* revealed that the death rate from bladder cancer due to smoking was rising as fast as cancer of the lungs. . . . Doctors Cobb and Ansell, writing in the *Journal of the American Medical Association* in 1965, suggested that the place where a cancerous chemical is excreted from the body may be just as susceptible as the place where it is ingested.

Dr. McCormick said that smoking even one cigarette destroys 25 milligrams of vitamin C, and if you smoke a pack a day you need at least an extra 500 milligrams just to replace the loss.

The American Cancer Society projects an estimated 52,000 new cases of urinary cancer per year, with an annual death toll of at least 17,500 lives. Both the ACS and HEW have fervent anti-smoking campaigns. Yet if they were really concerned about cancers caused by smoking, they would tell us about protective measures. In addition to all those warnings, they would publicize the fact that vitamin A protects against lung cancer, and vitamin C against cancer of the urinary tract.

Either they are totally ignorant of all the scientific evidence (which seems preposterous, in view of the billions they reap to spend on "research") or they prefer to keep *us* in ignorance.

Even some of the research that *is* done would appear to be redundant.

In 1972 our government allotted millions for a program to research ways to prevent and treat bladder cancer. Yet scientists at Tulane University had already provided significant answers four years previously. In 1968 Dr. J. U. Schlegel and his colleagues found that simply adding ascorbic acid to drinking water prevented bladder tumors. As reported both in *Medical World News* and in the *Journal of Urology,* pellets containing carcinogens were inserted into the bladders of two groups of mice. One received plain drinking water; the other, water containing 250 milligrams of vitamin C. As expected, the second group did excrete large amounts of vitamin C. But *they did not develop cancer.* The others did. It was the large amounts of ascorbic acid in the urine which detoxified the chemical and kept the tumors from forming. The scientists demonstrated further that ascorbic acid could prevent the recurrence of bladder tumors. And their results have been confirmed in actual practice by a number of other urologists and patients ever since.

A favorite crack of vitamin critics is that they "just go through the body and enrich the sewers." The studies at Tulane and elsewhere show that we need enough vitamin C so that it *will* spill into the urine, where it becomes a powerful protector against both bladder and rectal cancer. The oft-quoted Dr. Klenner says he is convinced that vitamin C can prevent cancer of the bladder and will control myelocytic leukemia.

"One can only speculate on what massive therapy will do in all forms of cancer." Writing in the *Journal of Applied Nutrition*, he cites the enormous doses of penicillin that are used over long periods and asks, "How long must we wait for someone to start continuous ascorbic acid drip . . . for various malignant conditions?"

The Cameron-Pauling Cancer Experiment

In 1971 Linus Pauling's Institute of Science and Medicine in Menlo Park, California, began a collaboration with Vale of Leven Hospital, not far from Glasgow, Scotland. There a program was begun, administering massive doses of vitamin C to terminal cancer patients.

Dr. Ewan Cameron, the hospital surgeon, had been working on a different theory when he heard of Pauling's work with vitamin C. Pauling's idea was based on the fact that a high intake of vitamin C helps the body produce more collagen. That by strengthening these collagen fibers in the intercellular cement, the cancer might be controlled. As later reported in their book *Cancer and Vitamin C,* Cameron's first reaction was "sheer incredulity."

> It seemed quite ludicrous to suggest that this simple, cheap, harmless powder, which could be bought in any drugstore, could possibly have any value against such a bafflingly complex and resistant disease. . . . But the ideas continued to make sense, together with the general idea that a high intake of vitamin C might make all the body's natural protective mechanisms more effective.

In the five-year trial, 100 cancer patients were given large doses of ascorbic acid and nothing else. They were matched against a control group of 1,000 equally hopeless cancer patients in the same hospital, who did not receive the vitamin but were otherwise treated the same. In the fall of 1976 the results were announced:

• Out of the 1,000 patients who did not receive vitamin C, only two were still alive. (They have since died.) . . . Out of the much smaller number, 100—18 were still living and 16 considered cured. (Three have since died.)

• Out of those remaining, 90 per cent lived three times longer, and 10 per cent lived twenty times longer than doctors expected.

Dr. Cameron stated, "It is our conclusion that the administration of ascorbic acid in amounts of about 10 grams a day to patients with advanced cancer leads to about a fourfold increase in life expectancy. Vitamin C increases the effectiveness of the body's natural resistance to disease, and this in turn seems to increase the survival time." Furthermore, the patients had far less *pain*—some had none; their appetite improved, they were alert, cheerful, lively. One man went back to his job as a truck driver after only six weeks. Thinking he was cured, he stopped taking the vitamin, only to have the cancer come back. This time he was given 20 grams, and again his X rays were clear. It was definitely the ascorbic acid that was keeping his cancer in remission.

The results of these clinical trials were reported in the most distinguished medical and scientific journals around the world. Even the National Cancer Institute was impressed. Yet when Dr. Pauling went to the NCI for funds to repeat the project in the United States, he was told he would first have to furnish proof with animal studies. (Never mind that you've already built a space ship—go back and reinvent the wheel.) But to his dismay, even his application for funds for the animal studies was refused. "I applied again and again. . . . Once a year for five years I've applied and they've turned me down each time," says this two-time Nobel Prize winner.

Meanwhile, however, further studies were launched at two hospitals in Scotland, this time using more patients, and this time patients who had not been pronounced incurable. And the Mayo Clinic here in the United States undertook to duplicate the Cameron-Pauling experiment with 150 patients.

To Dr. Pauling's dismay, the Mayo findings, published in the *New England Journal of Medicine,* purported to show no evidence that large doses of vitamin C were of benefit. Dr. Pauling

has challenged that report, insisting the patients investigated
were so different from those in the earlier study as to make the
report meaningless. That although he had strongly urged
against it, nearly all the Mayo patients had received chemotherapy, which damages the immunity system; whereas only 4 per
cent of those treated by Dr. Cameron had been subjected to
chemotherapy. "The Vale of Leven study showed that large
doses of vitamin C have great value for cancer patients who
have not received chemotherapy."

Cancer and Vitamin C puts such conflicts in perspective:

> Vitamin C is not a miraculous cure for cancer, but it goes a long way
> toward the therapeutic goal. . . . It significantly prolongs the life
> of the cancer patient. Moreover, it improves the condition of the
> patient to such an extent that his life during his remaining months
> or years is comfortable, contented, useful, productive, and satisfy-
> ing. Because of the low cost of vitamin C and the decreased need for
> special care, the financial burden of the treatment to the patient
> and his family is small. We believe that supplemental ascorbate can
> be of real help to all cancer patients and of quite dramatic benefit to
> a fortunate few.

Vitamin C and Energy

To move from the extremes of cancer to the common fatigues of
every day: Vitamin C is an invaluable ally when it comes to
energy.

We all know in a general way that our energy comes from our
food, primarily fats and carbohydrates. (The natural carbohydrates found in fruits and vegetables; *not* white sugar, which is
only a misnamed drug containing no food value whatever.) We
also know that our bodies somehow manage to convert that
food into energy-giving fuels. Less generally known is the fact
that this can't happen without certain enzymes, which have to
be constantly activated by vitamin C. Dr. Ayub Khan, writing in
Current Science, said that his studies revealed—"the onset of
fatigue was not due to the exhaustion of energy-yielding sub-
strates, but rather due to the inactivation of metabolic enzymes.
Ascorbic acid level was found to greatly alter during muscular

fatigue." In plain English—we get tired not because the fuel supply is low, but because our supply of vitamin C is low.

The Russians have recognized this for years; they give their athletes quantities of vitamin C, especially before competition. But sheer physical exertion isn't the only consumer of this vitamin—so are the trials and strains that assault our nervous system. Vitamin C fortifies us against their damage as faithfully as it fights to defend us against disease. What's more, it keeps us alert, reinvigorated. Dr. Klenner goes so far as to say that enough ascorbic acid taken daily "will sharpen an individual's perception, enabling him to accomplish more in less time. He'll find his mind will be clearer, his memory more retentive, his body less tired."

This makes sense when we remember that old Geritol commercial about "tired blood." Studies have shown that ascorbic acid keeps the blood lively; that large amounts increase the production of white blood cells (leukocytes), which fight infection, and the red blood cells (hemoglobin), which carry oxygen to all the cells. For vitamin C mobilizes the cell-building, energy-giving iron. Without enough vitamin C we simply aren't able to draw that pep and energy from the iron. Furthermore, large amounts of vitamin C are not "wasted," as is generally supposed, but reinvigorate the cells.

The result is indeed, as Pauling expressed it, an increased sense of vitality and well-being.

The Most Important Supplement

I consider vitamin C the most important supplement you can take. It is non-toxic. The body doesn't store it more than an estimated five hours; any it can't use is excreted. Yet the body is a voracious user. Every nerve, cell, tissue and process demands a large supply of ascorbic acid at all times.

Three outstanding vitamin C authorities, Dr. Klenner, Dr. Irwin Stone (who first influenced Pauling) and Dr. Pauling himself, all recommend ten grams a day or more. That seems a lot; but they remind us that animals produce quantities of vitamin C for their daily needs. "A goat, for instance, the size of a human adult, normally can produce 13,000 milligrams of ascorbate a day and will make much more under stress," says Dr. Stone in *The Healing Factor, Vitamin C Against Disease.* All of them deplore as ridiculous the recommended daily allowance of only 60 milligrams. "They are recommending 300 to 400 times less than the normal daily mammalian production, a bare subsistence level. If the other mammals produced this low amount, it is unlikely they would even survive."

No vitamin (or anything else) should ever be taken in large amounts without a knowledgeable doctor's direction. Vitamin C gives a few people diarrhea, if they're not used to it. It is also very drying. Excessive amounts could put a burden on the bladder and kidneys. But it can do you nothing but good if you use simple common sense.

I take three full grams of vitamin C a day (one after every meal). Sometimes, if I'm under stress or feel the threat of a cold, I take another 500 milligrams between meals. In the summer, when an abundance of fresh, organically raised fruits and vegetables is available from the garden, I cut back on the amounts of supplementary vitamin C. But taking vitamins and minerals is like any other good habit; the only way not to get careless and lazy or forget, is simply not to stop.

Around the end of his life, about 1780, James Lind, the man who had futilely tried to arouse the world to the fact that citrus fruit could prevent scurvy, remarked bitterly: "Some persons cannot be brought to believe that a disease so fatal and so dreadful can be cured or prevented by such an easy means."

Will it be another three hundred years before "some people" can be brought to realize that many diseases can be cured or prevented by such an easy means as vitamin C?

13

Vitamin E, for Youth, Heart and Energy

Vitamin E is my favorite, next to vitamin C. Each morning, swallowing that golden capsule, I am reminded of a trim, vivacious little Iowa bookseller with whom I was having lunch once years ago. I guessed her to be about fifty, maybe less. And when she told me she was about to retire I gasped, "But you're not that old!"

"My dear, I'm way past retirement age. Promise you won't tell anybody? I'm nearly seventy-four." Her secret, she confided, was vitamin E. Along with a happy outlook and exercise. She had begun to take vitamin E after reading Dr. Evan Shute's book *Alpha Tocopherol (Vitamin E) in Cardiovascular Disease.* "My husband had died of a coronary. I'm a curious soul, I wanted to know *why.* And the more I read, the madder I got that we hadn't been *told* what this vitamin can do. Anyway, I decided to take it myself for protection. At that time I was rundown, subject to bronchitis, had varicose veins, just about everything. In just a few months I was like a new person, and I've hardly had a sick day since. I know vitamin E has not only kept me healthy, it's helped keep me young." She shuddered faintly. "When I look at some of my contemporaries—!"

I agreed. Her bright eyes and thick shining hair, that scarcely wrinkled skin; even her lovely speaking voice. *Something* had helped this woman hold back age.

As if reading my thoughts, she said, "Have you ever noticed how older people's voices often get furry or cracked? Well, vitamin E has not only prevented that, thank heaven, it's actually improved my singing voice!* And let me tell you something else. My daughter had been married seven years and wanted a baby so bad. I persuaded her and her husband to take vitamin E too—not for that reason, just to protect them from what happened to her dad. Believe it or not, Betty was pregnant before the year was out." She opened her purse, proudly handed me snapshots. "Here are my three grandchildren."

Now, infertility has certainly never been my problem—and no amount of vitamin E will ever get me into a choir. But of one thing I'm convinced: those amber vials of vitamin E hold at least one answer to mankind's search for the elixir of youth.

Can We Get Enough Vitamin E in Foods?

Those who stubbornly spout the cliché of the "balanced diet" claim we don't need to take more vitamin E since it's so widely distributed in foods. What they fail to realize is that the amounts are extremely small, and easily destroyed. Wilfrid E. Shute, M.D. (Evan Shute's younger brother) writes in his book *Health Preserver,* "We get less vitamin E than in any age before, and we need more vitamin E than any people ever needed before."

All of the following things destroy vitamin E:
• Storage . . . Cooking and freezing.
• Air pollution.
• Medication (especially the Pill).
• Oils: Rancid oils . . . Mineral oils . . . *Polyunsaturates.*
Yes, the very margarines and vegetables oils we are downing in

---

* I took this remark lightly until reading *Health Preserver* (published by Rodale Press). In it Dr. Shute tells the story of a professional singer who developed scar tissue on her vocal cords and was told she would never sing again. Megadoses of vitamin E restored her voice within a few months. In another case, a man developed hoarseness and lesions after the removal of a nodule from a vocal cord. Vitamin E healed the lesions and returned the voice to normal.

our frenzy to avoid cholesterol. Polyunsaturates lose most of their vitamin E in refining; and when we consume them we need extra amounts of vitamin E to keep them from oxidizing in the body and forming free radicals. (Destructive particles which many scientists link to aging, and some relate to cancer.)

• Inorganic iron. The very mineral added to "enrich" bread. Actually it inhibits the vitamin E in our system. For this reason anyone who takes iron for anemia is likely to be deficient in vitamin E. In fact, the Shutes advise that if you take a vitamin E supplement you should separate it from the iron by eight to twelve hours. (Take your iron in the morning, for instance, all your vitamin E at night—or vice versa.)

• Finally, but fatally, processing. It is the processing which has most devastatingly raped, robbed and slain vitamin E.

The Rape of the Virgin Wheat

The oft-told story goes back to the late 1800s when the milling industry introduced a bolting cloth which separated and discarded the chaff (bran) from the wheat. It was the first step in devitalizing flour. Another "improvement" followed—high-heat and high-speed rollers which finely ground the grain. Since the hot wheat germ gummed the machinery, it too was discarded. What remained for human consumption was a starchy substance which was bleached and refined by a growing list of chemicals which now number nearly 100—most of them rank poisons.

Those early bakers, however, were delighted. This flour—almost pure starch—didn't turn rancid; and since all the life-giving elements had been stripped from it, even rodents and insects wouldn't touch it. Bread, the very staff of life, had been so weakened it could no longer *support* life. Yet people loved this spongy white stuff and began to devour it, along with cakes, pies, cookies and other pastries, all laden with refined white sugar (which once had been scarce and expensive). White flour also brought macaroni, crackers and dozens of other products to our tables, almost all pure starch. It can scarcely be a coincidence that it is only in the years since this began that America (and every country which has followed our example) has been cursed by so many degenerative diseases.

A century ago almost all deaths were due to accidents or infectious diseases. Cancer was so rare in 1876 that even the city of New York could report only a few cases. Heart disease was unknown. In 1890 several cases were described in scientific journals, but the symptoms were so strange nobody recognized their cause. When Dr. Herrick of Chicago reported six cases in 1912, doctors came all the way from Europe to study the phenomenon, finally called coronary thrombosis. In one of his many diatribes against our modern way of living, Dr. Little told me, "Coronary thrombosis was not even brought up when I was in medical school. I had not even seen a case until I'd been in practice almost twenty years."

Cancer, heart disease, arthritis—all diseases which now rack and kill our people—did not even manifest until after the refining of wheat. And what happened to the discarded bran and wheat germ? It was fed to the livestock, which thrived. For it was the discards which contained the precious proteins and enzymes, the minerals and vitamins—particularly the B vitamins and vitamin E. In his blindness man cheated himself of the very treasure a wise and loving creator had provided. For the wheat germ is the tiny inner nubbin of the seed, packed with nourishment to support that seed until it can sprout and draw sustenance from the soil. And its most abundant nutrient is what we call vitamin E.

Any good farmer knows that without vitamin E his breeding stock will be infertile or miscarry, his pigs and chickens will die. It would be unthinkable to feed them the same kind of empty-calorie foods he and his family probably eat themselves. Experiments have proved it. In Gaye Deamer Horsley's book *Commercial Foods Exposed,* she tells the story of a New York senator who also had a pig farm, and once arranged with a hotel to get their stale bread to feed his pigs. "Before long his pigs became runty and diseased. The brood sows had small litters or aborted." Even the chickens got sick. Suspicious, the senator began feeding only half his pigs the white bread, the other half whole wheat and corn. The contrast was so shocking the senator stopped feeding his family white bread.

As I mention elsewhere, a similar experiment was conducted by the famous biochemist Roger Williams using typical commercial breads, some widely advertised for their body-building properties. Rats fed the stuff all died of malnutrition within a few weeks, or were severely stunted—despite the fact the breads had been "enriched and fortified."

White bread can even harm strong bodies. Vitamin E, the protective anti-oxidant, has been removed. Then oxidizers such as chlorine bleaches are actually *added*. We are then powerless before the process of peroxidation or rancidity in the blood, which causes the free radicals that can attack the heart muscle and are also causes of cancer.

The Enrichment Hoax

The very term *enrichment* is deceptive. It creates the impression, "Hooray, I'm getting a bonus—look at all these nutritional goodies they're giving me." Because most people don't realize that some twenty-five vitamins and minerals have been removed. "Fortified" or "enriched" merely means that four or five have been put back synthetically, cheaply and usually in very small amounts. As Adelle Davis expressed it in one of her books, "It's as if somebody robbed you of $100 and then expected to be praised for giving you carfare to get home."

The government made enrichment of bread flour mandatory near the time of World War II, when the draft revealed that an appalling number of young men were physically unfit for service. Mills were ordered to restore at least a handful of bread's missing nutrients: the least expensive B vitamins, and inorganic iron. Which doesn't make much sense when we realize iron is the one mineral the body has the most trouble assimilating, and which will actually inhibit vitamin E. The travesty is compounded by the fact that there is *no* compensation whatever for the most tragic loss of refining—the vitamin E. Not even a fragment of this precious vitamin has been restored; probably because the process of extracting it is more complicated and expensive. (It takes a whole vat of vegetable oils to achieve approximately one cup of pure vitamin E.)

Joe D. Nichols, M.D., discussed all this in a memorable address before a bankers' convention in Galveston, Texas, some years ago:

> What is enriched bread? First they take a perfectly good grain of wheat and remove all the vitamins and minerals. Then they start out with raw starch and put back into it three little dead synthetic chemicals: niacin, thiamine and riboflavin, plus inorganic iron. These three synthetic vitamins are a part of the vitamin B complex. But natural B complex—and the wheat germ is one of the very best sources—contains twenty known parts besides the still unknown factors.
>
> The germ is also the richest source of natural vitamin E, which has proved to be essential to a normal cardiovascular system. . . . In Canada it is against the law to enrich bread. The Canadians are right and we are nuts. I tell all my patients they should never buy any food that has been enriched. . . . If the food is so sorry to start with that synthetic chemical vitamins have to be added, then it is not worth their money. This removes about 90 per cent of the breakfast foods.

Natural Sources of Vitamin E

I'm no pusher of any product if the original is available in nature. When it comes to vitamin E, however, nature isn't enough.

Vitamin E is found in root vegetables and leafy vegetables. In eggs and butter and organ meats. In the germs of all grains. In nuts and seeds and cold-pressed vegetable oils (with the exception of olive oil). Why should anybody need more?

But wait. The vitamin E in most vegetables is concentrated in the skin or coarse outer leaves, which most of us toss away. The organ meats—liver, kidney, heart and brains—are not many families' favorites. (For that matter, it's *raw* meat that contains most vitamin E.) Nuts and seeds are rich sources, but not a large part of most people's diet. The cholesterol scare, which Dr. Shute calls a catastrophe, has made many people avoid butter and eggs. As for vegetable oils—how often do you examine a bottle to make sure it hasn't been highly processed, canceling out its vitamin E? In fact, these polyunsaturates, touted as so much better than butter, are actually *one of the heart's worst enemies* unless the body can disarm them with plenty of vitamin E.

It is, in short, not easy to get even a bare minimum recommended daily allowance of 30 international units without putting forth a lot of effort, shopping with great care and changing most of your cooking and eating habits. Furthermore, it would be necessary to consume a lot more food. To prove this, four scientists bought foods believed typical of an average diet but considered highest in vitamin E. The breakfast they served included tomato juice, two eggs, cooked cereal, two slices of ham, two slices of whole-grain bread with margarine, coffee with cream and sugar. Lunch and dinner were equally generous. They then analyzed the foods, only to discover that the total of vitamin E added up to only 7.4 international units. Less than half the official recommendation set by the Food and Nutrition Board of the National Research Council in 1974.

Small wonder, then, that a deficiency of vitamin E is believed to be more widespread than any other, including vitamin C. That, in the words of Dr. Evan Shute, pioneer in its clinical use and one of the world's foremost authorities, "Americans are in a state of chronic vitamin E starvation."

The Bonds Between Vitamin C and Vitamin E

Vitamins C and E have a lot in common. They are synergistic— they work as a team. Neither can accomplish its job effectively without the other. Both are anti-oxidants. And the body's highest concentration of both is found in the adrenal glands. This indicates their tremendous importance. For it is these glands which produce two of our most vital hormones:

Our sex hormones, the steroids. (Which also produce cortisone, so important in cases of arthritis.)

Our adrenaline. Which affects the nerves controlling involuntary muscles, *especially the heart.* Adrenaline controls the exact muscles and organs to which the heart shoots extra blood in times of emergency, and enables the body to burn its sugar for energy. (Not white sugar, note, but glucose.)

Explorers used to be puzzled by the fact that people like the Eskimos suffered none of our degenerative diseases. This despite the fact they ate almost no fruits and vegetables, but lived primarily on raw meats and animal fats—the very stuff we're told to avoid. (They were spared our diseases, that is, until our sugars and starches got to them.) Where did they get their vitamins? Then it was observed that the first pieces claimed in a fresh kill were the liver—which stores vitamins A, D, E and K. And the two morsels located just above the kidneys. These two morsels, the adrenal glands, so well stocked with vitamins C and E, were considered a delicacy.

Such people, in their primitive wisdom, know the source of both creation and survival. That it lies in those two glands which God, in *his* wisdom, locates strategically together and nourishes with vitamins C and E.

The History of Vitamin E

In 1922 two researchers, Katherine Bishop and Herbert Evans, both M.D.'s, discovered a puzzling thing. Some mysterious substance in wheat germ seemed to be necessary for reproduction in rats. Without it females aborted or simply failed to conceive. When the rats were fed the whole wheat or its oil, however, the females were fertile and produced healthy young. Later this substance was extracted and identified by its chemical properties. For its name, a professor of Greek proposed *tokos* (meaning "childbirth") and *pherein* (meaning "bring forth") with the suffix *-ol* (indicating an alcohol). The final version became tocopherol; its more common name vitamin E.

The E stands for *essential. Essential for the very creation of life itself* in both animals and man.

In fact, its first fame was as a fertility vitamin. Unfortunately. For in our national obsession with sex, that fact got the most attention—along with the usual wisecracks and skepticism. Meanwhile, the other roles of vitamin E in the body, many of them just as impressive, were being demonstrated as more and more physicians and researchers began to study its properties and discover for themselves what this vitamin could do. Years of controlled experiments and a wealth of clinical data have now established the many roles and capabilities of vitamin E.

The Heart

Vitamin E provides the best possible protection against heart attacks. It can help heal the damaged heart. It is able to do this for a number of reasons:

• Vitamin E is a natural anti-oxidant, decreasing the oxygen requirement of a muscle by at least 43 per cent. (The heart is a muscle.)

• It is a natural anti-thrombin (dissolver of blood clots).

• It is a natural dilator of blood vessels, able to open up new pathways around blocked or clogged circulation.

I will illustrate this later in a discussion of the work of the Shute brothers. For now let me say that before discovering vitamins my husband suffered three serious heart attacks. I am convinced that vitamin E, working with its partner vitamin C, saved and prolonged his life.

The Respiratory System

Vitamin E protects the lungs and bronchial tubes from air pollution. It has been called one half of an umbrella or gas mask to protect us from the assault of chemical poisons most of us are breathing every day. (This time its primary partner is vitamin A.) Smoke, exhaust fumes, factory wastes, even seemingly harmless hair sprays and air "purifiers" take their toll of both our lungs and our atmosphere. When the ozone becomes saturated it turns to smog. Combined with the sun's ultraviolet rays it turns into a poison that has been compared with phosgene, the deadly mustard gas used with such terrible effects in World War I. In California they call this "photochemical smog," and when its ugly fumes are prevalent my granddaughters have been kept indoors; schools are sometimes closed. It attacks the mucous membranes; eyes and throat burn; it can lead to emphysema and pulmonary edema (fluid in the lungs). All this in turn strains the heart. Doctors have found a direct relation between air pollution and heart disease.

For proof that vitamin E can protect us, we again look to the lowly rat. Dozens of experiments have proved this. A team led by Dr. D. Warshauer, of the University of California at Davis, exposed rats and mice to various levels of ozone pollution. Half had been fed diets containing additional vitamin E; half were given none. The unfortified victims lost twice as much weight, had more than twice as many lung bacteria and showed far greater cellular damage than those given extra vitamin E. Many of them died.

Even so, the diet of the victims *had contained more vitamin E than the recommended daily allowance for human beings.*

Two years of extensive studies at the laboratories of Battelle Pacific Northwest, Richland, Washington, produced the same results not only with rats but also with pigs and goats. In one experiment conducted by Dr. Jeffrey N. Roehm, a control group of goats subjected to uranium dust, diesel fumes and other pollutants died within six weeks. The other group, which had been given vitamin E, not only survived but showed few ill effects.

In addressing the American Chemical Society's annual meeting in March 1971, Dr. Roehm said, "Vitamin E works as an anti-oxidant against effects of nitrogen dioxide on lung tissues. However, vitamin E-supplemented diets will not cure already diseased lungs. . . . Our experiments are designed to *prevent* obstructive respiratory diseases." He deplores the fact that so few physicians are even aware of what scientists have so clearly shown: that diet has something to do with respiratory illnesses, and that people should be advised to protect themselves against them with plenty of vitamin E.

Circulatory Diseases of Feet and Legs

Vitamin E has been a godsend to people who suffer from arterial diseases: Restless legs. Night cramps, rectal cramps. Intermittent claudication—those painful leg cramps which seize people while walking. (Once more its partner in this is vitamin C.) Vitamin E has even saved limbs.

Denise, a friend of ours, raises horses. Her mother was a model, she told me. "She developed arteriosclerosis so bad she lost all circulation in her legs, it became gangrene. The doctors removed all the veins and arteries from her heart and to both kidneys and legs, replacing them with Teflon. Then phlebitis set in, they didn't expect her to live through the night, they wanted to amputate both legs. Those beautiful legs had fed me for years —I knew I had to do something," she said. "Mother wouldn't want to go on living without them. The doctors didn't believe in vitamins, but I'd been smuggling them in. Now I doubled the vitamin E, and dolomite, which is so good for the heart. And I talked to her—the talking is just as important—to make her want to live.

"Together we held on, and the vitamin E saved her. She was fifty-five years old at the time. Another woman only thirty-three had the same operation and lost both legs, then died. My mother is alive today after eleven years, her beautiful body not mutilated."

Denise says it's the same with animals. "I've saved almost every known animal with love and vitamins. Especially vitamin E. Dogs and horses with tumors; a valuable racehorse that had broken its leg in two places and was dying. The vet said he couldn't be saved. I looked up what Adelle Davis said to do for broken bones, and multiplied everything ten times. I crushed the vitamins and minerals, mixed them with honey, and shoved it down his throat, then rubbed his legs with castor oil. Within a few hours he revived—there was a difference even in his coat! In five weeks he was jumping."

This same horse also tore his chest open running into barbed wire. "I treated it with vitamin E, didn't even have it sewed up, and it healed without a scar. With a black horse, when there is scar tissue the hair grows in white. Even this didn't happen, his hair grew back as black and glossy as before."

No doubt those surgeons who "don't believe in vitamins" are still sawing off legs. *Vascular* surgeons. Evidently they have never heard of the world-famous vascular surgeon Dr. Knut Haeger and what he has accomplished with the vascular agent vitamin E.† In a detailed article in *Prevention* he describes his long experience in these areas.

He and a colleague once conducted a clinical study of several

† Dr. Haeger was once a Halsted Fellow in Experimental Surgery at Colorado General Hospital, was chief surgeon in the Department of Vascular Surgery of Malmö General Hospital in Sweden and is now Assistant Medical Research

hundred patients. "We compared the effect of alpha-tocopherol with that of vasodilator agents (drugs which dilate blood vessels), anti-coagulant therapy, and vitamin tablets without vitamin E." It was found that patients who received vitamin E increased their walking distance far beyond the other groups, and 38 per cent were able to double the distance without pain.

To me, the account which follows is strangely moving—probably because I remember how my mother and father both suffered from aching legs and cramps in later years. Also, because I have been close to three different people who suffered the tragedy of amputations.

> We then asked the patients to rate their own improvement in terms of how far they could walk, how much their legs bothered them and to what extent they were troubled with coldness and numbness of the feet, both of which are symptoms of impaired circulation. Once again, the patients who took the vitamin E scored much higher, particularly those who had exercised. . . .
>
> During the years in which we conducted this study, it was necessary to amputate 12 legs because of intractable pain and/or gangrene. This was, of course, done as a last resort, only after more conservative treatment and operative techniques had failed.
>
> *In the group of patients who were taking vitamin E, there was only one amputation case out of 95 surviving patients.* [Italics mine.] But of 104 patients who did not receive vitamin E there were 11 amputations. This difference is very significant.

Arthritis

Vitamin E can help arthritis.

There are a number of clinical studies to prove its benefits, especially for rheumatoid arthritis. But my own conviction comes from the personal experience described in an earlier chapter. A truly nutritious diet supplemented by all the vitamins and minerals, but particularly wheat germ and vitamin E, can overcome other forms of this agony as well.

To me, nothing could be more logical in view of the fact that

Director of the Schering Corporation, Scandinavia. He has published hundreds of articles in medical journals.

the body's highest concentration of both vitamin C and vitamin E is in the adrenals. The very glands which manufacture *cortisone,* a substance which in drug form is used to treat arthritis. It simply stands to reason. A deficiency of alpha tocopherol (vitamin E) could lead to a deficiency of cortisone. The greater its supply of vitamin E, the more cortisone the body can manufacture for itself.

Burns and Afflictions of the Skin

• Vitamin E ointment or oil is one of the best treatments for burns, as we found out that time our furnace blew up. . . . It also hastens the healing of ulcers—another very important thing we discovered during bouts with those vicious ulcers caused by X-ray burns on my husband's back.

• Vitamin E heals cuts and abrasions. . . . It can relieve the itching of poison ivy and other afflictions—even the torment of shingles, especially if taken internally as well as used externally.

• Vitamin E ointment or cream is the most effective treatment yet known for preventing or minimizing scars from accidents, burns or surgery. If used at once it keeps the flesh pliable and hastens the healing process. (Once the scar has formed, however, even vitamin E can't help.) It's especially recommended for use before and after plastic surgery.

• The stretch marks of pregnancy can be prevented or greatly helped by applying and taking vitamin E. . . . Taken internally, this vitamin can help people who bruise easily.

• Vitamin E is also the best thing you can put on your skin to keep wrinkles at bay. If possible, start before the crow's-feet and other lines are set; but late is better than never. I alternate between a vitamin E face cream and an undiluted oil, whose stimulating action I can feel immediately. There is warmth and sometimes a flushing, at least for me.

It may seem strange that anything which so profoundly affects the heart can do all this as well. But not so strange when we remember that vitamin E enables the blood to deliver oxygen to every tissue and cell through the capillaries. And this includes those capillaries closest to the surface of the skin.

Energy, Speed, Endurance

The call letter of this vitamin is appropriate to some other lively contributions: energy, speed and endurance. This has been proved repeatedly with both animals and athletes.

Rats given vitamin E were able to swim far longer than rats without it; they could withstand higher altitudes twice as long, and could run the treadmill harder and longer. In autopsies later their vital organs failed to show the damage that was present in the rats deprived. Racehorses given vitamin E were able to outdistance, outbreed and outlive identical horses without it.

In *Vitamin E, Your Key to a Healthy Heart* (which I consider one of the best books on vitamin E yet written), Herbert E. Bailey gives an in-depth report on the experiments undertaken at the Windfields Farm, Toronto, Canada, and the National Stud Farm in Oshawa, where this was established. Furthermore, it was discovered that the horses hit their peak when the original doses, already effective, were doubled or tripled. Again we ask how and why? F. G. Darlington, manager of the farms, and their veterinarian, Dr. J. B. Chassels, stated in published reports:

> It enables the tissues of the body to do the same job on less oxygen; it is as if one strapped an aqua-lung (with oxygen) on the horse's back. It opens up huge reserves of capillary circulation, sets of vessels not ordinarily used but waiting there for emergency demands. It helps to control the passage of fluids through the walls of blood vessels. It may even be a direct stimulant of muscle power.

What vitamin E can do for animals it can do for man. Athletes the world over are now being routinely fed wheat germ and given vitamin E to improve their performance. The Russians and Australians were in the early vanguard of training with vitamin E and wheat-germ oil for the Olympics. They found that no matter how much their athletes ate, they had to have these supplements to excel. In Canada, Dr. Wilfrid Shute administered vitamin E to world pairs skating champions and to the champion swimming team. He says, "We could even manipulate the times of the top four in any event by the giving or withholding of vitamin E, or varying the dosage level." (His daughter Karen, incidentally, was one of the stars on the swimming team.)

Dr. Thomas E. Cureton, who coached the Australian swimming teams to smashing victories, is now head of the Physical Fitness Laboratory at the University of Illinois, where he uses the same technique: Vitamin E with exercise will improve *anybody's* performance. There he conducted an experiment with a cross section of 200 student athletes and run-down middle-aged men. Results in extra energy, drive and endurance exceeded his expectations. The swimmers and wrestlers surpassed themselves, and the older men became rejuvenated!

Keeping Young

Energy and rejuvenation. Those two faces of vitamin E probably have the most popular appeal. Vitamin E is gaining a reputation for keeping people young.

Let's face it, we're all mortal, we all will die someday. But it seems to me absolute folly not to do everything humanly possible to stay vigorous, yes, and attractive as long as the Lord allows. Surely if science can offer us any safe method or substance that will help, why not take it? And despite the familiar jeers from those who refuse to experiment themselves or contribute to fresh knowledge, biomedical researchers continue to produce evidence that one definite method and substance is vitamin E.

Let's look at only a fraction of their findings. Dr. Jeffrey Bland is a young associate professor at the University of Puget Sound in Tacoma, Washington. Red blood cells, he learned, could be "aged" by exposure to light and oxygen. Oxidation caused them to swell and burst, much like overinflated tires. He then asked the blood donors to take vitamin E for a period before samples were drawn. This time, although exposed to light and air, their blood cells failed to blow up or "age." To make sure that it was the vitamin E and not something else, he then drew blood from donors who had *not* taken vitamin E, and put their cells in test tubes which contained vitamin E solutions. These cells were also exposed to light and air. Again there was almost total resistance to membrane destruction. Obviously vitamin E, whether it reached the blood cells by mouth or was provided in a solution, had the power to keep those cells from succumbing to oxidation.

Reproducing cells outside the body is a common procedure to determine their reactions; but after about 50 divisions the multiplication halts. By adding vitamin E (the only substance that will do this) cells have reproduced through 120 generations.

I am always fascinated by how things *work*. Biologists tell us each cell is surrounded not by a single membrane, but by a whole complex of compartments, like a tiny factory, each working away to see that the precious cell receives its precise amount of nutrients. There is even a process of selection and rejection. Dr. Bland says vitamin E sits in the middle of the fat-rich membranes like the filling in a sandwich, protecting the fats from reacting to the oxygen. Other scientists, particularly Dr. J. Lucy of the department of biochemistry at the Royal Free Hospital of Medicine in London, describe vitamin E as a powerful "sink," trapping oxidants which otherwise would chemically change and cause damage.

Dr. A. L. Tappel, biochemist at the University of California at Davis, is an expert on aging. He conducted studies comparing:

> Animals who were definitely old
> Animals heavily dosed with radiation
> Animals with vitamin E deficiencies

All showed the same kind of damage, especially to cell membranes.

Aging, he and other experts believe, is mainly due to the gradual accumulation of the destructive results of free radicals in the system. Enzymes can't function. The cell's energy source is crippled. Cells can't fight back. Cells begin to die and there aren't enough replacements. The speed with which this happens varies with individuals; but a lot of it depends upon the amount of vitamin E we have. For it is vitamin E that is forever pitted against these free radicals.

A "free radical" (what an apt name) is an incomplete bit of a molecule gone wild; a highly reactive fragment that forms whenever oxygen combines with something else. A graphic illustration is the butter that turns rancid when exposed to air. Chemicals like BHA and BHT can slow rancidity down— they're often listed among the ingredients of cereals and cooking oils. Vitamin E is the natural substance which accomplishes the same thing, although it takes more of it. In the body vitamin E keeps oils and oxygen from combining and in essence becoming rancid (peroxidizing)—the process which creates free radicals.

"Aging," says Dr. Tappel, "is due to the process of oxidation, and since vitamin E is a natural antioxidant, it can be used to counteract this process in the body."

(Free radicals have been blamed not only for aging but for cancer, since their primary purpose is to attach themselves to cells; unless sloughed off they can form tumors. This was the conviction of the German scientist Dr. Otto Warburg, who won the Nobel Prize in 1966. In his lecture *The Prime Cause and Prevention of Cancer,* he presented evidence that lack of oxygen at the cellular level could cause bits of cells to go wild and attack other tissues. Vitamin E, the regulator and defender of oxygen, can prevent this from happening.)

Menstruation and Menopause

Songs may claim that diamonds are a girl's best friend. But even diamonds don't look very bright to the woman suffering menstrual cramps, or the hot flashes, nervousness and other miseries of menopause. Certainly any female would trade her diamonds (if she had them) to be spared breast surgery or a hysterectomy. And no gems can ever compensate for the heartache of not being able to have a baby.

A few years ago *Prevention* magazine conducted a survey, asking readers to report on their own experiences with vitamin E. Of the 20,000 responses, 2,000 women volunteered that it had helped them through every known symptom of menopause. Many had been on hormones, to no avail. . . . Anecdotal medicine? Then consider only a minor sampling of professional testimony: Henry A. Gozen, writing in the *New York State Journal of Medicine,* said that vitamin E had helped 59 out of 66 patients.

W. H. Perloff, in *American Journal of Obstetrics and Gynecology,* stated that he had used vitamin E to treat 200 women with serious menopausal problems, had helped more than half and felt that results would have been even better if doses had been higher. Dr. N.R. Kavinoky, in *Annals of Western Medicine and Surgery,* reported similar success with 92 patients.

Hundreds of other letters received in the *Prevention* survey recounted relief from menstrual problems; and such letters continue to appear regularly in the "Mailbag" column. (One of the most interesting features of this invaluable magazine.) Other letters have reported on that terror of all women, breast cysts and lumps. Typical is the following: "About 10 months ago I consulted a physician about very painful lumps in my breasts. His diagnosis was fibrosis. The only remedy he could give was painkillers and if necessary a mastectomy." This writer began to take 600 IU of vitamin E three times a day, and more before the start of menses, when the pain was worse. "There are now no lumps and no pain."

Drs. Evan and Wilfrid Shute, the Canadian physicians famous in the fields of both heart and gynecology, have used vitamin E for years for all vascular problems and find it their most effective aid.

Alas, too many doctors have tried to treat purely female afflictions with tranquilizers and/or the hormone estrogen. Synthetic hormones burst upon the scene in the sixties and were considered practically a panacea. Hormones for conception and contraception, for menstruation and menopause, hormones to keep you sexy. Sales soared from some $17 million in 1962 to over $70 million in 1973. I took them myself until their link with cervical cancer became too threatening to ignore. Six separate studies in three years, the largest from Johns Hopkins University in 1979, have established that women who take estrogens run a risk of uterine cancer six times above normal. Estrogens are also associated with thromboembolism (clotting), strokes, heart disease, even deaths. The evidence became so alarming that in 1977 the FDA was forced to order pharmacists and physicians to issue warning inserts about their possible side effects. A move that was vigorously opposed by both the Pharmaceutical Manufacturers' Association and the AMA.

It's hard to understand why these hormones, known killers and cancer causers, should remain a legal drug which doctors are still prescribing and millions of women are taking—at the same time the FDA tries to disparage and even restrict the sale of vitamin E. The contradiction seems incredible because, as Dr. Shute explains to his patients, *every woman who is taking estrogens* has a far greater *need* for vitamin E than women who aren't.

And the irony of all this is compounded when we realize that we already have a powerful natural hormone factory in our own bodies—the adrenal glands. In which are found (remember?) *the body's richest concentration of vitamin E.*

Fertility

My uncles were farmers. They had never heard of vitamin E, but they were using it for their livestock long before it was discovered and written up in *Breeder's Gazette.* They knew that if sows were to have healthy litters, if stallions were to sire or mares to conceive, the creatures had to be fed plenty of freshly ground wheat. My aunts, who raised chickens, knew the same thing. Plenty of fresh wheat meant a big "hatch," and also an abundance of eggs. We realize now that it was the vitamin E in the rich germ of the wheat that accounted for all this fertility.

Since then scientists have confirmed that vitamin E is indeed absolutely essential to normal reproduction. "Veterinarians have known this for 30 years," Dr. Joe Nichols went on to tell those bankers in his Galveston address, "and have fed pure wheat germ oil to the barren heifer and to the bulls. . . . Rats, if they get pregnant and if we remove all the vitamin E from their diet, will abort every time on the thirteenth day. One of the reasons we have so much sterility in our young women is no doubt because 80% of the food they eat has had all the life taken from it."

Carlton Fredericks, who has been writing the truth about nutrition for generations, says in *Food Facts and Fallacies:* "The popular medical treatment of the infertile woman currently revolves around large doses of hormones, usually administered without regard to the couple's nutritional status. We may liken this to fertilizing a field without regard to the quality of the seed to be sown." Even primitive societies know better. In that landmark book *Nutrition and Physical Degeneration,* Dr. Weston Price reported:

> A very important phase of my investigations has been the obtaining of information from these various primitive racial groups, indicating that they were conscious that such injuries [sterility, aborting, birth defects] would occur if the parents were not in excellent physical condition and nourishment. I found that the girls were not allowed to be married until after they had had a period of special feeding. In some tribes a six months' period of special nutrition was required before marriage.

Sterility affects one out of six couples in the United States. In view of this one must ask—whatever happened to vitamin E? For since I began this book both Washington, D.C., papers, the *Star* and the *Post,* have carried lengthy articles deploring that tragedy, listing numerous attempts to solve it, but neither even *mentioning* vitamin E. On my desk lies the December 1977 issue of *Reader's Digest,* containing an article titled "New Hope for the Childless." I read it with a sense of anticipation and urgency, seeking in vain at least some word about the importance of nutrition. Everything else was suggested as possible causes—psychological tensions, operations and previous illnesses, infected or faulty Fallopian tubes, adolescent mumps in the male. But not even a glance was given to a possible lack of proper nourishment.

The authors, Emily and Per Ola D'Aulaire, wrote:

> Persistent infertility problems often require the detective work of fertility experts, who painstakingly eliminate one factor after another. It's a process that can be emotionally taxing and expensive— as much as several thousand dollars for a lengthy evaluation. . . . "Fertility patients are often desperate," says Dr. Marshall. "They will go anywhere and try almost anything."

The "almost anything's" include: taking of temperatures; the timing of intercourse; use of a hand calculator called an Ovu-Guide; microscopic examination of both sperm and cervical mucus; a biopsy of tissues from the uterine wall; X-ray screenings; and surgical procedures to examine the reproductive duct-work via dyes or little lighted telescopes.

I can't help but wonder about those sterile rats. Where would we be today if the puzzled early scientists had subjected the poor creatures to all *that?* Or, likewise, any livestock which didn't bear properly? The world would have no wool, no milk, no meat!

The reproductive process is identical in all mammals. To create new life, healthy male sperm must unite with healthy female egg in a healthy womb. Yet specialists dealing with the very same problem in human beings don't seem to have even *heard* of the simple substance that gets results among our fellow creatures. Obviously, a discovery which held so much promise and which has actually helped so many couples achieve their families, has gotten lost in an avalanche of drugs, devices and dazzling new technology. Does it not go back to the all too familiar: Why use something simple and inexpensive when so many careers and so much money depend on sheer complexity? To quote Herbert Bailey once more:

> Official medicine will go to any lengths to prove anything it wishes, but is it not astounding that it did not choose to validate the already existing European and Canadian studies concerning sterility in the human? The European studies are so conclusive as to the value of vitamin E in sterility that it is almost impossible to believe they were not followed up in this country.

In those studies *both* men and women were given vitamin E several months before attempted conception, and the woman given vitamin E throughout her resulting pregnancy. West German medical doctor R. Bayer, working with 100 couples, got *100 per cent results.* Bailey goes on to point out:

> It is most interesting to note that *in not one of the experiments where the man and wife were under intensive vitamin E therapy has there ever been recorded the birth of a monster or even a mentally retarded child.* [Italics mine.]

Dr. Shute believes we should not overlook the fact that in these studies vitamin E was first given to the *male.* It has been his observation that in a large percentage of cases it is the male who is responsible for inability to conceive.

Certainly vitamin E is very important to the expectant mother, for it assures her baby of the oxygen it needs to develop properly. She also needs vitamin E to provide rich milk for her baby. Little new babies are born with low levels of this vitamin. Cow's milk is a poor source, and most commercial formulas contain iron and unsaturated fats which destroy vitamin E. New babies are susceptible to infant anemia, particularly if very small or premature. To forestall this it's now routine medical practice to immediately give them this critically important vitamin.

The Versatile Vitamin

Those who responded to the *Prevention* magazine survey described a broad array of other conditions for which vitamin E had proved a godsend, often after years of needless suffering. The experience of any doctor who has *tried* it (as the Shute brothers have for more than thirty years) backs up such testimony. In his book *Health Preserver: Defining the Versatility of Vitamin E,* Dr. Wilfrid Shute gives dozens of case histories. Here are some of the many afflictions that have yielded to vitamin E:

Hay fever	Stomach ulcers
Diabetes	Acute or chronic nephritis
Cataracts	Muscular dystrophy
Skin diseases	Epilepsy
Ulcerative colitis	Hyperactivity
Bone diseases	Arthritis

All these in *addition* to those we've already discussed. And among the estimated 300 research papers on this vitamin which pour out every year, we find more. One just published in the *Journal of the American Geriatrics Society* reports an experiment in Tel Aviv where patients with osteoarthritis "experienced marked relief of pain" by taking 600 IU of vitamin E. Another, from the National Cancer Institute, reports that "vitamin E lessens the harmful effects of the widely used anticancer drug Adriamycin on heart muscle." Despite all this interest, vitamin E remains controversial; more respectable in the laboratories or professional journals than in the hands of those whose profession is to minister to the health of human beings. Meanwhile, people suffer and die for lack of it.

Dr. Evan Shute acknowledges that its very versatility may be one of its major obstacles to acceptance. "No substance known to medicine has such a variety of healing properties." It's just too much to ask people to believe that anything that can heal burns, keep the heart and lungs healthy and prevent miscarriages can also be so useful in so many other areas.

Yet it is *not* illogical. The Bible tells us over and over that "the life is in the blood." Every cell and tissue of these marvelous bodies depends on blood. Clean, properly circulating blood. Vitamin E is a vascular agent. Just as vitamin C is anti-viral; and the B vitamins are neural, affecting the nerves; vitamin E is vascular, having to do with the blood vessels.

It dissolves blood clots. It keeps poisonous peroxides from forming in the blood. And one of its major jobs is to see that the blood delivers a steady, ample supply of oxygen to the cells. Unless all this happens the cells will die; in countless ways the body will fight back. All this depends on vitamin E. Without it the body sickens; and when vitamin E is restored the body responds.

The Shutes: Pioneers of Vitamin E

No discussion of vitamin E would be complete without the story of a distinguished Canadian family of physicians, the Shutes. As gynecologists, the father and two sons Evan and Wallace were among the first to use vitamin E in treating infertility and problems of pregnancy. Their success was so great that, after some initial resistance from colleagues, they were eventually honored, both at home and abroad. But they were to achieve even more in the field of cardiology (the specialty of the other brother, Wilfrid); only to encounter almost incredible opposition.

In 1945, quite by accident, Evan and Wilfrid discovered that alpha tocopherol relieved their mother's angina pains. Encouraged, they tried it on other heart patients. Within a few years they had successfully treated over 10,000 cardiac sufferers, many pronounced hopeless previously. Rejoicing that they had found the weapon to overcome a killer, they wrote up their data, confident the medical profession would welcome such a major breakthrough. To their astonishment, no journal would publish their findings. The facts, despite incontrovertible evidence, were perhaps too phenomenal to believe.

Wilfrid Shute writes, "We Shutes were really naïve." They had expected their discovery to be welcomed, "not only for the rapid and significant improvement it affords but also for its promise of preventing heart disease . . ." They were denounced by doctors who had neither read their papers nor even tried vitamin E; more appallingly, others who were using this vitamin in their own practice or referring patients to the Shutes, refused to stand by them.

As related in their books, they had hoped to bestow this boon on the medical profession and go on to other matters. When it was rejected they could not abandon so vital a project. A nonprofit research clinic, called the Shute Institute, was founded in London, Ontario, where they continue to treat thousands of victims of cardiovascular diseases. Here too they have gathered worldwide evidence on the value of vitamin E in treating other problems.

The credentials of these men are superlative. Their degrees, honors and titles would fill this page. Yet, like almost every genuine medical pioneer, they have been pilloried and persecuted. The treatment of the Shutes has been particularly disgraceful in the United States. In Detroit some years ago, a number of former patients attempted to form a society and disseminate information about this vitamin which had helped them so much. They were accused of conspiring to promote a worthless product, their publications were seized and mail to their headquarters was returned marked "fraudulent."

The Shutes themselves have been victims of vicious propaganda claiming they own companies which manufacture vitamin E and their only motive is to make a fortune from it. Actually, they have spurned offers from such companies. For years their institution operated at a deficit; they have poured their own time, genius and money into a single cause for a single reason—to alleviate suffering and save lives. Meanwhile, the medical establishment, the drug industry, the food industry and the FDA continue to use the media to maneuver public opinion into believing that vitamins are generally useless, and the claims for vitamin E particularly false. . . . Why? We are entitled to ask. In heaven's name, *why?*

The answer is so obvious and familiar it's almost redundant: *Profit.*

If the true value of vitamin E were generally recognized and utilized, such inroads would be made on heart and lung diseases, on such human tragedies as infertility and muscular dystrophy, the financial impact would be devastating. Medical specialists would have to change their fields. Fund-raising organizations like the Heart Fund would have to find something else to raise money for (the way the March of Dimes grabbed birth defects after Salk vaccine conquered polio; or the Christmas seal people latched on to respiratory ailments in lieu of TB).

If, instead of expensive drugs, people knew that one economical vitamin could wipe out a large share of their ailments, the pharmaceutical houses would see their vast fortunes fading. They're not *about* to let that happen. Nor can the food industry —guilty of taking vitamin E out of our bread and of destroying it in processing other products—stand idly by and let the public realize we're being deprived of something our health depends on.

It's in the interest of all these forces to spread the lie via magazines and newspapers, radio and television. (Which they largely control, thanks to billions of dollars in advertising.) In this our own government cooperates. Consider again that slick FDA publication (paid for by our taxes): *Myths of Vitamins.* Its cover warns consumers that the kind of testimony and claims we've been discussing "result from mere guesswork, confusion, and often outright fraud." As for vitamin E—this bureaucracy which for twenty years denied that vitamin E had *any* biological usefulness (until it had to recant in 1959) repeats the falsehood it's touted for another twenty years: That it's almost impossible to produce vitamin E deficiency in people, since vitamin E is so readily available in foods.‡

As for all the evidence I've presented—the studies made, the scientists named, as well as hundreds there is no room for—in short, more than fifty years of medical research—all this is dismissed with these words and a sarcastic cartoon: "There is virtually no scientific proof for the majority of these claims. In fact, the new interest in vitamin E is based on *misinterpretations of animal research.*"

Italics mine. . . . So much for science!

Small wonder the general public has been brainwashed. Or that even conscientious doctors are often afraid to give it their stamp of approval, even though they may be taking vitamin E themselves or prescribing it for their patients. (The number of such doctors is growing, and an ever increasing number *are* speaking out.) But they know the penalties of bucking the establishment—ridicule, ostracism, loss of hospital privileges, even dismissal from their medical societies.

The only comfort is that truth eventually prevails. In concluding his book, *Health Preserver,* Dr. Shute says it is unlikely he will write another book on vitamin E.

> The need for authoritative information will not cease, but there are now enough people interested in vitamin E treatment to carry on what we Shutes started so long ago. . . . The thousands who flocked to us from literally all over the civilized world . . . and have received help where there was no help, these are our satisfactions. These also have made it impossible for the philistines to ignore vitamin E and the final capitulation appears to be near at hand. Indeed, many of the enemies of vitamin E have already surrendered. . . .
>
> We have experienced the jealousies and hatreds of little men. . . . However, we have also had experiences granted to very few

‡ No diets were ever more carefully planned and "balanced" than those for the astronauts on the fourteen-day Gemini II flight in 1965. Yet when the men were examined on their return they had lost 25 per cent of their red blood cells. (One fourth the body's supply in just two weeks.) Their physician, David Turner, realized even those special diets hadn't provided enough vitamin E. From then on the men on all space flights received extra vitamin E. When they returned their blood cells were normal, and they were not fatigued the way their predecessors had been.

physicians . . . namely involvement in a medical discovery of
great importance.

He speaks of eyesight restored to patients facing blindness,
burns healed without painful skin grafts, limbs saved, chronic
invalids restored to long productive lives—only a fraction of
what they have been able to do.

> Latterly, we have seen the concepts we first enunciated, of the
> various actions of megavitamin E, applied by other bold imagina-
> tive clinicians, to many and various other disease entities in their
> specialties. . . .
>
> Fortunately, the publication of a book about vitamin E by a lay-
> man, and the frequent references to our work in one or two health
> magazines, interested large numbers of the public who were then
> anxious for more authentic information.* That is the reason for the
> books I've written. . . .
>
> As a result, it was reliably estimated three or four years ago that
> between 30 and 35 million Americans were taking vitamin E in
> megadoses. One result was that approximately 10,000 middle-aged
> American males were saved from death by cardiac disease in one
> year. I am certain that vitamin E and vitamin E only is responsible
> for the sudden decrease in deaths from heart disease. It will con-
> tinue as more and more people become acquainted with the pre-
> ventive aspect of vitamin E therapy.

How tragic, however, that ultimate acceptance always takes
so long. In the words of Alexander Fleming, who discovered the
antibiotic most commonly used today: "Penicillin sat on the
shelf for twelve years while I was called a quack. I can only
think of the thousands who died needlessly because my peers
would not use my discovery."

How to Buy and Use Vitamin E

Vitamin E is the common name for the chemical term tocopherol. Actually, vitamin E consists of a number of tocopherols
known as alpha, gamma and delta. Alpha tocopherol is the most
active biologically, and the only one the Shutes consider effec-

* *Vitamin E, Your Key to a Healthy Heart,* by Herbert Bailey, Arc Books.

tive, at least for therapeutic use. Other authorities recommend mixing tocopherols for average daily needs.

Twice a day I take two capsules containing 400 IU of d-alpha tocopherol plus the others normally present in mixed tocopherols. Because of my husband's injured feet and circulation problems, I began giving him double this amount when one of his feet began to discolor and swell. We also massaged the foot with vitamin E oil. Within a few weeks the condition cleared up, but I continued the dosage just to be sure.

Even the FDA admits vitamin E is safe in any amounts except for people with rheumatic hearts or high blood pressure. Such people should take vitamin E in small amounts and increase only under a doctor's supervision. For others, "toxicity symptoms have not been reported even at intakes of 800 IU per kilograms of body weight daily for 5 months," according to the Food and Nutrition Board. (A preposterous quantity for anybody.) We buy only the natural, which is more potent, although it costs a little more.

Vitamin E should be taken before meals. And I don't think you can get enough from the usual vitamin-mineral capsule. One of the most popular brands has only 15 IU of vitamin E and 18 milligrams of iron, which is actually considerably more iron, and which some authorities—particularly the Shutes—consider incompatible with vitamin E. In fact, they say that if you are taking any iron preparation it should be separated from the vitamin E by at least eight hours. (The iron in such foods as liver or spinach, however, doesn't seem to interfere.) Just to play safe, I take my vitamin E in the morning, the multiple at night.

I also take wheat-germ capsules and use lots of wheat germ in cooking. Wheat germ isn't the same as vitamin E, but it contains generous amounts of this golden treasure which protects our hearts, prolongs our youth and gives us energy.

14

The Magic Minerals and Organic Foods

Health is the most natural thing in the world . . . because we are a part of nature—we are nature. Nature is trying hard to keep us well, because she needs us in her business.

ELBERT HUBBARD

As a child, I knew cousin Jennie was anemic—she had to have iron for her blood. Mother's friend Mrs. Hanke had a goiter; she wore amber beads and took iodine for it. Our parents said to drink our milk—it was good for our teeth, had calcium in it. That, for many years, was the sum total of my knowledge about minerals. Like most people, I had no idea that every day of my life my body was doing business with twenty or more different minerals gotten from food and water, and that my health, energy and ability to resist disease depended on them.

Until recently vitamins have gotten the headlines; they've been the stars of the nutritional show. But without a large supporting cast of minerals the show literally couldn't go on. After years of neglect, scientists are now saying minerals are every bit as important. And not just the well-known minerals like iron and calcium, but the "trace" minerals—so called because we need only a trace of them. Yet those tiny amounts could be the missing pieces in the giant jigsaw puzzle of health and longevity: Why some people have more pep; why some families just don't get sick as often as others, or die off as fast; why some people stay young longer.

I'm so sold on minerals I could just as well have called this book *God and Minerals*. Because the Lord made minerals too, and stored them in the earth, like the treasures they are. We call them inorganic because they are themselves without life. When mined they can be turned into things like copper kettles and chromium chairs and the steel girders of buildings. Yet, miraculously, he also gave us plants which can take these hard, dead substances and transform them into the malleable stuff of life. The very liquid that flows in our veins, plant or animal, is largely mineral. Iron forms the hemoglobin or red blood cells of man; copper the blood of fish; magnesium the chlorophyl of vegetation. Minerals also give us substance. The skeleton that holds us up, the teeth which grind our food—all are built from calcium.

But minerals do far more. They control body fluids, regulate the heartbeat, stimulate the brain, determine the health of the glands. In fact, every life process depends on them. Scientists tell us that every body cell contains some 5,000 enzymes performing at least *two million* biochemical reactions every minute. And that *none* of these reactions can happen without the minerals. Vitamins are necessary, of course—they act as coenzymes. But the minerals must be present in proper balance to trigger the whole thing. Without them we will get tired, rundown, have trouble with hair, skin, nails and teeth, break bones easily, have little resistance to disease.

Even vitamins can't prevent these problems; not alone. Our creator gave us both, and designed our remarkably complex bodies so that his vitamins and minerals must work as a team.

Back to the Farm

My farming uncles knew about minerals, though—at least when it came to their stock. Minerals went into their daily feed. And if a horse began to gnaw its stall or a cow kept trying to reach the clover on the other side of the fence, the animals got some more. Once a heifer was so desperate in her efforts she tore her shoulder on barbed wire, yet kept right on. "She's trying to tell me something," Uncle Harrison said. "That pasture's about worn out, needs lime and so does she."

Meanwhile, my aunts threw the scraps to the chickens and fed the garbage to the hogs. And every spring and fall the manure that had accumulated in barns and pens would be loaded up and spread on the garden and the fields. I can still see the arched forks of those manure spreaders and remember the tangy aroma—faintly ammonia, not unpleasant—of their rich brown loads. Ecology? Recycling? We'd never heard the words. They were just doing what came naturally, giving back to the earth what would otherwise be wasted, to be transformed into mineral-rich eggs and meat and fruit and grains again. Practicing what the English agricultural scientist Sir Albert Howard called "the doctrine of return." Giving their own instinctive push to what he diagrammed as the Wheel of Life, "with man and animals at the top and the soil at the bottom." Robert Rodale describes it in *Prevention:*

> To the left, on the way up in the cycle were plants. On the right side, on the way down to the soil, were vegetable and animal wastes. No society could be healthy, he said, unless this wheel was kept turning. The crucial part of the cycle of return, Sir Albert pointed out, was the return of the vegetable and animal wastes to the soil. If that was done, the mineral health of the soil would be continually stimulated naturally. It would then be unnecessary to use synthetic fertilizers and poisonous pesticides, which have potential for harm.

It was this man who inspired Robert's father, J. I. Rodale, to experiment and start his *Organic Gardening and Farming* magazine, which actually launched the organic movement in the United States. From the very beginning he said, "The answer to health will be found in the soil. . . . There are other factors, but the condition of the soil in which our food is raised may well be the most important one."

Where the Farmers Failed

This should be evident to any thinking person. Minerals *must* come to us from the soil. And nature has provided only three ways for them to reach us: Through our drinking water. By eating the plants that change minerals into living matter; or by eating the animals that have eaten the plants. If our drinking water is soft, we've already lost one source. And if the soil is mineral-poor, we've lost another. Because plants simply cannot get, transform and bestow on us something that isn't *there.* Neither can they help us if chemicals have locked up the minerals so the plants can't use them; or killed the earthworms and microorganisms that bring the minerals up into their roots to be changed into the form the plant must have.

Paradoxically, agriculture, which we've always trusted to provide us with all the precious nutrients we need, has actually been the destroyer of that first fundamental step in the food chain or wheel of life. Long ago my uncles' methods of farming went out of style. Instead of rotating crops, plowing under the cornstalks and generally restoring humus to Mother Earth, farmers yielded to the fervent claims of salesmen and their own farm agents: "Science has got something better. You can raise bigger crops and make a lot more money by using pesticides and chemical fertilizers."

It sounded great. These guys had degrees from the agricultural colleges. (All generously but quietly endowed by the chemical companies.) This also became the dominant message of their helpful farming journals. (Supported even more liberally and quite obviously by chemical industry advertising.) And hooray, it worked! Crop yields *were* bigger for a while, and so were the farmers' bank accounts.

But the insects were smart too. Before long they became immune to all that poison; new and even more voracious species appeared. And the land took more and more fertilizer. Farmers began to realize they were "on a chemical treadmill leading to bankruptcy," as expressed by Dale Bottrell, entomologist with the Council on Environmental Quality. He's quoted in a lengthy Washington *Post* article by Daniel Zwerdling, which explores this whole disaster in depth. It brings out the fact that since pesticides first came to the farms after World War II *pest damage hasn't decreased, it has actually tripled.* "Little wonder that cornbelt farmers are spending nine times as much money per acre as they did only a decade ago." But farmers are scared to kick the chemical habit; they're on a treadmill they can't get off. And of course the chemical companies aren't complaining. Their profits have skyrocketed.

The Department of Agriculture launched a research program on IPM (Integrated Pest Management using biological controls). But its total budget for six years was only $14 million—a scant 7 per cent of what the chemical poison research companies spend in a year. The government also allotted 100 extension agents to teach IPM methods to farmers. Meanwhile, the Environmental Protection Agency found over 4,000 pesticide salesmen in Iowa alone.

The *Post* article appeared, coincidentally, at about the same time as a Tractorcade of desperate farmers rolled down Pennsylvania Avenue, demanding audiences with President Carter and Secretary of Agriculture Bob Berglund, threatening to strike if their demands for parity prices weren't met.

Certainly the economics of agriculture are very complex. Farmers *are* the victims of a lot of things—inflation, middlemen, government red tape and mismanagement. But don't their direst problems go back to that first forced overfeeding of an already rich and productive land? To that initial poisoning of weeds and insects that may seem obnoxious, but which are actually serving us in ways we don't fully understand? For they are a part of the chain of life which we break at our peril. And the tragedy is—it was so unnecessary! As the article points out, "Some major commercial growers are astonishing the agriculture industry by going completely organic." And doing handsomely, thanks, and finding they have "eliminated the need for any pesticides at all."

My friend Ken Hinde could have told them that years ago. Ken has farmed the same 240 Iowa acres for forty-five years and never added anything to the soil but natural fertilizer, rock phosphate and organic trace minerals, and he's never had any need for pesticides. "I may be old-fashioned," he said in an interview in our hometown paper, the Storm Lake *Pilot Tribune,* "but I think rotation is better for the soil. I've never lost a crop to bugs yet."

As I mentioned in an earlier chapter, Ken and Pearl "cry all the way to the bank." They heard the address given by Joe D. Nichols, M.D., before the Atlanta Bankers Convention some years ago, and obtained a copy for me. How eloquently Dr. Nichols expresses all this:

> The end result of chemical farming is always disease, first in the land itself, then in the plant, then in the animal and finally in us. Everywhere in the world where chemical farming is practiced, the people are sick. The use of synthetic chemicals does not make land rich. It makes it poorer than before.
>
> There is only one way to make land rich, and that is just exactly like the good Lord does on the floor of the forest. He puts back into the land dead plant matter and dead animal matter. This is what leaf mold contains . . . the major elements plus the trace elements, plus dead and decaying organic matter, and all in the proper proportions.
>
> And when we say dead and decaying matter, that presupposes that at one time the material had life. . . . This is of tremendous importance. You must have death and decay if you expect to have life and growth. This is a natural cycle that no chemist can get around, no matter how many degrees he may have behind his name.

Why People Are Going Organic

Rodale chose the word *organic* to describe his methods and philosophy because it focuses on the living or organic factors in the soil. To be healthy we must cooperate with nature. This means growing our foods uncorrupted from the start, and then not corrupting them by unnecessary processing later.

He was an explorer, a crusader, and like anybody who challenges the status quo, he was called a nut. Turn your back on technology, go back to farming the way our grandparents did? Spurn the wonderland of Cokes, sugared cereals and other additive-laced goodies on supermarket shelves? Raise or demand fruits and vegetables free of fungicides and pesticides, and hopefully still retaining a few vitamins and minerals? Insist on meats that haven't been pumped full of cancer-causing hormones, and antibiotics that could interfere with our bodies' own immunity system? Scientists smiled, the FDA jeered and the food and chemical companies were furious. And almost every branch of the government backed them to the hilt.

But this man was not only looking backward, he was prophesying that if we didn't, disease and devastation lay ahead. The chemicals we were using and consuming so wantonly would poison not only our people but our planet. His wasn't the only voice, of course, but his was perhaps the most resented because so many people began to listen, to start their own little compost piles and gardens, to ask questions of their doctors, to *think*. A few farmers *did* get off the chemical treadmill in time and found a ready market for all their natural, uncontaminated products. Natural food stores began to proliferate. And these were not just other so-called kooks, but people smart enough to see the connection between the soaring disease statistics and our way of life. If the medical profession has made such strides with its dazzling new technology and more and more potent drugs, why were so many people *sick?* And with so many dreadful, seemingly incurable diseases?

Gradually the organic movement grew. Primarily because, despite government critics and industry disclaimers, there is simply no way to keep the American people from reading and watching the news. And here are just a few of the stories that have made upsetting headlines during only two or three years:

• KEPONE FELLS WORKERS AT VIRGINIA PLANT. "All fish in the James River believed to be poisoned . . ."

• MILLIONS POISONED WITH CRIPPLING CHEMICAL DUMPED IN CATTLE FEED. "Former State Senator Donald Albosta said, 'I think it accurate to say that pretty much every person in Michigan is contaminated with PBB.' "

• CALIFORNIA PROBING PESTICIDE LINK TO STERILITY, CANCER. "A widely used pesticide, DBCP, is alleged to cause sterility, birth defects and cancer among chemical workers, farm laborers and consumers . . ."

• SCHOOL FOOD FOUND RADIOACTIVE. Citywide Lunch Program Closed.

• 400,000 HENS, ONE MILLION EGGS POISONED WITH PCB.

• VIRGINIA RAINS BADLY BEFOULED BY CHEMICALS . . . CHEMICAL COMPOUND SUSPECTED AS MARYLAND OYSTER KILLER . . . PCB'S RUIN HOUSATONIC

. . . TOXIC CHEMICAL FOUND IN DRINKING WATER. . . .

• SCIENTISTS WARN OF CONTAMINATED MILK FOR INFANTS. "A Senate subcommittee was told it is difficult if not impossible to find uncontaminated milk for babies. A study of mothers' milk revealed residues of pesticides and other chemical contaminants which can cause cancer and other diseases . . ."

• HEALTH AIDES ADVISE CLEARING POLLUTED AREA NEAR NIAGARA FALLS. "Citing a 'great and imminent peril,' the New York State Health Commission has recommended that pregnant women and infants up to two years of age leave their homes and that the public school not open in the fall . . ." (After that first grim warning so many health problems were found in the entire Love Canal population that President Carter declared an emergency; other residents were evacuated, homes boarded up. Worse, it was discovered that thousands of tons of waste containing deadly dioxin had been dumped throughout the entire county for years.)

The situation is not unique. An ABC-TV news special titled *The Killing Ground* portrayed an appalling picture of the chemical cesspools "that have been buried in *over 32,000 sites* all over America. But they don't stay buried forever. They seep into our rivers and streams, making water supplies deadly. They seep above ground, destroying our land and our homes, and poisoning our children."

Whole Species Are Dying

Those are just a tiny fraction of the horror stories that have to do with people. There are hundreds more about what's happening to our wildlife. Whole species are dying out because they can no longer reproduce—often creatures geographically far from the original source of pollution. For the poisons are carried by wind and water; entering the food chain, they are even threatening the plankton in the ocean on which life depends for a large part of our oxygen. As for those nitrogen fertilizers? Research scientists now warn that they pose more of a threat to the earth's critical ozone shield than spray propellants or supersonic planes.

Dr. John Gille of the National Center for Atmospheric Research in Boulder, Colorado, says that if the increased use of nitrogen fertilizers continues, there could be a 30 per cent depletion of ozone within a century. The Academy of Sciences has predicted that such an ozone depletion means an increase of skin cancer, a dire effect on world crops, and on the ocean's basic food source, those photoplankton.

Such stories have been appearing for years; I have accumulated an enormous file of them just since I began thinking about this book. But it took the government twenty years even to ban DDT, and by then there were thousands of other destructive chemicals to take its place. Federal officials don't even know how many; estimates range from 60,000 up—30,000 of these pesticides alone. Far more than can even be tested for safety.

William Tucker, writing in the Washington *Star,* reports that six years after the 1972 Federal Environmental Pesticide Control Act, the required testing hadn't even begun. "On top of all this, Congress has passed the Toxic Substances Control Act, which charges the EPA with monitoring all 70,000 existing chemicals, plus the more than 1,000 new chemicals that are introduced each year." A survey by the National Institute of Occupational Safety and Health shows that one of every four Americans is exposed at work to substances toxic enough to cause illness or death.

Yet about all Big Brother has been able to do is to pass seemingly unenforceable laws, and set "permissible" or "safe" standards. But safe for whom? and for how long? Even when they don't make headlines, toxic substances interact, and build up in the system. As Einstein once demanded, "Who gave them permission to *permit?*"

Science writer Wil Lepkowski, covering a conference sponsored by the National Institute of Environmental Health Science, says:

> The grim parade passes and lengthens. The short term effects are pain, damaged organs and death. Over the long term, the threat is cancer. . . . And those who control research funds and understand

the facts of epidemiology and toxicology know that setting "safe" standards for each carcinogen or potential carcinogen, is an economic nightmare. . . . For the cancer control issue comes down to thresholds. The sorry truth is that each person has his own threshold. Research is continually raising the ethical issue over, literally, which of the weakest ones will die.

For this reason alone our government should have been back of the organic movement long ago, and be vigorously urging everyone to join it now. Instead, our government has sided with the same groups that scorn natural foods, and who actually condemn the use of the very things that can *protect* us from these seemingly inescapable poisons: vitamins and minerals. To most of our federal agencies, the very term *organic* is a fighting word.

The Public Attack on Natural or Organic Foods

During his term as Secretary of Agriculture, Earl Butz denounced organic farming as "faddism" and said if we turned to it Americans would starve. (This was between his jobs as a paid director of Ralston Purina and his employment as consultant to Conagra, the second-largest flour mill in the United States.)

As for the products themselves, in 1973 the FDA struck out at anyone marketing organic foods. The order went out that any food should be deemed misbranded if its labeling represented or even *implied* that its nutritive quality had anything whatever to do with the soil on which it was raised; or that such food was affected in any way by its storage, processing or cooking.

Ironically, the edict was issued within a few weeks of a published report from West Virginia University based on research experiments with corn. There Dr. Robert Keefer and Dr. Rabindar Singh established that fertilizers did indeed alter the nutrient values in some food soils.

> The changes occur in the amounts of trace elements contained in the grains and leaves. The most important trace elements from a nutritional point of view are iron, manganese, copper and zinc . . . extremely important in the human diet. . . . One of the most interesting results of the studies on sweet corn is that the more phosphorus applied to one of the soils the less zinc found in the grains.

Results of this nature suggest that one should examine carefully the long term effect of heavy fertilization rates from the standpoint of human health.

The report notes that *similar surveys conducted in eleven midwestern states* revealed that the iron, copper, zinc and manganese content of grain had dropped in the last four years and "could have far-reaching effects on the health of animals and men that consume them."

Did the Department of Agriculture respond by hastening to warn the public? Hardly. The very next year they sent top officials to a convention to *attack* such nonsense. "The Food Supply and the Organic Food Myth" was its theme. Jim Hightower tells about it in *Eat Your Heart Out,* a book no concerned American should miss. All other speakers were food industry people and their scientists; nobody to present the organic side of it was allowed.

> Why all this ado over so little? Not because organic food threatens to become a significant factor in major food markets, but because the very existence of naturally produced, basic foods causes people to think about the manufactured stuff they are getting from the brand name food companies. . . . With billions of advertising dollars spent to develop an image, the food goliaths are not anxious now for eaters to start questioning it. . . .
>
> Sales of organic food are about $500 million a year. That is a mere four-tenths of one per cent of the total $161 billion food industry. . . . To put the dollar figure of organic sales into perspective, it is less than the combined advertising budgets of the six leading food advertisers.

It is these huge food companies that have been wiping out the family farmer. The American Agricultural Marketing Association estimates that by 1985 three fourths of our food will be raised and controlled by a handful of these monopolies. "Corporate control," writes Hightower, "has a tight grip on the growing of many of the things people like best. . . . The objective is not to produce the best-tasting tomato or the most nutritious chicken, but to produce an acceptable product at the cheapest cost to the company, leaving the rest up to the advertising departments. . . . The corporate crop is built on chemicals and hormones. . . . Most damning, the officials of government have chosen to side with the power of the corporations against the competitiveness and efficiency of family farmers."

These oligopolies, as Hightower calls them, are the biggest users of chemical poisons in growing our food. Then, to compound the crime, the milling process destroys not only whatever vitamins the plant may have but also the trace elements so essential for life:

> 78% of the zinc
> 86% of the manganese
> 40% of the chromium
> 89% of the cobalt
> 68% of the copper
> 48% of the molybdenum

Finally, they add sugar, salt, more chemicals, process it beyond recognition and spend millions of dollars selling it to us on TV and in newspapers and magazines. Naturally they are outraged that even a small but vocal minority should insist that this is all wrong, in fact a major cause for our terrible toll of degenerative diseases. And their propaganda mills fight back by way of spokespeople in the media where they advertise so heavily. In fact, concerned by mounting criticism, Monsanto launched a massive public relations campaign "to convince America that some chemicals are good for you," reports Jack Anderson in his syndicated column, "even though they are suspected of inducing cancer.

"With sales revenues of $4 billion a year, Monsanto is easily able to pay for a combined television and magazine drive to gloss over scientific findings that the chemicals that preserve your food and safeguard crops may be hazardous."

How Truth Is Perverted

"Without chemicals life itself would be impossible," claim the now familiar slogans. Which contain enough truth to confuse; as if the concoctions of Du Pont, Dow Chemical or Monsanto were somehow as vital to our existence as the very elements with which God made the world.

And take the true-false quizzes, the question-answer exchanges in many a nutrition column. Q. "My sister is convinced she should buy or raise organic foods. Are they really any better?" A. "No, just more expensive. There is no evidence whatever that plants raised 'naturally' have more nutritional value; or that meats from animals that eat such plants are any different or more healthful. They just cost more." (Track down the author and you'll find a consultant to the American Grocers Association and a director of Monsanto, which manufactures preservatives, pesticides and artificial fertilizers.)

Or this from *Diabetes Forecast:*

> Poor soil is largely the farmer's headache, not the eater's. . . . The vitamins in our foods are manufactured by the plants themselves, they don't come from the soil. . . . Aren't foods grown with natural, organic fertilizers such as manure, more nutritious? No. The preference for "natural" over "chemical" fertilizers may be perceived by health food marketers, but it's not a distinction recognized by the plant world. Organic fertilizers can't be used directly by the plants. They must first be broken down by soil bacteria into inorganic compounds. The inorganic compounds actually taken up by the plant are identical to those supplied by man-made fertilizers.

What a distortion. Because it's the inorganic (hard, dead) compound which must be broken down into *organic or living* substance which the plant or animal can use; and those soil bacteria so necessary to the process are crippled or destroyed by chemical fertilizers. Fertilizers such as nitrogen and phosphorus do produce luxurious plants, but only because their roots have been overstimulated. Their energy goes into size, instead of reaching out and drawing in the zinc, selenium, copper and other minerals we need so critically.

The *Journal of the American Society of Horticultural Science* reports a study at Kansas State University where the iron in spinach was greatly increased by using only manure instead of the usual commercial fertilizers. "Our results likely came from decomposing organic fertilizer forming organic acids that caused iron to chelate into forms more readily absorbed by the plants."

Even if naturally raised foods were *not* higher in vitamins and minerals (which they are), surely anyone writing about health or nutrition should remind the reader that at least they are not drenched with poisonous insecticides or filled with dangerous drugs and chemicals. Yet these facts are ignored.

Natural Foods and the Diabetic

Now if there's one person who needs all the unpolluted, vitamin- and mineral-rich nutrients he can get, it's the diabetic—especially the minerals chromium, zinc and selenium. His arch-enemy is ordinary sugar, ever present in processed foods. And the last thing he needs is meat from animals that have been pumped full of hormones and antibiotics. The hormones can upset his own highly sensitive hormone balance (since insulin is a hormone secreted by the pancreas); and the antibiotics play havoc with his own immunity to disease. As for minerals, they are so important to the body's natural ability to produce and utilize insulin, many doctors now consider diabetes a mineral-deficiency disease.

There are an estimated 6 million diabetics in America, three fourths of them maturity-onset cases (the kind that usually strikes about middle age). In his early forties my husband joined their ranks. For years he was hooked on insulin, and for years rode the terrifying seesaw that this toxic medication propels: going into insulin shock from getting too much (disorientation, dizziness, fainting), or risking actual coma from getting too little.

In the more than fifty years since insulin was first isolated, it has been considered a lifeline to millions, a way to control an ancient and supposedly "incurable" disease (the body's inability to handle sugar). Recently insulin has come into serious question. In their book *Live Longer Now*, based on extensive research from the Longevity Foundation of America, authors Leonard, Hofer and Pritikin state: "Although insulin was considered a medical breakthrough . . . its complications—blindness, heart disease, and so forth—tarnished the insulin image. In addition, it became known in modern years that injected insulin has a way of seriously damaging the pancreas and the body's own insulin-producing capacity, so that once started on it, a diabetic often had to continue using it despite its dangers." Dr. Henry C. Bieler has stated that insulin "has a harmful effect on the blood vessels. Its continued use causes different types of arterial disease."

In any case, despite insulin and other diabetic drugs, diabetes is the third leading cause of death in America; and 70 per cent of the deaths among diabetics are due to a vascular disease. My husband's diabetes followed the usual pattern, leading to the three heart attacks that nearly killed him.

All this, however, was before we discovered minerals and vitamins, especially vitamin E—and began buying or raising our own organic foods. Thanks to them he was able to get his heart troubles under control; to live a full active life despite the presence of cancer; and gradually, to control his diabetes—so that for most of his last five years, he had almost no need for insulin. (Except for rare occasions such as Christmas when he "cheated" by eating sweets.)

It was a long, slow process of eliminating all possible pro-cessed foods, then meats and dairy products, and finally living almost exclusively on whole-grain breads and cereals, together with the fruits and vegetables from his own mineral-rich or-ganic garden. It took more self-discipline than most of us could muster, but he had so much more energy, felt and looked and slept so much better, he wanted to shout its wonders to the world. And one of the greatest blessings of all was that he was no longer enslaved to those daily shots of insulin.

Why Natural Foods Are So Important

I realize not everybody is lucky enough to have garden space. But there are other ways to produce many of your own natural, uncontaminated vegetables, at least. Before we moved to the country we dug up part of the lawn, edging flower beds with carrots and lettuce, growing peas and tomatoes against a fence. Our apartment-dwelling daughter uses window boxes and pots on a balcony. A cousin raises tomatoes in her sunny windowsills all winter and gives them as Christmas presents. Friends have glassed in a porch for a greenhouse. Anybody can grow sprouts, the purest form of vegetable protein, in glass jars. At Ann

Wigmore's Hippocrates Health Institute in Boston, they grow all the vegetables for some sixty weekly guests, in the kitchen. They even make their own compost there! And because so many green things are growing, the air is always sweet and clean. A breath of spring, in fact, compared to the heavy pollution on the busy street just beyond their doors.

A word of caution in this respect: City gardeners are being warned to scrub and peel any vegetables from gardens close to busy streets. In Boston, New York, Washington, D.C., and other cities, thousands of people have been gardening (often in groups) partly to combat the high cost of food. Now tests reveal that exhaust fumes from cars may be contaminating both soil and vegetables with lead and cadmium—two minerals which are actually dangerous. Parents are being urged to have children's blood checked for lead levels. (Proving that the soil and its products *do* reflect whatever goes into them.)

The irony of this is underscored by the fact that the Environmental Protection Agency will also warn you to scrub and peel any fruits and vegetables bought at the supermarket. A spokeswoman for the toxicology branch says the amount of pesticides on them varies; some will rinse off easily, others actually penetrate the product so deeply that if you eat it you've *got* it. How much is anybody's guess—or how great a threat to your health. The amounts may be infinitesimal, but they build up in time. *There are no safe levels.* If a poison is lethal enough to kill insects in seconds, surely it is sheer arrogance to think, "Oh, but it wouldn't hurt *me!*"

Following are precautions *Consumers' Research Magazine* has published for handling pesticides:

Be sure not to apply them where there are foods, dishes, or cooking utensils.

Do not apply them in a room where an aquarium, bird, dog, cat, or other pet is present.

Keep them away from and positively out of the reach of children at all times.

Do not smoke or prepare food or eat while you handle a pesticide. If you accidentally spill some of the product on your skin, wash immediately with plenty of soap and water.

If you spill some on your clothing, take the garment off immediately, and launder it before you wear it again.

Once you have finished the job, wash your hands and face thoroughly.

These, remember, are the products that have already actually been *sprayed* on your fruits and vegetables!

At this writing the House Commerce Oversight and Investigations Subcommittee is urging Congress to broaden the Delaney Amendment to include not only those pesticides which cause cancer but also those which have been shown to cause genetic mutations, birth defects and other serious injuries. They called EPA's system for setting pesticide tolerances "outdated, ineffectual," and scolded the FDA, labeling its chemical residues programs "seriously inadequate." The agency was urged to "substantially increase its surveillance program for chemical residues in food." The panel also attacked the USDA's monitoring of animal drugs known to leave residues in poultry and meat, stating, "The combined efforts of FDA and USDA do not effectively regulate the occurrence of toxic levels of animal drugs in meat."

If you can't raise natural, uncontaminated foods, try to find a trustworthy health store that has them, or a farm where they are grown. Because this is difficult, I think it's imperative that we take supplements to counteract the abuses our bodies will suffer otherwise. The vitamins and minerals that see that our cells are properly nourished; that fortify our immunity system; and that detoxify these poisons we do ingest every day, no matter where or how we live.

Natural foods are not only rich in both vitamins and minerals, they taste the way God meant them to. And their flavor can't be duplicated by the chemical trickery that has meant millions to the food industry. (For instance, Flavor and Fragrance Systems manufactures a line of pie filling flavorings known as TNT—True Natural Taste. Imitation Apple No. 28005 and Tart Red Cherry No. 34-02 are just two that are presented in *Food Product Development* as a way to reduce the actual content of fruit in the pie and save costs to the manufacturer.)

Belatedly, the big companies have rushed to cash in on the natural foods trend; some merely capitalizing on the word (as you'll find if you read the labels), others making honest reforms. I am personally heartened by the number of breads, ice creams and other products becoming available courageously claiming, "Nothing artificial, no additives." Hooray for them. High time. Because actually most companies have so perverted our palates through excessive salt and sugar, artificial flavors, fake foods, junk foods and foods processed beyond recognition that an honest old-fashioned tomato or apple, or the leg of a chicken that has been allowed to peck at Mother Earth, may taste a little strange at first.

But they *are* better for you, and they *don't* cost any more in the long run. Not if you value your health enough to spend the time, energy and a few extra dollars to keep it, instead of thousands trying to get it back once it's gone.

15

Nine Supplements
That Can Save Your Life

In addition to vitamins, I take other supplements, mainly for their minerals. The body *is* the temple of the spirit, and the good Lord built it strong. For the solid substance of our bodies is proteins and minerals. Especially calcium.

But minerals have other critical jobs to perform; in fact, even vitamins would be helpless without them.

Here are some marvelous food supplements that guarantee those minerals. They can give you energy and save your life.

Bone Meal

If I never took another vitamin, even C, I would take bone meal. It's the best single source of calcium. And calcium is the most important mineral. Our very skeleton and teeth are made of it; what's more, *every physical process depends on it.* Calcium is the one thing our body demands every instant, and *must have* or we die.

Calcium is the most abundant mineral within us. Ninety-five per cent goes into our bones and teeth—which are not static, but must constantly be rebuilt by fresh supplies; while the calcium already stored in the bones is continually withdrawn in small but critical amounts to keep us going. Every breath, every reflex, every digestive process, every movement—from the flick of an eyelid to hard physical labor—requires calcium. Even every heartbeat. In fact, it is the push-pull mechanism triggered by calcium and magnesium that *enables* the heart to beat.

Calcium is so vital that if its supply runs low the body will actually cannibalize its own bones to survive! That's why so many people are susceptible to broken bones, especially in later life.

Calcium deficiency is a subtle, long-time thing. It can go unrecognized for years as people live on "borrowed bone." With less bone to support them they may tire easily, have back problems, arthritis, begin to stoop. Often they actually shrink. Edward Banner, M.D., writing in *Postgraduate Medicine,* says studies have shown that "postmenopausal women may lose from one to six inches in height." All too often a bone will suddenly snap—generally in thigh or hip.

Osteoporosis (the condition of porous, fragile bones) has become almost an American epidemic. Each year 6 million people suffer bone fractures because of it; and of those who break hips, one out of six victims will simply waste away in hospitals and die. Partly because being immobilized for any length of time will severely further drain the body of calcium. The situation seems ironic when we realize that a five-person team of physicians and surgeons conducted a ten-year study of literally thousands of patients in two New York hospitals, and presented their findings in the *New York State Journal of Medicine* in 1975. They had found that calcium could not only prevent this disease, but actually reverse it.

This should be common knowledge to any doctor. Yet quite recently in one of the most famous medical teaching institutions, I was shocked to encounter a friend being wheeled down the hall with her leg in a cast. She'd been there three months, she told me, after breaking her femur. Medicated. In therapy. In traction. But bone meal? Calcium? The doctor hadn't mentioned them. Another friend is going through the pain and expense of having an artificial hip implanted. A surgical procedure that has been hailed as a great advance, and is becoming very popular. Yet it grieves me to think how many people are being subjected to such misery when they might be spared if they only *knew* about bone meal.

The prime victims of osteoporosis are women past menopause, when estrogen slows down. (Estrogen helps keep calcium in our bones.) Trying to compensate by taking estrogen only substitutes the risk of cancer. Bone meal, however, has no side effects. And men need it too—for their own teeth and bones; and because calcium protects the heart. Calcium in any form is also critically important to anyone taking cortisone— *one of whose side effects is bone loss.*

Bone Builds Bone

Our bodies have the remarkable ability to use the tissues of other creatures' organs to replenish our own. Liver for liver, brain for brain, bone for bone. Quite literally. When my husband had that terrible two-story fall from our balcony, his feet were so badly shattered the doctor didn't think he'd ever walk again. But he'd been taking bone meal; and though he landed upright *he broke no leg, hip or back bones.* And I increased his daily supply for healing. The orthopedic surgeon grinned when we told him.

"Yeah," he said, preparing to cut away the bandages from those poor broken feet, "I understand bone meal is pretty good . . . for gardens." When he actually saw the feet, however, he gasped. The heels had improved so much he decided not even to put on a walking cast. "You know," he admitted. "Maybe there *is* something to that stuff you're using."

"That stuff," however, is *not* the same bone meal you use in your garden—that's toxic to human beings. Rather, bone meal that is made from the ground leg bones of cattle. It's better than consuming calcium alone, as bone meal also contains the right proportion of phosphorus (necessary for calcium to work), as well as the trace minerals copper, nickel, manganese, magnesium and fluoride in safe form. Better than milk, because you'd have to drink a quart of milk a day to get enough—and think of the calories. Besides, today's milk isn't always safe from pesticides or radioactive fallout.

Very few foods provide calcium in significant amounts. They

are primarily dairy products and dark molasses. Small amounts are found in leafy vegetables, but it's usually insoluble and hard to absorb. Animals get their calcium from chewing bones; and when some zoos fed their wild animals only muscle meats, they found their lions and tigers breaking hips and developing arthritis—a condition that was corrected by giving them bone meal. Our primitive ancestors also chewed bones, and boiled them down for soups and gravies. The rest of us almost have to depend on calcium tablets or bone meal.

Bone meal can help keep you young. That's very important to me. I want to hang on to my teeth. I don't want to become arthritic or palsied. I want to keep right on dancing and swimming and skipping rope. I don't want to break a hip or get a dowager's hump or begin to stoop and shrivel. (I'm already short, I can't afford to lose even a fraction of an inch.) These are all symptoms we see so often in people past fifty or sixty that we've come to believe they're an almost inevitable part of aging.

They needn't be, and aren't. Not if we supply the body with the nutrients it needs. Especially the kind of calcium and other minerals available in bone meal.

Dolomite

Marching hand in hand with bone meal is dolomite. A natural limestone which not only contains calcium, but is the richest source of another extremely important mineral, magnesium. One of magnesium's major jobs is to see that the right amount of calcium is deposited in teeth and bones instead of wandering off to clog arteries, or cause bursitis or kidney stones. (And oh, boy, did I have bursitis in my pre-dolomite days!) Magnesium is also one of the heart's best friends, for it lowers blood fats, protects the heart muscle and helps trigger and control our very heartbeats.

Researchers have found that heart attack victims have from 19 to 42 per cent less magnesium in their hearts than normal, depending on the severity of the attack. In *Electrolytes and Cardiovascular Disease*, Drs. H. A. Nieper and L. Blumberger reported that in treating 100 heart patients with a magnesium compound they had saved all but one life. This was far better than the previous year's record of losing 60 out of 196 cases treated with anticoagulant drugs.

The name dolomite comes from the Dolomite Mountains in northern Italy, of which Goethe wrote, "All that struggles for existence in the mountains is here full of life and energy. One turns again to belief in a beneficent power." It is the magnesium in dolomite which gives us that feeling of life and energy, and can even inspire the calm that stirs our faith "in a beneficent power." For this mineral has the miraculous ability both to revitalize and to relax. It takes the edge off frazzled nerves, yet renews vigor. It is extremely important in combating stress. And the more stress we have, emotional or physical, the more we need.

As for sleep, calcium and magnesium are nature's tranquilizers. It's said that hibernating animals like polar bears have large quantities of magnesium in their system. In fact, when the quieting effects of magnesium were first discovered early in the century, doctors used to give it by injection to control convulsions, epileptic seizures, and to induce sleep. Insomnia can often be traced simply to a lack of those two minerals, calcium and magnesium. Physically, the brain cells and the entire nervous system may be begging for them; that's why you toss and turn, why your mind won't quiet down. It may also be because you're worried, overtired or overstimulated; but remember that such are forms of stress which seriously deplete these very minerals.

Lelord Kordel has an excellent chapter on this in his book *Health Through Nutrition*. "It is all very well," he says, "for the writers to talk about 'learning to relax' in their treatises on insomnia. I, for one, say let's have more emphasis on the chemical-mechanical processes that permit us to relax sufficiently so that sleep may come in its natural way." (He also recommends vitamin B_6 and a low-salt diet.)

For me, the best assurance of a good night's sleep is to take several dolomite and/or bone meal tablets, together with a little orange juice and yogurt, as recommended in Naura Hayden's delightful book, *Everything You've Always Wanted to*

Know About ENERGY But Were Too Weak to Ask. The juice and yogurt make for quick assimilation; if I go to bed at once I feel their relaxing effects within a few minutes. If I wake up later I may take some more. I can't recommend specific amounts— each of us is so different. But I can tell you these completely natural substances are not toxic, and they *won't* "turn you into stone," as a doctor half jokingly scolded. Certainly they have none of the deadly hazards of the sedatives and sleeping pills he dispenses so freely.

Magnesium is also found in foods—seeds, nuts, wheat germ, soybeans and green vegetables. But most of it is milled out of flour, lost in food processing, and a high-protein diet takes further toll. Drugs destroy it; diuretics will flush it out of the system. So do perspiration, diarrhea, bleeding. And unless magnesium is replaced after the stress of surgery, patients can actually die from the loss. Athletes and people who do hard physical work use up enormous amounts. Long-distance runners are so aware of this they fortify themselves with dolomite before and during a race, says Air Force author-physician Dr. Kenneth Cooper, who has measured results. It gives them more endurance and speed.

Dr. Mildred S. Seelig, in a comprehensive magnesium study published in the *American Journal of Clinical Nutrition,* says the average intake of magnesium is barely 250 milligrams. She recommends up to 700 milligrams a day for maintaining excellent health. And according to medical texts, the average adult loses an approximate total of 320 milligrams of calcium a day just through perspiration and evacuation. Government surveys show calcium deficiency to be one of our most common and serious nutritional problems.

No wonder millions of people are limping through life tired, nervous, weak, dizzy, sleepless, depressed, hypertensive, drug-dependent, in danger of dropping over from a heart attack. Far too many because of a simple but critical lack: too little calcium and magnesium in their bodies. The more tragic because vitality, energy, calm and even "increased speed and endurance" are in most cases so readily available so cheaply—merely by replenishing these vital minerals.

Some people say bone meal and dolomite duplicate each

other, since they both contain calcium and magnesium. The difference is: bone meal also contains the so essential phosphorus. Dolomite doesn't. But dolomite contains a lot more magnesium. To play safe, I take both, usually in a combination tablet. About 1,000 milligrams a day.

Desiccated Liver

My mother loathed liver. Our relatives didn't seem to like it much either, because whenever they'd butcher that's what they'd always bring us. Mother would thank them sweetly; but after they'd left she'd shudder and feed it to the cat. I didn't even know what it tasted like until I went to college, where I became almost as crazy about it as our lucky cat. For liver has been known as a source of strength and energy since the beginning of time.

Liver (although they didn't know it then) is a treasury of vitamins and minerals, especially iron. And iron is critical to the production of hemoglobin, the most vital part of our red blood cells; the part which enables them to snatch the precious oxygen from our lungs and rush it to all the tissues of our body. Which *must* have oxygen or they sicken; and the red blood cells themselves must be replaced every day. For this they depend on a continual supply of iron.

That's why lack of iron can cause so many problems. Why you may feel so weak, so *tired.* Dizziness, ringing in the ears (and how I used to suffer from those!). Inertia, loss of appetite. Learning difficulties, mental confusion. (The brain, above all organs, demands its oxygen.) These are all signals of anemia; and when the iron shortage is severe the anemia can become pernicious— and kill.

Years ago it was discovered that large amounts of raw liver would cure the condition. Drs. George Whipple, George Minot and William Murphy won the Nobel Prize for this in 1934. But it wasn't until the 1940s that the other healing elements in liver were recognized. Primarily, the vitamins B_6 and B_{12}. These two vitamins must be present if the iron is to do any good. So must vitamin C and the mineral copper. The good Lord put them all in liver, plus lots of protein and the detoxifying agents vitamin

A and zinc. (Other food sources of iron are eggs, meat, beans, prunes and raisins, but few of them have the necessary vitamin B6.)

Iron is most urgently needed by women (especially pregnant women) and children; yet government studies have revealed that *most* are getting very little. Iron is so important doctors prescribe it; a great many people take iron supplements. But the program of fortifying bread, pastries, cereals and baby foods with iron has been ridiculous, because the cheap iron salts commonly used are in a form the body can't assimilate. It's said that manufacturers prefer this inert form because it doesn't discolor or reduce the shelf life of the product, although easily absorbable iron compounds are available at slightly more cost. When doctors at the University of Washington School of Medicine tested babies to see how much iron they were actually getting from such fortified cereals, says *Pediatrics,* they found it was less than 1 per cent.

The iron in liver presents no such problems. Like my mother, however, many people are revolted by liver; besides, how could you eat *enough?* The answer to that is desiccated liver—which is simply raw liver from which fat and fiber have been removed. It is then vacuum-dried in a low-heat process that doesn't destroy its precious nutrients. In fact, a mere teaspoon of desiccated liver packs more concentrated iron and vitamin B than a whole pound of cooked liver.

Concentrated liver is not only a terrific energizer, it can help detoxify the poisons that now assault us from almost everything we eat, touch or even breathe. (And isn't this logical, since liver is the organ in man or animal which filters and purifies?) Biochemists at the University of Michigan Medical Center have isolated definite elements in liver which protect against pollutants. *Proceedings of the British Medical Society* even reports that large doses of desiccated liver have retarded the growth of chemical-caused tumors in test animals.

That this marvelous stuff does provide super-energy has also been laboratory-tested. One of the most fascinating experiments was that of Dr. Benjamin Ershoff of Loma Linda Medical University in southern California, and reported in several scientific journals. He subjected different groups of rats to different diets, to test their endurance and fatigue. After six weeks they were placed into vats of water where they had to keep swimming or drown. The rats that had been given the desiccated liver outswam the others ten times over; in fact, they were still swimming vigorously (and finally rescued) hours after the other rats had died.

I don't consider myself a rat, but I want the joyous vigor and endurance that comes from what they got. Desiccated liver is an absolutely safe natural energizer; taken in sufficient amounts, it will enable you to work and play circles around what you did before.

Don't take it at night, however, unless you're planning to drive. Its energy is so potent it will keep you awake. It's therefore excellent for truck drivers or anyone else who faces long hours at the wheel. Certainly far better than the coffee and dangerous amphetamines on which many people depend to stay alert.

Zinc

Zinc is one of the few minerals you can buy in tablet form, and the only one I take just for itself. Zinc is one of the most miraculous and versatile of all God's natural gifts.

When I was a child about all anybody knew about zinc was that a mild white salve called zinc oxide was the quickest way to heal cuts, burns, blisters, and was even good for pimples. It was years before scientists discovered that zinc is one of the two most essential trace minerals, found in more places in the body than any other except iron. Working with both vitamins and enzymes, it is vital to the synthesis of proteins and the nucleic acids RNA and DNA; as such, zinc affects every cell in the body. Here are just some of the things that depend on zinc:

Growth. . . . Wound healing. . . . Shiny hair, strong nails, healthy skin. . . . Sexual health, especially for men. (The largest amounts of zinc are concentrated in the prostate, seminal fluid and sperm.) . . . Energy and vitality. . . . Mental alertness. . . . Resistance to disease. . . . Taste and smell. . . . Zinc has even been found to destroy body odors.

Conversely, a lack of zinc can cause dwarfism, impotence,

infertility, birth defects, and is closely related to prostate cancer. Low zinc levels can mean bad skin, fatigue, forgetfulness and the entire range of human afflictions. Diabetics are notoriously low in zinc, which is necessary to the production of insulin.

Zinc *should* be plentifully available in foods—whole grains, fruits and vegetables, meats. But here again chemical fertilizers and poor soil have robbed both our plants and the animals that eat them; and what little zinc is left can be destroyed by food processing. Also, alcohol will flush zinc out of the system. Zinc deficiency is therefore very common—but easily prevented and corrected. I take 50 milligrams of zinc a day, but more during times of stress. Zinc is vital to the health of the nerves, and like calcium and magnesium, it is a natural tranquilizer. I often take zinc at bedtime as well as dolomite.

Lecithin (and the Cholesterol Scare)

In our refrigerator sits a large can of lecithin granules. I use them as a thickening agent in cooking. Beside them is a jar of lecithin capsules. I take one every day. The labels on these containers bear the statement, "The need for lecithin in human nutrition has not yet been established." That "yet" sounds promising; but the scientific studies proving lecithin vital to health date back to the forties.

In *Proceedings of the Society of Experimental Biology and Medicine*, Volume 49, 1942, H. D. Keston and R. Silbowitz report that lecithin prevented hardening of arteries in rabbits. . . . Dr. Francis Pottenger, writing in the April 1944 issue of *Southern Medical Journal*, deplores the loss of lecithin in processing fats and cereals, and reports on its effectiveness in treating skin diseases. . . . *Gastroenterology*, Volume 1, 1943, says there is an unknown factor in lecithin that helps in the synthesis of fats and vitamin A. . . . There are others. One can only wonder how many more years must pass before that need *is* "established."

For me it already has been. I began adding lecithin to our diet after my husband's third serious heart attack. In the eight years that followed, until his final illness, he never had a recurrence.

We attributed this to God and minerals and vitamins (especially vitamins C and E) and the cholesterol-controlling properties of lecithin.

Lecithin is an emulsifier; it keeps cholesterol fluid, moving through the bloodstream as it was meant to, instead of clogging artery walls. But let's get one thing straight: cholesterol is *not* that mean little man who pops up on TV to spoil dinner parties. And whose seeming villainy is defeated because the people are using margarine instead of butter. I wince every time I see that commercial; it gives a totally false impression.

The body *itself* creates and constantly uses both lecithin and cholesterol. It is the cholesterol in our skin that enables the sun to give us vitamin D. Cholesterol is necessary for our hormones and our digestive juices. It is a normal component of almost every tissue in our bodies. Without cholesterol we would have no sex life, no blood, no nervous system, no brain. Take away all cholesterol from that TV dinner and the people themselves would collapse.

Beyond the body, cholesterol is found in fatty foods—which are to be avoided for many reasons. They overload the digestive system; evidence is accumulating they may cause cancer. But it's absurd to give up things as nutritious as butter and eggs and avocados because they too contain high levels of cholesterol. The Lord in his wisdom also planted *lecithin* in those foods as a regulator. The very word *lecithin* comes from the Greek word *likithos, meaning egg yolk.* In fact, the first lecithin used by German researchers was actually extracted from egg yolks until cheaper sources like soybeans could be obtained. And if the food companies had let the Lord's products alone, we'd never have to buy it. But their processing not only destroys the vitamins and minerals, it ruins the precious lecithin oils.

In any case, the mad rush to substitute polyunsaturated fats makes no sense unless those fats are accompanied by plenty of vitamin E to keep them from oxidizing and causing more damage.

The whole cholesterol scare is so full of contradictions it's fought about among the best authorities. For instance, the African Masai have unusually healthy hearts; yet their heavy meat and milk diet gives them twice the cholesterol count recommended by the American Heart Association. The same is true of the Congo pygmies; it was also true of the Eskimos before the advent of white flour and sugar. And why is heart disease the major killer of physicians, many of whom are ardent proponents of low-cholesterol diets?

Light has been shed on this by a number of research projects, dating back to 1951, when Dr. David Barr, then of Cornell University Medical College, suggested the relationship between lipoproteins and heart attacks. More recent is the widely publicized work of Dr. William P. Castelli, director of laboratories for the Framingham, Massachusetts, Heart Study. He discovered that the clogging of arteries is not caused solely by cholesterol, but by the type of molecules called lipoproteins which carry it through the bloodstream. It is the job of the low-density lipoproteins (LDL's) to pick up cholesterol from the liver, where it's manufactured, or from the diet, and deliver it to the cells. If these LDL's are overloaded they simply dump some off in the coronary arteries, where it can build up into plaques.

There are, however, *high*-density lipoproteins (HDL's), whose job is just the opposite—to coast around in the bloodstream, picking up after the LDL's. Any extra they find they rush back to the liver to be excreted.

"The most surprising finding in our study," Dr. Castelli has said in his interviews, "was the observation that as the HDL's went up, the rate of coronaries went down. This explains why we often see patients with blood cholesterol levels that seem very high, yet they don't have coronary problems. They don't fit the pattern. Lab tests reveal they have a higher than normal ratio of HDL's to LDL's. The HDL's are carrying the excess fat and cholesterol out of the system before they can do any harm."

Significantly, women, who generally have a higher rate of HDL's in their blood, have fewer heart attacks.

Lecithin (and What It Can Do for Us)

Back to lecithin. This substance too is a natural component of every cell in our bodies. And it too is manufactured by the liver. In short, lecithin and cholesterol are created to work as a team. But the liver can't manufacture lecithin without vitamin B, one of the vitamins lost in the milling and processing of foods, hence the ever present danger of shortage. We *must* replenish our lecithin somehow. For it has also been discovered that lecithin not only keeps cholesterol in line, but raises the ratio of those very important HDL's.

When Dr. L. A. Simons and his colleagues in New South Wales and Sydney, Australia, fed lecithin supplements to patients, they were excited to discover not only a dramatic drop in cholesterol levels, but that the drop was almost totally in the dangerous LDL's. Similar results were reported by Belgian doctors testing 100 patients. Almost every one responded to this simple, non-toxic food substance.

I didn't mean to spend so much time on the lecithin-cholesterol connection, because lecithin has other roles. But I must tell you what lecithin can do in dissolving cholesterol when it clogs the gallbladder.

Several years ago our daughter-in-law suffered agonizing pains which were diagnosed as gallstones. The doctor told her an operation was inevitable, but since she was teaching school it could probably safely wait until summer. Now I don't lure anybody away from doctors or even pretend to prescribe. But this was a family matter, and we all plunged into the sizable body of medical literature I'd acquired by then, to find out what we could about gallstones.

We learned that gallstones are mainly deposits of hardened cholesterol; and over and over we encountered evidence to show that simple soybean lecithin can knock them. Among other things, we learned that dogs almost never get gallstones due to the fact that their bile has such a high concentration of lecithin. In fact, a human gallstone will dissolve if dropped into dog bile. Judy herself decided to try lecithin, taking a tablespoon of granules in orange juice, as well as three 1,200-milligram capsules a day. It worked. She had to call her doctor and tell him to cheer up and operate on somebody else. Despite his urgent warnings, she hasn't had an attack of gallstones in the six years since.

Another exciting contribution of lecithin is what it can do for the brain. For soybean lecithin is the most bountiful source of the B vitamin choline, on which the brain depends for the production of the neurotransmitter acetylcholine. Any deficiency of this substance can cause actual brain disorders. A number of studies have shown that learning disabilities, nervous afflictions and even some early senility yielded to large doses of lecithin. It was also useful in disturbances that resulted from psychiatric drugs. Curiously, the best results were obtained by using the lecithin itself, rather than the actual choline.

Because choline is so fast-acting, I believe that consuming some lecithin in the morning makes you more mentally alert for the day.

Here are some other things lecithin does for us:

It helps to cleanse the liver and purify the kidneys.

It's important to the nerves, for it's a component of the myelin sheath that shelters them.

It's been found to help abnormal bleeders.

It's crucial to smokers; also to newborn babies. To breathe properly they both need plenty of lecithin in the lining of their lungs. (Welsh researchers have measured the amount of lecithin in amniotic fluid, and found it will reveal whether or not a baby will have trouble breathing—which is very important in the case of premature infants. The lungs in the fetus don't develop enough lecithin until the last stages of pregnancy.)

Soybeans are the richest dietary source of this miraculous stuff. We eat them sprouted or cooked in various ways. The supplement lecithin is made from them.

Some people are afraid lecithin is fattening, since it is itself a fat. This may be true for some people, but quite the opposite for most. Lecithin acts as a solvent, not only for cholesterol but for other fats, drawing deposits of fat into the bloodstream, where the extra fat is chemically burned. Because of this, some doctors believe it is one of the most important things to be included in a reducing diet.

Wheat Germ

Wheat germ is the most valuable foodstuff you can have in your kitchen. Nutritionally it surpasses even milk, meat, fruits, vegetables and certainly bread. You can buy it as wheat-germ oil in liquid or capsule form. And you can get it as raw or lightly toasted flakes. They have a mildly nutty flavor and are good eaten like cereal with milk and fruit. Adding bran, lecithin and sunflower seeds makes them even better. I use them for dusting fish or chicken, add them to soups, salads, batters, meat loaf, stuffing; in fact, everything that comes to the table is enhanced by this super-source of protein, vitamins and minerals.

Wheat germ is the priceless element, remember, that is milled out of the flour to be consumed by mere human beings, then sold to farmers as a rich mineral and vitamin supplement for livestock! Fortunately, people got wise; they began demanding the right to be as well fed as hogs and chickens. Thanks to health leaders like the Rodales, backed by an impressive battery of scientists like Dr. Szent-Györgyi, a small portion of this vital wheat germ is rescued and packaged for health food stores and now even many supermarkets. Here's why it is so important:

• Wheat germ is the almost perfect protein, lacking only one of the eight essential amino acids. Ounce for ounce it contains more protein than most cuts of beef, and three times more protein than bread.

• It is the richest source of vitamin E, surpassing oatmeal, corn flakes and even whole-wheat grains.

• It is rich in unrefined polyunsaturated oils.

• Except for vitamin B_{12}, it contains the entire vitamin B complex, including B_6, which is so important to women, and which is *not* restored to bread. Wheat germ far surpasses bread in the B vitamins alone, even after that bread has been "enriched."

• It contains enormous amounts of magnesium and potassium, and generous amounts of iron and zinc.

Wheat germ should be stored in the refrigerator where it won't turn rancid. The capsules of cold-pressed wheat-germ oil are a highly concentrated form of nutritious energy so potent they're given to athletes. I not only use the dry wheat germ in cooking, I take the capsules two or three times a day.

Wheat germ is one of my secrets of health and vitality.

Brewer's Yeast

Brewer's yeast is a non-leavening yeast that comes in powder, flakes or tablets. Like wheat germ, I sprinkle it on foods to increase their nutritional value. I also take four tablets twice a day. It is a tremendous source of energy. And it far outranks cosmetics or creams in keeping your skin smooth and young.

Brewer's yeast has so many vitamins it's been called a vitamin factory. Mainly, it contains all the B vitamins, including several that are often missing from vitamin B complex products. It's especially rich in vitamin B_{12}, a fact important to my husband, who became a vegetarian. (Plants just don't have B_{12}.) But the primary reason I take brewer's yeast is that it contains *fourteen minerals;* and one of them is chromium in the form most helpful to diabetics.

Brewer's yeast also contains sixteen amino acids. It abounds in RNA (ribonucleic acid), which along with DNA (deoxyribonucleic acid) holds the secrets of life and possibly youth, through our genetic codes. Benjamin S. Frank, M.D., who has written books about aging, says, "If you nourish the body tissues with sufficient nucleic acid you can repair the damage to cells caused by age." He recommends sardines and brewer's yeast as two of the best sources of these nucleic acids.

Selenium

For many years selenium was considered almost a mystery mineral. Now this substance, "occurring in minute amounts in nearly all materials of the earth's crust," according to the U. S. Department of Interior, and needed in extremely small amounts in both animals and man, has become a kind of mineral celebrity. For researchers have discovered that those minute amounts are absolutely essential to the processes of nutrition. What's more, that selenium is a potent anti-oxidant, detoxifier, and one of our most important weapons against disease.

In fact, a number of diseases are now being associated with lack of selenium in the system. Among them, unexplained crib deaths. There have been crib (unexplained) deaths among young animals that weren't getting enough selenium. In human beings, crib death victims are usually boys, who have a much higher selenium requirement than girls. Dr. Donald Money has suggested, in both the *New Zealand Journal of Medicine* and *Medical World News,* that bottle-fed babies are far more susceptible to this tragedy than breast-fed, since mother's milk is much higher in the protective selenium and vitamin E. That when a "modest number" of the victims were examined for these elements, all were found to have far less than is considered necessary for protection from the pulmonary edema that accompanies this type of death.

Selenium boosts the effectiveness of vitamin E and helps the heart. Animals grazing on selenium-poor soil, or fed selenium-poor diets, develop the same high blood pressure and coronary problems as people. And researchers who compared the mineral intake with the deaths from heart disease in twenty-five countries, discovered a significant relationship: Deaths from arterial or heart disease were highest in every area where the selenium consumption was lowest.

Selenium is even credited with completely wiping out a type of heart disease that affects children up to age fifteen and is widespread in China. In one commune it was given to all the children; while the commune in a neighboring village received none, as controls. When the disease was eradicated in the first commune, the second village was given the selenium. There too the disease was stamped out.

Raymond J. Shamberger, Ph.D., who tells this story, is a researcher at the Cleveland Clinic Foundation, and one of the first to report the selenium-cancer connection. His own work and that of others, however, has convinced him, as he told *Prevention,* "The emerging link between selenium and heart disease may turn out to be a bigger and more important finding than the cancer link."

As for cancer, worldwide studies have shown that in Asian and South American countries, where the selenium intake is generally high (up to 300 micrograms a day), the deaths from a wide range of cancers are significantly lower than in the United States and Europe. Particularly breast cancer.

At a 1978 symposium at the National Cancer Institute, Dr. Gerhard Schrauzer, of the University of California at San Diego, pronounced selenium "one of the most significant cancer-preventing nutrients." In his own laboratories he was able to prevent mammary tumors in mice simply by adding selenium to their drinking water.

He recommends that people supplement their diets with 150–250 micrograms a day, since it's almost impossible to get enough from food. And that such supplementation start early. Particularly if there is a history of cancer in the family, or if you live in a chemically polluted environment or an area where the soil content is poor. "Too many people wait until it's too late before even trying to prevent disease."

Selenium is one of the vital trace elements that, like iodine, is unevenly distributed; erosion and chemical fertilizers have also stripped it from the soil. In some states the pigs and cows and chickens were becoming so stunted and sickly from eating the plants raised on such poor soil, the farmers themselves petitioned and were granted the right to add selenium to animal feed. Recommended allowances were even established for most farm and domestic animals; and finally provisional RDA's of 50 to 200 micrograms per day were set for people. (A microgram is one thousandth of a milligram.)

The best food sources of selenium are liver, seafood, eggs, garlic, mushrooms, asparagus, whole grains and brewer's yeast. Careful surveys have shown that most people don't get even *half* as much selenium as they should in their diet.

Selenium can be toxic, however. Never take more than 200–300 micrograms a day except under the direction of a knowledgeable doctor.

Kelp

Kelp is a seaweed harvested from oceans all over the world, and available for home use in powder or tablets. I take two or three tablets a day, and use the powder as a light seasoning. It has a mildly salty taste.

The Lord has packed so many nutrients and healers into kelp it could very well one day be both medicine cabinet and cupboard for a sick and starving world. It's hard to realize that stringy green-brown stuff piled up on beaches, or swirling round your legs in swimming, actually contains fats, proteins, carbohydrates and vitamins! More remarkably, it is a treasure trove of minerals. In the incredible design of this planet, little is wasted; those precious trace elements washed from the soil in silt are faithfully carried by rivers and streams until they reach the oceans, where both fish and seaweed reclaim them. That's why seafood is so very good for us. Or used to be. Now that man is polluting even these precious waters, seafood is often contaminated—especially shellfish like clams and oysters.

Algae or seaweed isn't. It's a different form of life, bent only on vigorous growth. Almost as if kelp is there in such abundance, growing away so fast in order to *save* us from our folly. For it contains two critically protective substances, selenium and iodine.

Iodine is a mineral so important the whole world has been mapped to show where it is lacking in the soil. Such areas are known as goiter belts because many women there have thyroid problems, causing their throats to swell. In fact, goiter was fairly common in Iowa, where I was raised. Several prominent women in our town had it and wore amber beads in the belief they helped. As a child, I actually thought goiter a mark of distinction because of those beautiful beads. . . . In places like Japan and Iceland, however, where seaweed is a popular food, there is very little goiter.

Even more significant to us today is the fact that in such countries there is *almost no breast cancer.* Researchers have discovered that iodine is active in breast tissues; their studies strongly suggest that lack of sufficient iodine is a contributing cause to this tragedy which attacks over 100,000 American women every year. Thousands of these women will lose one or both breasts, and according to the American Cancer Society, 35,000 of them will die. "Breast cancer remains the foremost site of cancer incidence and death in American women."

Closely related to this is the evidence that iodine protects against the cancers caused by estrogens. Despite many warnings, these dangerous steroids are still being given to women for birth control or to help them through menopause. Dr. Bernard

Eskin, gynecologist of the Medical College of Pennsylvania, says that physicians should not prescribe estrogens without first checking the patient's iodine levels, and if necessary using iodine therapy.

The iodine in kelp can help prevent breast cancer.

The main reason we became avid kelp takers, however, is that the iodine and other minerals in kelp are effective in fighting radiation. And my husband, as I've said, was subjected to far more X rays than most people get and live.

Add to this time bomb the silent, invisible, odorless, tasteless radiation all around us. From microwave ovens, smoke detectors, TV sets. From mercury-vapor lamps on streets, in stores and gyms. From the incessant bombardment of X rays ordered by dentists, doctors and hospitals. Processors are even irradiating many of our foods. While nearly every newspaper carries stories about possible or actual strontium 90 fallout from more and more nuclear plants. The mere problem of disposing of their radioactive wastes has become a national nightmare.

There is literally no place to hide. And in the sobering words of John W. Gofman, M.D., a co-discoverer of uranium 233 and member of the Manhattan Project: "There is no reasonable doubt in my mind or to my knowledge from the scientific literature on the part of anyone that radiation is a cause of leukemia or cancer. There are more deaths now, and there will be more, the more that gets out of containment."

It's no use pretending all this doesn't exist or that it will go away. What *does* make sense is to inform ourselves about what we can do to prevent personal damage; and then to fortify our bodies with every agent that can protect us:

Every vitamin and mineral that can build up our resistance and strengthen our immunity system.

And every substance, every supplement known to detoxify poisons and pollutants, including radiation.

16

Foods that Help You "Eat Healthy"

My dad had a saying, "Eating healthy." Whenever he'd bite into an apple or start cracking peanuts between meals, he'd fend off Mother's scolding that he was ruining his supper—"No, Rose, I'm just eating healthy. Now if it was a candy bar or a piece of pie, I'd agree. This just keeps me healthy till supper."

He was right. I'm sure one reason most of us had so much pep is that we were great snackers and nibblers. I know plenty of authorities warn, "Don't snack." But that's because snacking, if you're not careful, is an insidious but inevitable way to pile on the pounds. Too many snack foods are simply empty, no-energy calories laden with fat, salt and sugar. Nutritional studies have shown, however, that taking food in small amounts throughout the day is far better than overloading the system at meals. When the stomach has to cope with too much food there is a strain on the rest of the body. Instead of feeling energetic you feel tired. And the surplus can only be stored as fat.

My aunts and uncles snacked too, but the fat ones were those who couldn't miss their afternoon cookies, or cake and coffee. Mother didn't bake as often as my aunts (we didn't even *have* a cookie jar). So the stuff we were always popping into our mouths was actually "eating healthy." Carrots, a piece of cabbage or raw potato, a handful of raisins. Celery, apples, peanuts, pop-corn—anything that crunched. Dad was crazy about peanuts, cheese and the big tart wealthy apples from a tree in our back-yard. Mother's favorite not-so-secret snack was an onion sand-wich. (This was only when Dad was out of town. She felt rather guilty about this strange indulgence, and would chew parsley or urge us to join her so she wouldn't offend.)

Actually, we all loved onions and ate them every possible way. Fresh and green from the garden, boiled, fried, pickled. And if any of us were coming down with a cold, Mother always fried onions for supper and/or made us eat slices of raw onions at bedtime, which usually knocked it. If we coughed, the cooked onions were mixed with honey for cough syrup. If a cold settled in the chest, onions went into the mustard plaster. The doctor was rarely called for even the complications of a cold. And about the only medications in the house were Mentho-latum and Castoria. Certainly not aspirin, which my parents considered a dangerous poison. (Their opinion makes more sense every day.)

Simple Meals, Busy Teeth

Despite orgies of eating at picnics, big family gatherings and on holidays, the pattern of meals at our house was usually simple. Mother quite frankly didn't like to cook, and mostly settled for the basics: Inevitably potatoes, a couple of fresh or home-canned vegetables, meat on Sunday and two or three other times a week. Friday or Saturday she generally set some fruit Jell-O and baked a pie or cake—which would be gone by Mon-day. If we had dessert at all it was a pudding or more often fresh or canned fruit. We loved sliced bananas with cream. Fresh pears, peaches or white grapes were a treat. Oranges appeared more often at supper than breakfast. Dad showed us the best way to peel them, inserting a spoon beneath the skin and fol-lowing their juicy curves. Then when our plates were sur-rounded by the bright curls, we kids would skin their velvety white linings with our teeth and eat it. Then we'd eat the seeds.

Like chipmunks, we had tough busy teeth which we used to extract every morsel. Apples were seldom abandoned until we'd chewed the core and savored its faintly bitter kernels. Peach and plum pits were always saved and left on the sill to dry. Later we'd put them on a flatiron, break them open with a hammer and eat the almondy centers. They were a good substitute for nuts, which we were mad about but usually had only at Christmas. We even cracked the delicate bones of chickens and sucked the dark sweet marrow. . . . Were we greedy—or instinctively guided toward the extra nourishment and healing factors so cunningly hidden in skin and seeds and even bones? One thing sure, with all that roughage we had healthy bowels— and strong healthy teeth.

The whole family downed gallons of milk and quantities of eggs. Quite often fried or scrambled eggs substituted for meat. We ate a lot of oatmeal too, which wasn't processed then and had all its vitamins and minerals. With raisins, brown sugar and milk, oatmeal sometimes served as dessert.

Since supper was usually light, we were often hungry later. This meant popcorn once or twice a week. Somebody would be sent to the basement for the bulging sack of prickly ears. When we'd shelled enough we shook the kernels in a long-handled black screen popper, over the coals in the kitchen stove. If the fire was out we used a skillet on the gas flame. Anyway, the toasty fragrance of it filled the house. We devoured it by the dishpanful, without the faintest idea that we were "eating healthy," as Dad would say.

Now let's look at why these old-fashioned foods, and some others, were and still are so good for us.

Raisins

When we raided the cupboard for raisins we were doing more than satisfying our craving for sweets. We were getting a carbohydrate pickup from their natural sugar. Fructose. This is far different from the refined white sugar, sucrose. We were also getting minerals—calcium, phosphorus, sodium, potassium, magnesium and iron. Also some of the B vitamins; and if we ate a whole cup, 32 units of vitamin A.

When my own children were toddlers I would put them

down for their naps with a picture book and a little dish of dry raisins. They would nibble and gaze until they fell asleep; then wake up happy and lively. (Never do this with sticky raisins, though; it isn't good to have even natural sugar deposited on the teeth.)

Nuts

When Dad brought home those heavenly smelling freshly roasted peanuts which brought us swarming like squirrels, he was providing not only pleasure but protein, carbohydrates and essential energy fats. Also a scattering of vitamins, especially the B vitamin choline; and several minerals, including magnesium, the one that contributes so much to vitality and a happy outlook.

The other nuts we were crazy about we usually got only at Christmas: walnuts, hazelnuts, almonds, and the black walnuts from Uncle Harrison's farm . . . we had no idea they contained such a rich treasury of health and vigor. That in these delicious treats the good Lord had hidden the very germ of life, and compressed for its use every substance it needed to grow. Every nutrient to produce roots, branches, bark and leaves—in fact, a new nut-laden tree: Protein, fats and carbohydrates. Calcium, phosphorus, potassium, magnesium and iron. Some of the B vitamins, a little C and generous amounts of vitamin A.

In protein alone nuts far surpass steak or potatoes or bread. Between their oil and their protein, a pound of nuts will supply enough calories for the day. It's the fat in nuts that scares some people. But remember, it is unsaturated fat, containing the essential fatty acids which the body *must* have to turn food into energy. Unsaturated fats are the good guys which keep cholesterol and saturated fats in line. EFA's (essential fatty acids) are vital to the health of nerves and arteries. A study released by scientists at the University of Maryland links infant retardation to lack of these fatty acids in the diet of pregnant women and young babies.

It is also reported in CNI (bulletin of the Community Nutrition Institute) that "EFA are needed for proper myelination, a process that produces membrane 'insulators' around nerve fibers that transmit brain impulses. Myelination occurs in the last three months of pregnancy in humans and continues for the first year of life."

Seeds

In our habit of cracking and eating seeds we were joining company with the healthiest people in the world. All long-lived, cancer-free people in still primitive areas are known to eat seeds. They eat them for the same reason we did—because they like them. But more, all seeds (as we've seen with nuts, which are a seed) contain every nutrient needed for new life. They are thus life-giving, a source of growth and strength and energy.

Many seeds also contain minute amounts of a protective substance known variously as nitrilosides, amygdalin, Laetrile or B_{17}. It consists of tightly combined molecules of sugar, benzaldehyde and natural cyanide. It is found in some 1,500 different plants—not just apricot seeds, as is commonly supposed. We get some when we eat whole-grain cereals; before hybridization, even corn used to have a lot. Certainly anything that God has scattered so widely in edible, nutritious foods cannot be toxic, but is perfectly normal to human metabolism. It's estimated that people who still live close to nature consume from 250 to 500 milligrams or more of it a day. They never get cancer— which strikes one out of four Americans. This highly protective agent is another casualty of technology and our overprocessed foods. Instead of letting the FDA denounce Laetrile as worthless and dangerous, our government should be concerned about the dangerous lack of it in our diet.

Dr. Dean Burk, who for thirty-five years was an official at the National Cancer Institute, reminds us amygdalin has been around for centuries. It was used as a medicine by the ancient Chinese; formal studies of its properties began in Germany in 1834. He cites worldwide experiments which have proved that amygdalin *does* work on animals with cancer as well as human beings, and is appalled that his own NCI took such a strong public stand against it a few years ago they can't or won't back down. Amygdalin has been studied for 130 years, he says, "and more is known about it chemically and pharmacologically than most drugs in general use."

Yet the FDA is so paranoiac about this perfectly natural substance it even tries to confiscate apricot pits.

I'm sure glad we didn't have to worry about Big Brother when I was growing up. Because if we could have gotten our hands on any fresh apricots, you know what would have happened to the seeds.

We missed a good bet, though, when it came to sunflower seeds. Sunflowers grew in pastures, beside the fence, along the railroad tracks. Tall beauties wearing hats of golden petals, whose round mysterious faces were always turned as if in worship toward the sun. In the fall, when they collapsed, sometimes from the sheer weight of their seeds, the birds swarmed down to gorge themselves. We had no idea that in other parts of the world—Russia, the Orient, the Middle East—people ate these seeds as avidly as the birds. Roasted them, carried little sacks of them around in their pockets to nibble on for a lift to both body and spirit. And did so even after migrating to America.

Now I know why. They are delicious. And no other food source is richer in nourishment. Those lovely faces drinking in the sun are actually using solar energy to create proteins and fats, vitamins and minerals. Compressed into that abundance of tiny seeds (at least a cupful to a single flower) are enormous amounts of potassium (so important to the heart), phosphorus, magnesium and seven other minerals. They contain as much vitamin B as wheat germ, and lots of vitamins A and D to protect the eyes. Vitamin E is also there, as it should be, to balance the polyunsaturates—for the seeds are some 50 per cent pure unsaturated oil. (A very digestible oil rich in linoleic acid, considered the most important fatty acid.) Sunflower seed oil has proved to be healing, especially for any problems due to a deficiency of EFA's.

It was years before I discovered sunflower seeds in health food stores. Raw or lightly roasted they're as hard to quit eating as popcorn. (Be careful, though, their calorie count is high.) With raisins, toasted soybeans and other seeds, they're great for party mixes. Mainly, I keep a jar of them in the refrigerator to sprinkle on salads, add to casseroles or breads (where they taste like nuts) and grind and mix with wheat germ as an extra nutritious coating for fish or chicken.

We now grow our own sunflowers. And whenever I see them, heads ever lifted toward the source of light and life, I have a new sense of awe and wonder at how God can use even a humble if charming flower to bless us so abundantly.

Popcorn

The popcorn we devoured by the dishpanful was great for our teeth and bowels. Popcorn is *not* a junk food. It is whole grain containing the germ and bran. Because of its protein, fats and carbohydrates, the Department of Agriculture rates it high in food energy. It has no minerals, but three of the B vitamins—niacin, thiamine and riboflavin—as well as some vitamin E.

And popcorn *isn't* fattening unless you douse it with lots of salt and oil. Nutritionist Dr. Betty Alford of Texas Women's University at Denton, Texas, says a two-cup serving of fluffy kernels has no more calories than a thin slice of bread. A lightly salted quart provides only 220 to 250 calories. (The smaller the popped kernels, the more calories since you're actually consuming more.)

We like it dusted lightly with kelp or a vegetable salt, and don't even miss the oil. But when we do yield, we use real old-fashioned butter. Butter is rich in vitamin A and infinitely preferable to the hydrogenated fats in many margarines. Besides, there's simply no comparison when it comes to flavor.

Bran

There was always a cut-glass bowl of bran on the breakfast table. Dad bought it in bulk at the feed store, tough little brown curls we were ordered to add to our cereal. "Good for your bowels," he told us bluntly. Mother also made bran muffins at least once a week, and their sweet nutty fragrance brought us running. Served hot, with fresh butter and homemade grape jelly, their richness was better than cake. A fond gustatory memory of childhood. (I make them too, but they never taste quite that good.)

We knew only in a general way that bran prevented constipation. Now it is known that fiber in the diet, but especially bran, helps the body excrete fats, thus lowering cholesterol; helps lower blood sugar; and reduces the loss of calcium in elimination. We know that people who eat plenty of fibrous, unrefined foods seldom if ever get cancer of the colon. This has been established in a number of studies, and was dealt with in a popular book, *The Save Your Life Diet,* by David Reuben, M.D.

Furthermore, contrary to a popular misbelief, bran is *not* just a broom to sweep out the intestines, but is highly nutritious itself. In fact, with the exception of wheat germ, it contains more nutrients than any grain or vegetable—surpassing even wheat germ in vitamin B. According to the *U.S. Department of Agriculture Handbook, No. 8,* it is very high in protein and contains iron, phosphorus and potassium. *All* natural unprocessed foods have food value, and contribute nutrients to the body before the fibrous material leaves.

When We Skinned Those Orange Peels

We'd never heard of bioflavonoids, of course, as we sat nibbling the velvety white linings of oranges and lemons. Nobody had. Because it wasn't until later that Dr. Albert Szent-Györgyi, the Hungarian scientist (who isolated vitamin C), discovered their presence and value and labeled them vitamin P. Now we know these substances are critical to the health of our capillaries—those tiniest of blood vessels which are the final step in delivering nutrients to the cells. They must be permeable for the nutrients to ooze through, but they must also be strong.

Without bioflavonoids the capillaries grow frail and collapse. The result is bruising and bleeding. For years doctors found bioflavonoid preparations effective against miscarriages, heavy menstrual periods, nosebleeds—in fact, any form of hemorrhaging, as well as varicose veins and other conditions caused by capillary breakdown. Dr. B. F. Hart, a Florida physician, reports remarkable results with them in treating diabetes retinitis, phlebitis, kidney infections, stroke and other ailments. "I learned many years ago," he writes in *Let's Live* magazine, "that these so-called vitamin stepchildren are perhaps the most underrated substances in human nutrition."

The bioflavonoids are always found in the same fruits and vegetables which contain vitamin C. They both work to maintain collagen, that inner cement which holds us together. Without it, Dr. Hart tells us, the capillaries stretch and even rupture. A factor in cataracts, as well as many eye and blood vessel problems.

Using hesperidin (the bioflavonoid from the white underskin of oranges), Dr. Hart extracted a water-soluble form, which was carefully clinically tested on both animals and patients. "We did all the FDA required studies, and it was approved by the head of the department." Meanwhile, he had offered the whole process to any drug company, without pay. After some cost accounting, all concluded "that the profit margin was not good enough."

Even so, he and other doctors continued its use with great success—until the 1950s and the Thalidomide disaster. The FDA panicked. In an effort to prove its vigilance, it banished, among other things, the bioflavonoids! Not dubbing them dangerous, merely "useless." And they decided there was no such thing as vitamin P. It was forbidden as a medication, and health food stores were warned against even implying that bioflavonoids contribute to health in any way.

This despite the fact European doctors had been using the flavonoids for years. French doctors in particular have reported them highly effective in dealing with female bleeding or any gynecological problems, and an excellent substitute for hormone therapy. The irony is compounded by the fact that since the FDA decree, scientists at another government center, the National Eye Institute, have pronounced bioflavonoids the most effective substance tested to date in preventing cataracts in laboratory animals. Once this knowledge can be freely adapted to human beings it will surely prove a blessing.

But why wait, when this pure and simple nutrient is already available in nature and can do so much for us? If you don't care for the rather tasteless lining of citrus peels, at least eat or drink the whole fruit containing the pulp. Bioflavonoids are there too. Other sources are plums, apricots, blackberries and green peppers. Especially peppers—if you eat those velvety white inner fibers, which contain the most.

And don't forget to eat the seeds.

Bring On the Eggs

As I've said earlier, the whole Holmes clan devoured eggs morning, noon and night. And to my knowledge, nobody had high blood pressure; certainly nobody was ever rushed to the hospital with a heart attack.

Eggs, like nuts and seeds, are the cradles of life. Actually, we should eat them with awe as well as gusto, for in them our creator has stocked everything necessary to nourish a complete new being. Eggs are the perfect food. Their B vitamins are important to the nerves. (They are especially rich in the B vitamin choline, which feeds the brain.) Their vitamin A is essential to body tissues, lungs and eyes. Their generous proteins are in the form ideal for utilizing that vitamin A. Their yolks contain the rare and precious vitamin D. They are a treasury of minerals, especially phosphorus.

Both the yolk and the white of eggs contain protein of the highest grade, albumin, which enables the blood to distribute vitamin A. (Without protein vitamin A is useless.) I'm personally convinced the body *needs* the cholesterol found in eggs or God wouldn't have put so important a substance in so precious a container, along with the lecithin which helps it do its job of nourishing the cells. Eggs provide energy without a lot of calories. They are *not* fattening, a fact I didn't know in the days when I was foolish enough to try egg substitutes.

The makers of fake egg products have loudly embraced the cholesterol scare. One popular brand claims to have 25 per cent less cholesterol, which really isn't much less, not when you consider that most synthetic eggs contain a lot of starch and sugar. Also, in addition to corn oil and non-fat dry milk, they're asking your body to cope with mono- and di-glycerides, cellulose and xanthan gums, aluminum sulfate, ferric orthophosphate and artificial colors.

No, thanks. I'll feel safer with some old-fashioned God-given eggs.

Generations of doctors have found eggs valuable in preventing and treating both tuberculosis and rheumatic fever. Eggs are so digestible and restorative they have been used for convalescents since the beginning of time. In my own family, whenever anyone doesn't feel well, nothing is more healing and comforting than a couple of poached or soft-boiled eggs on milk toast.

Garlic

Despite Mother's passion for onions, she would have been horrified at having their first cousin, garlic, in the house. In those days anybody who ate garlic was "foreign" and probably lived down by the railroad tracks. We had no idea that garlic had been used as medication by all the ancient civilizations—the Chinese, Babylonians, Egyptians, Romans, Greeks; that in other parts of the world garlic was relished by both princes and peasants, or that the best cooks wouldn't be without it. In fact, the famous French chef Louis Diat once said, "Garlic is the fifth element of living and as important to our existence as earth, air, fire and water."

While I wouldn't go quite that far, my own enthusiasm for garlic is fervent. Because garlic is not only a marvelous flavoring agent, it's one of the most potent protectors God ever gave us. Here are just some of the things that both ancients and moderns have discovered garlic is good for:

> Indigestion, gas pains, diarrhea. Worms.
> Skin diseases: fungus, psoriasis, acne.
> Dizziness. Headaches.
> Colds, bronchitis, pneumonia, influenza, TB.
> Typhoid. Cholera. Diptheria.
> Infections. Wound healing.
> High blood pressure. Clotting. Heart problems.
> Arthritis. Aging. Cancer.

Richard Lucas tells us in *Nature's Medicines* that Dioscorides, second-century physician to the Roman armies, specified garlic for all lung and intestinal disorders. And when the plagues ravaged Europe during the Middle Ages, "those who ate garlic daily were not affected." In fact, people who took care of the dead bodies protected themselves with garlic. During both world wars the British and the Russians bought tons of garlic with which to treat their wounded. Garlic is still so popular in the Soviet Union it's sometimes called "Russian penicillin." Because now we know that this member of the Siberian lily family contains a powerful disinfectant and antibiotic. *Germs can't live in its presence.*

Laboratory tests have revealed that when garlic juice is introduced into colonies of bacteria, the germs stop moving and are dead within minutes. In other experiments this powerful antidote, known as allicin, even prevented mice who'd been injected with cancer cells from developing malignant tumors. The half given garlic remained healthy; the others died.

More common is the knowledge that garlic is good for high blood pressure, hence strokes and cardiovascular diseases. It's believed to do this by lowering cholesterol, cleansing the kidneys and possibly dilating the blood vessels. Anyway, countries like Italy or Spain, which consume quantities of garlic, have a far lower mortality rate from heart disease than we do. America is finally waking up to the wonders of garlic, however. Anne Crutcher, food editor of the Washington *Star,* writes that after years of Victorian inhibitions, "the garlic revolution, like its sexual counterpart, spread quickly once it started," until now we've become the most garlic-using country in the Western world.

Certainly we're crazy about garlic at our house. I use it as juice, oil, powder or bulbs fresh from the market or our own garden. When garlic is cooked there's almost no problem of breath odor; when you eat it raw in salads, all you have to do is chew parsley or a chlorophyl tablet. We also take capsules of garlic and parsley oils. These are deodorized, and especially good for people whose digestion can't cope with fresh garlic. Both garlic and parsley are energizers. (It's said that the Romans fed large quantities of parsley to both soldiers and horses before going into battle, or to give them vitality for the long marches.)

I consider garlic almost as important as vitamin C when it comes to fighting off infections or a cold. I would no more be without garlic than vitamins, minerals or bone meal.

Yogurt

We helped Mother make a lot of cottage cheese (hanging the clabbered milk to drain in a little cloth bag, then squeezing out the whey), and we sometimes joined Grandpa in drinking buttermilk; but we'd never heard of another form of fermented milk called yogurt. Yogurt didn't make its American debut until the forties; its tangy flavor caught on fast (especially when laced with sweet fruits) and its health properties were quickly embraced. Now yogurt, fresh or frozen, is almost as popular as ice cream.

Actually, this "new" discovery in "eating healthy," as Dad would say, has long been commonplace in the rest of the world. The Persians claimed it grew hair; the beautiful girls of the Middle East eat it and use it for facials; in Italy, Bulgaria, Romania, France, yogurt is associated with sexual prowess and regarded as an elixir of youth. In France it's been called *lait de la vie eternelle* or the milk of eternal life.

Yogurt is good for many of the same ailments as garlic is—especially disturbances of the intestinal tract. And (here we go again) it has even been found to be a tumor retardant. The *Journal of the National Cancer Institute* reported that when mice with tumor transplants were given yogurt mixed with their drinking water, there was a 28 per cent reduction in cell growth. Whereas in a control group that didn't get the yogurt, all the tumors grew rapidly. It was also reported in *Medical World News* that researchers at the Bulgaria Academy of Sciences cured several types of cancer by injecting one of the organisms which turns milk into yogurt (*Lactobacillus bulgaricus*).

It is these beneficial bacteria which give yogurt its healing and protective powers. They keep the digestive flora in balance. Paradoxically, yogurt cures diarrhea quicker than drugs, without their side effects (antibiotics always kill off the intestinal flora); yet yogurt gives relief from constipation. Another paradox—people who can't tolerate milk because they lack the proper enzyme to handle its lactose, can enjoy and benefit from natural *Lactobacillus* yogurt.

The fresher the yogurt, the higher its bacterial count. And it's quite easy to make your own. Just buy some plain yogurt to start, from any good food store; after that you can use your own yogurt as culture. The process consists of heating then cooling the milk until it forms a custardy curd, a matter of only a few hours. It isn't absolutely necessary to have a yogurt maker (some people use the oven or a heating pad), but yogurt makers are cheap and a big help in maintaining the right temperature.

Fresh homemade yogurt is sweeter than the store-bought kind. Also much cheaper. And you know its bacteria are lively. I use yogurt in sauces, salad dressings, on baked potatoes instead of sour cream. There are countless ways to turn yogurt into dessert, with fruits, nuts and toppings. Or it's good plain. Just going to the refrigerator and eating a tablespoonful of this tangy delicacy give me a feeling of doing something nice for my body. And, like the girls of Iraq and Iran, I've found there's nothing more refreshing than a yogurt facial.

How wonderful that this simple substance holds so many living secrets eager to work for us. I only regret it took me so long to discover them.

Sprouts

Sprouts too have burst belatedly on the American scene. Yet like garlic, yogurt and sunflower seeds, they've been a staple in the diet of others for generations. The Asiatic civilizations have always used sprouts. So have primitive peoples like the Hunzas, noted for their long vigorous lives. They not only eat seeds winter and summer, they live all winter on their sprouts. For when seeds are moistened, the life components stored there are swiftly released into their most effective state.

In his book *Survival Into the 21st Century*, Viktoras Kulvinskas likens this to suddenly activating a powerful enzyme factory. When eaten at this stage, "This rich enzyme concentration induces a heightened enzyme activity in your metabolism leading to a regeneration of the bloodstream and digestive process."

Sprouted seeds double their weight in three days; and their vitamins and minerals are enormously increased. The vitamin C in wheat multiplies by 600 per cent; the B vitamins, as well as vitamins A and E, double and quadruple. What's more, sprouted grains and legumes produce protein in its most complete, digestible form. It has already been converted into the essential amino acids. It is therefore a predigested food, quickly assimilated. There is no gas, and no undesirable mucus.

Sprouts are so capable of sustaining life they could well be the quickest, cheapest, most transportable way of providing protein for a hungry world.

Sprouts are also regenerating. Researchers at the Agricultural Experimental Station at Beltsville, Maryland, found sprouted oats restored fertility to sterile cattle. Dr. J. J. Fayne writes in a Department of Animal Husbandry bulletin:

> The success was no less than amazing. In every case tested the cows that had lost or outgrown their ability to reproduce became mothers again, giving birth to fine, normal, healthy calves. The same sprouted grain diet was given to another group of cows that were so completely sterile they had never reproduced, although they had been bred many times. . . . they all became mothers with every evidence of healthy reproductive ability. Bulls that had become sterile were also restored to normal fertility again in every case tested.

In other experiments some years ago, when old, decrepit rats were fed a diet of bean sprouts they too became revitalized and even reproduced.

I've never heard of such fertility experiments with people. But we do know sprouts are in a fresh new stage of life, their "youth"; and because of this they can flood our cells with that same fresh new life.

Furthermore, in their swift emergence from seeds, sprouts contain the same nitrilosides, amygdalin or B_{17} as seeds, which can help protect us from cancer.

Sprouts are remarkably easy to grow. Almost any seeds will do, although the most popular (partly because they can be grown in jars) are mung beans, soybeans and alfalfa. Other seeds, such as sunflower, wheat and buckwheat, are better grown on trays. These seeds should be soaked a few hours before sowing (on about an inch of topsoil mixed with peat moss), then covered lightly. They grow to three or four inches within a few days, and can be cut for tender, succulent salad greens.

You can buy all such seeds at your health food store. They are very cheap, and a few teaspoons of mung beans, soybeans or alfalfa will fill a fruit jar with their fluffy wonders. Some people prefer sprouters, but fruit jars work just great. Simply wash the seeds, put them in a jar and fill the jar with lukewarm water, to stand overnight. Next day pour out the water and cover the jar with a paper towel held by a rubber band; or with a screen-top lid, which makes it easier to wash them. Rinse two or three times a day, saving the nutrient-filled water for soups or juices (or drink it).

We lay the jars on their side by a warm windowsill where they will get the light to manufacture chlorophyl. By the third or fourth day tiny leaves and delicate tendrils will be almost bursting out of the jars. Sprouts are then ready to eat—roots, seeds, leaves and all. Eat them by the handful, or in salads and sandwiches, or added to anything you cook.

The Fun of "Cooking Healthy"

Like Mother, I was never any great shakes in the kitchen. True, like most brides, I spent ecstatic hours clipping out and trying exotic recipes. But the results were often disastrous. And as the children arrived and time to write became more valuable, I began to share Mother's half-whimsical, half-apologetic philosophy: "I hate to spend hours making something that'll disappear in ten minutes. If only people didn't have to *eat!*" So nobody welcomed package mixes and TV dinners more ardently than I. I blush to remember the years I fed my hapless family on all the drugged, devitalized, poisoned, fat- and sugar-drenched junk I now deplore. No wonder one or all of us were continually ailing or downright sick.

Since waking up to the wonders of "cooking healthy," however, my whole attitude has changed. The kitchen is no longer a prison to get out of as fast as possible, but a place to work imaginatively with the incredibly varied and delicious products of God's earth. Talk about gourmet recipes—the health food cookbooks and magazines are filled with them. And when you create dishes using carob and tahini and tofu and millet—a whole myriad of things you'd scarcely heard of before, let alone used—there is a sense of adventure and challenge. But more—of purpose. Of moving in harmony with the eternal wheel of life.

You are preparing something that tells the body you cherish it. Not just something that may look and taste good for a few minutes, then vanish, perhaps to damage it—but something that both tastes good and *is* good for it. This is especially important when cooking for those you love.

There is no space in this book to give you our favorite recipes (besides, I keep trying new ones). But you can find your own in the many marvelous cookbooks that are constantly being published and reviewed. Here are just a few that I wouldn't be without:

The Rodale Cookbook, published by Rodale Press, Emmaus, Pennsylvania.

Ten Talents, by Dr. and Mrs. Frank J. Hurt (who are Seventh Day Adventists), Chisholm, Minnesota.

Nature's Own Vegetable Cookbook, by Ann Williams-Heller, Arco Publishing Company, New York City.

More-with-Less Cookbook, by Doris Janzen Longacre (suggestions by Mennonites on how to eat better and consume less of the world's limited food resources), Herald Press, Scottdale, Pennsylvania.

Managing Your Personal Food Supply, Rodale Press, Emmaus, Pennsylvania.

Pure & Simple, Delicious Recipes for Additive-free Cooking, by Marian Burros, William Morrow & Company, New York City.

The Deaf Smith Country Cookbook, by Marjorie Winn Ford, Susan Hillyard and Mary Faulk Koock, Collier Books, Macmillan, New York City.

The Natural Foods Cookbook, by Beatrice Trum Hunter, Pyramid Books, New York City.

The Health Food Dictionary and Recipes, by Anstice Carroll and Embree De Persus Vona, Weather Vane Books, New York City.

17

None of Us
Needs to Get *Old!*

And thine age shall be clearer than the noonday; thou shalt shine
forth, thou shalt be as the morning.

JOB

When we are young we can't imagine ever getting old. Impossible! Look at us, so full of vigor and beauty and joy; so in love. We
are immortal. And age is simply a dread affliction that applies to
a totally different segment of society, almost a different breed.
Even gazing at early photographs of parents or grandparents is
an amusing shock. We refuse to believe they were ever that
young. How *could* those bright eager faces be the wrinkled,
often worried ones we know? That lovely flying hair—how can
it now be so gray—or gone? Those lithe bodies dancing, canoeing, playing tennis—now heavy, hurting, infirm? Preposterous
that such should ever be our fate. *Not me, not me!*

I remember saying those very words to my mother. And her
laughing reply: "It just happens, honey. You can't stop it." She
was partly right. Life does scribble its story on our faces. The
body does change with every passing year; eventually its marvelous machinery halts. But although we will all grow older,
there's no reason for anybody to grow *old.*

Youth itself—if youth would only hang on to it—has the perfect antidote: *I can't, I won't.* Because half the battle of staying young in mind and body is *simply wanting to enough.*

Now by staying young I don't mean dressing and acting like a teen-ager, or refusing to value and enjoy the rewards of our own maturing. (I wouldn't go through the horrible insecurities of youth again for all the treasures of King Tut.) I mean simply caring enough about your own glorious body to keep it as attractive, healthy and vigorous as possible. Learning how it works. Refraining from what will harm it. Doing what will help it. And, quite inseparably, caring enough about that miracle your own mind, to do the same for it.

But alas, how quickly vanish the fierce bright resolves of youth. Marriage, family, jobs crowd in, demanding so much sheer physical energy and attention that a time when we actually looked and felt young becomes a kind of mournful memory. Now it is our own pictures we look at with dismay: Cheerleading. Backpacking. At a prom. On our honeymoon. . . . What a contrast to the picture that accuses us from the mirror. Sometimes we wonder, startled—"Where'd I *go?*"

And usually one of the first things about us to *go* is our figure.

A Practically Painless Way to Keep Your Figure

We Americans glorify youth, but we also love to eat. Schizophrenically, the two categories that constantly top best-seller lists are cookbooks and books on losing weight. Dieting is almost a national obsession. Organizations like Weight Watchers and Tops (Take Off Pounds Sensibly) attract millions. The efforts are certainly commendable. Pride in appearance *is* important to a healthy, happy life; and the hazards of being overweight are too well documented to belabor here. If you have already developed a serious weight problem, follow your doctor's advice. These remarks are not for you.

Neither are they for those who have been fat all their lives. It's some people's *nature* to be fat. I think if that's your nature and you've tried every possible program, doctor and diet, you should stop torturing yourself. So do some obesity specialists, like Dr. Abraham Friedman, who says doctors are discovering that "not all fat people should lose weight." There is now even a

National Association to Aid Fat Americans. Chapters meet throughout the country to proclaim their rights, yes, pride and pleasure in being fat—and to them I say hooray.

Rather, I am talking to the people, especially young women, who don't as yet have a weight problem: You don't have to. Not ever. The trick is in caring enough not to lose your figure in the first place. Here are some things that helped me:

1. *Make the decision.*

Everybody told me I was built just like Aunt Eva and I'd look like her someday. In a way it was a compliment; Aunt Eva was pretty and witty, but short like me—and fat. All Dad's people were on the fat side; Mother's were lean. I decided to take after my mother's people. Maybe my spirit decided—because I believe there *is* an inner spirit that directs one's life if we let it. Deep in my soul I resolved never, never to be fat.

2. *Keep busy.*

I was born busy. I held down law office jobs all through high school and college and still participated in every possible activity. "You burn it all off," people said, and they were right. Sheer activity does consume the calories. Also, there was simply no time to hang around the Sugar Bowl downing malted milks with friends.

"Wait till you settle down," Mother lovingly predicted. But luckily I never have. With four children to raise and a career to pursue, I've had to bypass the coffee klatches, the luncheon clubs and bridge parties with their goodies. And my work is so absorbing it seldom even occurs to me to eat between meals.

So get involved, pursue your dream. It's idle hands that reach into the refrigerator, and restlessness and lonely brooding that often impel them to.

3. *"Never gain the first pound."*

Our daughter's dancing teacher told me that. I was still nursing my second baby and felt justified in the five or six pounds gained. "Take it off as soon as you can and don't put it back," she said. "The secret is to weigh yourself every day." I've done this ever since. Of course, there are variables—but any gain beyond three or four pounds should be dealt with right away. It's surprising how little you have to give up to lose them; and far easier than going on crash diets in frantic attempts to get rid of more.

4. *To lose weight, eat less.*

Serve your plate with your normal portion, then divide and put half back. I know a man who took off sixty pounds in the course of a year by this simple method. "It wasn't what I ate," he told me, "it was just that I was eating too darned much!"

5. *Eat slowly, with awareness.*

Once you become aware of what you are eating you will eat less of it. Learn to savor instead of stuff. Most of us take bites too big and eat too fast. The mouth is too full for the taste buds to appreciate flavor, and the food is often swallowed before it's thoroughly chewed. We then reach for more. And suddenly there is a sense of fullness without real satisfaction. (*"I can't believe I ate the whole thing!"*)

6. *Try never to compensate with food.*

To "let yourself go" in the body is closely related to a letdown of the spirit. Life seems disappointing, we get discouraged, or emotionally exhausted from coping with mates, children, the demands of our jobs. Sometimes we just don't have the energy or will power to fight the battles of the flesh. "I deserve this," we reason, reaching for the consolation of another piece of cake. But food as a substitute for love and attention, for success or peace, is a sure way of *not* getting what you really want.

7. *Exercise every day.*

This is just as important as stepping on the scales. It takes an awful lot of exercise to take off unwanted pounds. But once you have your ideal weight, exercise helps keep it there. And it keeps you fit in several ways. Your clothes fit better, your *life* fits better.

8. *Don't become a girdle prisoner.*

Girdles are instruments of torture never meant for healthy bodies. Some bodies may need them to disguise the worst. But the only thing a girdle can do for an already firm and trim figure is to flatten the hips slightly and help hold the stomach in. Don't depend on a girdle to do this for you. By holding the rib cage high and tucking in the hips you can do this for yourself.

Whenever I've watched women struggling into girdles and heard their gasps of relief when they got out of them, I've thanked my lucky stars that I was too poor to buy a girdle when I was first married. And by the time I could afford one I was glad I didn't have one.

To summarize: Get into the right eating habits. Exercise every day. Above all, listen to the voice of your inner spirit insisting that you will always keep your body slender, supple and young.

It's Not How Long You Live, But How Well

There is a Greek myth about Tithonus, who begged the gods to let him live forever. He forgot to specify what kind of life, however, and found himself trapped in a state of perpetual old age. In his misery, he now begged for release. It was not eternal life he really wanted, but eternal youth. The lesson applies to all of us. A long life offers few rewards to the bedridden, the senile, the mentally and physically tormented. *It isn't the length of time we live that really matters so much as the length of time we live WELL.*

This is the one overriding quality of those primitive peoples who capture headlines because they seem to live so long: The amazing villagers of Vilcabamba, Ecuador. The Abkhasians and other tribes of the Russian Caucasus. The Hunzas of the Himalayan Mountains of Pakistan. They remain bright-eyed, alert, productive, happy and physically active until they die. That's what should excite us, quite apart from the remarkable ages they claim to achieve—some as high as 160 years.

Whether or not these claims are valid may be established by Dr. Jeffrey Bada, a San Diego chemist who has developed a bone-dating process believed to be more accurate than carbon dating. Called "racemization," it is based on the configuration of molecules as they react to polarized light. Ken Ringle, writing in the Washington *Post,* says that racemization occurs most obviously in places like teeth, and may be a key to the aging process itself. Dr. Bada's "quest for a tooth from the Caucasus is thus more than a move to debunk some questionable claims to long life. It is part of his continuing investigation of racemization and the aging process." But the Soviets are reluctant to give up a tooth for testing. The longevity of these people is part of their claim to fame. They don't want to risk any evidence of exaggeration.

But isn't that in itself one clue to their well-being? Imagine living in a society where age is so admired that you actually bragged about yours! Where old people aren't patronized, made fun of in comedy sketches, shunted off to "homes." And isn't *that* very attitude because (so far, at least) people in those places have not been subject to the same debilitating diseases that make so many infirm and helpless elsewhere?

What are the common denominators that produce these results? What can we learn from them that all our conferences and committees on aging fail to tell us? Here are the basics, as reported by Grace Halsell, Dr. Sula Benet and others who have visited them.

• They don't take drugs as we know them. Natural plants and herbs provide any medicine they may need.

• They eat a light, low-calorie diet, generally high in vitamin C.

• Food is always prepared fresh. Fruits and vegetables are picked as near mealtime as possible. Meat is freshly killed, not aged. Any leftovers are fed to the animals. Day-old food is considered unhealthy.

• Much of their food is eaten raw. Cooked food is never served hot, only lukewarm. They eat whole foods—seeds and often the bones.

• They eat slowly, lingering over meals. They don't overeat. Overweight is considered an illness.

• Any food put away for winter is pickled instead of canned. (This provides lactic acid and preserves the enzymes.) They eat sprouts.

• They drink buttermilk and are fond of yogurt. Many are bee keepers, but instead of eating the honey they love the "scrap" or pollen at the bottom of the hives. (Pollen is a highly energizing, almost complete food, rich in amino acids.)

• They are free of emotional stress as we know it. They don't have to worry about crime. They have strong family and religious ties. They are cheerful, they love to laugh and dance and sing.

• They live close to nature, and always return to the earth what they take from it. They have been spared pollution of their air, water, soil, and the chemical pollution of their food.

• They exercise. Most of their work is hard physical labor done in the open air.

• They seldom retire. They keep busy and useful to the end of their lives.

Scientists are saying the true value of studying the Hunzas or the people of Soviet Georgia is not that some of them may live beyond one hundred, but that so many of them past seventy go right on living vigorous, happy, productive lives without the afflictions of age so common to the rest of the world.*

We can't hope to achieve their pure environment or enjoy their freedom from stress. But we *can* emulate many of the other things that have helped to let them live so long—and yet stay so young.

Get Outdoors

I think we begin to age when we stop wanting to be outdoors. It is evidence that the child within us has died. The child who begged to romp in snow or sand or sea; the youth who was happiest swimming, biking, climbing mountains. Who would make any sacrifice, suffer any hardship just to be one with nature. And so long as he continues to do this he can't and won't get "old."

For there is a life-force in nature that sustains us if we let it, that renews and refreshes us. I have friends and correspondents in their eighties and nineties who, like the Hunzas, are still going strong. Almost every one of them has a garden. One dear man, now almost a hundred, tends two hundred rosebushes,

* Tragically, this way of life is succumbing to "progress" in some places. A highway built through Vilcabamba has caused the death rate to jump. Peasants who once trudged behind mules are riding tractors; sugar and processed foods are luring people away from natural crops. Diabetes, cancer and heart disease are appearing. The *National Enquirer* quotes the eminent Ecuadorian cardiologist Dr. Joseph M. Izquieta as saying, "It's tragic but true. The ancient, peaceful, orderly, healthful, hard-working life they've had for centuries . . . has been shattered because the highway brought in all the worst of civilization."

plants a thousand bulbs in the fall. "I dream about them all winter," he says. "You can't worry when you're in the garden, not when the birds are singing, the sun is shining and there's so much to be done. And it keeps me healthy. If the doctors depended on me for business they'd starve."

Outdoor exercise, surrounded by growing things. Seeds and sun and soil. To work with them is to draw their precious secret energy into your own being. To hold life in your hands.

Being outdoors also lets us breathe fresh air. God never meant us to stay cooped up all winter, or locked away from summer with doors and windows closed. Even though my husband's business was air conditioning, I simply refused to let this happen. And wherever we lived, as many meals as possible were eaten on porch or patio or in the yard. There too I've done a great deal of my writing.

We *are* the air we breathe, just as much as we are the food and water we eat and drink. Life itself began when God breathed into the nostrils of man. In his marvelous little book *You Are Greater Than You Know,* Lou Austin wrote: "With every breath of air, you breathe in life-giving oxygen for your body and you also breathe in the Spirit of God. The Latin word 'spirare,' meaning to breathe, is the root of the English word 'spirit.' . . . Air is the one physical thing that unceasingly, uninterruptedly flows between you and your Maker."

He points out that we can live weeks without food, we can even live a few days without water; but "without breath there is no life. It is true from the beginning. An infant emerges from the womb, sucks in the life-giving air, lets out a wail, and begins life on earth. The aged person gives a faint gasp, ceases to breathe, and life is over. Life is a series of breaths."

So breathing, whether we are aware of it or not, unites us inescapably with God. How tragic that we have let this precious lifeline become so polluted in many places. And how sad that so many people huddle indoors breathing stale air . . . and disease and age and death. (Call on them and you can sense it, smell it.)

No, no—God wants us to breathe in his cool sweet fresh air of life and youth and health. So fling the windows wide, open the doors. Turn off the television, get up out of that bed or chair.

Walk, or run if you can, into the sunlight. Into the healing embrace of nature. Into God's glorious outdoors!

Get Away from Drugs

For at least two hours every evening Americans are captive to TV commercials which create the impression that everybody over forty is miserable and falling apart. One I simply can't *stand* is that forlorn-looking sixtyish woman who struggles bleakly into robe and slippers and, hanging on to the rail, creeps painfully downstairs, while a bright young voice marvels, "Mother's a wonder!" and catalogs all the things good old Mom still bravely does for her family in spite of her age and her arthritis. (Of course, she just couldn't manage all this without her Bufferin.)

But good old Mom isn't much worse off than the sorry parade of characters with nagging backaches, constipation, gaseous stomachs, hemorrhoids, insomnia and false teeth. Naturally, these models are seldom the beautiful young sex symbols used for selling everything else from shampoos to champagne. The victims of such wretched maladies are generally middle-aged and beyond. Creating the impression that life after forty is just "patch, patch, patch," as somebody has said, and the only way to endure it is to use Doan's Pills, Ex-Lax, Alka-Seltzer, Preparation H or dozens of other products proffered so eagerly by the solicitous sponsors.

The pity of it is that so many people *believe* this. We Americans are now spending more than a billion dollars a year for over-the-counter drugs, 75 per cent of which do absolutely no good, according to the National Academy of Sciences; and some of which—like laxatives and mineral oil—can actually contribute to the further crippling and aging of the body. Furthermore, pharmacists are filling some 2 billion drug prescriptions a year (nearly seven apiece for every man, woman and child) at a total cost of nearly $9 billion.

What makes all this preposterous if not downright criminal is the fact that the World Health Organization has reported that of 160,000 drugs available, only about 200 are considered essential (anesthetics, pain killers, antibiotics, etc.). And that despite the vast increase in pharmaceutical products, "there has not been a proportionate improvement in health." In fact, all drugs have undesirable side effects with a potential for causing more harm than they relieve.

In my own pre-God and vitamin days, I often traipsed to my doctor for various maladies and a listening ear. (Not Dr. Little. This was after we moved.) He was a delightful man who always examined me briskly but thoroughly, listened patiently and signaled the interview's end by reaching for his prescription pad—or a handful of samples. One day, about to take the sample capsule for what we'd both decided must be nervous anxiety, I chanced to read the company's warning, which usually only doctors see. *No less than sixty-eight possible adverse reactions were listed,* ranging from mouth dryness, dizziness, drowsiness, shortness of breath and hives, to such serious threats as jaundice, blindness, violent behavior, cardiac arrest and stroke.

Yet this drug also carried the assurance that it had been classified by the FDA as effective and safe! (Can you imagine what would happen to a *vitamin* if it was known to have even one such side effect?) And it seems to me almost beyond belief that *doctors,* people to whom we turn for help and healing, would tolerate our taking such monstrous poisons into our systems— let alone prescribe them. Yet they are glowingly advertised in every medical journal, and glut the shelves of almost every medicine cabinet.

The Dangers of "A Pill for Every Ill"

We are a pill-gobbling society; taught that doctor can fix it, doctor has a pill for every ill. *McCall's* magazine conducted a survey of readers, druggists and 1,000 physicians. After results were tallied, Alice Lake wrote, "The medication the doctor orders may be ineffective or inappropriate, too costly, even dangerous. Instead of getting better, it may make you worse. What's more, the likelihood that you will take the drug as intended is only about fifty-fifty." One doctor acknowledged, " 'Too often I've ordered a drug, not because it was clinically indicated but because the patient wanted it—*or I couldn't think of anything else to do.'* Several asserted that patients 'deserve' a prescription as a form of bonus for an expensive office visit."

Drugs can interact with each other and with things like tobacco and alcohol. All too often we forget what "Take as directed" was supposed to mean. Yet drugs taken at the wrong time in the wrong amounts or in conjunction with other drugs can be both ineffective and dangerous. While drugs like tranquilizers, anti-depressants and sleeping pills can be addictive and sometimes fatal.

The National Institute on Drug Abuse estimates that at least 2 million people a year become seriously dependent on prescription drugs. A great many of these are older women. Betty Ford's courageous admission that she had become hooked on drugs blew the lid off a delicate but serious situation. The Institute says it has reached "epidemic proportions." In the words of Muriel Ellis, author of its study, *Drugs, Alcohol and Women's Health,* "Women tend to believe that if a drug is prescribed for them, it is good for them. They don't question their doctor." This attitude is true of both men and women; and overmedication becomes the norm.

The science of gerontology, like nutrition, gets scant attention in medical schools. Many doctors simply don't know that the bodies of older people absorb and excrete drugs at a much slower rate, that they need smaller doses, just as children do. Furthermore, many doctors, sympathetic to the loneliness and depression of elderly patients, keep them on sedatives and mood-changing drugs. This has created a whole new geriatric syndrome; what psychiatrist Wendell R. Lipscomb of Berkeley, California, calls "the spaced-out grandma." I have personally seen this happen. And despite those TV sketches, it's *not* funny, but pathetic and heartrending.

One of the most appalling aspects of all this is that drugs can create symptoms of actual senility. Dr. K. Warner Schaie, director of the University of Southern California's Gerontology Institute, has stated that one out of four presumably senile people, in or out of institutions, is simply disoriented by drugs. Nationally this adds up to a million Americans who are suffering drug-induced senility.

Wean Yourself from Drugs

Fortunately, the new U. S. Commissioner of the Food and Drug Administration does *not* believe in "a pill for every ill." Dr. Jere Goyan, appointed in late 1979, although himself a former dean of the School of Pharmacy at the University of California Medical School, has told the press: "The less drugs people take, the better off they are. . . . I mean, people should take drugs if they have to, but the idea that there's a pill for every disease— that just isn't true. . . . I am very strongly in favor of the patient taking care of himself."

Remember, nobody ever got sick for lack of a drug. And although *some* drugs are essential in some cases, most only mask symptoms. It's the body's own remarkable defense system and powers of recuperation that restore health. Drugs, however, destroy the very vitamins and minerals your immunity system must have to work for you.

God has better medicine than all those bottles and boxes of expensive capsules and liquids that choke the bathroom shelves. Claim his many healing promises in the Bible. But also pray for guidance in how to keep your body vigorous, vital and well. Then do your part. It's ridiculous to lean either on God or on your doctor if you don't cooperate.

By exercising and eating plenty of fresh, natural, bulky foods you'll never have need for laxatives or stomach remedies. By getting enough calcium, magnesium and vitamin B your nerves will calm down. Vitamins A, D and C will guard your eyesight, strengthen your resistance and minimize the spotting, wrinkling and other ravages of age. (Vitamin C builds collagen; without enough collagen we begin to shrink, wrinkle, sag.) Vitamin E provides the blood with oxygen, so important to the heart and brain. (One cause of senility is too little oxygen reaching the brain.) Vitamin E also fights those free radicals believed to be a major cause of aging.

Arm yourself with all the information you can. Libraries, bookstores and health stores abound in material that is exciting and scientifically sound. Consult a good doctor who treats the whole person with orthomolecular (natural) methods. He can give you tests to determine your body's individual needs, then design a diet and supplement program that will *keep* you almost as well and raring to go as you were at twenty. Maybe more.

Go Barefoot

One of the best ways to stay young and healthy is simply going barefoot.

Like most small-town kids we went barefoot as early as parents would allow; and despite the hazards of cut feet or stubbed toes, played in a barefoot rapture till fall. (Most parents encouraged this; it saved shoes.) I will never outgrow the thrill of caged feet at last released from shoes and stockings, the joyous feeling of cool prickling grass and earth and sand beneath their nakedness. As an adult I began going barefoot indoors and out whenever possible, just because I still enjoyed it. Now I realize that this old-fashioned, peasanty habit has actual physical benefits.

For one, it's a way to prevent the most common agonies of age: Cold, crippled, arthritic feet. Bunions, ingrown toenails, metatarsal tenderness. Extremities so stiff and ailing "it's hard to get about"—hence the inactivity that breeds even more ailments and depression.

Dr. Paul W. Brand, public health official and orthopedic surgeon, has said, "Both health and joy of living would be enhanced if every American spent a part of each day barefoot in his or her own garden or yard." In studying foot problems around the world for thirty years, he found the healthiest feet were always among people who had no shoes. He says we rush children into shoes too fast. In their book *Understanding Arthritis and Rheumatism,* Malcolm I. V. Jayson and Allan St. J. Dixon, both M.D.'s, say shoes are the beginning of that most crippling and painful affliction, arthritis of the feet. That, ideally, children should spend the first years of life running around all day on green grass.

Notice how children appreciate their feet. A baby is fascinated by his toes, he even tries to eat them; youngsters fondle and pick at them. How sad that adults neglect them, except when they hurt. Try to recapture that childlike pleasure; marvel at your own—every homely, lopsided toe of them. Thank the Lord for giving you two of them (each equipped with 26 bones, 20 muscles and 33 joints!). Wiggle them, stretch them, take a stiff brush and scrub them—feel the tingle of blood responding. In your shower lift each of them for its turn of vigorous pounding. For the feet, being so far from the heart, need all the help they can get in maintaining good circulation. And poor circulation in the feet is a symptom and a hazard of age.

Baby your feet with comfortable but attractive shoes. (Pride is important too; you *don't* have to wear ugly, "sensible" shoes.) But free your feet as often as you can. Going barefoot stimulates circulation, strengthens arches, improves your posture and gives feet invaluable exercise. By going barefoot the weight is properly distributed, podiatrists tell us; the fatty cushion that pads the bottom of the foot is toughened. In elderly people this cushion often shifts away from the weight-bearing area, with only thin skin protecting their frequently damaged joints, so that every step is painful. If you eat properly and run around barefoot most of your life, this just doesn't happen. (Diabetics should be careful about going barefoot, however. Even a slight injury to the feet could cause them serious trouble.)

Going barefoot also triggers responses in the thousands of tiny nerve endings in the feet. Medical science is belatedly coming to recognize what the ancient Greeks, Persians and Chinese have used in healing for centuries: that we are an infinite network of reflexes and vibrations, so that to touch one part of the body will set up an instant reaction in another part. This is the principle back of acupuncture and all the related arts known as zone therapy—acupressure, finger pressure, reflexology. Through needles, massage or manipulation pain can often be relieved in the associated organ, and health restored.

Strangely, every organ and gland in the body has a zone in the feet. Charts have been made of these reflex areas, and by pressing or massaging the proper spots, help can be obtained for almost every known ailment. I have heard and read of countless people who claim remarkable benefits. Except for acupuncture, I can't speak from experience.† But I am con-

† Acupuncture relieved my husband of the terrible pain in his crushed heels after his fall. . . . Acupuncture also temporarily restored hearing to my left ear, which had baffled doctors for years. (They had finally decided it was irre-

vinced that going barefoot every day is a constant form of acupressure that helps *prevent* such ailments.

. . . Dear feet, how we take you for granted! Yet it is you who keep us upright, faces to the life-giving light. And you who ground us firmly to the life-giving earth. . . . So there is a mystique about going barefoot, especially outdoors. We draw energy from Mother Earth—her rocks, her grass, her soil. We are revitalized, made young in body and spirit.

You're as Old as Your Sense of Adventure

Age is also a matter of attitude. Jesus said, "As a man thinketh, so is he." I wince whenever I hear people using phrases like: "At our age." "We're slowing down." "Over the hill." "Declining years." I could shake them. Declining years, indeed! The later years of life ought to be ascending years, a time to reach new peaks of adventure, enjoyment, fulfillment. To think of them otherwise is a quick way to become *old.*

Mary Frances, a friend in Covington, Louisiana, wrote me she'd been doing volunteer work at a nursing home. "And one 'little old lady' really clings to me. Every week she wants to tell me about her grandchildren and pine for 'the good old days.' Then one day she got out her high school annual and I about flipped. I discovered she's five years younger than *I* am!"

---

versible nerve deafness.) To my amazement, *one treatment* brought sounds back clear as a bell. And two months of weekly treatments maintained hearing for a year. The next year when it began to dim I simply went back for more. A third set of treatments, however, proved disappointing. I turned the problem over to God and lived with it. Then one day several years later, after a lot of prayer, the phone rang and again I could hear brightly through the long blocked ear! Was it God and vitamins along with the delayed results of acupuncture? I only know how glad I am. And if ever necessary again, I'll try all three.

I think it's wonderful that most American doctors are no longer resisting acupuncture; many even want to learn it. Acupuncture is a delicate, highly skilled art, however, that can't be mastered in a few weeks' crash course. If you decide to use it, make sure you get a medical doctor who has also had years of training in the Orient. Ours, Dr. Chi Chin Huang, was not only a graduate of Tokyo University's medical school, he had grown up in Taiwan, where his training in acupuncture had begun as a boy.

Emotionally, I think such people are born old. They've never had a sense of adventure. Other people "get that way." Here is a reader's letter which I published in my Washington *Star* column:

My wife and I took a trip to Florida on a sit-up car. We had the time of our lives wandering all over the train meeting these strange and wonderful people, people from all walks of life whom we'd never have met otherwise. We arrived dead tired, of course, but both agreeing it was the most delightful trip we'd ever had. Some friends took this same trip, only they had a private compartment. When they arrived all they could talk about was how the door rattled, the place was drafty, rough and noisy, and how bad the service was.

And I got to wondering—at what point in life does a person lose his sense of adventure and begin getting more pleasure out of complaints? Why does it so often follow that once you reach a point where you can afford a few luxuries, you feel you can also afford to find fault? Is there a kind of curve of life where even our satisfactions begin to descend, to take a negative, critical approach? Or is it purely a matter of the spirit, of our emotional age?

It is surely a matter of the spirit, of emotional age. I'll never forget something Dorothy McCardle once said to me in the early days of our long friendship: "I think the true test of keeping the vitality of youth is whether or not you're willing to try new things."

Dorothy covered five administrations as a top reporter for the Washington *Post.* No assignment was ever too tough for her, no trip too far. Interviewing, lecturing, meeting deadlines, driving home alone late at night, she outlasted many colleagues. We had a merry telephone conversation the very night she died. "Marj, I'll be seventy-five next week," she said, "but the *Post* wants me back for another year. I'm going to Guatemala next week, but I'll call you when I get back. I'm taking swimming lessons—maybe we could meet at the gym. Anyway, I want to talk to you about the book I've started."

She didn't get to finish her book—the Lord called her on a bigger assignment. But how Dorothy had lived her words! She was never old a day of her life because each day was a new adventure.

Even if you've had to postpone adventures, it's never too late to start. One year I participated in Georgetown University's Traveling Writer's Conference. We taught, studied and visited literary shrines in the British Isles. And the cheeriest person on the bus was Helen Sheppard, eighty-three. She was also the first one off, scurrying up steps and hills and through the hedges to the homes of Kipling, Dickens, Jane Austen. Between stops she quoted Shakespeare, Plato, Dylan Thomas, and could tell us more about Stonehenge than the guide.

Even more remarkable was the fact that Helen had lived in the same house in the same sleepy Massachusetts village for nearly fifty years before she had the time, money and freedom to travel. But, boy, when she did! This was her seventh trip abroad. Meanwhile, shortly after her breakaway in her seventies, she decided to move to Washington, D.C., where she got herself a job with best-selling author Frances Spaatz Leighton, co-author of *Backstairs at the White House, My Life with Jacqueline Kennedy,* etc. (And Frances herself is so vital you can't be *around* her without having a ball.) . . . I saw Helen the other night at a press party. Now ninety, she's still enthusiastically working, learning, adventuring.

The papers are filled with stories of everyday people unwilling to settle for sickness, self-pity or waiting for somebody to pay attention to them. Such people keep young because they never lose their sense of adventure, they're always willing to try new things.

Keep Growing and Giving

In his "Words to Live By" series, which appeared for many years in the Sunday supplement *This Week,* Wilferd A. Peterson wrote: "Stay young by continuing to grow. You do not grow old, you become old by not growing."

Closely related to that is giving. I've never known anyone who kept mentally young by learning who didn't rejoice in sharing his knowledge and skill with others.

For years Pat Foster, a wonderful man in his eighties, sent me tapes of his lively tunes. He'd been a harmonica champion in his youth; now he played at hospitals for crippled children. He also gave magic shows, worked with the deaf and taught the art of making jewelry out of shells and stones. "I've raised a fine family," he wrote, "and now I want to make other people happy as long as the good Lord lets me. . . . The hard part, though, is those little tikes with cancer. How it warms my heart to see their eyes light up when I come in. But how it hurts to go back and find so many of them gone. Poor little things—before they even had a chance to live! Health, life, those are the real riches, and I thank God for mine every night on my knees."

Myrtle Lee, once a prominent educator, Mother of the Year, and also a very wealthy woman, gave away her fortune and moved to Hawaii in order to teach poor Asian immigrants how to speak. Using the Laubach method, thousands of others were taught to read. At eighty-four she wrote me: "Rather than living in despair at the human predicament—and this includes so-called 'old age'—I bounce back and live in joy via serving the people. I expect to do it through all eternity. Change and giving are part of growth."

Top psychologists agree. Dr. Robert Kastenbaum, editor of the *National Journal of Aging and Human Development,* says the brain in a normally healthy body does *not* disintegrate with age. It's possible to be just as productive mentally as you were in your thirties if you just keep learning, and especially if you teach somebody else. But the brain, like the body, must be exercised. In her book *Better Than Ever,* Dr. Joyce Brothers cites studies which prove that intelligence in many people actually *increases* with age.

Keep Doing the Work You Love

Everyday people or famous people—those who live life to the hilt to its very end are those who never stop doing the work they love. Often their productivity reaches new heights the longer they live: Goethe finished *Faust* at eighty. Benjamin Franklin was eighty when he helped compose the Constitution. Titian, Da Vinci, Michelangelo, all painted their greatest masterpieces in their last late years. Within our own century we have had Albert Schweitzer, Bertrand Russell, Shaw, Stokowski, Picasso, Charlie Chaplin, Pablo Casals—to name only a few.

Not long before his death at ninety-six Casals appeared in

Washington, D.C. At the last minute he was unable to perform, but after the concert he was escorted onstage, and to the joy of the wildly cheering audience, spoke: "I am a very very old man," he said, "and I remember the first concert that I gave here at the beginning of the century. It was very touching for me. I was a young man and I was astonished to receive so much of your applause. But now I feel younger than ever because I play Bach every day; every day I play after having prayer to that fantastic, fantastic nature. Nature first, and then prayer. . . . And so, despite my age, I am still a musician. And I would like to give you more."

I am still a musician. An actor, a banker, a builder, a doctor, a useful person—*and I would like to give you more.* Not a has-been, jerked out of the mainstream, set aside to die—but still ready and eager to give my talents, energy and experience to the world every precious day that I have left. Enforced retirement, once believed to be a panacea, has caused more pain than arthritis, shortened more lives than heart disease.

Retired Senator Sam Ervin, himself in his eighties, said in an address before the Leonard Davis School of Gerontology at the University of Southern California, that he had known "aged individuals who are only twenty-five and young people who are ninety-one. It is tragic that such a small number of active employees today are over sixty-five." Right now the mandatory retirement age has been raised to seventy, and there are movements underway to abolish it altogether. As Harvey Wheeler expresses it in *Modern Maturity,* this would "end the myth that only the first six-and-a-half decades of life were good for anything."

The fact that people in the arts haven't been so hobbled is precisely why so many of them are still dancing while others their age may be using walkers; still publishing, performing, while people no older endure bleak and pointless days in rest or retirement homes. When Horowitz played in Washington recently at seventy-three, he said he had no plans for taking things easy. "Every year I play something new, something I have not played before." Such people are too busy using the talents God gave them to be sick and "old." They also recognize the value of their own precious bodies, which must be equal to the strain of long rehearsals or hours at the typewriter, public appearances, travel.

It's certainly true that many people look forward to retirement and thoroughly enjoy it. To many it's a well-earned reward. But usually these people are so full of plans for golf, hobbies, gardening, volunteer work, study, that we often hear them say, "I'm so busy I wonder how I ever had time to go to the office." My husband was one of them. After a long successful career with his company he was only too happy to turn the responsibility over to younger successors. But *he went right on doing other work he loved.* Holding back age and death doesn't necessarily mean doing the same work, but only projects so constructive and absorbing there's something to look forward to each morning, and the days aren't long enough.

And many times people are late bloomers. Talents that have lain dormant during the years of raising a family, making living, can manifest and provide second careers. To discover them, however, you must be willing to *try* things. As an outstanding example, Peggy Mann, writing in *Reader's Digest,* gives us Harry Lieberman, 101, whom critics have called another Chagall. Yet he'd never touched a paintbrush until one day at the Golden Age Club, where "he was sitting disconsolate waiting for a chess partner" when a volunteer urged him into the art room to paint a picture. Within a few years his pictures were hanging in galleries.

Of that volunteer he says, "She made me again into a man. . . . Boredom is the main thing that makes a man go down to death." And to those gathered for his twenty-second one-man show: "Don't think how old you are. Think only of what you can accomplish. Go, *do!* This alone is the living."

Choose the Nightmare or the Dream

That's the idea, *the dream that could be realized by oh so many more of us.* But what is the reality—or more accurately the nightmare for America's 22 million people over sixty-five? Let's look at some of the grim statistics:

• At least a million of them are occupying the nation's 22,000 nursing homes.

• One third of the federal budget is spent on the aged; of every dollar spent, 40 cents goes to these nursing homes.

• There are now more beds in nursing homes than in hospitals. Yet there is still a desperate shortage of beds for the aged.

• Hotels and boardinghouses provide for another million elderly. Many of these places are "geriatric ghettos" whose horror stories include rats, improper sanitation and fires.

Most nursing homes are far too expensive for people who have only social security; and even some of them are understaffed and poorly run. There have been scandals of Medicare frauds, where patients don't get food and medicines paid for, instances of gouging by organized crime. Even those operated by skilled and dedicated people (and there are many) are at best usually a forlorn finale to life for people who need care and have no other solution. Dr. Robert N. Butler, director of the National Institute on Aging, says: "Even more than cancer, what most people fear most is growing old, losing their mind and being put away."

What greater incentive than that could we have for taking care of our minds and bodies *now?* Now, now, *now,* while there is still time!

We dare not and must not wait on government to do it for us. Gummed by politics and profit, reforms can take years—if they ever come at all.

Besides, genuine reform must come from each individual. You. Me. Nobody else can forestall old age for us; nobody else can prevent its loneliness, frustrations and infirmity. Physically, mentally and emotionally we are preparing our own fate.

Dr. Olga Swanson, a researcher at the University of Iowa, says in *Let's Live,* "What we will be in 10, 20 or 30 years depends on the food choices we make now."

It will depend on whether or not we keep the cells of our bodies supplied with all the vitamins, minerals and other nutrients they need. It will depend on whether or not we've kept our bodies free from dangerous, nutrient-destroying drugs. It will depend on *whatever* we take in by way of air or food or drink.

And it will depend on whether or not we exercise, or let these marvelous bodies atrophy.

It will also depend on our habits of thought. Whether we are negative, worried, dwelling on the past, criticizing the present, unwilling to try new things . . . or thanking God for the gift of life and the glorious adventures of each new day.

Remember, we *are*

> The food we eat. The water we drink.
> The air we breathe. The muscles we use.
> *And the thoughts we think.*

Vitamins, exercise, diet and faith have changed my life. They have made me a more healthy, happy, vital, productive and loving human being. They can do the same for anyone who really wants them to.

References and Suggested Reading

CHAPTER ONE

Frederick Price, *How Faith Works.* Tulsa, Oklahoma: Harrison House, 1976.
William Standish Reed, M.D., *Surgery of the Soul.* Old Tappan, N.J.: Fleming H. Revell, 1969.

Suggested Further Reading

S. I. McMillen, M.D., *None of These Diseases.* Old Tappan, N.J.: Fleming H. Revell, 1963.

CHAPTER TWO

Kathleen Maxa, "Sound Body, Sound Mind," a series in the Washington *Star*, June 1978.
An Introduction to Physical Fitness, The President's Council on Physical Fitness and Sports, 1973.
Leonard Lear, "Gym Class Goes Natural," *Prevention*, 1976.
Hal B. Richerson, M.D. and Paul M. Seebohm, M.D., "Nasal Airway Response to Exercise," *Journal of Allergy*, May 1968.
Herbert de Vries, *Vigor Regained.* Englewood Cliffs, N.J.: Prentice-Hall, 1974.

Suggested Further Reading

"The Fitness Mania," *U.S. News & World Report,* February 27, 1978.
Dr. Max Warmbrand, *Add Years to Your Heart.* New York: Pyramid
House, 1956.

CHAPTER THREE

Joseph Wolffe, M.D., paper presented to the Annual National Recre-
ational Congress in Philadelphia, 1962.
Kenneth Cooper, M.D., *Aerobics,* 1968. *The New Aerobics,* 1970. With
Mildred Cooper, *Aerobics for Women,* 1972. All published by M.
Evans & Company, New York.
Michael Clark, "Strengthen Your Bones With Exercise," *Prevention,*
August 1973.
Marguerite Agniel, 1) *Body Sculpture.* 2) *Your Figure.* 3) *Creating Body
Beauty.* Penobscot, Maine: Traversity Press, all undated.

Suggested Further Reading

Greg Campbell, *The Joy of Jumping: A Complete Program of Skip-
Rope for Health, Looks and Fun,* New York: Richard Marek, 1978.
Albert E. Carter, *The Miracles of Rebound Exercise.* Snohomish, Wash-
ington: Snohomish Publishing Co., 1979.
Dr. James Counselman, *Swimming,* 1976; *Aquarobics,* 1979. Both New
York: Atheneum Publishers.
James Fixx, *The Complete Book of Running.* New York: Random
House, 1977.
Michael Minick, *The Kung Fu Exercise Book.* New York: Simon &
Schuster, 1974; New York: Bantam Books, 1975.
George Sheehan, M.D., *Running and Being.* New York: Simon &
Schuster, 1978.

CHAPTER FOUR

Fred Soyka with Alan Edmonds, *The Ion Effect.* New York: E. P. Dut-
ton, 1977; New York: Bantam Books, 1978.
Guy Remsen and Lawrence G. Blochman, *Wake Up Your Body!* New
York: David McKay, 1969; New York: Pocket Books, 1970.
Melvin Page, D.D.S. and H. Leon Abrams, Jr., *Your Body Is Your Best
Doctor!* New Haven, Conn.: Keats, 1972.
Henry A. Schroeder, M.D. A survey linking soft water with cardiovas-

cular disease, *Journal of American Medical Association,* April 23, 1960 and January 10, 1966.

Ray Wolf, "Drinking Water Dolomite and Longer Life," *Prevention,* April 1974.

John N. Cole, "Twilight of a Species," *Reader's Digest,* April 1979. Condensed from *Striper, A Story of Fish and Man.* Boston: Atlantic Monthly Press, 1978.

David Reuben, M.D., "If It Sounds Terrible, It *Is* Terrible," *National Health Federation Bulletin,* March 1979.

CHAPTER FIVE

Melvin Page, D.D.S., *Degeneration-Regeneration,* St. Petersburg, Florida: Biochemical Research Foundation, 1949.

Robert Rodale, "Prevention Is One Man," *Prevention,* June 1970.

Esther Nelson, M.D. A report on her survey of nutrition courses taught in medical schools. *Journal of the American Medical Association,* November 29, 1976.

Dr. Roger J. Williams, *Nutrition Against Disease,* New York: Putman & Co., 1971; New York: Bantam Books, 1973.

Diet Related to Killer Diseases, Hearing Before the Select Committee on Nutrition and Human Needs of the United States Senate. U. S. Government Printing Office, 1977.

Ronald J. Glasser, M.D., *The Body Is the Hero.* New York: Random House, 1976.

Dr. Roger J. Williams and Dr. Dwight K. Kalita, *A Physician's Handbook on Orthomolecular Medicine.* Elmsford, N.Y.: Pergamon Press, 1977.

Morton Mintz, "The Medicine Business," a series in the Washington *Post,* April–July, 1976.

Alan H. Nittler, M.D., *A New Breed of Doctors.* New York: Pyramid House, 1972.

William McKay, with Maureen Mylander, *Salesman Surgeon.* New York: McGraw-Hill, 1978.

Suggested Further Reading

Mark Bricklin, *The Practical Encyclopedia of Natural Healing.* Emmaus, Pa.: Rodale Press, 1976.

Linda Clark, *Get Well Naturally.* Old Greenwich, Conn.: Devin-Adair, 1965; New York: Arco Pub., 1978.

Joe Graedon, *The People's Pharmacy.* New York: St. Martin's Press, 1976; New York: Avon Books, 1977.

Ivan Illich, *Medical Nemesis.* New York: Random House, 1976; New York: Bantam Books, 1977.

Joe D. Nichols, M.D. and James Presley, *"Please Doctor, DO Something!"* Old Greenwich, Conn.: Devin-Adair, 1972.

CHAPTER SIX

Isaac Asimov, *The Chemicals of Life,* Abelard Schuman. New York: New American Library, 1954.

Dr. Richard Passwater, *Supernutrition—Megavitamin Revolution.* New York: Dial Press, 1975.

Nutrition-Minded Doctors in the U.S. and Canada. Buena Park, Cal.: Alacer Corp. (Undated).

J. I. Rodale and staff, *The Complete Book of Vitamins.* Emmaus, Pa.: Rodale Press, 1966.

Dr. Isobel Jennings, *Vitamins in Endocrine Metabolism.* New York: Charles C. Thomas, 1970.

Suggested Further Reading

Ruth Adams and Frank Murray, *Mega-vitamin Therapy.* New York: Larchmont Books, 1973.

Herbert Bailey, *The Vitamin Pioneers.* Emmaus, Pa.: Rodale Press, 1968; New York: Pyramid Books, 1969.

Lloyd Crain, *Magic Vitamins and Organic Foods.* Crandrich Studios, 1971.

Martin Ebon, *Which Vitamins Do You Need?* New York: Bantam Books, 1974.

Dr. Roger J. Williams, *The Wonderful World Within You.* New York: Bantam Books, 1977.

CHAPTER SEVEN

Joan Dye Gussow, *The Feeding Web.* Palo Alto, Cal.: Bull Publishing, 1979. "Children Vs. The Gross National Product," *Nutrition Action,* November 1977.

Senator George McGovern, *Dietary Goals For the United States,* U. S. Government Printing Office, 1977.

Weston A. Price, D.D.S., *Nutrition and Physical Degeneration,* The Price-Pottenger Nutrition Foundation, 1945.

Dominick Bosco, "White Man's Food Bad Medicine For Indian," *Prevention,* January 1976.

Dr. Michael Fox, "The Hidden Costs of Factory Farming," *The Humane Society News,* Winter 1978.

Marian Burros, *Pure & Simple.* New York: William Morrow, 1978.

Beatrice Trum Hunter, "Dietary Fiber: A Panacea?" *Consumers' Research Magazine,* July 1977.

John M. Ellis, M.D., "Recent Changes in Concepts of Nutrition," *Natural Food and Farming.*

Ronald J. Glasser, M.D., *The Greatest Battle.* New York: Random House, 1978.

Lawrence Galton, "Childhood Arthritis—the Neglected Disease," *Parade,* August 14, 1977.

Jack Anderson, "Best Fed—But Starved," Washington *Post,* March 6, 1977.

Susan Parry, "Whatever Happened to Apples and Oranges?" *Nutrition Action,* November 1977.

Allan Cott, M.D., *The Orthomolecular Approach to Learning Disabilities.* New York: Academic Press, 1977.

Greta Bunin, "Objective Science Groups or Industry's Puppets?" *Nutrition Action,* February 1979.

Charlotte Gerson Straus, Speech for the National Health Federation Convention, November 1978.

Suggested Further Reading

Letitia Brewster and Michael F. Jacobson, *The Changing American Diet.* Center for Science in the Public Interest, 1978.

William Dufty, *Sugar Blues.* Radnov, Pa.: Chilton Book Co., 1975; Warner Books, 1976.

Dr. Carlton Fredericks, *Nutrition Handbook, Your Key to Good Health.* Canoga Park, Cal.: Manor Books, 1976.

"The Great American Food Debate," *U.S. News & World Report,* November 28, 1977.

Hucksters in the Classroom, The Center for Study of Responsive Law, 1979.

Dr. Michael Jacobson, *Nutrition Scoreboard.* New York: Avon Books, 1975.

Deborah Katz and Mary T. Goodwin, *Food, Where Nutrition, Politics and Culture Meet.* Center for Science in the Public Interest, 1976.

William Longwood, *The Poisons in Your Food.* New York: Simon & Schuster, 1960; New York: Pyramid House, 1969.

Gary Null and Steven Null, *Poisons In Your Body.* New York: Arco Pub., 1977.

Thomas Porter, "School's Switch to Natural Diet Improves Performances in Class," *National Enquirer*, January 10, 1978.

CHAPTER EIGHT

Myths of Vitamins, HEW Publication No. (FDA) 77-2045, U. S. Government Printing Office, 1977.

Dr. Jacqueline Verrett and Jean Carper, *Eating May Be Hazardous to Your Health*. New York: Simon & Schuster, 1974.

Jack Anderson, "Regulating Those Conflicts of Interest," Washington *Post*, February 19, 1978.

Senator William Proxmire's testimony on vitamin legislation, *Congressional Record*, May 8, 1975.

Lea Thompson, "Baby Formula: The Hidden Dangers," Transcript, News Center 4, WRC-TV, Washington, D.C., October 25, 1979.

Suggested Further Reading

Dr. Arnold Pike, "Vitamins A & D— A Defeat For FDA," *Let's Live*, December 1977.

Harold J. Taub, "FDA Wants to Stop Your Vitamin Supplements," *Prevention*, September 1972.

"Vitamin and Mineral Drug Product For Over the Counter Human Use," *Federal Register*, March 16, 1979.

CHAPTER NINE

John Ott, *Health and Light*. New York: Devin-Adair Co., 1973; New York: Pocket Books, 1976.

The Merck Manual of Diagnosis and Therapy, 13th Edition, Merck Sharp & Dohme Research Laboratories, 1977.

John J. Straumfjord, M.D. A report on the use of vitamin A in treatment of 100 acne patients, *Northwest Medicine*, August 1943.

Elizabeth Macfarlane Hatfield, "Estimates of Blindness in the United States," *The Sight Saving Review*, Vol. 43, Summer 1973.

Harold A. Kahn, M.D., et al., *The Framingham Eye Study*, The Johns Hopkins University School of Hygiene and Public Health, 1977.

Arthur Alexander Knapp, M.D., "Blindness: Forty Years of Original Research," *Journal of the International Academy of Preventive Medicine*, Vol. IV, No. 1, July 1977.

First Health and Nutrition Examination Survey, United States, 1971–72, Dietary Intake and Biochemical Findings. U. S. Department of Health, Education and Welfare.

U. R. Saffiotti, et al., "Studies of Experimental Cancer of the Lung; Inhibition by Vitamin A." *Cancer* 20: 1967.

Michael B. Sporn, et al., "Prevention of Chemical Carcinogenesis by Vitamin A and Its Synthetic Analogs (Retinoids)," *Federation Proceedings,* April 15, 1975.

E. Bjelke, "Dietary Vitamin A and Human Lung Cancer," *International Journal of Cancer:* 15, 1975.

Jean Carper, "Learning to Outwit Cancer and the Poisons Within Us," Washington *Post,* February 4, 1979.

Gail Fisher, M.D. and Penn G. Skillern, M.D., "Hypercalcemia Due To Hypervitaminosis A," *Journal of the American Medical Association,* March 25, 1974.

R. M. Russell, M.D., et al., "Hepatic Injury from Chronic Hypervitaminosis A," *New England Journal of Medicine,* August 29, 1974.

Eli Seifter, M.D., "Vitamin A's Protective Role in Shrinkage of the Thymus," *Federation Proceedings,* National Cancer Institute, March 1973.

Vitamin A. Talk Paper, Food and Drug Administration, August 23, 1979.

The Vitamins, Vol. I. New York: Academic Press, 1967.

CHAPTER TEN

Diet Related to Killer Diseases: Mental Health and Mental Development, Select Committee on Nutrition and Human Needs of the United States Senate, 1977.

Abram Hoffer, M.D., with Morton Walker, *Orthomolecular Nutrition.* New Canaan, Conn.: Keats, 1978.

Lelord Kordel, *Health Through Nutrition.* Cleveland, O.: World, 1950; Canoga Park, Cal.: Manor Books, 1971.

Carlton Fredericks, with Herbert Bailey, *Food Facts and Fallacies.* New York: Arc Books, 1965.

Jonathan Winer, "Vitamins: RX for Schizophrenia?" Boston *Sunday Globe,* October 1, 1978.

Roger J. Williams, *Nutrition Against Disease.* New York: Pitman, 1971; New York: Bantam Books, 1973.

John M. Ellis, M.D., with James Presley, *Vitamin B6: The Doctor's Report.* New York: Harper & Row, 1973.

Robert M. Atkins, M.D., with Shirley Linde, *Super Energy Diet.* New York: Crown, 1977. "Too Much Sugar?" *Consumer Reports,* March 1978.

Dr. Carlton Fredericks, *Psycho-Nutrition.* New York: Grosset & Dunlap, 1976.

Suggested Further Reading

Ruth Adams and Frank Murray, *Megavitamin Therapy.* New York: Larchmont Books, 1973.

Marian Burros, "Diet and Behavior, The Link to Mental Disease," Washington *Post,* June 30, 1977.

E. Cheraskin, M.D. and W. M. Ringsdorf, Jr., with Arline Brecher, *Psychodietetics.* New York: Stein & Day, 1975; New York: Bantam Books, 1976.

H. L. Newbold, M.D., *Meganutrients For Your Nerves.* New York: Peter H. Wyden, 1975.

William H. Philpott, M.D., *The Physiology of Violence: The Role of the Central Nervous System,* The Huxley Institute for Biosocial Research, April 23, 1976.

Dr. Harold Rosenberg, with A. N. Feldzamen, *The Book of Vitamin Therapy.* New York: G. P. Putnam's, 1974.

Timothy D. Schellhart, "Can Chocolate Turn You Into a Criminal?" *The Wall Street Journal,* June 2, 1977.

CHAPTER ELEVEN

Dr. Richard Passwater, *Supernutrition for Healthy Hearts.* New York: Jove, 1978.

Brenda Forman, *B-15: The "Miracle Vitamin."* New York: Grosset & Dunlap, 1979.

Judge Orders FDA to Return Apricot Kernels, *National Health Federation Bulletin,* September 1977.

"Prescription Drug Use," *OTA Priorities, 1979,* Congress of the United States, Office of Technology Assessment.

Dr. Harold W. Manner, *The Death of Cancer.* Chicago: Advanced Century Publishing Co., 1978.

———, Lecture for the National Health Federation Convention, 1978.

Arlin J. Brown, *Cancer Victory Bulletin.* Fort Belvoir, Va., Arlin J. Brown Foundation, January 1978.

"Fanfare Fades In the Fight Against Cancer," *U.S. News & World Report,* June 19, 1978.

"Second Opinion Special Report: Laetrile at Sloan-Kettering," *Second Opinion,* November 1977.

"Chad Green and Parent Rights," Transcript, "The Phil Donahue Show," NBC-TV, November 16, 1979.

John Hofbauer, address before the Annual Cancer Victory Convention. Washington, D.C., September 1978.

Ed Griffin, *World Without Cancer*, American Medics, 1974.

James J. Kilpatrick, "Laetrile and FDA Tyranny," Washington *Star*, April 1, 1977.

Gary Null, et al., "The Suppression of Cancer Cures," *Penthouse*, May, September, October, November 1979 and January 1980.

Physician's Desk Reference, 33rd Edition, Medical Economics Co., 1979.

Victor Cohn and Peter Milius, "They Make Good by Making Well," Washington *Post*, January 7, 1979.

Suggested Further Reading

Ralph W. Moss, *The Cancer Syndrome*. New York: Grove Press, 1980.

Anatomy of a Cover-up, Successful Sloan-Kettering Amygdalin (Laetrile) Animal Studies. The Committee for Freedom of Choice in Cancer Therapies, 1975.

"Environmental Defense Fund and Robert H. Boyle," *Malignant Neglect*. New York: Alfred Knopf, 1979.

Samuel S. Epstein, M.D., *The Politics of Cancer*. San Francisco: Sierra Club, 1978.

Dr. Carlton Fredericks, *Breast Cancer: A Nutritional Approach*. New York: Grosset & Dunlap, 1977.

Daniel S. Greenberg and Judith E. Randal, "Waging the Wrong War on Cancer," Washington *Post*, May 1, 1977.

Virginia W. Livingston, M.D., *Cancer: A New Breakthrough*. San Diego: Production House, 1972.

Eydie Mae, with Chris Loeffler, *How I Conquered Cancer Naturally*. Irvine, Cal.: Harvest House Publishers, undated.

Dr. Richard Passwater, *Cancer and Its Nutritional Therapies*. New Canaan, Conn.: Keats, 1978.

John A. Richardson, M.D. and Patricia Griffin, R.N., *Laetrile Case Histories*. New York: Bantam Books, 1977.

O. Carl Simonton, M.D., Stephanie Matthews-Simonton, James Creighton, *Getting Well Again*. J. P. Tarcher, New York: St. Martins Press, undated.

CHAPTER TWELVE

Dr. Linus Pauling, *Vitamin C, the Common Cold and the Flu*. San Francisco: W. H. Freeman, 1970.

————, "On Fighting Swine Flu," New York *Times*, June 5, 1976.

T. W. Anderson, D. B. W. Reid, G. H. Beaten, "Vitamin C and the Common Cold: A Double Blind Trial," *Canadian Medical Association Journal*, 107, 1972.

Theodore Cooper, M.D., interview in *Medical Tribune*, November 3, 1976.

Richard Neustadt and Harvey Fineberg, *The Swine Flu Affair*. Department of Health, Education & Welfare, 1978.

Dominick Bosco, "Boost Your Immunity with Vitamin C," *Prevention*, May 1977.

Robert Cathcart III, M.D., Lecture for the California Orthomolecular Medical Society, February 1977, reported in *Nature's Way*, August 1977.

Clement A. Herbert, M.D., "A Case of Scurvy," *Annals of Thoracic Surgery*, August 1977.

Joan Jennings, "Vitamin C and Stroke," *Prevention*, July 1976.

W. J. McCormick, M.D., "Ascorbic Acid as a Chemotherapeutic Agent," *Archives of Pediatrics*, Vol. 69, 1952. Ibid, "The Rheumatic Diseases: Is There a Common Etiologic Factor?" Vol. 72, 1955.

James Greenwood, M.D., "Optimum Vitamin C Intake as a Factor in the Preservation of Disc Integrity," *Medical Annals of the District of Columbia*, Vol. 33, 1964.

Norman Cousins, *Anatomy of an Illness As Perceived by the Patient*. New York: W. W. Norton, 1979.

Dr. J. U. Schlegel, et al., "Studies on the Etiology and Prevention of Bladder Carcinoma," *Journal of Urology*, Vol. 101, 1969.

————, "Ascorbic Acid: An Anticancer Vitamin?" *Medical World News*, June 21, 1968.

R. F. Klenner, M.D., with Fred H. Bartz, *The Key to Good Health Vitamin C*, Graphic Arts Research Foundation, 1959.

Ewan Cameron, M.D. and Dr. Linus Pauling, *Cancer and Vitamin C*, Linus Pauling Institute of Science and Medicine, 1979.

Dr. Irwin Stone, *The Healing Factor, Vitamin C Against Disease*. New York: Grosset & Dunlap, 1972.

CHAPTER THIRTEEN

Wilfrid E. Shute, M.D., *Health Preserver*. Emmaus, Pa.: Rodale Press, 1977.

Gaye Deamer Horsley, *Commercial Foods Exposed*. Salt Lake City, Utah: Hawkes, 1975.

Adelle Davis, *Let's Get Well*. New York: Harcourt, Brace & World, 1968.

Joe D. Nichols, M.D., Address: "A Concept of Totality." Published in *Texas Bankers Record,* May 1952.

Knut Haeger, M.D., "Vitamin E and the Circulation: A Surgeon's Success Story," *Prevention,* March 1975.

————, "Longtime Treatment of Intermittent Claudication With Vitamin E," *American Journal of Clinical Nutrition,* Vol. 27, 1974.

Jane Kinderlehrer, "Breathe Easier with Vitamin E," *Prevention,* September, 1974.

Herbert Bailey, *Vitamin E, Your Key to a Healthy Heart.* Radnor, Pa.: Chilton, 1964; New York: Arc Books, 1966.

Dr. Jeffrey Bland, "How Vitamin E Can Slow Cellular Aging: A New Discovery," *Prevention,* June 1976.

A. L. Tappel, "Vitamin E as the Biological Lipid Antioxidant," *Vitamins Hormones,* Vol. 20, 1962.

Dr. Otto Warburg, *The Prime Cause and Prevention of Cancer.* Lecture for the Nobel committee, 1966. English edition by Dean Burk, National Cancer Institute, Cancer Control Society, 1969.

Evan V. Shute, M.D., and medical staff of The Shute Institute of Clinical and Laboratory Medicine, London, Canada, *The Heart and Vitamin E.* New Caanan, Conn.: Keats, 1956.

Emily and Per Ola D'Aulaire, "New Hope for the Childless," *Reader's Digest,* December 1977.

Suggested Further Reading

C. H. Chow, et al., "Effects of Dietary Vitamin E on the Red Blood Cells of Ozone Exposed Rats," *Federation Proceedings,* Vol. 35, March 10, 1976.

Erwin Di Cyan, *Vitamin E and Aging.* New York: Pyramid Books, 1972.

Carlson Wade, *Vitamin E, The Rejuvenation Vitamin.* New York: Award Books, 1970.

CHAPTER FOURTEEN

Robert Rodale, "Short-circuiting the Cycle of Life," *Prevention,* November 1969.

Daniel Zwerdling, "The Pesticides Plague," Washington *Post,* March 5, 1978.

"Hindes Farm the Organic Way," *Pilot Tribune,* Storm Lake, Iowa, February 8, 1978.

Bill Richards, "Nitrogen Fertilizers Seen as Threat to Earth's Ozone Shield," Washington *Post,* March 17, 1977.

William Tucker, "Environment Crusade Crushes Friends and Foe Alike," Washington *Star*, August 6, 1978.

Wil Lepkowski, "An Ethical Dilemma," Washington *Post*, September 19, 1976.

West Virginia University, Agricultural Experiment Station; results of studies by Dr. Robert E. Keefer and Dr. Rabindar N. Singh, News Release, March 4, 1973.

Jim Hightower, *Eat Your Heart Out.* New York: Random House, 1975; New York: Vintage Books, 1976.

Congressman Benjamin Rosenthal, "Feeding at the Company Trough," *Congressional Record,* August 24, 1976.

Jack Anderson and Les Whitten, "Pro-Chemical PR Blitz Readied," Washington *Post*, December 15, 1977.

"What's Your Nutrition IQ?" *Diabetes Forecast,* May–June, 1977.

Jon N. Leonard, J. L. Hofer, and N. Pritikin, *Live Longer Now.* New York: Grosset & Dunlap, 1974; Charter Books, (undated).

"What to Do About Those Annoying Household Pests," *Consumers' Research Magazine,* April 1977.

The Killing Ground, transcript of a broadcast by ABC News, New York, March 3, 1979.

Suggested Further Reading

A Plague on Our Children, transcript of a broadcast by NOVA, WGBH Educational Foundation, 1979.

Frances Moore Lappe, *Diet for a Small Planet.* New York: Ballantine Books, 1971.

Jethro Ross, *Back to Eden.* Santa Barbara, Cal.: Woodbridge Press, 1972.

Lee Fryer and Dick Simmons, *Earth Foods.* Chicago: Follett Pub., 1972.

Peter Tompkins and Christopher Bird, *The Secret Life of Plants.* New York: Harper & Row, 1973.

Lee Fryer and Dick Simmons, *Earth Foods.* Chicago: Follett Publishing Co., 1979.

CHAPTER FIFTEEN

H. A. Nieper, M.D., and L. Blumberger, M.D., *Electrolytes and Cardiovascular Disease.* Baltimore, Md.: Williams & Wilkins, 1966.

Lelord Kordel, *Health Through Nutrition.* Chicago: World Books, 1950; New York: Manor Books, 1971.

Naura Hayden, *Everything You've Always Wanted to Know About ENERGY But Were Too Weak to Ask.* New York: Simon & Schuster, 1976; New York: Pocket Books, 1977.

Benjamin Ershoff, M.D., *Proceedings of the Society of Experimental Biology and Medicine,* July 1951.

Mark Bricklin, "Dr. Ershoff and the Health Miracles in Natural Foods," *Prevention,* June 1976.

William P. Castelli, M.D., *Framingham (Massachusetts) Heart Study, 1950–78,* U. S. Department of Health, Education and Welfare.

Benjamin S. Frank, M.D., "Nucleic Acid Therapy in Aging and Degenerative Diseases," *Psychological Library,* 1969.

Dr. Raymond J. Shamberger, "On Selenium, That Natural Anti-Oxidant That Helps Protect You From Heart Disease," *Executive Health,* Vol. 15, March 1979.

John Feltman, "Selenium, The Double-Duty Protector," *Prevention,* June 1979.

Gofman, John W., M.D., and Dr. Ernest J. Sternglass, *Shutdown: Nuclear Power on Trial.* Summertown, Tennessee: The Book Publishing Co., 1979.

Suggested Further Reading

Stanley L. Englebardt, "New Light on Cholesterol," *Reader's Digest,* February 1978.

Bill Gottlieb, "Are You Shrinking?" *Prevention,* January 1978.

Max Huberman, "Radiation—The Hidden Hazard," *Let's Live,* May 1978.

CHAPTER SIXTEEN

David Reuben, M.D., *The Save Your Life Diet.* New York: Random House, 1975; New York: Ballantine Books, 1976.

Nutrition Search, Inc., *Nutrition Almanac.* New York: McGraw-Hill, 1973.

Bernice K. Watt and Annabel L. Merrill, et al., "Composition of Foods," *Agriculture Handbook, No. 8,* U. S. Department of Agriculture, 1975.

Dr. Dean Burk, Lecture for the Cancer Control Society, reported by Los Angeles *Times,* July 16, 1973.

Ernest Krebs, Jr., M.D., *The Laetriles—Nitrilosides in the Prevention and Control of Cancer,* The McNaughton Foundation, 1964.

Richard Lucas, *Nature's Medicines.* New York: Award Books, 1969.

B. F. Hart, M.D., "The Vitamin Stepchildren: Bioflavonoids," *Let's Live,* May 1978.

Shambhu D. Varma and Jin H. Kinoshita, "National Eye Institute Research with Flavonoids and Cataract," *The National Eye Institute,* November 1977.

Viktoras Kulvinskas, *Survival Into the 21st Century.* Wethersfield, Conn.: Omangod Press, 1975.

Dr. J. J. Fayne, "The Miracle of Alfalfa," *Bulletin, U. S. Department of Agriculture.* Undated.

S. D. Farlin, J. J. Dahmen, and T. D. Bell, "Effect of Sprouting on Nutritional Value of Wheat in Cattle Diets," *Canadian Journal of Animal Science,* Vol. 51, 1971.

CHAPTER SEVENTEEN

Ken Ringle, "In Search of an Old Tooth," Washington *Post,* March 5, 1978.

Grace Halsell, *Los Viejos.* Emmaus, Pa.: Rodale Press, 1976.

Dr. Sula Benet, *Abkhasia: The Long-Living People of the Caucasus.* New York: Dial Press, 1973.

————, *How To Live To Be 100.* New York: Dial Press, 1976.

Lou Austin, *You Are Greater Than You Know,* The Partnership Foundation, Capon Springs, West Virginia, 1955.

Alice Lake, "What Women Don't Know About the Medicines They Take," *McCall's,* June 1977.

Muriel Ellis, *Drugs, Alcohol and Women's Health,* National Institute on Drug Abuse, 1978.

"For Foot Health Go Barefoot," *Nature's Way,* May 1977.

Malcolm I. V. Jayson, M.D. and Allan St. J. Dixon, M.D., *Understanding Arthritis and Rheumatism.* New York: Dell Books, 1976.

Dr. Joyce Brothers, *Better Than Ever.* New York: Simon & Schuster, 1975.

"The Tragedy of Care for America's Elderly," *U.S. News & World Report,* April 24, 1978.

Peggy Mann, "Age 101—Motto: Go *DO!" Reader's Digest,* August 1978.

Suggested Further Reading

Mildred Carter, *Helping Yourself with Foot Reflexology.* West Nyack, N.Y.: Parker, 1969.

Benjamin S. Frank, M.D., *Dr. Frank's No Aging Diet.* New York: Dial, 1975.

Henry Legler, *How to Make the Rest of Your Life the Best of Your Life.* New York: Simon & Schuster, 1967; New York: Pocket Books, 1970.

M. F. Graham, M.D., *Prescription for Life.* New York: David McKay, 1966.

How to Live It Up and Live Longer! Emmaus, Pa.: Rodale Press, 1974.

Elmer A. Josephson, *God's Key to Health and Happiness.* Old Tappan, N.J.: Revell, 1962.
Gordon Lindsay, *The New John G. Lake Sermons.* Dallas, Texas: Christ for the Nations, 1971.

Index

Abdomen, exercises for, 22, 31, 35, 83. *See also* Stomach
Accidents, 83, 104, 137, 151, 235, 244
Acetylcholine, 168, 171, 291
Acne, 53–54, 60, 133–36, 150, 165, 170
Acupuncture, 328
Adrenal glands, 144, 168; C and, 217, 220, 223–25, 239, 244; E and, 238, 239, 244
Adrenaline, 238
Advertising, 57–58, 121, 211; food and drug companies and, 67, 75, 95, 97–98, 106–7, 111–13, 211, 270, 271, 323
Aging, 91, 129, 133, 136, 159, 161, 162, 168, 179, 207, 221, 281, 315–16; anti-oxidants and, 234, 236, 238, 240, 241, 247–48; avoiding drug use and, 323–27; C and, 207, 221, 326; E and, 234, 236, 246–48; 326; exercise and, 17–18, 318, 319, 321, 322, 326; keeping

young, 315–36; nucleic acid and, 159, 293; statistics, 334–35
Air pollution, 8, 37, 42, 83, 90, 103, 129, 131, 142, 151, 233, 240–41
Albumin, 125–26, 307
Alcohol (drinking), 44, 62, 83, 122, 131, 153–54; B and, 153–54, 155, 157–58, 174, 178, 179; C and, 207
Alcoholism, 9, 153–54, 155, 157, 158, 165; AA and, 158
Allergic conjunctivitis, 139
Allergies, 60, 110n, 163; B and, 163, 168–69; C and, 207, 212, 217; exercise and, 16; synthetic vitamins and, 90
American Cancer Society, 203–4, 226
American Medical Association (AMA), 60, 62, 65, 68, 69–70, 113, 114, 249; and C, 213; and cancer, 196, 203; Council on Food and Nutrition, 62; *Journal*, 62, 72
Amino acids, 125–26
Amputations, 241, 242, 243
Anecdotal medicine, 60, 135, 219

Anemia, 160–61, 170, 284–85; C
 and, 218; E and iron and, 234;
 liver and, 284–85; pernicious,
 160–61, 162, 164, 284–85
Antibiotics, 83, 99, 169, 225, 265,
 273, 323; garlic and, 309; yogurt
 and, 310. *See also* specific kinds
Anti-depressants, 153, 163, 325
Antihistamine, C as, 212, 217
Anti-oxidants, 236, 238, 240, 241,
 247–48, 293
Anxiety (despair, fear, worry), 5, 9,
 40, 60; exercise and, 18, 19. *See
 also* Depression; Stress
Apples, 277, 298, 299–300
Apricot pits, 180–83, 194, 302, 303
Arms, exercises for, 22
Arteries (arterial problems), 222,
 241–42, 274, 289, 294; E and,
 241–42; exercise and, 15–16;
 lecithin and, 287, 289. *See also*
 Cardiovascular problems;
 Circulatory system
Arthritis, 5, 69, 85, 104, 126, 327; B
 and, 85, 166–67, 168, 170, 171; C
 and, 85, 207, 222; in children,
 105; E and, 85, 235, 238, 243–44,
 253; niacin and, 166–67; statistics,
 93; sunlight and D and, 127, 130;
 supplements for, 85–86
Artificial preservatives, 76, 101
Aspirin, 205, 223–24
Autism, 167, 174, 178

Babies, 37–38, 84; birth defects, soft
 water and, 46; crib deaths, 293–
 94; D and calcium and, 129, 130;
 food (formulas), 122–23, 158, 169,
 285; iron and, 285; thalidomide
 and, 72. *See also* Children
Backache, 207, 212, 222, 223
Bacteria, 133, 143–44, 310–11
Balanced diet, 23, 61–62, 63, 92–
 114, 115; myth of, 23, 61–62, 63,
 92–114, 115, 256–57
Barefoot, going, 327–29

Basic Four food groups, 93–94
Bathing, 37–44, 51–52
Beef heart, 165, 172
Behavioral problems, 109–11; B and,
 155–57, 174–76, 178
Benzaldehyde, 202
Beriberi, 65, 66, 79, 160, 165
BHA, 122, 248
BHT, 122, 248
Bicycling, 34
Bioflavonoids, 84, 305–7
Biotin, 172
Birth control pills, 134, 145, 157,
 170, 171, 233
Bladder cancer, 225–27
Blindness, 127, 136–38, 141–42, 258;
 night, 136–38, 139; "smoker's,"
 162
Blood, 45, 55, 78; circulation *(see
 Circulatory system)*; exercise and,
 15–16. *See also* Red blood cells;
 White blood cells
Blood clotting: C and, 207, 222; E
 and, 240, 254; K and, 84; Q and,
 79
Blood pressure, high, 46, 283, 309
Blood serum injections, 202–3
Blood sugar problems, 273–74; B
 and, 155–57. *See also* Diabetes;
 Hypoglycemia
Blood vessels: C and bioflavonoids
 and, 221, 222, 305–7; E and, 240,
 241–43, 254, 257. *See also*
 Arteries; Circulatory system
Bone meal, 57, 59, 278–81, 282, 283
Bones (bone problems): C and, 207;
 calcium and D and, 128–30, 140,
 278–84; E and, 242, 253; exercise
 and, 17, 29, 30; skipping rope
 and, 29
Brain (brain function), 41, 284;
 aging and, 326, 332; B and, 155,
 157, 159, 161, 162, 165, 166, 169,
 171, 172, 173–74; C and, 231. *See
 also* Mental problems
Bran, 234, 235, 304–5

Bread, 75, 97, 100–1, 277, 292; E and, 234–37, 238; "enriched," 236–37

Breast (mammary) cancer, 183, 185, 195, 196, 198, 200; iodine and, 296–97; mammography and, 74, 183; selenium and, 294–95

Breast lumps and cysts, E and, 249

Breathing, exercise and, 16, 22. *See also* Lung(s); Respiratory system

Brewer's yeast, 135, 154, 160, 164, 172, 180, 293; using, benefits of, 293

Burns, 207, 218–19, 244, 258

Bursitis, 61, 85–86, 281

Butter, 90, 131, 151, 162, 237, 248, 288, 304

Cadmium, 275

Caffeine, 103, 113

Calcium, 60, 101, 278–84; bone meal and dolomite and, 278–84; D and, 128–29, 130, 138–40; drinking water and, 45, 46, 51; exercise and, 17, 29; and eyes, D and, 138–40; food sources, 280

Cancer, 47, 69, 104, 105, 113, 121, 147, 148–49, 161, 166, 172, 269, 335; A and, 87, 145, 146–49, 151–52, 226; B and, 161, 166, 170, 180–206; C and, 87, 149, 152, 202, 206, 207, 208, 222, 225–29; chemicals and, 50, 266, 267, 268–69, 271, 276; cholesterol and, 288; cover-up in war on, alternative therapies and, 183–206; E and, 206, 234, 248, 249–50, 296–97; estrogen and, 296–97; iodine and, 296–97; preventing and overcoming, 205–6; selenium and, 294–95; statistics, 93, 104, 105, 189, 192, 203–4, 296; sunlight and, 127, 172. *See also* specific kinds

Candy, 98, 105–6, 108, 109, 110, 111, 116

Carcinogens, 47, 147, 148–49, 226, 269. *See also* specific kinds

Cardiovascular problems, 104–5; B and, 167, 178; drinking water and, 45–46; E and, 237, 241–43, 254, 255, 258; exercise and, 13, 25, 29; garlic and, 309; magnesium and, 281–82. *See also* Arteries; Circulatory system

Carpal tunnel syndrome, 170

Carrots, 99, 102, 125, 126, 131

Cataracts, 136, 139, 142, 166, 207, 253, 306

Cat Arch exercise, 32

Cereals, 49, 75, 98, 101, 106, 108, 111, 116, 120, 238, 265

Cervical cancer, 249

Cheese, 162

Chemicals (chemical poisons, pollutants), 90, 178, 205, 263–77 *passim;* detoxifying, vitamins and, 83, 209, 210, 240; fluorides and, 48–51; in food and water, 83, 94, 99–102, 103, 109, 116, 263–77 *passim. See also* Poisons; specific kinds

Chemical versus organic fertilizers, 263–77 *passim*

Chemotherapy, 186, 187, 188, 191, 192, 193, 198, 204, 205, 225, 229

Cherries, 98, 101

Chicken, 98–99, 127, 262, 277, 300

Children (adolescents, teenagers), 104–14, 127, 157, 293–94; A and D and, 129, 135–36, 142; acne and, 135–36; autistic, 167, 174, 178; B and, 155, 156, 157, 162, 164, 167, 168–69, 178; "balanced diet" and, 104–14; behavior and learning problems and, 104–11; cancer in, 105, 186–93; food industry and, 94–114; hyperactive, 60, 93, 109, 111, 155, 253; iron deficiency in, 119; lead in, 275; selenium and, 293–94; vision in,

141–42; vitamin "poisoning" and, 123–24. *See also* Babies

Cholera, 64, 69

Cholesterol, 62, 113, 125, 128, 151, 172, 178, 287–91; bran and, 305; C and, 207, 221; E and, 234, 237; eggs and, 307; food sources, 288–89; garlic and, 309; lecithin and, 287–91

Choline, 161, 171–72, 290–91

Chromium, 156n., 271, 273, 293

Circulatory system, 15–16, 41, 55, 64, 166, 230, 328; E and, 240, 241–43, 254, 257; exercise and, 15–16, 17, 19, 22, 25, 30, 328; niacin and, 166. *See also* Arteries; Blood vessels

Citrus fruit, 231, 305–7

Climbing stairs, 24–26

Cod liver oil, 128–29, 134

Cokes, 49, 106, 154, 265

Colds, 20, 61, 73, 103, 180, 209; and flu, C and, 61, 207, 209–18, 231

Cold water bathing, 51, 52; showers, 38–40, 51, 52

Colitis, ulcerative, 253

Collagen, 219, 221–25, 227, 306, 326

Convulsions, 169–70, 282

Cooking (cookbooks, recipes), 314

Copper, 269, 270, 271, 272

Coronary thrombosis, 104, 235

Cortisone, 131, 157, 168, 171, 217, 219, 238, 244

Cramps, E and, 241, 243

Cream, chemicals in, 101–2

Crepe label, 118

Crib deaths, 293–94

Cyanide, 181–82, 188, 194

Dancing, 32–33; pliés, 33; square, 27–28

Darvon, 73, 180

Dentists, 53–56

Depression, 41, 42, 60, 84, 87, 103, 293; B and, 153–54, 162, 165, 168, 170–71, 173, 174

Dermatitis, 166, 172

Desiccated liver, 154, 164, 284–86

Diabetes, 54, 69, 93, 97, 131, 171, 272, 273–74, 328; C and, 207; chromium and, 273–74, 293; drugs for, 173, 274; natural foods and, 273–74; zinc and, 287

Diarrhea: C and, 218, 231; yogurt and, 310

Dieting, 316–19

Digestive system: drinking water and, 45; exercise and, 16, 17; teeth and, 55

Disc lesions, 207, 212, 222

Disease(s), 65–67; "balanced diet" and, 92–114; degenerative, 69, 103, 106–7 *(see also* specific kinds, problems)*; vitamin deficiencies and, 65–67; vitamins for resistance to, 90 *(see also* specific nutrients, problems)*

DNA, 286, 293

Doctors (medical establishment), 61–75, 81, 87, 211, 212–18 *passim,* 224–25; and "balanced diet" myth *(see* Balanced diet); choosing, 326–37; and cover-up in war on cancer, 183–206 *passim;* and drug industry *(see* Drug companies); new breed of, nutrition-minded, 64–67, 69–71, 88, 141, 224–25, 326–37; public rebellion and, 71–72; and surgery, 73–74 *(see also* Surgery); and vendetta against supplements *(see under* Supplements)*. See also* specific developments, groups, individuals

Dolomite, 57, 59, 242, 281–84

Donuts, 98, 107

Dowager's hump, 281

Drinking water, 4, 8, 37, 44–51; fluorides and, 48–51; hard, importance of, 45–46, 262; pollutants and, 47–48, 267

Drug companies (drug industry), 67–69, 72–75, 323–27; doctors and,

67–69, 72, 75, 224–25, 249–50; and interferon, 216–17; and vendetta against supplements, 115–24 *passim*, 179–205 *passim*, 208–18 *passim*

Drugs (drug use), 72–73, 131, 135, 180, 207, 323–27; addiction, 155, 157, 323–27; aging and use of, 323–27; side effects, 324. *See also* Prescription drugs

Eggs, 90, 125–26, 129, 135, 151, 154, 171, 300, 307–8; cholesterol and, 288, 307; fake, 307; as source of B, 154, 160, 162, 172, 307; as source of D, 138; as source of E, 237, 238, 250; value of, 126, 307–8

Emotional problems, 8, 83, 131, 320; B and, 155–57, 159, 162–63, 164, 165, 169–71, 173–76

Endurance, 245–46, 257, 284

Energy, 78, 85, 89, 90, 91, 94; B and, 154, 165, 171, 178, 284, 285–86; C and, 207, 229–31; and drinking water, 37, 39, 41–42, 43; E and, 245–46; liver and, 284, 285–86; magnesium and, 283; staying young and, 315–16

Environmental Protection Agency (EPA), 46, 47, 264, 268, 275

Enzymes, 81–82, 131, 186, 190, 191, 194, 195, 197, 198, 199, 205, 261

Epilepsy, 207, 253, 282

Epithelial system, A and, 132–33, 144, 146

Estrogen, 83, 171, 249–50, 280, 296

Exercise, 3, 4, 9, 10–23, 24–36; Cat Arch, 32; circulation and, 15–16, 17, 19, 22, 25, 30, 328; heart function and, 15, 19; isometrics, stretching, 31–32, 33, 35; respiration and, 16, 22, 322–23; staying young and, 17–18, 318, 319, 321, 322, 326; valuable,

examples of, 12, 22–23; work and, 34–35

Eyeglasses, 126, 130, 141

Eyes (eyesight), 127, 136–42, 162, 258; A and D and, 125, 129, 132, 136–38; B and, 162, 165, 166; D and calcium and, 138–40; exercise and, 30, 35; nutrition and, 140–42, 326; tobacco and, 162

Faith, 4, 224, 225

Farming (agriculture), 261–77; organic, 56, 57, 76, 260–77 *(see also* Organic farming)

Fast foods, 92–93

Fatigue, 84, 87, 93, 103, 286; B and, 162, 168, 170; C and, 229–31; E and endurance, 245–46, 257; liver and, 284, 285–86

Fats, rancid, 83, 233–34

Fatty acids, 97, 101, 106, 113; 237, 238, 239, 287, 288, 301; cholesterol and, 288 *(see also* Cholesterol); EFAs, 301–2, 303

Federal Drug Administration (FDA), 68, 69, 79, 102, 115–24, 130, 249–50, 259, 324, 326; and C, 208, 212, 213; and food poisons, 265, 269, 276; and laetrile and cancer *(see* Laetrile); *Myth of Vitamin* booklet, 256–57; and RDAs, 86; and vendetta against supplements, 115–24, 139–40, 149–50, 177, 179, 181–205 *passim*, 208–18 *passim*, 249–50, 301–2, 306

Feet (foot problems): circulation, E and, 241–43; exercise for, 23; going barefoot, 327–29; and hands, B_6 and, 170; zone therapy and, 328–29

Fertility (infertility): E and, 145, 233, 239, 249, 250–53, 254, 312. *See also* Pregnancy; Reproduction; Sex

Fertilizers, 58, 76, 99, 151, 262–73

Fiber, 100–1, 106, 108, 305

Fish (seafood), 171, 293, 296; D
    from, 128, 130; oils, 128–29, 130,
    135; pollutants and, 48–49, 99,
    296
Flour, 96, 100–1, 116, 234–37;
    white, 96, 97, 100–1, 154, 156,
    159, 168, 234–37; whole-grain,
    154, 158, 234–37
Fluoridation, 48–51, 83
Folic acid (folate), 164
Food (diet), 23, 58–59, 60, 229, 233–
    39, 241, 280–81, 295; additives
    (see Food additives); aging and,
    316–18, 320, 326, 335; allergies
    (see Allergies); balanced diet and,
    23 *(see also* Balanced diet); Basic
    Four groups, 93–94; cancer and,
    186, 198, 200, 204, 265; chemical
    poisons in *(see Chemicals);*
    cholesterol scare and, 288–89;
    clinical nutrition and *(see*
    Nutrition, clinical); cooking
    (cookbooks), 214–15; doctors and,
    61–75; fads, 96; healthful, 298–
    314; hospitals and, 71–72; junk
    (see Junk food); organic, 8, 56–57,
    58–59, 76, 205, 260–77 *passim;*
    shopping and, 97–102
Food additives, 83, 94, 109, 111,
    116, 121, 158, 265; dyes, 116
Food industry: and "balanced diet,"
    94–114, 115; and chemical poisons
    in food, 94–95, 263–77 *passim;*
    influence on FDA, companies
    listed, 120; lobby, 106, 120; and
    vendetta against supplements,
    117–24
Free radicals, 234, 236, 247–48, 326
Fruit, 82, 84, 90, 93, 100, 106n.,
    135, 156, 162, 164, 170, 172, 180,
    186, 205–6, 220, 221, 229, 231,
    275–76, 298–300; healthful, 265,
    298–300, 305–7

Gallstones, 172, 218, 290
Garlic, 59, 308–9; uses, 308–9

Gastric ulcers, 79
Germs, 65, 83, 84, 138; A and, 143,
    144–45; garlic and, 309
Ghost surgery, 73–74
Ginseng, 121
Glaucoma, 136, 142
God, 2–6, 8, 14, 15, 30, 31, 32, 35,
    37, 40, 45, 52, 61, 96, 152, 158,
    173, 197, 206, 216, 218, 322, 326,
    333; Jesus, 5, 173, 329; worship
    and exercise and, 35–36
Grain(s), 270; E and, 234–37, 238;
    sprouts, 311–13; unprocessed, 90,
    93; whole, 154, 160, 162, 206,
    221, 234–37, 238
Growth, B and, 157, 162, 165

Hair, 168, 172; baldness and
    graying, B and, 168; PABA and,
    172
Halibut, 128; liver oil, 128, 135
Hands and feet, numbness or
    tingling in, B and, 170
Hard and soft water, 45–46
Hay fever, 16; E and, 253
Healing, 284, 328–29; healthful
    foods and, 298–314, 326; water
    and, 37, 40, 41–42, 43; worship
    and exercise and, 36; zone
    therapy and, 328–29. *See also*
    specific nutrients, problems
Health care costs, 68, 69, 71–72, 93
Health food stores (industry), 69,
    75–76, 88, 265, 276
Hearing problems, 166, 167
Heart problems, 69, 178, 207, 222,
    289, 309; calcium and, 279, 281–
    82; choline and, 161, 171;
    drinking water and, 45–46; E and,
    60, 235, 236, 238, 240, 244, 255,
    258, 274; exercise and, 15, 19, 25,
    26; free radicals and anti-oxidants
    and, 236, 240; magnesium and,
    281–82, 283; statistics, 93, 104–5;
    See also Cardiovascular problems
Hernia, C and collagen and, 222

Hip problems, 129, 130, 279–80; calcium and, 129, 130, 279–80
Hodgkins disease, 189–93
Holistic (wholistic) medicine, 88, 190; defined, 88
Honey, 153, 320; pollen, 320
Hormones, 128, 133, 145, 265, 273; B₁ and, 165, 168; C and, 217, 238; E and, 238, 249–50
Hospitals, 68, 71–72, 73–75; costs, 68, 71–72; food in, 71–72; unnecessary surgery in, 73–74
Hunzas, 95, 181, 319–21
Hyperactivity, 60, 93, 109, 111, 155, 253
Hypertension, 46, 283, 309
Hypoglycemia, 155–57, 163
Hysterectomies, 145, 153–54, 248

Illness, 5–6, 26, 55; "balanced diet" and, 92–114; psychosomatic, 5; supplements and, 65–67, 79–91 (*see also* specific kinds). *See also* Disease(s)
Immune system, 152, 265, 297, 325–26; A and, 142–44, 151, 152, 195; B and, 162; C and, 216–18, 225, 228; cancer and, 195, 199, 202, 205–6, 228–29
Infections, 65, 103, 104, 235; A and, 132, 136; C and, 207, 212–18, 220, 230; garlic and, 309
Influenza (flu), 61; swine flu vaccine, 213–14, 218
Inositol, 172
Insanity, 163, 166
Insomnia, 165, 168, 282–83
Insulin, 273–74
Intelligence, B and, 165, 172
Interferon, 216–17
Intermittent claudication, 241
Intravenous feeding, 71
Intrinsic factor, 162
Iodine, 295, 296–97
Ions, negative and positive, 41
Iron, 45, 94, 100, 101, 119, 125, 131, 261, 269, 270, 272, 284–85; anemia and, 284–85; C and energy and, 230; E and, 234, 236, 259; food sources, 284
Isometrics, 31–32

Jogging, 26–27, 36
Junk food, 59, 87, 92–94, 96–114 *passim*, 117, 135, 155, 170, 277

Kelp, 59, 295–97
Kidney stones, 218, 281

Labels, 22, 76; crepe, 118
Laetrile, 79, 177, 181–205, 302
Lead, 275
Learning problems, 109–11, 172, 291
Lecithin, 59, 125, 171, 287–91
Legs: circulation, E and, 241–43; exercise for, 22
Leukemia, 187–88, 297
Light, 29–30, 126–30
Lipoproteins, 289; HDLs and LDLs, 289, 290
Little, A. B., 5, 19–23, 27–28, 31, 39–40, 51, 53, 70, 235, 324
Liver, body's, 82, 130, 131; alcohol and, 157; B and, 157, 160–61, 164, 172; lecithin and, 289
Liver (food), 135, 284–86; B in, 154, 164, 172, 180; desiccated, 154, 164, 284–86; iron in, 284
Lung(s), 16; C and, 209–18; cancer, smoking and, 146–47, 151–52, 225–26; E and, 240–41. *See also* Breathing; Respiratory problems

Magnesium, 94, 281–84; in dolomite, 57, 281–84; food sources, 283; and heart problems, 281–82; water and, 45, 46, 51
Malnutrition, 63, 136; hospital food and, 72; processed food and, 236
Mammography, 74, 183
Manganese, 269, 270, 271

Meat, 90, 98–99, 113, 135, 162, 165, 170, 171, 172, 205, 237, 272; hormones and antibiotics in, 122, 265, 276

Memory, B and, 157, 165, 172

Ménière's disease, 46, 61

Menopause, 297; E and, 248–50

Menorrhagia, 145

Menstruation, 134, 144, 170, 248–50

Mental problems, 155–57; B and, 155–57, 159, 161, 164, 165, 167, 169–71, 173–76; retardation, 164, 170; senility *(see* Senility). *See also* specific kinds

Mercenene, 202

Metabolic doctors, 98, 200, 206

Metabolic nutrition, 67, 71

Metabolic therapy, 184, 192, 196

Metabolism, 81–82, 83

Milk, 90, 93, 98, 99, 101, 108, 116, 162, 168, 267; baby formulas and, 122–23, 169, 285; calcium and D in, 129, 130, 280; mother's, 294; skimmed, 130; soy, 162; whey, 101, 160

Mineral oil, 83, 131–32, 233, 323

Minerals, 260–77, 278–97; balanced diet and, 92–114; "enrichment" hoax and, 236–37; enzymes and, 81, 82; trace, 125, 260–61, 264, 271, 278–97 *passim;* using supplements, benefits of, 76, 80, 81–82, 85, 260–66, 278–97; vendetta against supplements, 116–24. *See also* Supplements; specific kinds

Mucous membranes, A and, 132, 146

Muscles (muscle problems), 172, 253; C and, 207, 222, 229–30; E and, 238; exercise and, 16–17, 18, 25, 29, 35; spasms, 222

Muscular dystrophy, 172, 253

Myelination (myelin sheath), 162, 172, 301–2

Myopia, 139, 142

National Cancer Institute, 87, 146–47, 189, 194, 200, 203–4, 228

National Health Federation, 175, 191, 196

Natural food industry, 75–76, 116, 262–77

Natural health movement, 75–76, 261–77

Natural versus synthetic vitamins, 57, 76, 89–90, 118, 148n.

Nervous system (nervous disorders and stability), 43–44, 84, 90, 155–57, 163, 165; B and, 154, 155–57, 159, 161, 162–63, 164, 165, 168, 169–71, 172, 173–76; E and, 248; magnesium and, 282

Neuritis, 165, 170

Neuroses, B and, 163, 165

Neurotransmitters, 159, 173

Niacin, 66, 102, 154, 155, 161. *See also* Vitamin B₃

Niacinamide, 166–68

Night blindness, 136–38, 139

Nitrates, 116, 122, 126; fertilizers, 126, 151

Nitrilosides, 206

Noise pollution, 8, 103

Nucleic acids, 159, 286, 293

Nursing homes, 335

Nursing mothers, 83, 157

Nutrition, clinical, 55–56, 58–59, 60, 62–64, 70–71, 118; medical profession and, 62–64, 66–67

Nuts, 90, 180, 237, 301–2

Oatmeal, 165, 300

Oils, 116, 233–34, 237–38; E and, 233–34, 237–38, 248; fish, 128–29, 130, 135; polyunsaturates, 233–34, 237–38, 288, 307. *See also* Vegetable oils

Onions, 125, 299

Oranges, 299, 305–7

Organic farming (agriculture, foods, movement), 8, 56–57, 58–59, 69, 76, 205, 260–77 *passim*

Orthomolecular medicine, 67, 70, 88, 161, 326–27; defined, 88
Orthomolecular psychiatry, 161, 163, 167, 174; agencies, listed, 175–76
Osteomalacia, 128
Osteoporosis, 279–80
Oxygen (oxygenation), 322–23; C and, 221, 230; cancer and, 205; E and aging and, 240, 244, 245–48, 254, 326

PABA, 172; ointment, 172
Pain (aches), 84, 85–86; C and, 207, 212, 219, 222, 223, 224, 228; E and, 243–44; zone therapy and, 328–29
Pantothenic acid, 85, 168–69
Parkinson's disease, 169
Pastries (cakes, cookies), 107–8, 116, 234
PCBs, 99, 266–67
Peanuts, 168, 170, 298, 301
Pellagra, 65, 66, 79, 160, 166, 169
Penicillin, 81, 202, 227, 258
Pesticides, 83, 99, 116, 263–77
Phlebitis, 19
Plastic surgery, E and, 244
Poison ivy, E and, 244
Poisons, 99–100, 234; detoxifying, C and, 209, 210, 212, 219; war on supplements and claims, 115, 118–20, 123–24. See also Chemicals; Pollution; Toxicity; specific kinds
Pollution (pollutants), 47–48, 83, 84, 90, 103, 152, 266–70; E and, 233, 240–41; in food, 94–95, 99–102. *See also* specific kinds, problems
Polyunsaturates, 233–34, 237–38, 288, 303. *See also* Oils; Vegetable oils
Popcorn, 300, 304
Pork, 165
Postnasal drip, 142–43
Potatoes, 99, 165, 299

Poultry, 167–68, 276. *See also* specific kinds
Prayer, 2, 61, 153, 154, 173, 326
Pregnancy, 83, 105, 157, 162, 164, 165; E and, 244, 250–53, 254; iron and, 285; stretch marks, E and, 244. *See also* Fertility; Reproduction; Sex
Prescription drugs, 72–73, 211; dangers, avoiding, 72–73, 180, 323–27; side effects, 324. *See also* Drugs
Preventive medicine, 53–77 *passim*, 88. *See also* specific aspects
Processed (refined) food, 95–114 *passim*, 116, 117, 151, 234–37, 270–77, 288; E and, 234–37. *See also* specific kinds
Protein(s), 131, 169, 205, 301, 307. *See also* specific kinds
Psychiatry, 161, 163, 167, 174, 175–76
Psychosomatic illness, 5, 162–63
Pulmonary edema, 240, 294
Pyridoxine. *See* Vitamin B$_6$

Radiation, 205, 225, 227, 297; kelp and, 297; therapy, 183, 186, 197, 198–99. *See also* Radioactive fallout; X rays
Radioactive fallout, 122, 280, 297
Raisins, 300–1
RDAs, 87–88, 94, 119–20, 151
Rectal cancer, 227
Red blood cells (hemoglobin), 164, 261, 284; E and, 246–47, 257
Rejuvenation, E and aging and, 246
Relaxation: exercise and, 18, 23, 28; square dancing and, 28
Reproduction, 145–46, 312. *See also* Fertility; Pregnancy; Sex
Respiratory problems, 16, 165, 322–23; A and, 142–44; C and colds and flu and, 209–18; E and, 240–41; exercise and, 16, 22, 322–23; lecithin and, 291. *See also* Lung(s)

Retina, 138–39

Retinitis pigmentosa, 139

Retinoids, 148–49

Reuben, David, 49, 305

Revici, Emanuel, 203

Rheumatism, 222

Rheumatoid arthritis, E and, 243

Riboflavin (Vitamin B₂), 165–66

Rice, 79, 97; brown, 160, 180

Rickets, 65, 66, 79, 128–29

RNA, 286, 293

Rose hips, 57, 90

Running, 17–18, 26–27, 36; stationary, 27

Saccharine, 122

Salt (sodium chloride), 46, 49, 83, 98, 99, 101, 102, 103, 113, 277

Sardines, 128, 293

Scars (scar tissue), 242, 244

Schizophrenia, 60, 79, 80–81, 134, 155, 161, 167, 174; Associations, listed, 175–76; C and, 207

Scurvy, 65–66, 79, 212, 220–21, 222; intermittent, 221

Seeds, 90, 206, 237, 302–4; sprouts, 311–13

Selenium, 99, 121, 203, 204, 206, 272; food sources, 295; toxicity, 295; using, benefits of, 293–95, 296

Senate Select Committee on Nutrition and Human Needs, 63, 67, 68, 95, 110, 113, 155, 161

Senility, 326; B and, 157, 167, 174; C and, 221; drug-induced, 325

Sex (sexuality), 145–46, 312; A and, 145–46; E and, 239, 249, 250–53. *See also* Fertility; Pregnancy; Reproduction

Showering, 38–44

Skating, 34

Skin (skin problems), 34, 90; A and, 132–33, 146; acne, 53–54 *(see also* Acne); A and D and complexion, 133–36; B and, 166, 172; burns,

244 *(see also* Burns); cancer, 127, 172, 268; D and, 126, 128, 129; E and, 244, 253; exercise and, 22; lecithin and, 287; water and, 41, 42, 43–44

Skipping rope, 29–30, 36

Sleep, 90, 282–83; aids, 83, 121, 325; calcium and magnesium and, 282–83. *See also* Insomnia

Smallpox, 64, 69, 81

Smoking, 16, 62, 83, 131, 135, 147, 151, 162; B₁₂ and, 162; C and, 207, 225–26; cancer and, 147, 151–52, 205, 225

Snakebite (stings), 212, 219

Soft and hard water, 45–46

Soft drinks, 44, 49, 75, 108, 109, 111, 113. *See also* specific kinds

Soybeans, 291; milk, 162

Sports, 11, 13, 14, 27, 34

Square dancing, 27–28

Stair climbing, 24–26

Steroids, 157, 171, 238, 296

Stomach problems: exercise and, 22, 31, 35, 83; ulcers, 79, 253

Stress (tension), 6, 8, 45, 103, 131, 282, 320; A and D and, 131, 144–45, 151; B₅ and, 168–69; C and, 217, 220, 223–25, 231; exercise and, 14, 18, 19

Stretching exercises, 31, 33, 35

Stroke(s), 207, 305, 309

Sugar, 83, 94, 96, 101, 102, 103, 104, 106, 108–9, 111, 113, 229, 234, 238, 265, 273, 277; B and, 154, 156–57, 158, 162, 168; raisins, 300–1

Sunflower seeds, 128, 303–4

Sunlight, 29–30, 126–30, 134, 135, 142; burns, PABA and, 172

Supplements, 57–61, 84–91, 278–97; benefits of, 90, 278–97; buying, 57; natural versus synthetic, 57, 76, 89–90, 118; RDAs, 86–87; vendetta against use of, 115–24, 149–50, 179–205, 208–18, 249–50

Surgery, 73–74, 83, 131, 145, 162, 169, 199–200, 225, 242, 244; ghost, 73–74; plastic, 244; unnecessary, 73

Sweets, 135, 154, 158–59, 300–1. *See also* Candy; Pastries; Sugar

Swimming, 30–31, 36, 38, 51–52, 128; E and endurance and, 245

Swine flu, 74, 213–14, 218; vaccine scandal, 213–14, 218

Teeth, 48–51, 53–56, 95–96, 126, 222, 299–300; calcium and, 278–79, 280, 281; D and, 128, 129, 130; dentists and, 53–56; fluorides and, 48–51; nutrition and, 95–96, 97

Tennis, 34

Thiamine. *See* Vitamin B₁

Thymus, 144

Toes, exercise for, 23

Tomatoes, 99, 277

Toxicity, 83, 87, 149–50, 295. *See also* specific nutrients

Toxins (toxic chemicals), 266–77 *passim*. *See also* Chemicals; Poisons

Tranquilizers, 72, 83, 153, 155, 163; magnesium as, 282; zinc as, 287

Tryptophan, 121, 169

Tuberculosis, 69

Turkey, 168

TV, 9, 13, 14, 17, 18, 155; food industry and, 98, 106, 111, 112–13, 121, 270, 271, 323

Ulcerative colitis, E and, 253

Ulcers, 54, 79, 93; E and, 244, 253. *See also* specific kinds

Urinary tract cancer, 226

Uterine cancer, 249

Vaccines, swine flu scandal and, 213–14, 218

Vaginal area: A and, 132, 133, 147; tumors, 147

Vegetable oils, 116, 233–34, 237–38, 239; E and, 233–34, 237–38, 239. *See also* Fatty acids; Oils

Vegetables, 82, 84, 90, 93, 100, 106, 135, 156, 160, 162, 164, 170, 172, 186, 198, 205–6, 220, 221, 229, 231, 298–99; A from, 131; E from, 237; organic, 265, 274–77; poisons and, 99–100, 265, 274–77

Viruses, 143–44; C and, 213–18

Vitamin A, 51, 59, 82–83, 101, 102, 125–26, 130–38, 151, 307; and cancer, 87, 145, 146–49, 151–52, 195, 196–97, 206, 226; and D and complexion (acne), 133–36; and D and eyes, 125, 136–38, 141–42; emulsified, 195, 196–97; and epithelial system, 132–33, 144, 146; and immune system, 142–44, 151, 152, 195; nature and work of, 131–38; restrictions, 121; and sex, 145–46; and stress, 144–45; toxicity, 83, 87, 149–50, 151

Vitamin B complex, 59, 66, 79, 82, 100, 118, 119, 125, 135, 153–76, 177–206, 235; and arthritis, 85, 166–67, 168, 170, 171; "enrichment" hoax and, 236–37; food sources, 154, 160; need for, 157–59; nervous disorders and, 154, 155–57, 159, 161, 162–63, 164, 165, 168, 169–71, 172, 173–76

Vitamin B₁ (thiamine), 102, 157, 160, 164–65; food sources, 165

Vitamin B₂ (riboflavin), 165–66

Vitamin B₃ (niacin, niacinamide, nicotinamide, nicotinic acid), 66, 102, 154, 155, 161, 166–68

Vitamin B₅ (pantothenic acid), 85, 168

Vitamin B₆ (pyridoxine), 169–71, 284, 285

Vitamin B₁₂, 161, 162–63, 164, 181–82, 284

Vitamin B₁₅ (pangamate), 177–81, 206

Vitamin B₁₇ (amygdalin, laetrile), 79, 177, 181–205, 302

Vitamin C (ascorbic acid), 51, 59, 66, 70, 76, 82, 90, 101, 102, 118, 122, 130, 135, 142, 155, 158; and arthritis, 85, 207, 222; bioflavonoids and, 305–7; and cancer, 87, 149, 152, 202, 206, 207, 208, 222, 225–29; and colds and flu, 209–18, 231; and collagen, 219, 221–25, 227; dosage, 230–31; E and, 238–39; and energy, 207, 229–31; natural and synthetic, 57, 90; and scurvy, 65–66, 220–21, 222

Vitamin D, 59, 82–83, 168; A and, 130–33; and A and complexion, 133–36; and A and eyes, 125, 136–38, 141–42; and bones, 128–29; calcium and, 128–29, 130; and calcium and eyes, 138–40; and rickets, 66, 129; and skin, 126, 128, 133–36; and sunlight, 128–30; toxicity, 83, 87, 121, 130, 140, 149

Vitamin E (tocopherol), 51, 59, 76, 82, 94, 102, 116, 122, 125, 135, 142, 232–59; and aging, 246–48; and anti-oxidants, 234, 236, 238, 240, 241, 247–48; and arthritis, 85, 235, 238, 243–44, 253; and burns and skin problems, 219, 244; C and, 238–39; and cancer, 206, 234, 248, 249–50; and energy, speed, and endurance, 245–46; and fertility, 145, 233, 239, 249, 250–53; and heart disease, 60, 235, 238, 240, 244, 255, 258, 274; and iron, 234, 236, 259; kinds, buying and using, 258–59; menstruation and menopause and, 248–50; restrictions, toxicity, 122, 150, 259; selenium and, 294; sources, 233–39

Vitamin K, 84

Vitamin P, 84, 305–7

Vitamin Q, 79

Vitamins, 78–91; amount, kinds to take, 84–88; benefits of, 90–91; deficiency-diseases, 65–67 *(see also* specific kinds); enzymes and, 81–82; natural versus synthetic, 57, 76, 89–90, 118, 148n; need for, 82–84, 86–88; used up by (list), 83; vendetta against supplements, 115–24, 155, 159, 174, 179–205 *passim,* 208–18 *passim*

Vitamin U, 79

Voice (vocal cords), E and, 233

Walking, 9, 10–11, 18–19, 24, 35

Water, 37–52; bathing and, 37–44, 51–52; drinking, 4, 8, 37, 44–51; fluoridation, 48–51; hard, importance of, 45–46; healing quality of, 37, 40, 41–42, 43; negative and positive ions in, 41–42; pollution, 47–48, 83, 84, 90, 296; skiing, 34; softeners, 46

Weight problems (obesity), 78, 316

Wheat, E and processing of, 234

Wheat germ, 85, 241, 250, 259, 291–92, 305

Wheat-germ oil, 85, 241, 250, 259, 291–92

White blood cells, 217–18, 230

Worship, exercise and, 35–36

Wrinkles, 123, 132, 172, 244

X rays, 53–54, 61, 64, 134, 169, 183, 197, 198–99, 205, 297. *See also* Radiation

Yogurt, 310–11, 320

Zinc, 59, 76, 94, 99, 206, 269, 270, 271, 286–87

Zone therapy, 328–29